ROCKETS AND MISSILES OVER UKRAINE

ROCKETS AND MISSILES OVER UKRAINE

UKRAINE

THE CHANGING FACE OF BATTLE

Mihajlo S. Mihajlović

FRONTLINE BOOKS

ROCKETS AND MISSILES OVER UKRAINE
The Changing Face of Battle

First published in Great Britain in 2023 by

Frontline Books
An imprint of
Pen & Sword Books Ltd
Yorkshire – Philadelphia

Copyright © Mihajlo S. Mihajlović, 2023

ISBN 978 1 39904 810 1

The right of Mihajlo S. Mihajlović to be identified as
Author of this work has been asserted by him in accordance
with the Copyright, Designs and Patents Act 1988.

A CIP catalogue record for this book is
available from the British Library

All rights reserved. No part of this book may be reproduced or
transmitted in any form or by any means, electronic or mechanical
including photocopying, recording or by any information storage and retrieval system,
without permission from the Publisher in writing.

Typeset in 10.5/13 pt Palatino by SJmagic DESIGN SERVICES, India.

Printed and bound in the UK by CPI Group (UK) Ltd.

Pen & Sword Books Ltd incorporates the imprints of Pen & Sword Archaeology, Atlas,
Aviation, Battleground, Discovery, Family History, History, Maritime, Military, Naval,
Politics, Social History, Transport, True Crime, Claymore Press, Frontline Books,
Praetorian Press, Seaforth Publishing and White Owl

For a complete list of Pen & Sword titles please contact

PEN & SWORD BOOKS LTD
George House, Units 12 & 13, Beevor Street, Off Pontefract Road,
Barnsley, South Yorkshire, S71 1HN, England
E-mail: enquiries@pen-and-sword.co.uk
Website: www.pen-and-sword.co.uk

or

PEN AND SWORD BOOKS
1950 Lawrence Rd, Havertown, PA 19083, USA
E-mail: uspen-and-sword@casematepublishers.com
Website: www.penandswordbooks.com

Contents

Preface vii
Acknowledgements viii
Note to the Reader ix
Special Military Operation x

Chapter 1   Introduction to Warheads... 1
             Missile and Rocket Explosion Effects 2
             Cratering 6
             Blast Effects...11
             Fragmentation.. 13
             Piercing Through the Armor – Shaped Charges..................... 17
             Thermobaric Warheads.. 23

Chapter 2   Operational-Tactical Missile Systems........................... 24
             Tochka-U 25
             Iskander 35

Chapter 3   MLRS... 49
             BM-21 (9K51) Grad... 58
             BM-27 (9K57) URAGAN 76
             BM-30 (9K58) Smerch... 88
             M270 and M142 HIMARS 112
             Improvised Launchers.. 127

Chapter 4   Thermobaric Weapons 132
             Technological Background 132
             Formidable TOS.. 139

Chapter 5	Guided Missiles	155
	Kh-22 and 32 Family	156
	Kh-55 and 101 Family	162
	Kh-59	172
	3M-14E and 3M-54 "Kalibr"	175
	Kh-29 and 38 Family	184
	P-800 Oniks/Yakhont	185
	R-360 Neptune	188
	Harpoon	190
	Kinzhal	193
	Anti-Radiation Missiles	198
	Storm Shadow/SCALP	206
Chapter 6	Surface-to-Air Missiles	209
	Long-Range AD Systems	209
	Medium-Range Systems	224
	Western "Wonder Weapons"	234
	SHORADs	241
	MANPADS	247
Chapter 7	Anti-Armor Systems	256
	Javelin	256
	NLAW	260
	Stugna	263
	Brimstone	265
	9K121 Vikhr	267
	9K135 Kornet	268
	Izdeliye-305	270
Chapter 8	Air-to-Air Missiles	272
Appendix	Abbreviations	278
Notes		283
Bibliography		287
Index		290

Preface

This book examines the most common rockets and missiles in use in the war in Ukraine and is written at a level that will be understandable to the average reader with an interest in technology and the military. The author has been able to inspect some of these munitions and systems personally. The book has 200 illustrations and diagrams. To summarize:

- Chapter One introduces the warheads and their explosive effects,
- Chapter Two covers the operational-tactical missile systems,
- Chapter Three details Multiple Launch Rocket Systems (MLRS),
- Chapter Four surveys the thermobaric weapons,
- Chapter Five addresses in detail the guided missiles launched from the air, land and sea,
- Chapter Six covers the surface-to-air missile systems,
- Chapter Seven describes the anti-armor missile systems,
- Chapter Eight covers the air-to-air missiles,
- The Appendix lists the most common abbreviations used through the book,
- The Bibliography contains the extended list of references and recommendations for further reading.

Acknowledgements

The images in this work come from the files listed in the Bibliography, the Ministry of Defense of Russia and of Ukraine (MoD), public domain sites and the author's archives. Some of the contemporary photographs come from Russian military websites and publications. Some images are from other named sources. As with all published works, the author has relied on friends for assistance in reviewing his work.

Note to the Reader

Due to the book's size constraints, this work is a very broad overview of the most common rockets and missiles used by both sides in the Ukrainian war. There are weapons such as the older anti-tank guided missiles, guided artillery shells, shoulder launched anti-tank rockets which are not specificaliy mentioned due to the constraints of space. The author has chosen to use the original designations pairing them with the Western designations when they appear for the first time.

This book is written so that every chapter can be read without necessarily having read the previous chapter. The text is aimed at the ordinary reader who is interested in military technology, especially rockets and missiles, and their applications in the war in Ukraine. It may also be interesting to engineering professionals as well as the intelligence community and military analysts.

Special Military Operation

On 24 February 2022, at 0530 Moscow Time, state television channels began broadcasting the address of Russian President Vladimir Putin.[1]

The program named *On Conducting a Special Military Operation* featured a televised address by President Vladimir Putin, immediately preceding the beginning of the military operation against Ukraine, addressing the citizens of Russia and Ukraine, and the military personnel of both armed forces. The speech was intended to sway public opinion by describing Putin's motivations for the invasion. To justify the operation, Putin claimed that Ukraine was a neo-Nazi state and made references to Article 51 of the UN Charter.

President Putin stated that Ukraine was becoming an "anti-Russia" state, with it being supplied by other NATO members with "the most modern weapons," saying:

> Further expansion of the NATO infrastructure and the beginning of military development in Ukraine's territories are unacceptable for us. The problem, of course, is not NATO itself – it is only an instrument of US foreign policy. The problem is that in the territories adjacent to us – territories that were historically ours, I emphasise – an "anti-Russia" hostile to us is being created, placed under full external control; it is intensively settled by the armed forces of NATO countries and is supplied with the most modern weapons.
>
> We have been left no other option to protect Russia and our people, but for the one that we will be forced to use today. The situation requires us to take decisive and immediate action. The people's republics of Donbas turned to Russia with a request for help … In this regard, in accordance with Article 51 of Part 7 of the UN Charter, with the sanction of the Federation Council of Russia and in pursuance of the treaties of friendship and mutual assistance ratified by the Federal Assembly on 22 February of this year with the Donetsk People's Republic and the Luhansk People's Republic, I have decided to conduct a special military operation.

The purpose of the "operation" was to "protect the people" in the predominantly Russian-speaking region of Donbas who, according to Putin, "for eight years now, have been facing humiliation and genocide perpetrated by the Kiev regime." Putin said that "all responsibility for possible bloodshed will be entirely on the conscience of the regime ruling on the territory of Ukraine." Putin also stated that Russia sought the "demilitarization and denazification" of Ukraine.

Putin called on the Ukrainian military to "immediately lay down their arms and go home," saying, "All servicemen of the Ukrainian army who comply with this requirement will be able to freely leave the combat zone and return to their families. All responsibility for possible bloodshed will be entirely on the conscience of the ruling regime on the territory of Ukraine."

Addressing the citizens of Ukraine, he linked Russia's actions with self-defense against the threats created for it and "an even greater disaster than the one that is happening today," saying, "No matter how hard it is, I ask you to understand this and call for interaction in order to turn this tragic page and move forward together."

Putin stated there were no plans to occupy Ukrainian territory and that he supported the right of the peoples of Ukraine to self-determination, saying:

> Our plans do not include the occupation of Ukrainian territories. We are not going to impose anything on anyone by force. At the same time, we hear that recently in the West there is talk that the documents signed by the Soviet totalitarian regime, securing the outcome of World War II, should no longer be upheld.

At the end of the address, Putin warned other countries against intervening in the conflict, saying:

> Whoever tries to interfere with us, and even more so to create threats for our country, for our people, should know that Russia's response will be immediate and will lead you to such consequences that you have never experienced in your history. We are ready for any development of events. All necessary decisions in this regard have been made. I hope that I have been heard.

Chapter 1

Introduction to Warheads

The primary role of the missiles and rockets is to destroy enemy personnel and equipment, structures and fortifications, and perform special tasks. The working edge of them is a warhead (Figures 1-1, 1-2) which inflicts the most damaging effects on the target. Detailed descriptions and explanations of particular warhead types will be discussed in the corresponding chapters.

Damaging effect is defined as the ability of ammunition to damage a target provided that it is already close to it and all its elements have operated without failure. The effectiveness of the damaging effect of ammunition on the target and its combat effectiveness should not, therefore, be confused. Obviously, the combat effectiveness depends not only on the effectiveness of the ammunition near a target but also on the accuracy of ammunition delivery, the reliability of all its elements (the fuze in particular), the ability to withstand the enemy's defensive actions, and many other factors.

All ammunition is divided into the following types, depending on its main effects:[1]

- Fragmentation (with natural, controlled fragmentation, and preformed fragments; rod warheads; gunpowder and explosive shrapnel; case-shot),
- Penetrating (small-arms ammunition, armor-piercing, and concrete-piercing),
- Shaped charges (with single or tandem shaped charges; explosion-formed projectiles),
- High-explosive (blast) ammunition, including volumetric explosion ammunition (aerosol, thermobaric),
- Incendiary,
- Nuclear (based on fission or fusion),
- Unified by type of action.

Ammunition that does not damage targets but serves as a countermeasure to protect or reduce the damage from the enemy's ammunition can be identified as a separate group. For the same purpose, active protection of armored vehicles is developed to destroy enemy ammunition as it approaches the target.

There are also many auxiliary and special-purpose munitions: lighting, smoke, and others that will not be considered here as well as the nuclear one.

To ensure a damaging effect on targets, it is necessary to exert any action on them. It is usual to highlight the following:

- Action of fragment flow,
- Penetrating action,
- Shaped charge action,
- Action of a shock wave and explosion products,
- Incendiary action,
- Action of penetrating, and
- Electromagnetic radiation of a nuclear explosion.

Despite the large variety of rockets and missiles designs, there are just a few ways for ammunition to act on targets. For the most part, all of them are determined either by the kinetic energy of the munition itself or by the chemical energy of the explosive that the munition is equipped with.

Missile and Rocket Explosion Effects

Modern versions of artillery guns and mortars are capable of a relatively high level of accuracy in an indirect fire role within their effective ranges. MLRS projectiles are generally spread over a sizable area which increases as the distance to the target increases. This limits their technical suitability for use against smaller or moving targets, especially in populated areas. Most indirect fire weapon systems used in today's conflicts are incapable of achieving the high degree of accuracy required to hit a small point target with the first round, excluding the guided projectiles.[2]

Unguided artillery rockets fired from MLRS are neither accurate nor precise to some degree.

The main effects of high-explosive munitions comprise blast, heat and fragmentation originating from the munition, plus the secondary fragmentation and debris generated in the impact, or explosion of the munition, travelling at high velocity to considerable distance (see the next section for the technical description). These effects are compounded by firing a salvo of munitions simultaneously or sequentially and by their use in populated areas, which often results in large areas experiencing significant damage, as opposed to damage to a cluster of unconnected and localized points.

High-explosive munitions can cause a lot of damage to military objects, including the full destruction of the targeted object or area. In Ukraine,

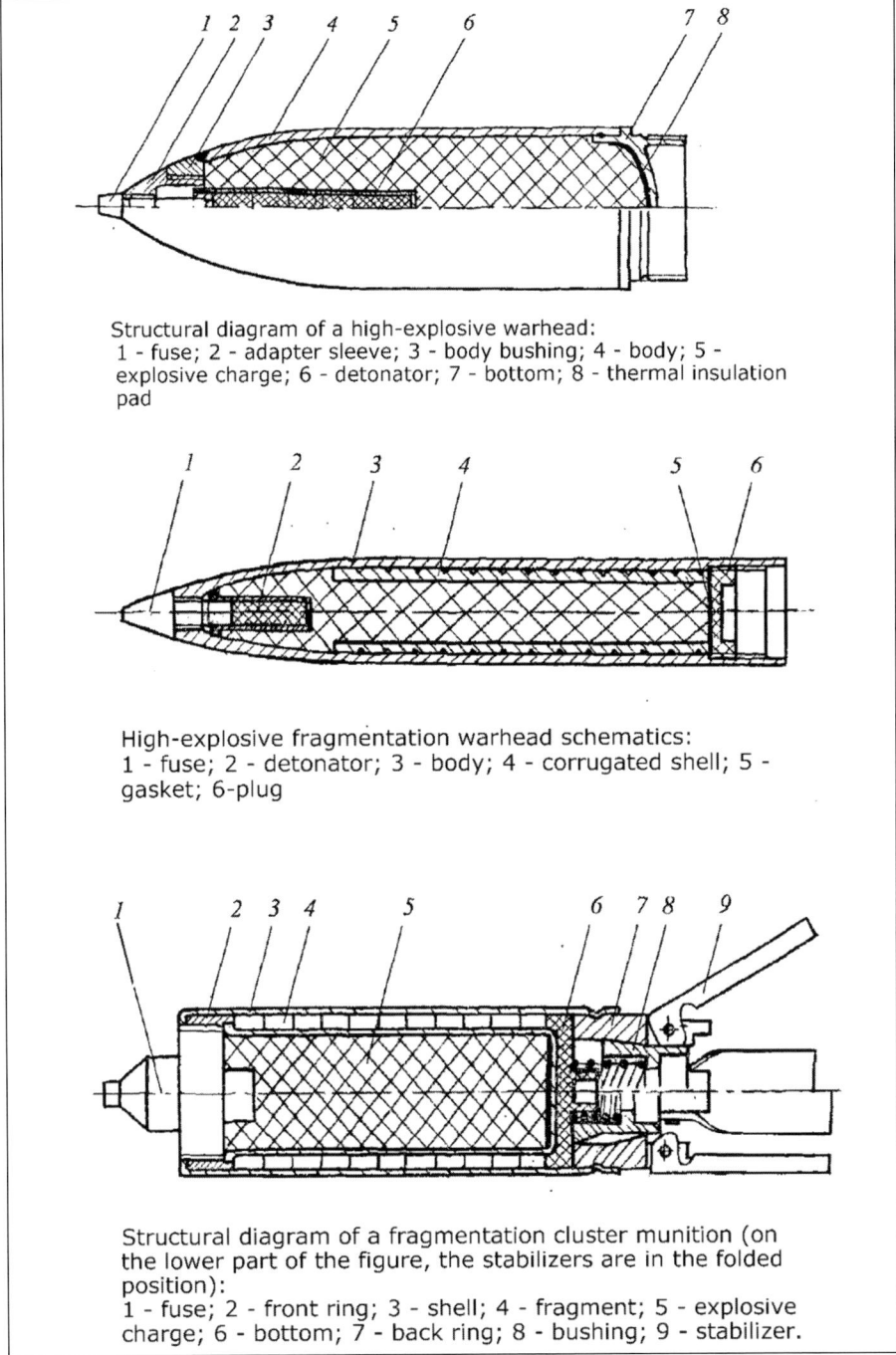

Figure 1-1: Warhead types: High Explosive – HE (top); High Explosive Fragmentation – HE FRAG (middle); cluster munition (bottom). (*Source*: A.P. Orlov, *Osnovi ustroistva i finkcionirovania snaryadov RSZO*, modified by author)

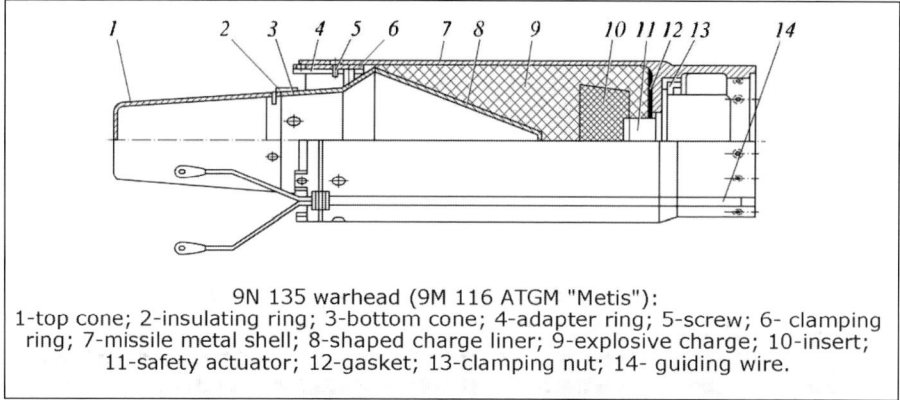

Figure 1-2: Shaped Charge (cumulative). (*Source*: A.P. Orlov, *Osnovi ustroistva i finkcionirovania snaryadov RSZO*, modified by author)

there are many urban areas used for military purposes such as factories and warehouses converted to ammunition depots and storage facilities. Many residential buildings such as schools, houses and buildings are used for military purposes. Explosives delivered either by unguided or guided munitions within populated areas are influenced substantially by the presence of built structures and geographical features. Structures may provide protection from primary and secondary explosive weapon effects, but also amplify these effects due to the channelling and reflection of blast waves. Buildings and vehicles may contribute bricks, concrete, glass, and other debris to the fragmentation originating from the weapon. Any fuel sources (liquid and gas) or toxic chemicals within the munition's impact zone may pose a further hazard to humans, as does the compromised structural stability of buildings which may be prone to collapse.[3]

The intuitive reflex among those targeted (both military and civilians) to seek shelter from an explosive-weapon attack in buildings, vehicles, and similar enclosed spaces poses a lethal risk. The intensification of the weapon effects in a populated area is mainly due to the reflecting blast waves and presence of a number of people and structures within the amplified effective range of a munition(s), as well as sources of secondary fragmentation. This results in a higher proportion of fatalities than would be likely in open spaces.[4]

Humans are particularly vulnerable to blast overpressure and reflected blast waves. Surviving an explosive-weapon attack with only surface bruises visible does not exclude ruptured eardrums, damaged lungs, internal bleeding, brain damage, infections and poisoning, and bone fracturing. Depending on the layout of structures in a populated area and the type of explosive weapon used in an attack, the probability of survival for a human may indeed increase when away from the proximity of structures (prone on the ground in a small depression or narrow ditch).

Mortar and artillery systems continue to be "walked on" to the target using the method of observing the impact location and thereafter correcting the aim. The first projectiles often impact areas outside the intended target. To maximize accuracy and precision during such procedures, extensive training, frequent weapon testing, access to modern technologies, and detailed intelligence are paramount, supported by robust targeting policies and comprehensive and competent collateral damage estimates.

Explosion Effects on Targets
The impact of explosive munitions can be broken down into the principal damage mechanisms and their primary effects, and the secondary and tertiary effects occasioned by these. This section focuses on the primary damage mechanisms and secondary effects of explosives.[5]

The primary effects of explosive weapons are defined as those "caused directly by the destructive effects that radiate from a point of initiation and include blast overpressure, fragmentation, heat and light." These are attributed directly to the principal damage mechanism of an explosive weapon – blast, fragmentation, and heat. The term "blast" refers to a high-pressure blast wave moving at supersonic speed, referred to as the shock wave, which is followed by blast winds. Primary fragmentation comprises fragments that originate directly from the explosive munition. The third damage mechanism is the thermal energy released during detonation of the explosive.

Most high-explosive warheads are not designed to deliver an augmented incendiary effect and the thermal effect is limited to the immediate area of the detonation, as well as by its extremely short duration. Generally, the primary thermal hazard posed by an explosive weapon is less significant than the blast and fragmentation threats. Secondary effects of explosive weapons derive from the environment in which the munition detonates. The most significant secondary effects include secondary fragmentation, firebrands, ground shock, and cratering.

Secondary fragmentation originates from objects that have been affected by the detonation and can include such objects as pieces of masonry or glass from structures, or bone fragments from human or animal targets. Secondary fragments are generally larger than primary fragments and tend not to travel as fast, or as far.

Ground shock results from the energy imparted to the ground by the shock wave caused by an explosion and can result from a detonation under or on the ground, or in the air above. Ground shock poses an additional threat to the structural integrity of buildings (which has significant effect in the urban areas), as the ground conducts the shock wave into the foundations and walls.

Cratering

Cratering refers to the buckling and deformation of the ground around the detonation point (Figure 1-3). Both ground shock and cratering can cause substantial damage to underground shelters and bunkers as well as critical infrastructure. This may be a deliberate effect of explosive munitions optimized for cratering, intended to obstruct avenues of approach or to disrupt infrastructure.[6]

Spalling presents an additional danger in urban environments. It is a stress-wave effect most commonly observed in materials more brittle than metal. This occurs when an impact strikes the outer surface of a solid body, causing fragments to break off from the inside surface. The projectile or the fragment does not need to penetrate the solid body; merely striking the outer surface with sufficient energy may result in spalling. A possible scenario resulting in spalling is a brick wall being struck by a blast wave, or in some cases a projectile or a sufficiently energetic fragment, causing secondary fragmentation inside the building. A significant hazard unique to urban environments is the risk of fatally compromised structural integrity of buildings caused by the blast

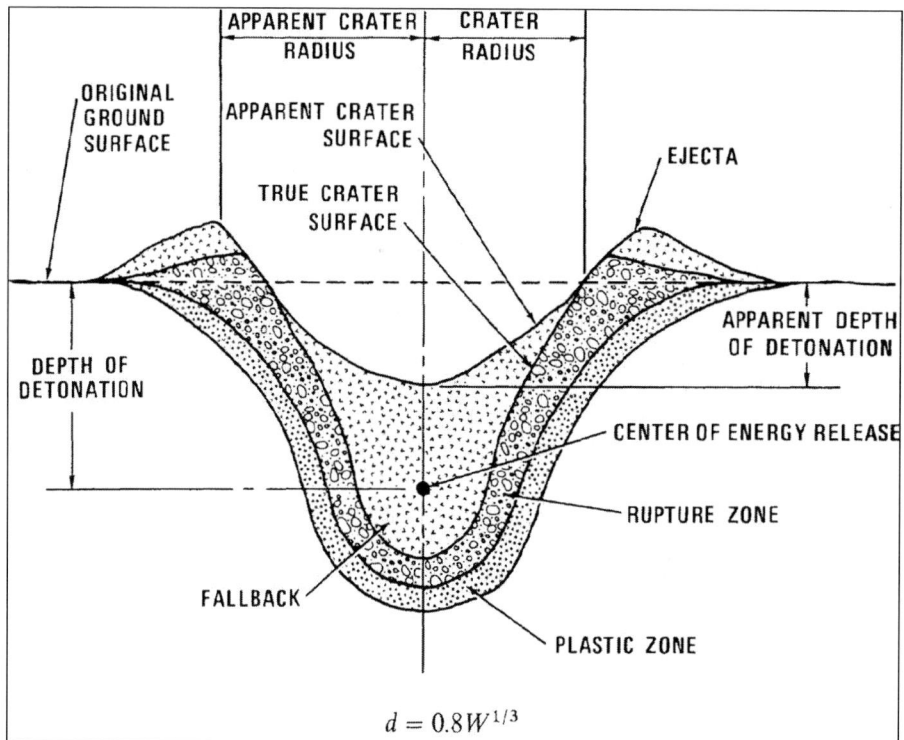

Figure 1-3: Typical crater from an explosion; "d" is the crater diameter, "W" is the crater width. (*Source*: G.F. Kinney and K.G. Graham, *Explosives Shock in Air*)

waves. Any people in and around those buildings and structures may be crushed by their partial, or complete collapse.[7]

An impressive aspect of a surface explosion is its resulting crater (Figure 1-4). The great variability in crater formation is indicated by standard deviations of about one-third the diameter given by equation in Figure 1-3.

The depth of the crater created by an explosion ordinarily is about one-quarter its diameter, but this depends on the type of soil present (Figure 1-4). The diameter of the crater from an explosion also depends on the location of the explosion relative to surface level. Thus, explosions above a surface may not create any crater at all. For explosions below the surface, crater diameter initially increases with depth of explosion, reaches a maximum, then decreases substantially.[8]

Figure 1-4: Tochka-U crater near Makeevka (top); a pool-size crater in Slovyansk after impact (bottom). (*Source*: Author's archive)

There is a comparatively good correlation between crater radius and sympathetic detonation distance (Figure 1-5), an observation that confirms the thought that sympathetic detonation is affected by the tangible physical means of missile or fragment impact (Figure 1-6).

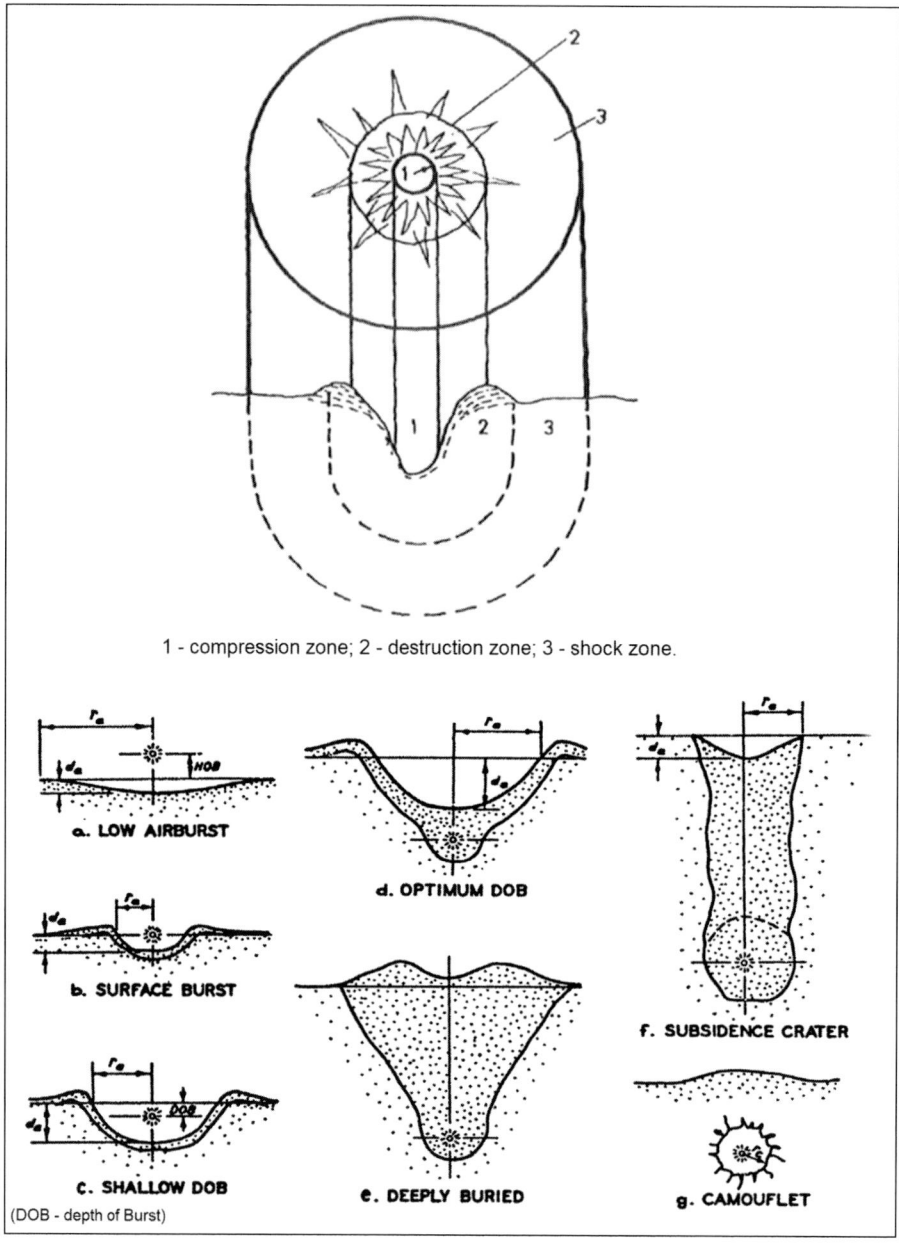

Figure 1-5: During the explosion in the ground three characteristic zones are formed (top). (*Source*: S. Jaramaz, *Physics of Explosion*); Crater shapes as affected by burst geometries (bottom). (*Source*: *Cratering by Explosion, Compendium*)

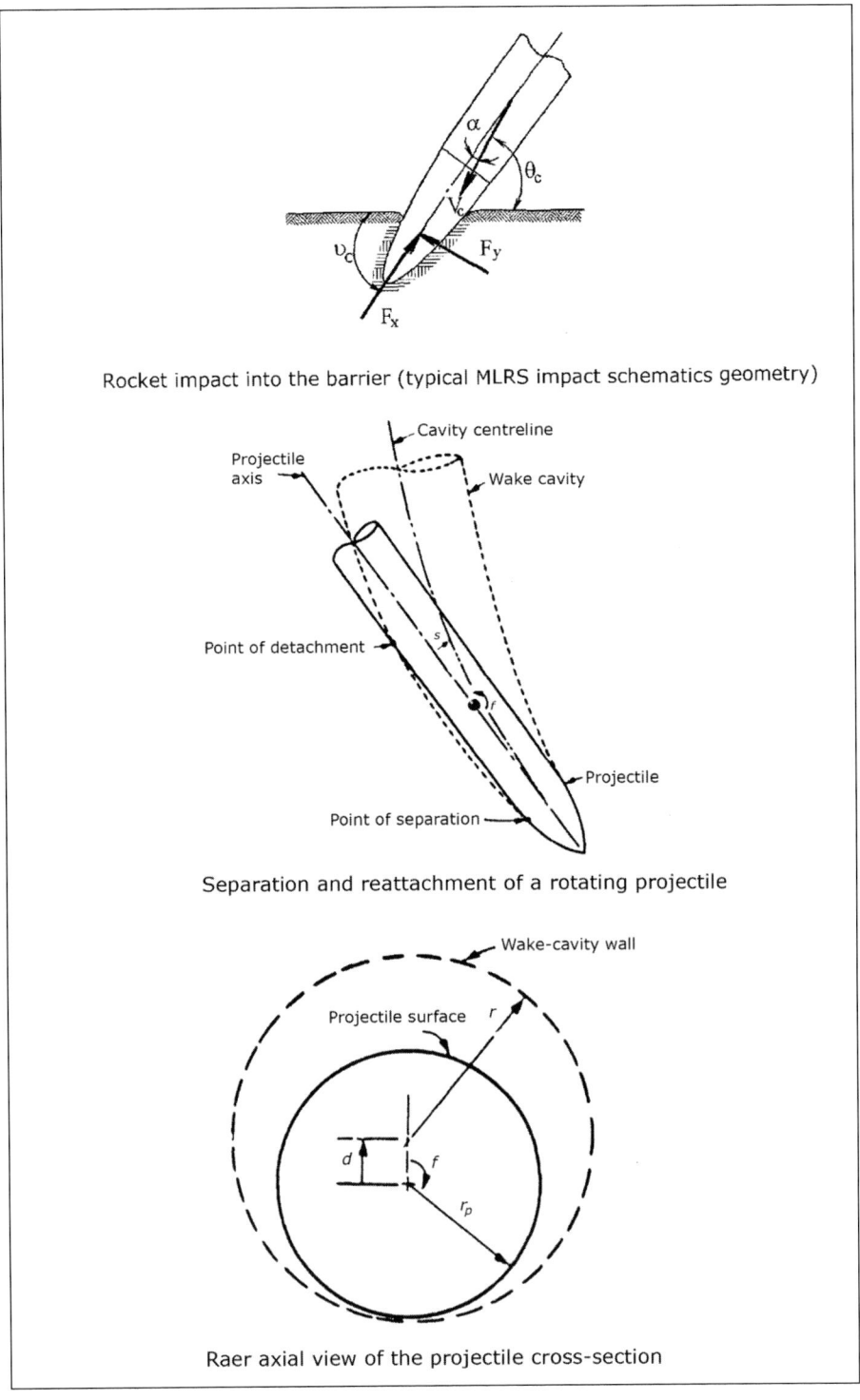

Figure 1-6: Impact geometry. (*Source*: *Cratering by Explosion, Compendium*)

One of the interesting cratering phenomena often misinterpreted in the media is when photos show a missile tail sticking out of the ground. Often this is interpreted as an unexploded missile which is not true. These kinds of photos present the motor/propulsion section of the unguided or guided missile fired from the MLRS which at a certain point in the trajectory is separated from the rest of the missile but continues on the ballistic trajectory with the spin which stabilizes it on the path. Upon impact, almost under some angle, it can penetrate deeply into the ground. Taking into consideration the mass and the velocity of the tail section, these impacts can cause significant damage even if there is no explosion involved, but rather a sheer momentum of inertia (Figure 1-7).

Figure 1-7: Unusual even in a war, this Russian BM-30 rocket propulsion section impact was so high that it tore open the truck side and penetrated into the ground half length. (*Source*: avia.pro)

Blast Effects

An explosive is a material that is capable of producing an explosion by releasing the potential energy contained within it. All high explosives produce heat and gas. When a high-explosive charge detonates, it produces a blast wave (overpressure) that consists of two parts: a shock wave and a blast wind. The blast wave pushes outwards from the core of the detonation at supersonic speed. The outer edge of the blast wave is made up of the compressed gases contained in the surrounding air. This layer of compressed air is more properly described as a shock wave or shock front. In open air, the blast decays extremely quickly with time and distance; typically it can be measured in milliseconds.[9]

The blast wave has two phases (Figure 1-8). The positive-pressure phase pushes a large portion of the surrounding air away from the core of the detonation at supersonic speed, leaving a broad partial vacuum behind it. When the blast wave of the positive-pressure phase loses momentum, the partial vacuum behind it causes the compressed and displaced gases to reverse their movement and rush inward to fill the void. The negative-pressure phase moves less quickly than the positive phase and it generally lasts approximately three times as long.

The effect of the pressure wave upon a structure depends on what the structure is composed of and how it is built. In essence, it is dependent upon

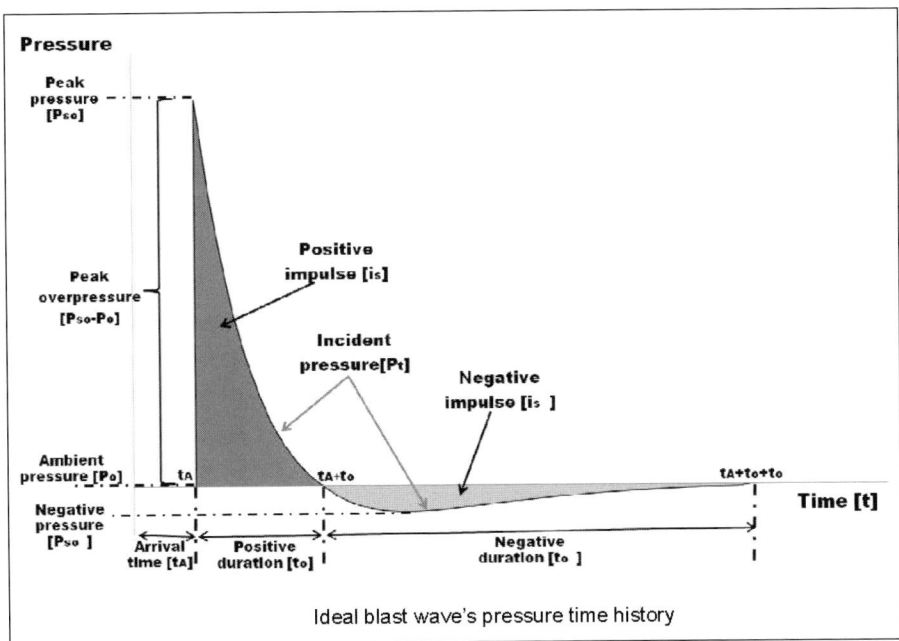

Figure 1-8: Blast scaling law, named Hopkins-Cranz law. (*Source*: V. Karlos and G. Solomos, *Calculation of Blast Loads for Application to Structural Components*)

the structure's natural frequency of vibration compared with the duration of the blast wave. When the supersonic shock front from a detonation encounters a solid structure, some of the energy is reflected, and some of the energy is transmitted into the structure; the relative amounts depend on the properties of the structure.

In the process of striking the target, the shock front will impart significant momentum to the exterior components (Figure 1-9). These components will be pushed towards the interior by the positive-pressure wave, straining

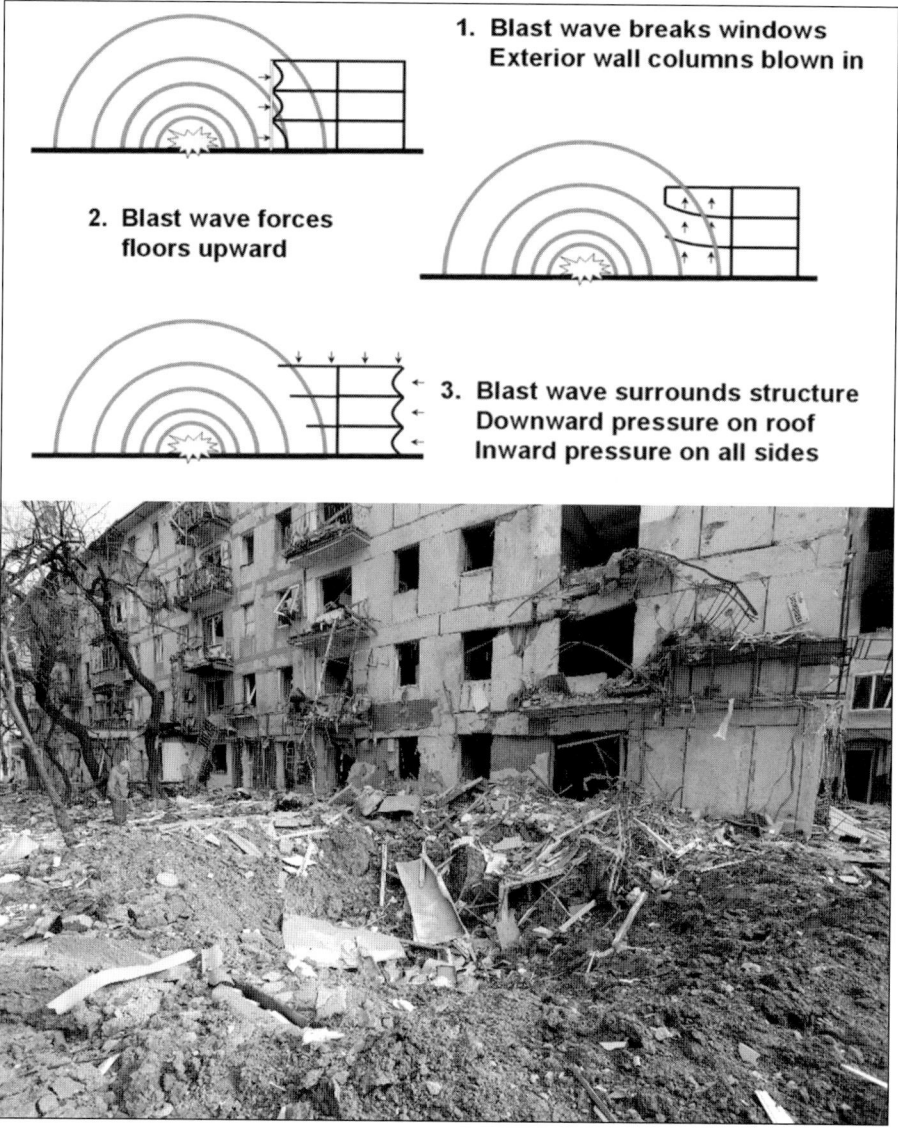

Figure 1-9: Damage pattern due to the nearby explosion (top), Mariupol building (bottom).

the resisting elements of the structure (such as support columns, building facades, etc.). Some of those resisting elements, windows in particular, will fail. As the negative-pressure phase of the pressure passes back through the structure, the direction of the energy is reversed. Unlike the reflection of sound waves, which have a negligible effect on the medium through which they are travelling, shock waves are moving at such high speed and contain so much energy that they change the medium itself. When the shock wave hits the ground, it is reflected back into the still-advancing blast wind. This amplifies the blast overpressure anywhere up to twenty times that of the initial detonation.[10]

Fragmentation

Primary fragmentation originates from the casing of the metallic shell surrounding the high-explosive charge. Fragments can take a variety of shapes and sizes, and are primarily effective in an anti-personnel capacity (Figures 1-10, 1-11).[11]

The type of steel used in the manufacture of the artillery shell plays a significant role in determining the nature of the natural fragmentation that is produced. High-explosive shells are typically made from either forged or cast steel or iron. Cast metals are melted down and poured into molds to form the shape of the projectile, whereas forged steel projectiles are formed by beating red-hot steel ingots into the desired shape. MLRS rockets have the thinner pre-formed shells or tight packed cubes to reduce the weight.

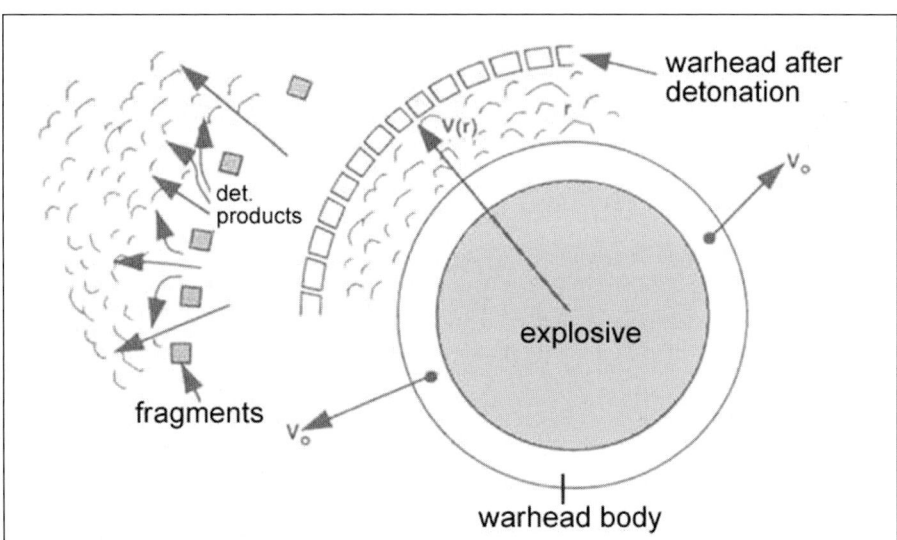

Figure 1-10: Schematic representation of the HE warhead detonation process. (*Source*: M. Lloyd, *Conventional Warhead Systems, Physics and Engineering Design (Progress in Astronautics and Aeronautics)*, Vol. 179)

The same is true of anti-aircraft missiles where the primary defeating elements are fragments.

Calculating the effects of primary fragmentation is more complicated than the blast effect, owing to the number of known unknowns. In many cases, the initial velocity (speed and impact angle) of the shell at the time of detonation is not known, nor is the exact shape, weight, and aerodynamic performance of each fragment. The type of fuze will also affect the fragmentation pattern. Due to the greater variation in the size and number of fragments caused by the explosion, natural fragmentation is more difficult to predict and model. The effect of fragmentation on human targets is particularly unpredictable, as the amount of exposed body area and the posture of the target can have a marked influence on the potential harm.[12]

The angle at which a munition impacts the target has a significant bearing on the size and shape of the lethal area. In simple terms, the higher the angle (toward vertical 90°) of fall, the larger the lethal area will be. In order to maximize lethal area, at higher angles of fall (45–90°) the optimal height for detonation is approximately 2m above ground, although even at just above ground, the lethal area is increased (Figure 1-11).[13]

Fragmentation is very important in surface-to-air missile warheads (Figures 1-12 top, 1-13). One of the variants of the fragmentation warhead is the one which uses rods (Figure 1-12 bottom). These types of warheads are in use in some anti-aircraft missiles.

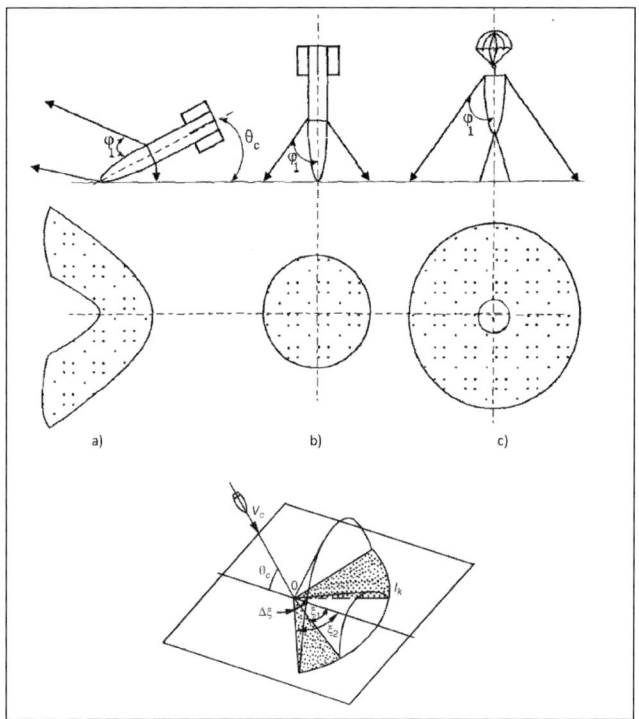

Figure 1-11: Warhead fragments distribution: a) angle impact; b) vertical impact; c) vertical impact with distance activation (top and middle). (*Source*: A.P. Orlov, *Osnovi Ustroistva i Funkcionirovaniya Snaryadov RSZO*); formation of damaging sectors on the ground (bottom). (*Source*: I. Balagansky, *Damaging Effects of Weapons and Ammunition*)

INTRODUCTION TO WARHEADS

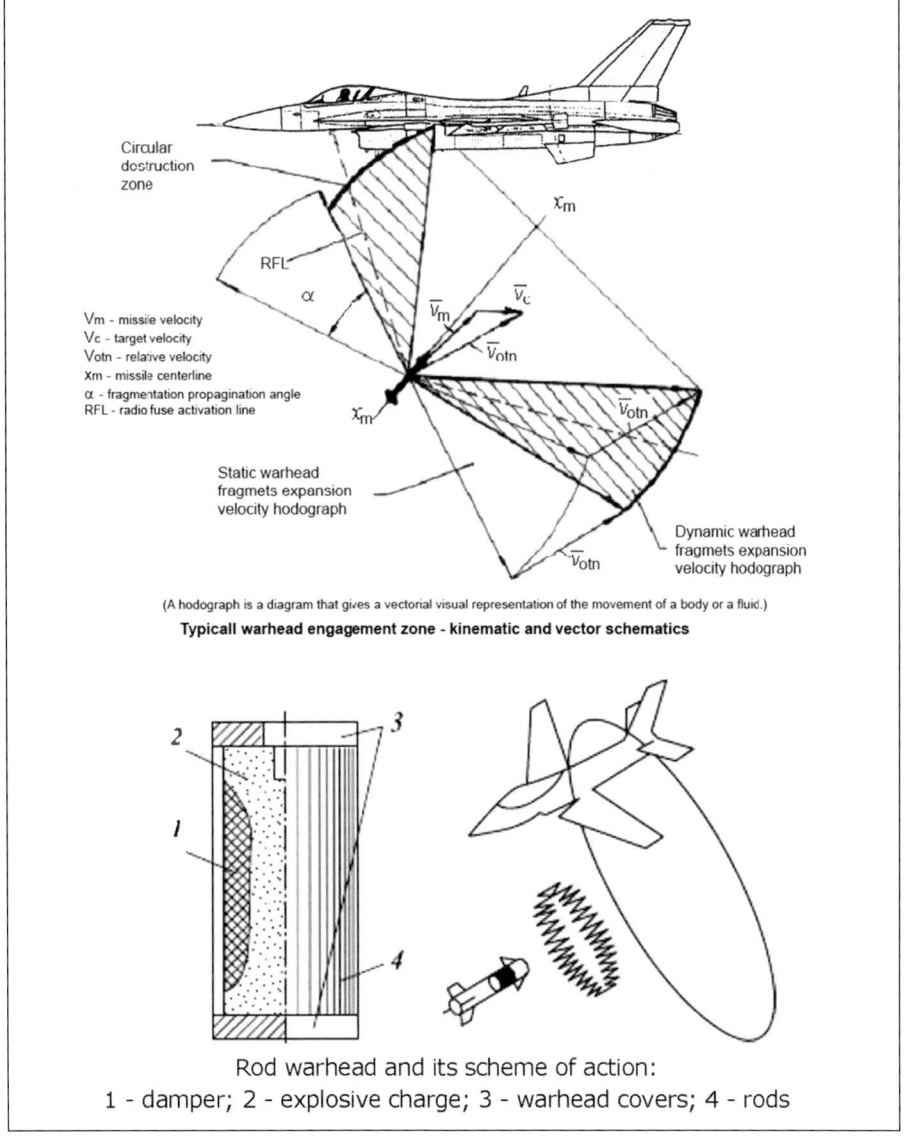

Rod warhead and its scheme of action:
1 - damper; 2 - explosive charge; 3 - warhead covers; 4 - rods

Figure 1-12: SAM Fragmentation warhead explosion kinematic schematics with fragment velocity distribution (top); rod warhead action (bottom). Rods are made in the form of steel rods of square or round sections, laid on the surface of the explosive charge, as a rule, at a slight angle to its central axis. The rods can be firmly connected (welded) alternately with upper and lower ends. In this case, when throwing a system of rods, a continuous ring is formed. If the rods are not interconnected, then a field with many long fragments is formed. To prevent destruction during the explosion of the charge, the rods are separated from the explosive charge by a damper. The damaging effect of such rod components is in making continuous cuts in the aircraft skin (like a can opener), fuel lines, airframe, and power units, which leads to the destruction of the structure, almost instantaneously after the target was hit.

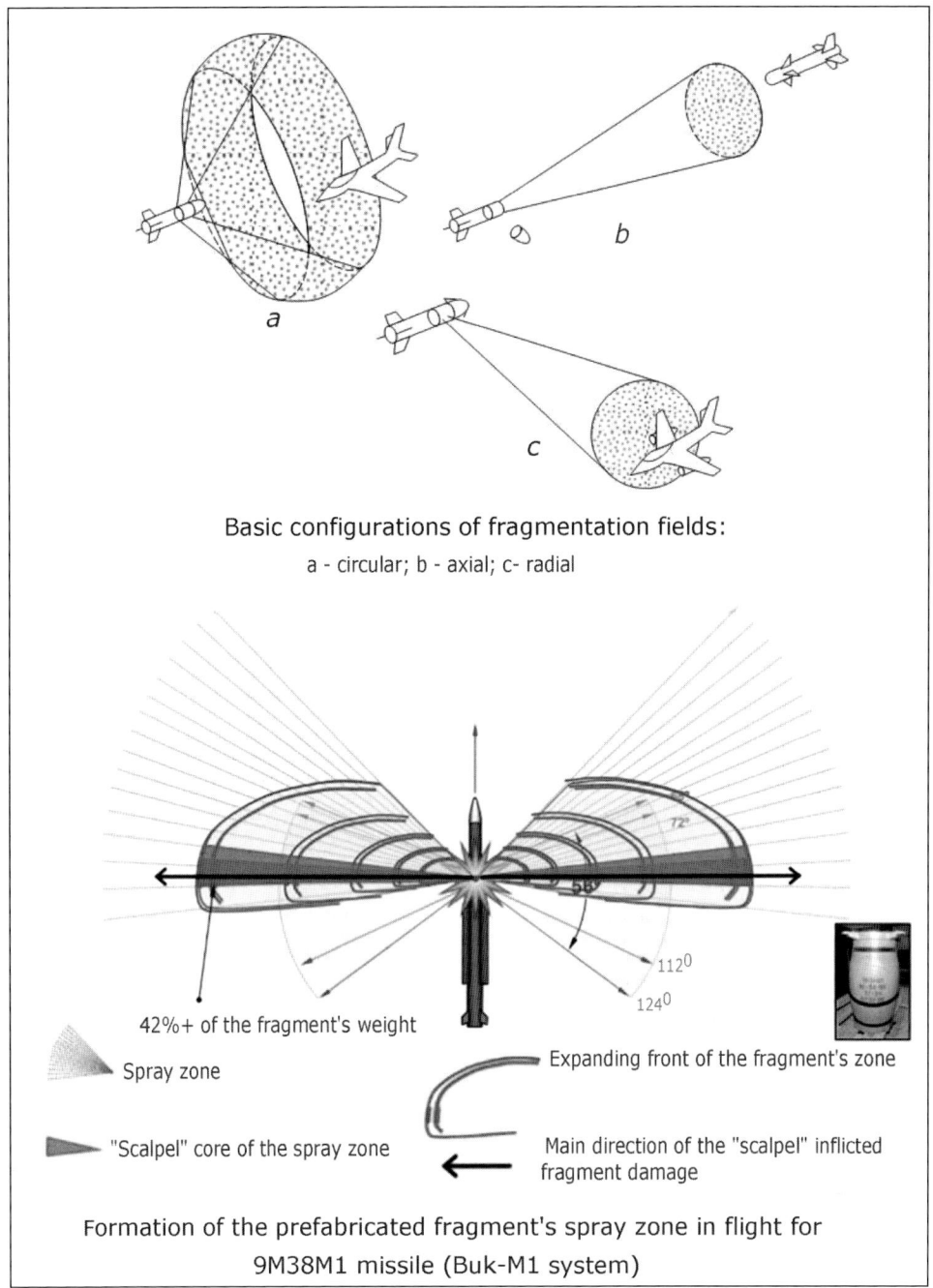

Figure 1-13: Fragmentation: circular, axial and radial (top). (*Source*: V.V. Selivanov, *Bopepripasi*, Vol. 1); 9M38M1 missile (from Buk-M1) fragmentation patterns (bottom). (*Source*: Almaz-Antey)

Piercing Through the Armor – Shaped Charges

Shaped charge warheads fall into the category of chemical energy warheads because they do not require any kinetic energy (KE) from the delivery system to be effective. This property makes them ideal for use in items such as shoulder fired weapons, grenades, mines, and even static cutting charges.

The process through which a shaped charge works is as follows:

1. An explosion is generated which passes a detonation wave over the liner,
2. The liner collapses from the rear forward and is squeezed by the pressure of the expanding gases,
3. A jet of material forms, the tip of which moves at high velocity toward the target,
4. The remaining liner material is formed into a slug which follows the jet at a much lower velocity (approximately one-tenth the tip velocity). The tip then penetrates the target material and the overall length of the jet is decreased until either the target is perforated or the entire jet is consumed.

This process generates high temperatures and pressures. This has led to several common misconceptions. Shaped charges do not burn through the armor plate. This idea is believed to have come about through the misunderstanding of the acronym HEAT, which actually stands for high-explosive anti-tank. Although high temperatures are generated during a penetration event, it is the KE of the jet that does the work. Shaped charges do not turn the liner into a liquid. When pressures are orders of magnitude above the yield strength of the material (and they are during a jet formation), the problem can be treated as a fluid dynamics problem even though the liner material is not really a fluid. If the detonation process can be frozen, what would be seen is a solid rod of material. The formation of a typical shaped charge jet is shown in Figures 1-14, 1-15 top and the penetration into the armor (bottom).

The standoff "A" (Figure 1-14) of a shaped charge is the distance from the base of the liner or cavity to the target. It is known that the standoff distance in shaped charges has an optimum value for armor penetration. The penetration performance is very sensitive to the standoff and performance rapidly decays if it is too large or too small. Explosive reactive armor is an effective way to defeat a shaped charge by breaking the jet up on impact, feeding additional material to erode the jet, and altering the standoff (Figures 1-16, 1-17).

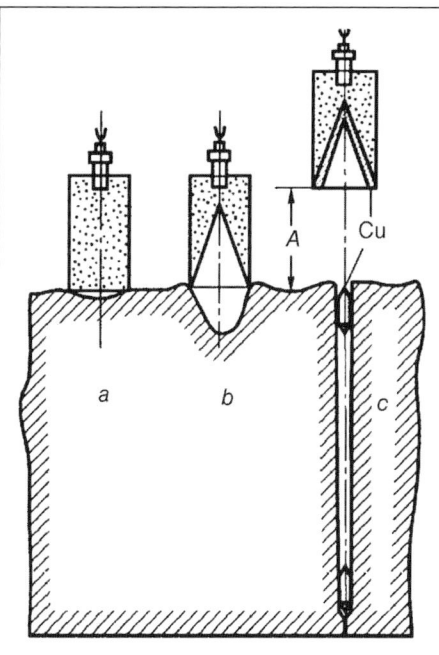

The action of high explosive (HE) charges on soft steel barrier: monolithic (a), hollow without liner (b), shaped charge with the copper lined cavity and standoff distance A (c).

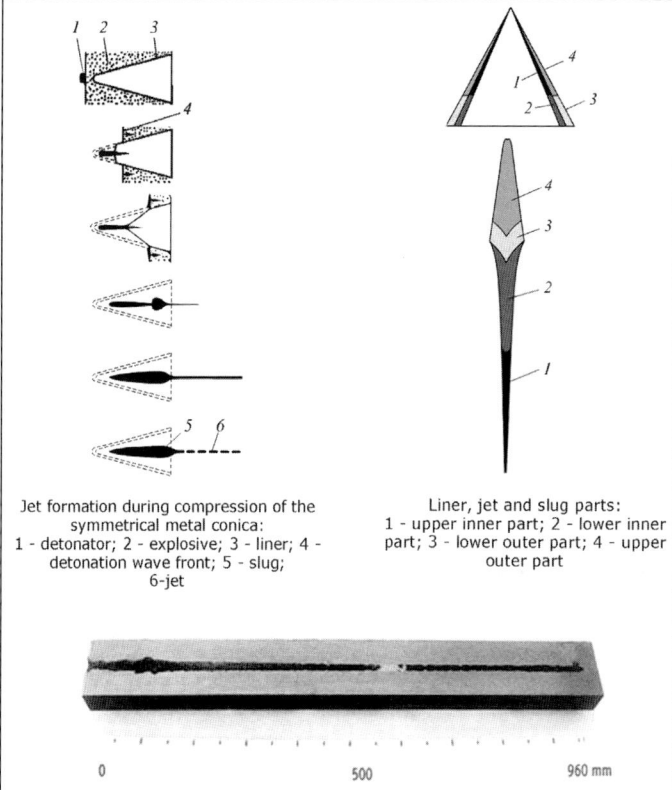

Jet formation during compression of the symmetrical metal conica:
1 - detonator; 2 - explosive; 3 - liner; 4 - detonation wave front; 5 - slug; 6 - jet

Liner, jet and slug parts:
1 - upper inner part; 2 - lower inner part; 3 - lower outer part; 4 - upper outer part

Above: Figure 1-14: Ordinary and shaped charges penetration effect comparison. (*Source*: V.V. Selivanov, *Bopepripasi*, Vol. 1)

Left: Figure 1-15: Shaped charge formation (top). (*Source*: V.V. Selivanov, *Boepripasi*, Vol. 1); armor piercing by tandem HEAT warhead (bottom). (*Source*: Author's archive)

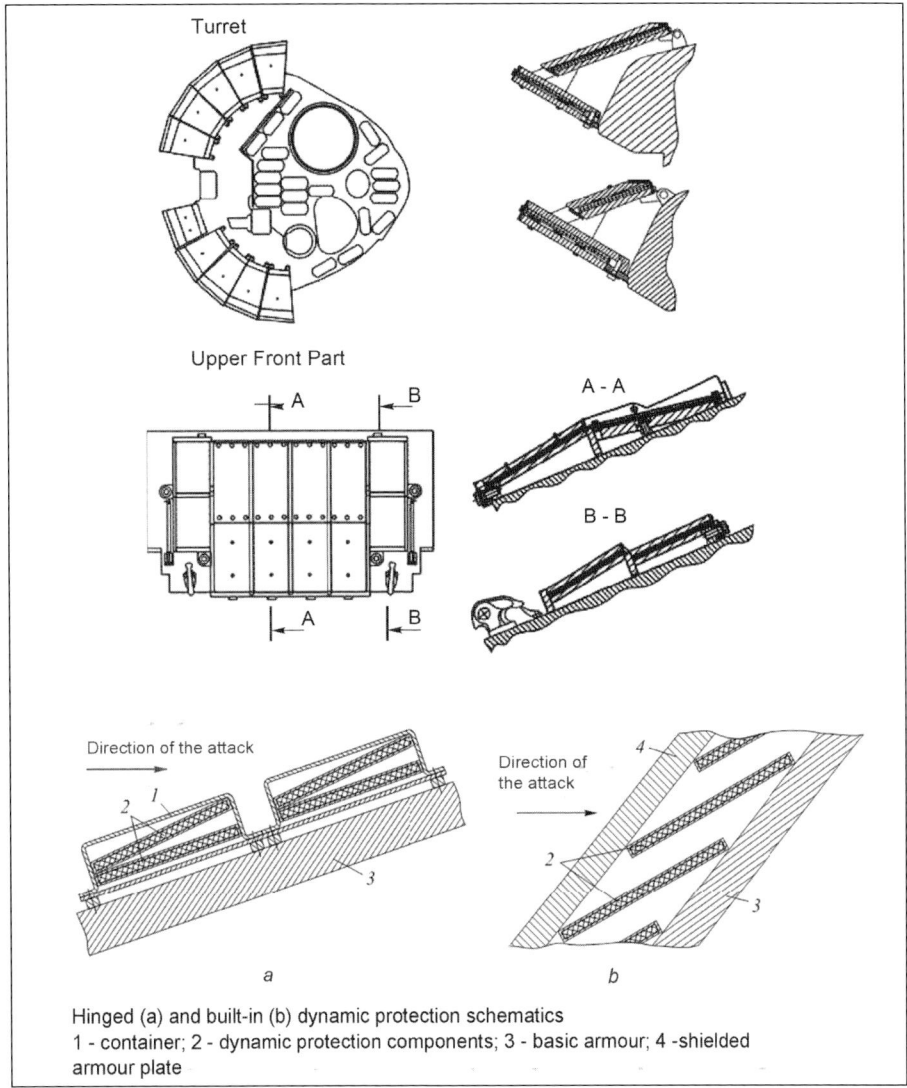

Figure 1-16: Reactive armor and installation on the tank (top and middle). (*Source*: V.V. Selivanov, *Boepripasi*, Vol. 1); multi-layered dynamic protection that can be with explosive or with the passive components (bottom).

Standoff plates and sandbags defeat shaped charges by respectively affecting the standoff or forcing the jet to be consumed. Standoff plates can be in different shapes such as slotted armor often seen in Ukraine (Figures 1-18, 1-19). One particularly interesting example is the "roof cage" seen over some of the Russian tanks which rolled into Ukraine. This is intended to defeat roof attacks by the most modern ATGMs and rockets, such as Javelin and NLAW that NATO poured into Ukraine prior to the Russian intervention.

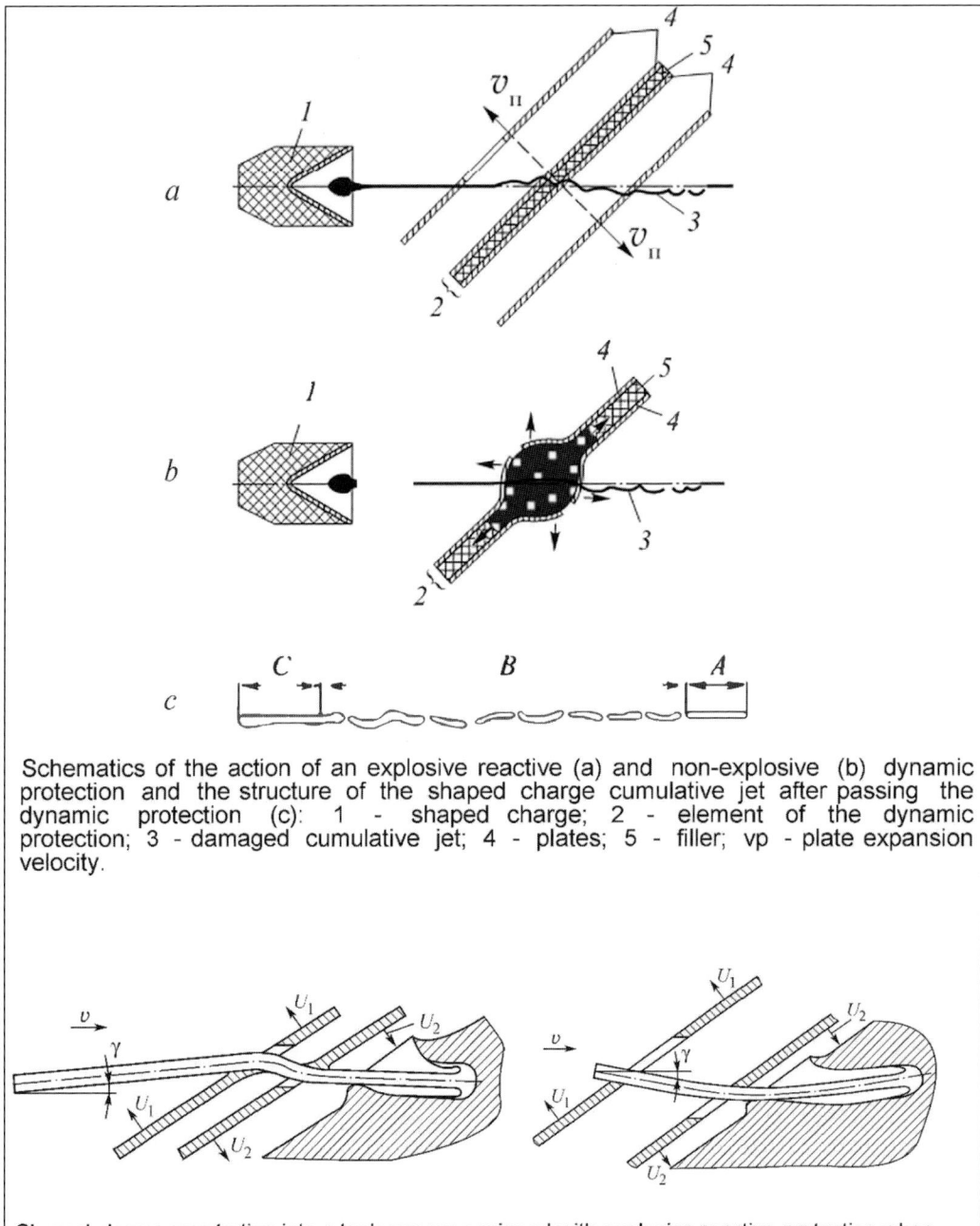

Figure 1-17: Interaction between shaped charge and reactive armor with breaking of the cumulative jet (top); shaped charge penetration through the tank armor when the explosive plates did not break the cumulative jet (bottom). (*Source*: I. Balagansky, *Damaging Effects of Weapons and Ammunition*)

In addition to standoff, detonation symmetry is also very important. A slight asymmetric geometry of the liner or charge ignition will result in inefficient or improper formation. This is why most liners designed for military use are machined to precise tolerances. Charge-to-liner mass ratio greatly affects the velocity of the jet. If this ratio is too high, the liner can

Figure 1-18: Destroyed Russian T-72B3 tank equipped with a rooftop cage armor (gur.gov.ua). In general, the working principle of the cage armor consists of short-circuiting the detonation chain of the warhead in such a way that current will no longer flow through the detonator upon the impact of the piezoelectric element on the target, generally the armored hull of a fighting vehicle. This short circuit is caused by the local deformation of the outer metallic cone by the cage armor. A very small current will still flow to the detonator due to the high resistance of the detonator and the fact that the short circuit, with very low resistance, and the detonator are forming a parallel circuit with the piezoelectric element as a power source. This very small current will normally be insufficient to trigger the detonator.

A secondary effect of the cage armor is the possible damage done to the liner of the shaped charge, even if insufficient damage has been done to the warhead to cause a short circuit in the detonation chain. Although this can significantly reduce the penetration capacity of the warhead, this is in most cases not sufficient to protect light armored vehicles from a complete perforation of the hull. However, for main battle tanks, this reduction in penetration capacity can be sufficient to avoid a complete perforation of their armor. A possible negative side-effect of the cage armor is the possibility that the explosive material in the short-circuited warhead still detonates upon impact on the main armor. This may be caused simply by the shock at impact or by the impact of the hot and possibly still burning rocket engine into the explosive material after impacting the vehicle hull. (*Source*: Frederik Coghe, "Efficiency of Different Cage Armour Systems," *Applied Sciences*)

fragment and fail to penetrate. If this ratio is too low, the jet velocity will not be high enough for efficient penetration. The liner geometry has a pronounced effect on the jet formation because it affects how the explosive wave collapses the liner and forms the jet.

Figure 1-19: Destroyed Ukrainian T-64BV (top) and Russian T-72B3 (bottom). Blown turrets as a result of an internal explosion. The autoloader on most Russian and Ukrainian tanks has the ammunition in a carousel under the floor (T-72, T-90) or sidewise (T-80, T-84, T-64). If the ATGM can score a top hit or just between the turret and hull, the jet may penetrate the armor (top armor is 25–50mm thick) and set off the ammunition initiating the explosion that may blow off the turret. The media often present tanks as Russian but the reality is that both sides have lost equipment in large quantities. (*Source*: Ukrainian and Russian MoDs)

Thermobaric Warheads

Thermobaric weapons are explosives optimized to produce heat and pressure effects instead of armor-penetrating or fragmentation damage effects. Explosives used in thermobaric weapons are generally oxygen-deficient; additional oxygen from the air is required to achieve complete combustion of the charge. Only part of the energy is released during the initial detonation phase, which generates high levels of fuel-rich products that undergo "after-burning" when mixed with the shock-heated air. The energy released through after-burning and combustion lengthens the duration of blast overpressure and increases the fireball. In conventional blast/fragmentation TNT-based munitions, no significant after-burn occurs. Fragments inhibit the mixing of detonation gases with air and the rapid expansion of the detonation has a cooling effect before mixing with atmospheric oxygen occurs.

The weapons are particularly effective in enclosed spaces such as tunnels, buildings, and field fortifications. Fireball and blast can travel around corners and penetrate areas inaccessible to bomb fragments. Blast waves are intensified when reflected by walls and other surfaces.

The primary injury mechanisms are blast and heat, with secondary effects through flying fragments and toxic detonation gases.

The kill radius for blast is usually greater than the kill radius for burns, so that protection against thermal injuries has little benefit (Figure 1-20).

Figure 1-20: TOS-1A point blank hit (top); stills from the Russian UAV showing the Ukrainian position hit with a thermobaric rockets. The soldier (circled) appears to be thrown more than 40m away (bottom).

Chapter 2

Operational-Tactical Missile Systems

A ballistic missile is a surface-to-surface missile that follows a sub-orbital ballistic trajectory to deliver one or more warheads to a predetermined target. A ballistic missile trajectory consists of three parts: the powered flight portion (boost phase), the free-flight portion which constitutes most of the flight time (cruise phase), and the re-entry phase where the missile re-enters the earth's atmosphere (descent-terminal phase).[1]

Ballistic missiles can be launched from fixed sites or mobile launchers, including vehicles (transporter erector launchers – TELs), aircraft, ships, and submarines. The powered flight portion can last from a few tens of seconds to several minutes and can consist of multiple rocket stages. Surface-to-surface ballistic missiles can vary widely in range and use, and are often divided into categories based on range. Various schemes are used by different countries to categorize the ranges of ballistic missiles. In the countries of the former Warsaw Pact classification of surface-to-surface ballistic missiles was as follows:

- Tactical (30–100km),
- Operational (200–1,500km),
- Strategic (3,000–12,000+km).

Missiles for operational-tactical and tactical purposes are used to destroy enemy combat assets such as missile systems, MLRS, long-range artillery, radars, and air defense systems, aviation at airfields, command and control centers, command posts, nuclear attack weapons, large concentrations of troops, and important civilian infrastructure facilities (railway junctions, bridges, power plants, factories, repair centres, etc.). In this regard, many missiles of these complexes, in addition to conventional ones, have nuclear warheads, are controlled on a flight path, and in some cases have detachable warheads that maneuver when approaching the target. Launchers provide the launch of one or two missiles at high angles and contain equipment in their design that provides pre-launch preparation of missiles. Modern OTRK are placed on wheeled or tracked chassis with high cross-country ability. Some launchers can swim across water obstacles. OTRK are transported by all modes of transport.

Operational-tactical missile systems[2] – an integral link in the chain of missile weapons of all modern armies – perform important combat work in Ukraine. These workhorses are Tochka-U and Iskander and the appearance of US-supplied ATACMS is still questionable at the time of writing.

Tochka-U

In March 1968 development work began on the creation of the Tochka operational-tactical rocket complex (OTK-21) designated as 9K79 to replace the outdated OTRK 9K52 Luna. Tochka entered into service in 1976. The firing range for the first model 9M79 was 15–70km and an average CEP of 250m. In this chapter, Tochka-U is designated a rocket because no guidance or correction is available.

In 1984, the modernization of the Tochka complex began with the intention to increase the range (up to 120km) and accuracy. The modernized complex was named Tochka-U, and the new 9M79M rocket was developed (Figure 2-1). A great improvement on the old rocket, an optical seeker is installed on the rocket, which ensures the defeat of point targets. The warhead can be equipped with an AA-60 nuclear warhead, a high-explosive and fragmentation (HE-FRAG) 9N123F warhead and 9N123K cluster warhead. The cluster warhead contains bomblets with fifty fragmentation submunitions. The head part does not separate from the rocket motor section in flight. The control system is autonomous, and inertial, with an onboard computer system. On the final section of the trajectory, flight control is carried out utilizing the GOS. Thus, the flight of the rocket is controlled throughout the trajectory, which ensures high accuracy. Upon reaching the target, the rocket is rotated and vertically dived at the target. To achieve the greatest efficiency of the HE-FRAG warhead, an air blast is carried out over the target.

The 9M79F rocket is equipped with the 9N123F HE-FRAG warhead (Figure 2-2). The warhead is designed to destroy targets by fragmentations and blasts. It consists of:

- Body with explosive and fragments,
- Proximity fuze 9E118,
- Two impacts sensor 9E128,
- Safety and initiating mechanism 9E117.

The weight of the warhead is 482kg. The body of the warhead is filled with explosives and fragments. The explosive filling charge consists of 162.5kg of high explosives. The bursting of the warhead creates 14,500 fragments

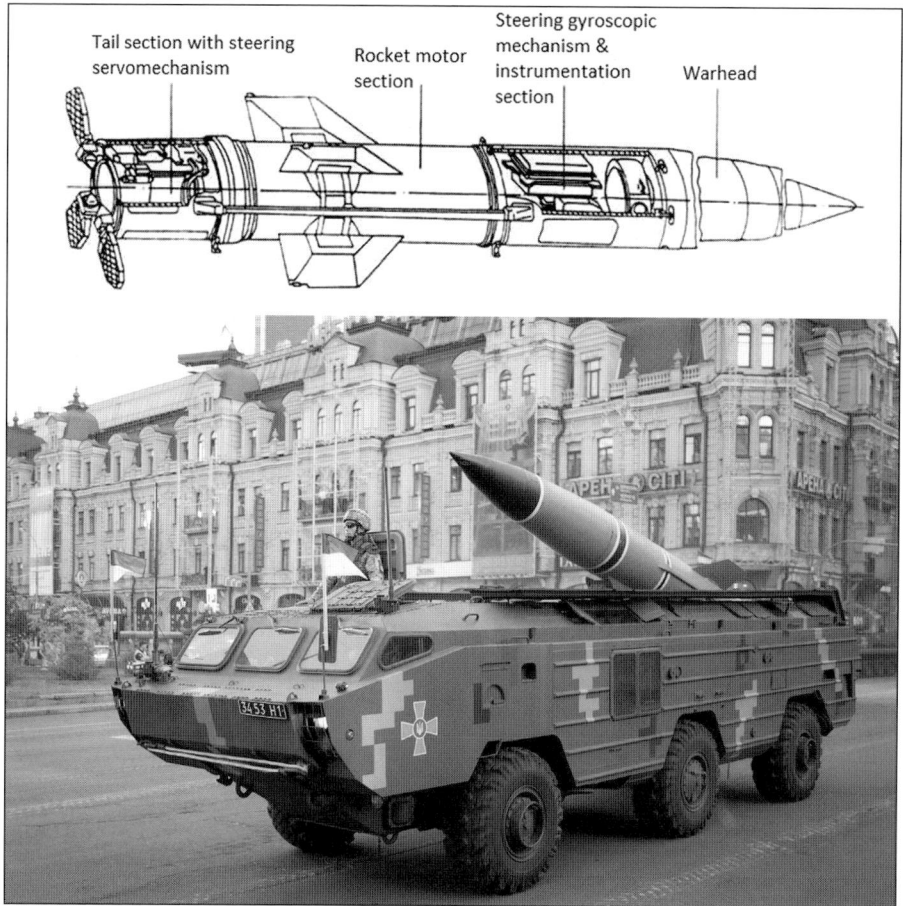

Figure 2-1: 9M79M rocket cutaway (top) and Ukrainian Tochka-U TEL (bottom). (*Source*: Author's archive, Wikimedia commons)

(6,000 pieces with a weight of 20.8g, 4,000 pieces with a weight of 10g, and 4,500 pieces with a weight of 5.47g).

Proximity fuze 9E118 is designed to send a switching command for the explosion of the warhead when the rocket is approximately 15m above the ground and prior to that at 450m above the ground sends an impulse to turn the rocket at the incidence angle of 80° to improve the effectiveness of the explosion. Proximity fuze consists of:

- Two altitude sensors, independent of each other,
- Radio sensor to turn rocket at the incidence angle,
- Laser sensor to send switching command.

Impacts sensor 9E128 is an impulse magneto-electric generator. It is designed to send electric impulses to safety and initiating mechanisms if the rocket hits the target and the proximity fuze fails. The electric impulse activates an electric detonator.

Safety and initiating mechanism 9E117 is electromechanical with two levels of safety which under the signal from proximity fuze or impact sensors produce detonation impulse to initiation explosive charge. The safety and initiating mechanism ensures safe handling and safe transport up to activation. The first level of safety is deactivated after the rocket launch. The second level of safety is deactivated in the descending phase of flight. Safety and initiating mechanism consists of:

- The safety actuation mechanism of first and second levels,
- Switch over mechanism,
- Initiation circuit.

An integral part of the safety and initiating mechanism is the booster, electric detonator, and two squibs.

The 9M79K rocket (Figures 2-3 to 2-5) has the 9N123K cluster warhead (Figure 2-2) designated to destroy the target by fragments from the 9N24 submunitions (bomblets). The warhead consists of:

- Body,
- Central bursting charge,
- 9N24 submunition,
- 9E117 safety and initiating mechanism,
- 9E326 radio sensor.

The weight of the warhead is 482kg. The body of the warhead is filled with a central bursting charge and fifty 9N24 sub- munitions. A central bursting charge is designed to open the body of the warhead and scatter the 9N24 submunition. The weight of the central bursting charge is approximately 2.5kg.

Construction of the 9N24 submunition is similar to the 9N22 submunition which is used in the 9M21 "Luna" rocket, except for the weight of the bursting charge. The central bursting charge consists of nineteen TNT cylinders. The weight of the bursting charge is 1.45kg high explosives. Safety and initiating mechanism 9E117 is the same as in the 9N123F warhead. However, there is one difference, the signal for activation is received from a radio sensor, not from a proximity fuze.

Radio sensor 9E326 sends an electric signal to safety and initiating mechanism 2,250m above the ground (by surface reflection).

The executive surfaces of the control system are "lattice-type" aerodynamic rudders on the tail of the rocket, controlled by steering mechanisms (Figure 2-3).

At the starting section of the trajectory, when the speed of the rocket is insufficient for the operation of aerodynamic rudders, control is carried out through gas-dynamic rudders. The rocket launch is carried out from

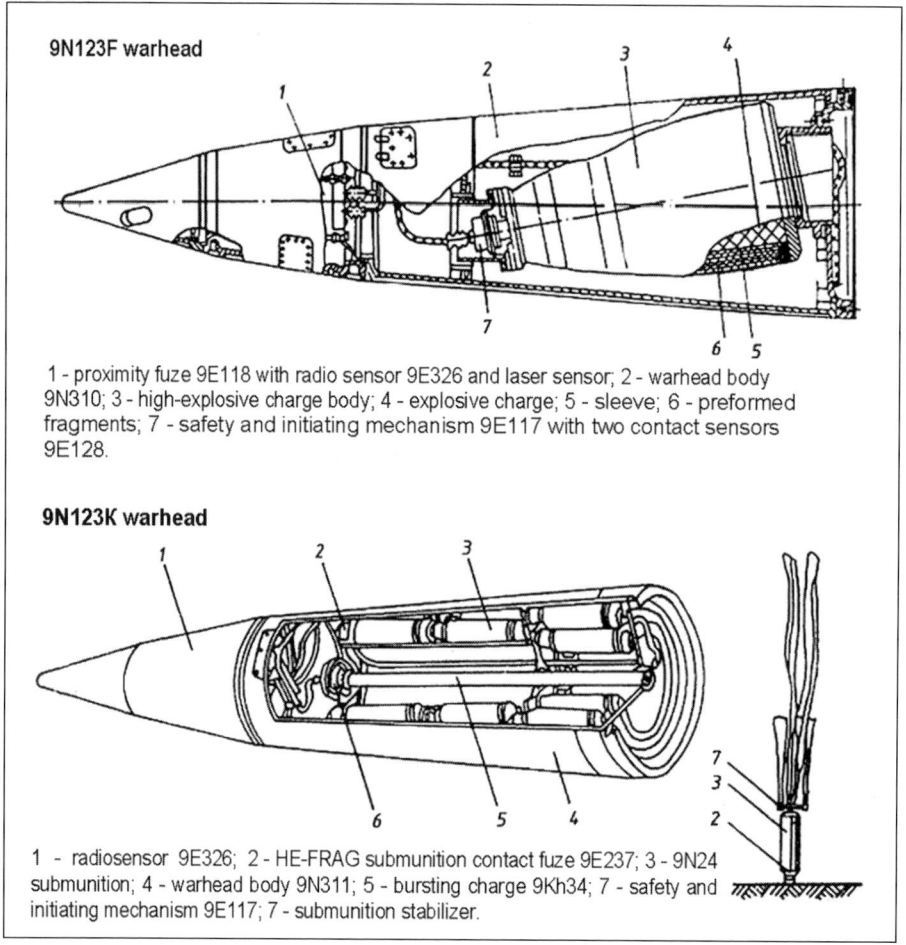

Figure 2-2: 9N123F HE-FRAG (top); 9N123K cluster (bottom). (*Source*: Author's archive)

an inclined guide, and after launch, the rocket makes a turn towards the target. The direction of the launcher position in relation to the target is +15°, which, when notching the trajectory, reduces the likelihood of an accurate determination of the starting point.

To direct Tochka-U at the target, digital maps of the area are used, created from the results of space or aerial photography of the enemy's territory. In Ukrainian use, photographs and information are obtained from domestic sources and NATO Intelligence Centres.

The rocket motor is a solid-propellant single-mode type. The launcher 9P129M-1 is mounted on a wheeled chassis model 5921, manufactured by the Bryansk Automobile Plant, structurally it is a closed sealed container, on the bottom of which the launcher itself is located. The main node of the launcher is a swinging beam with a hydraulic drive for lifting the

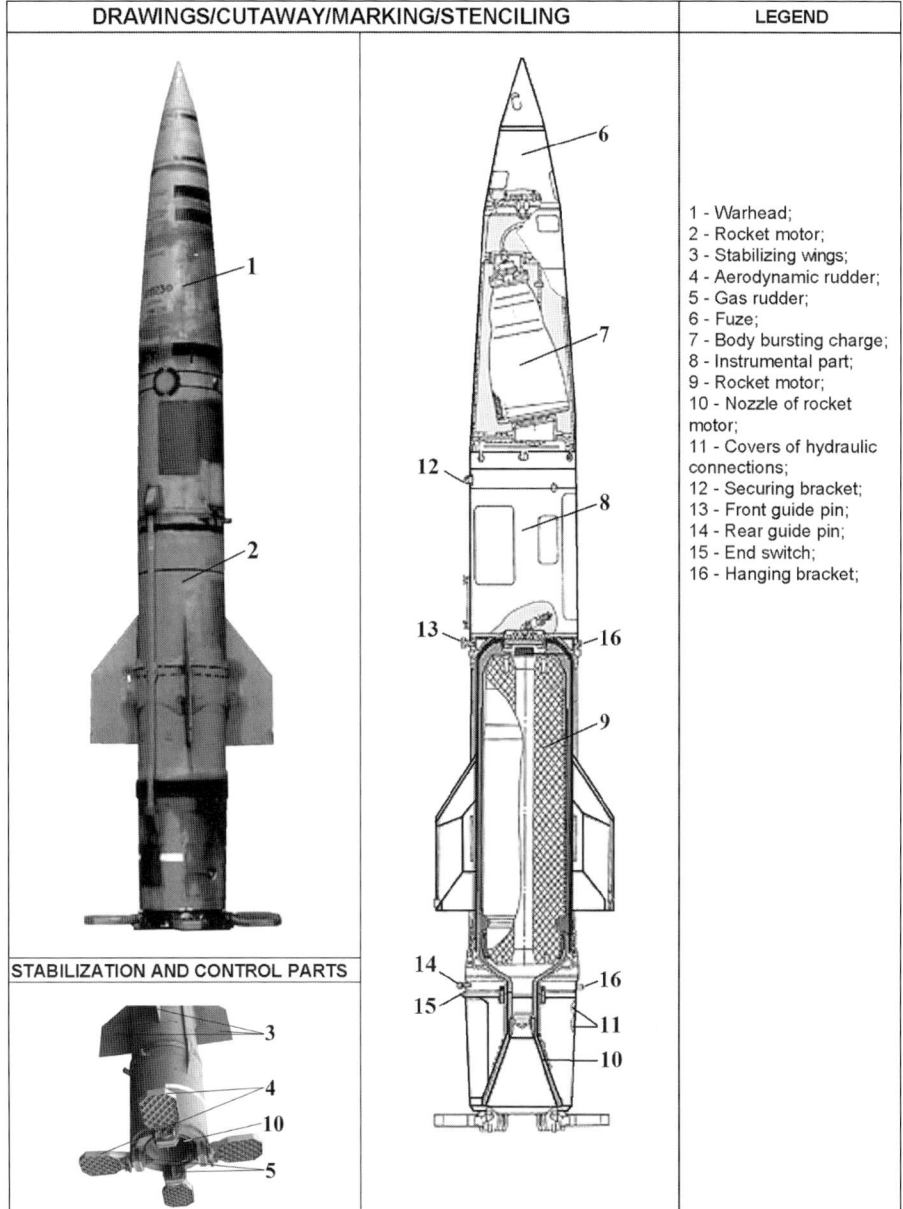

Figure 2-3: 9M79M ballistic rocket. (*Source*: former Warsaw Pact *Ammunition Handbook*, Vol. 2)

rocket to an elevation angle. From above, the container is closed with sliding lids.

The 9T218-1 transport-loading vehicle (TZM) was made in a similar way on the 5922 chassis. Inside the container, there are cradles for two rockets or four warheads. In the body of the TZM, there is a jib crane for reloading the

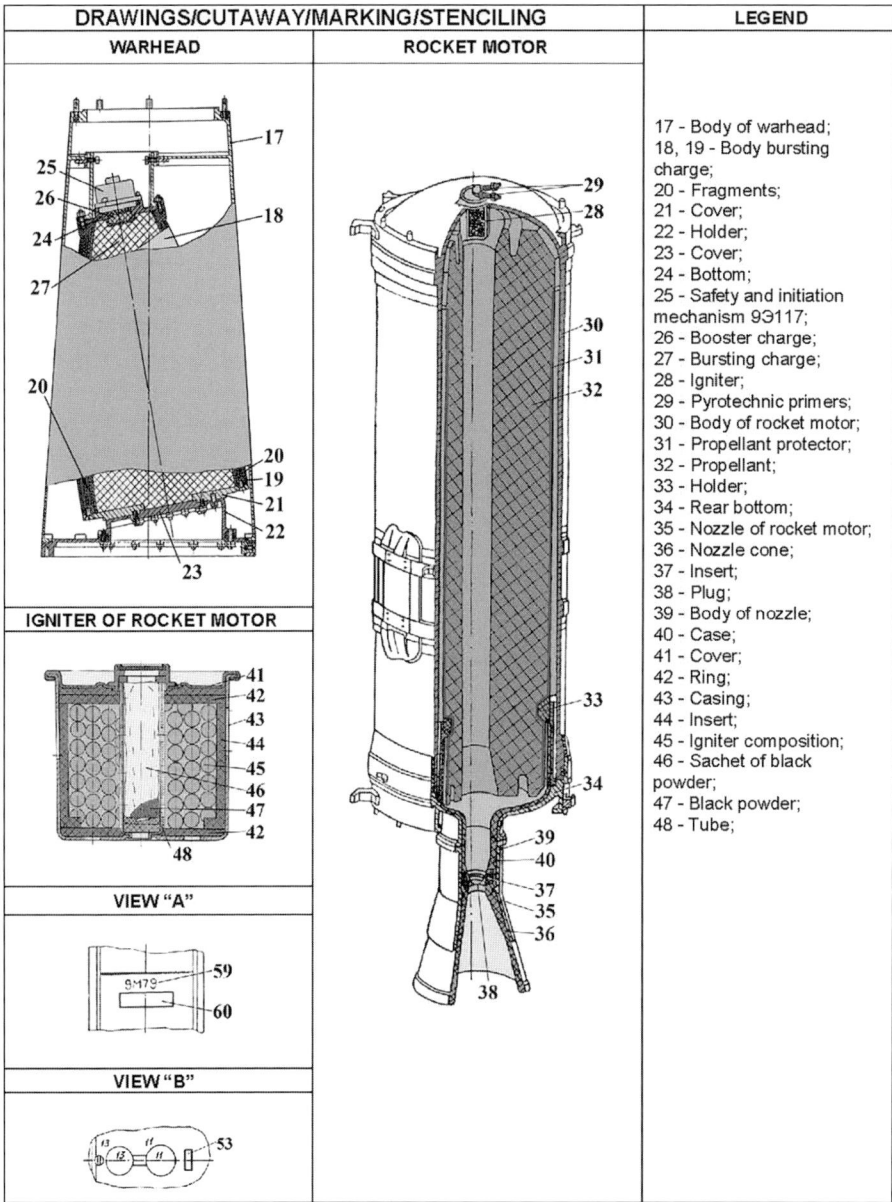

Figure 2-4: 9M791 warhead rocket motor section. (*Source*: former Warsaw Pact *Ammunition Handbook*, Vol. 2)

launcher. Both chassis are equipped with a 5D20B-300 six-cylinder diesel engine. All wheels are driven and tires with adjustable air pressure. Wheel suspension is independent of the torsion bar. The wheels of the first and third pairs are steerable. Propeller-type jet propulsion pumps are provided for the movement of the water. On the water, the chassis is controlled by

OPERATIONAL-TACTICAL MISSILE SYSTEMS

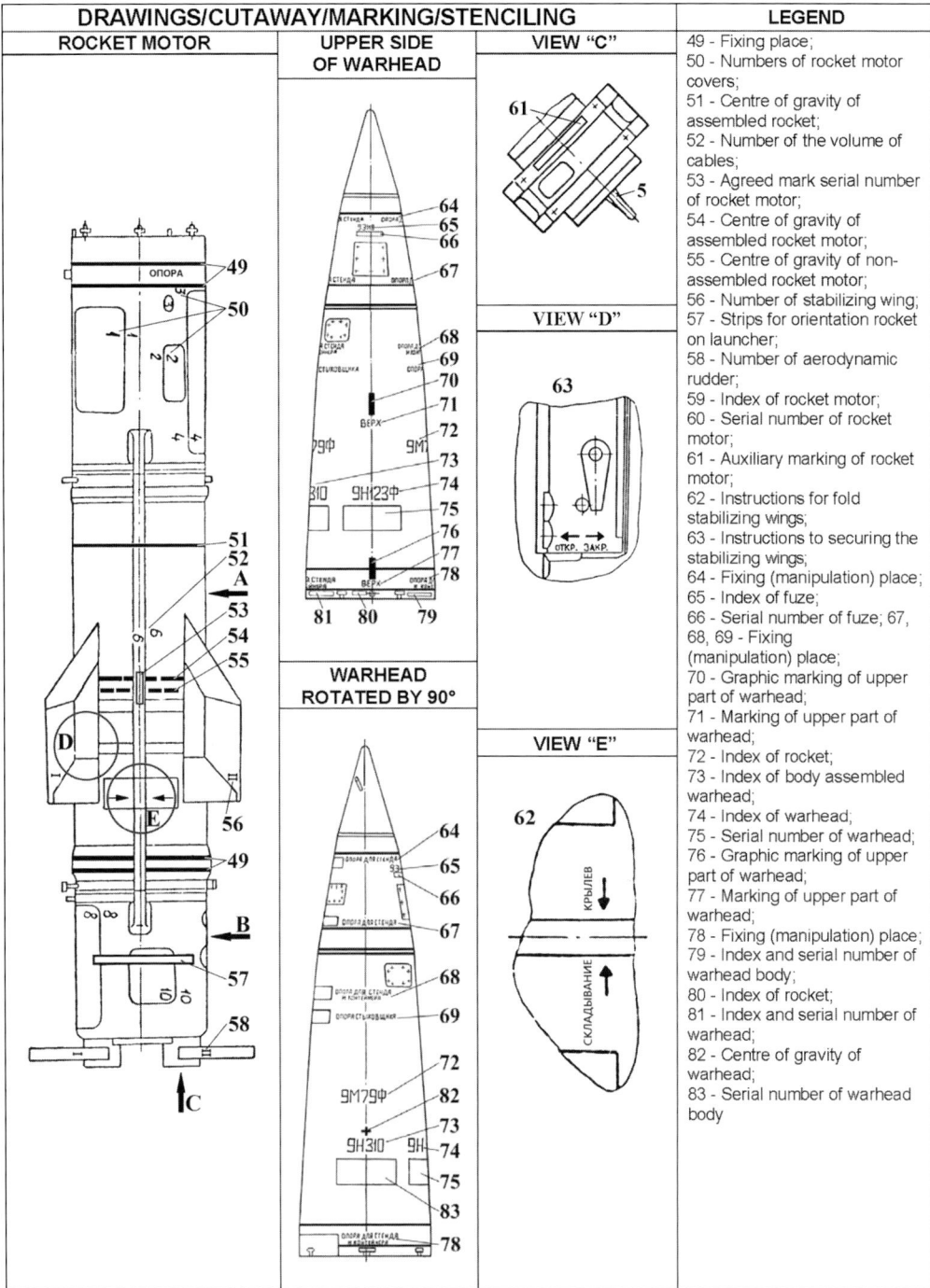

Figure 2-5: 9M791-1 markings. These markings with the missile inventory files are crucial in determining which side fired missiles. The blame game is ever-present in Ukraine. (*Source*: former Warsaw Pact *Ammunition Handbook*, Vol. 2)

water cannon dampers and channels built into the hull. Both launcher and loader can move on and off-road.

The 9P129M-1 launcher equipment independently solves all the tasks of tying the launch point, calculating the flight task, and aiming the rocket. The complex does not require topographic and geodetic and preliminary engineering preparation of the starting position and meteorological support. From 16–20 minutes after the launcher arrives at the launch position, the rocket can be launched towards the target, and after 1.5 minutes the launcher can leave the launch site. The rocket rises to the start 15 seconds before launch, which ensures high secrecy. The launcher can transport one rocket.

In the war in Ukraine, only the Ukrainian forces are using Tochka-U rockets (Figure 2-6). After independence, Ukraine retained about

Figure 2-6: Ukrainian 9P29M launchers ready for fire, eastern Ukraine (top left); 9P29M launcher which executed twelve 9M79M1 launches (top right); rocket launch (bottom). (*Source*: Author's archive)

90 launchers and about 800 older rockets. Since the outbreak of the civil war in the east, Ukrainian forces have actively targeted the rebel positions, infrastructure, and sometimes residential areas. After Russia launched its special operation, Tochka-U were launched against the targets in Russia hitting the military airport and destroying several fighters there. It was also credited with hitting Berdyansk port and sinking a Russian transport ship and damaging several others (Figure 2-8 top). One of the infamous events was the hit on downtown Donetsk, which killed numerous civilians, and the controversial hit on Kramatorsk railway station (Figure 2-7 bottom).

Figure 2-7: 9M79M stabilizer with characteristic "lettuce" stabilizers (top); rocket motor section with the words "for kids" written on it as found in Kramatorsk (the rocket was Ukrainian but likely downed by Russian air defence and fell onto the city) (bottom). Some damage from explosions is shown in Figure 2-8. (*Source*: Author's archive)

Ukraine accused Russia of intended targeting of civilian areas but Russia has not been using Tochka-U system for a while, rather the new one – Iskander. As the war progressed, Russian forces were able to neutralize the majority of the launchers and rockets. Occasionally, Ukraine launches some rockets but that has become rarer more recently. Russia's air defense (S-300V and Buk) is constantly intercepting and destroying Ukrainian rockets (Figure 2-7 top).

Figure 2-8: 9M791 impact on the Russian landing and supply ship *Orsk* in the port of Berdyansk (top); crater on the Donbas road. (*Source*: Author's archive)

Some of the hits in the residential areas are actually parts of the intercepted rocket out of which some bomblets may not be destroyed in the air and exploded upon impact. If the rocket is not intercepted, the damage at the target would be much greater.

Iskander

In the opening minutes of the "Special Military Operation," ballistic missiles struck key Ukrainian positions – command centers, communication nodes, airports, and ammunition storages. The initial "star" of the war was the 9K270 Iskander short- and medium-range operational-tactical missile system.

The Soviet Union started developing short-range ballistic missiles in the late 1950s. The very first one was the 9K52 Luna after which a generation of missiles followed. The latest is the 9K720 Iskander, which represents the core of Russia's modern precision strike capability. In Western military circles, for a long time the Iskander development was considered a response to Western missile defenses. Even today the Iskander is often described as a more sophisticated successor to the 9K79 (OTRK-21) Tochka. However, the direct technological predecessor of the 9K720 system was the 9K714 Oka (OTRK-23) short-range ballistic missile system. Behind the development was the idea to have a rapid deployable tactical ballistic missile that can be set up and launched in a very short time – up to 5 minutes.

As a result of the state of the Soviet technical development, the 9M714 missile was poorly suited to any precise conventional missions because of a circular error probable (CEP) of about 50–100m. The system relied on a combination of inertial guidance and an early digitized scene-mapping area correlator providing radar terrain contour matching for guidance in its terminal phase. This was a viable means of striking targets that were large, fixed, and on well-mapped terrain, but was less useful against camouflaged, time-sensitive, or mobile targets. Moreover, the missile was not sufficiently accurate to hit hardened or underground targets or to dispense submunitions reliably.[3]

The Iskander project was likely continued covertly in the 1990s by the Kolomna Machine Bureau under the aegis of a satellite programme. The 9M723 ballistic missile (Figure 2-9) fielded as part of the Iskander system represents the culmination of these efforts, providing Russia with a highly accurate prompt strike capability that can be used for both tactical- and theater-level missions. In addition, the system can launch cruise missiles – the 9M727 and 9M728.[4]

By formation, the Iskanders are assigned to Missile Brigades, which are separate from the Strategic Missile Brigades that employ the country's ground-based strategic missiles. The brigades are intended to support

Figure 2-9: 9P78-1 transporter-erector-launcher (TEL) with 2M723 missiles. (*Source*: Said Aminov)

the Russian ground troops with operational-tactical precision strikes. Regarding the numbers, one or more brigades are assigned to each of Russia's military districts.

Composition and Operation

The Iskander system was designated 9K270, and consists of the 9P78-1 transporter erector launcher (TEL) vehicles (each carrying two missiles); the 9T250E transporter loader vehicles; the 9S552 command post vehicle; and the 9S920 information processing station. The basic combat unit is a battalion equipped with four 9P78-1 TELs. An Iskander-M brigade is provided with three battalions for a total of twelve TELs per brigade (Figure 2-10).

The 9P78-1 TEL is based on an 8x8 MZKT-7930 all-terrain chassis from the Minsk Tractor Plant in Belarus and is fitted with a gas-turbine generator that provides power for the elevation and programming of the missiles. The gross vehicle weight of a 9P78-1 is 42.3 tonnes. It can attain speeds of 70km/h on roads, but is designed to be taken off-road to conduct engagements. The TEL vehicle can be made ready to launch a missile within 16 minutes of travelling, although this is reduced to 5 minutes if the vehicle is stationary. The TEL is crewed by three personnel, and the 9T250E that is also based on

Figure 2-10: Iskander system components.

the MZKT-7930 carries a crew of two. It uses a crane to reload missiles onto the TEL and can also dock or undock the missile warheads. Reloading the missiles requires a maximum of 16 minutes (Figure 2-11).[5]

The brigade support 9S552 and 9S920 vehicles are capable of receiving and processing real-time full-motion video from UAVs as well as targeting data from the "Strelets" reconnaissance command and control system. It allows targeteers to select areas on a map for targeted strikes by a range of Russian long-range assets. The coordinates are confirmed and then entered using a computer in the cab of the 9P78-1. There is a datalink in the rear of the vehicle that transmits the coordinates to the missile and programmes it for the engagement. The type of data varies depending upon the seeker used; some are capable of using synthetic aperture radar or optical imagery of the target to enable the seeker head to adjust the missile's course and ensure a high degree of accuracy.

Once the target coordinates have been programmed into the missile, it is elevated from the horizontal to the vertical position and then launched. Both missiles carried by the TEL can be launched within 1 minute of each other, and it may be possible for a single TEL to carry two different missiles such as the 9M728 and 9M723 with both launched to arrive at the target at the same time, further complicating any air defense efforts. Russian forces have also practiced the integration of Iskander and the Tornado-S multiple rocket launcher into a single reconnaissance-strike complex, the mass of the latter complementing the precision of the former.

At operational-strategic ranges, the missile is intended to strike important strategic targets such as headquarters, industrial and repair production facilities, critical infrastructure, and hardened storage sites such as underground bunkers and ammunition depots up to 500km range, which are widely used in Ukraine. Russia is moving their Iskander brigades to "encircle" the territory and put it under the range.

The adoption of UAVs by the Russian armed forces on a large scale, coupled with their use of automated systems such as the ISBU[6] to fuse and disseminate data, can allow information regarding mobile targets to be relayed in near real time. This is, however, subject to the significant caveat that it is probably only viable on a limited scale, in contexts where the Russians can saturate a compact battlefield with sensors and communicate across limited distances. It is noteworthy that the contexts in which Russia achieved this ideal – Donbas and Syria – are relatively small theaters, while the Russian forces have not achieved comparable effects across Ukraine. That said, the Iskander can likely now accurately strike targets of tactical-operational significance including brigade headquarters, supply depots, and communications nodes at very short notice in compact theaters such as Donbas, Kharkov, Nikolaev, or the Baltic states.

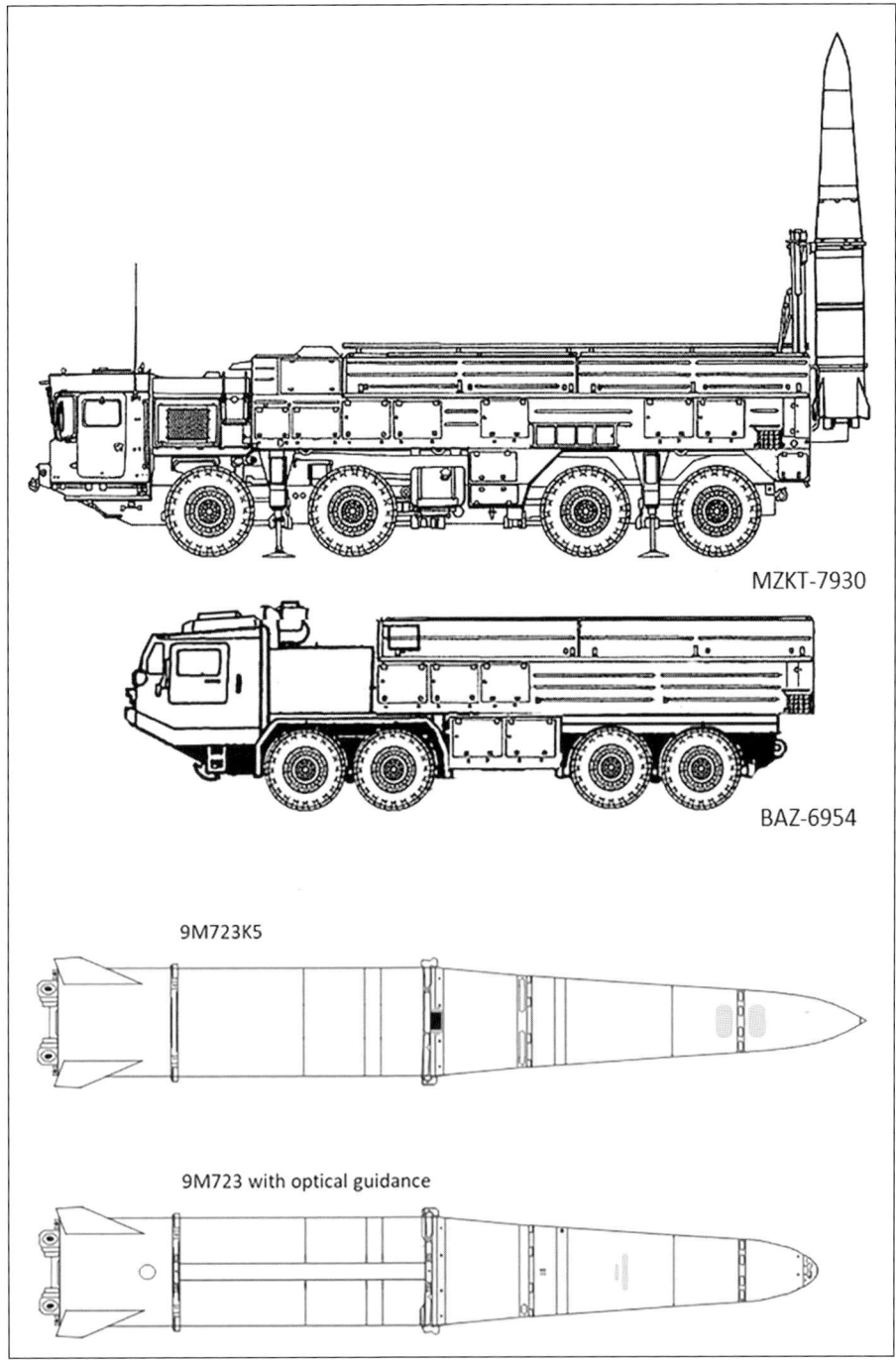

Figure 2-11: 9P78-1 transporter erector launcher (TEL) on MZKT-7930 chassis and BAZ-6954 chassis (top); 9M723 with 9M723K5 cluster warhead and 9M732 with optical self-guidance (bottom).

The Orlan-10 UAV is one of the assets that can be used to provide targeting data for the Iskander complex, although its range when remotely piloted is limited to 150km. This data may be combined with other sources such as radar, SAR, and information collected by special forces to inform an accurate targeting mission.

The Missiles
The 9K270 operates two types: the 9M723 series of quasi-ballistic missiles and cruise missiles derived from Russia's 3M-14 family. The 9M723 missile entered into service in 2006 and appears to have worked its way through several iterations to reach its current capability. The missile body can carry warheads weighing between 480kg and 700kg, and the warhead types include cluster munitions, unitary high-explosive warheads, and tactical nuclear payloads. While likely to have a range of roughly 500km if carrying a 700kg warhead, the missile's range can be doubled depending on the size of the warhead used and its trajectory (Figures 2-12, 2-13).[7]

In addition to work conducted on the missile's motor, the 9M723 received the electro-optical (EO) seeker which the Soviets planned to install on the Oka, reducing its CEP by an order of magnitude to 5–10m. An accurate electro-optical (EO) seeker and a more capable onboard computer called the Baget 62-04, which supports EO image processing in terminal phase, allow the missile to classify a range of mobile targets that could not have been hit by older systems – as illustrated in the conflict in Ukraine, where an Iskander was used to attack a Buk-M1 surface-to-air missile vehicle. The Baget 62-04 is used onboard both cruise and ballistic missiles fired from the Iskander. The JSC Serpukhov Metallist Plant specifically names it as a product manufactured for the Iskander-M in a 2013 report.

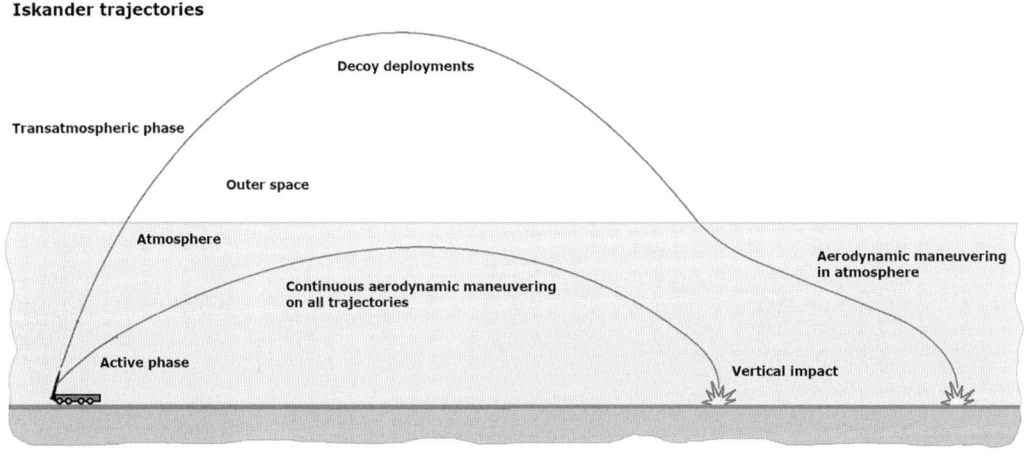

Figure 2-12: Iskander trajectories. (*Source*: L.N. Tsiginalo, modified by author)

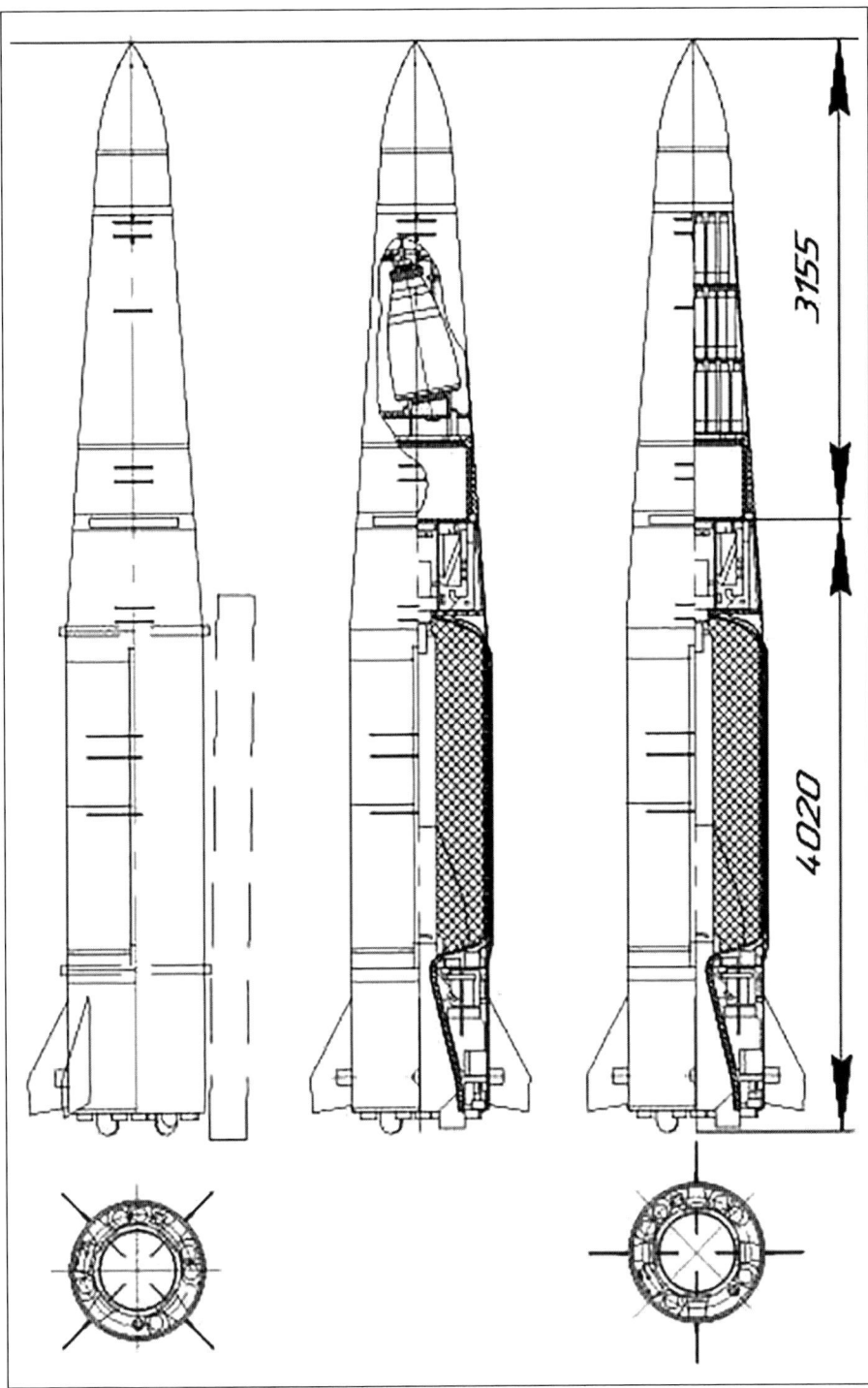

Figure 2-13: Iskander missile at launching rail (left); 9M723F (HE-FRAG warhead (middle); and 9M723K cluster warhead (right).

Assuming the practice of using common components across different missiles is consistent, the 9M723 likely also carries the Zarya, a system for processing radar feedback that is found on the 9M727. The use of EO seekers and possibly radar allows the 9M723 to be used against a wider range of targets. For example, the Russian Ministry of Defense reported in 2018 that Iskanders had been used to engage ships for the first time, illustrating how a combination of active and EO seekers enables them to hit moving targets. Functionality against ships also illustrates the capacity for high-g terminal phase maneuvers.[8]

The seeker used may be dependent upon the payload carried. The missiles that are not equipped with a seeker – those carrying cluster munitions – are able to strike within 30m of their intended target, which is sufficient for cluster munitions to take effect. Those carrying a seeker are much more accurate and may be capable of striking within 4m of the target.

In midcourse, the 9M723 relies on a combination of DSMAC, inertial guidance, and, potentially, satellite navigation systems (including the Russian GLONASS and US GPS systems). As of 2009, Russia was working to incorporate datalinks that could allow the system to draw on data from UAVs and satellite guidance for target designation. While there is no conclusive evidence of success in this regard, it appears likely on the balance of probabilities. The objective of incorporating datalinks on the missile was, after all, being pursued by the Soviets (on the Oka). It is also of note that the USSR had already succeeded in incorporating datalinks on supersonic cruise missiles such as the P-700 – though the task of maintaining communication using datalinks is simpler on a cruise missile's trajectory. Even working on conservative assumptions and assuming a slow and inefficient rate of product development by the Russian defense sector, an objective that has been the subject of several decades of work may well have reached fruition. The frequency of UAV footage of Iskander ballistic missile strikes might also lend itself to the idea that the Iskander can receive in-flight retargeting – though, of course, there is an obvious sampling bias (strikes conducted with no nearby UAVs are not filmed), and UAVs may be used for the simpler tasks of target designation and battle-damage assessment before and after a launch, respectively.[9]

In addition to ballistic missiles, the Iskander can launch cruise missiles – the 9M727 and 9M728 (Figures 2-14, 2-15, 2-16). The advantage of cruise missiles is that they are designed to fly a variable profile that is mostly at a low altitude to reduce the risks of detection and complicate countermeasures. Their slower speeds and more consistent altitudes also make tasks such as maintaining datalinks with satellites easier. The 9M727 may be an earlier version of the 9M728, however, both have been used in Ukraine, and it is not clear what differentiates them. The missiles are understood to fly at altitudes no higher than 6km, although this may be reduced to 6m on approach to the target. The missiles contain the Zarya and the Baget 62-04 which, respectively, process radar signals and TV guidance. It appears the 9M727 and 9M728 use the latter in their terminal phase. The missiles can carry a 480kg warhead and have a range of 500km, leading them to be given the designation R-500. Once launched, the missile maintains an altitude of 50–150m above land, and when within 20km of its intended target, the radar guidance system begins to search for the target. It can complete an engagement using either a combination of the satellite receiver and the inertial navigation system, or both of these together with the radar seeker. In the latter circumstance, the missile can strike within 1–3m of its target. The processing module onboard the 9M727 is the SN-99 – a guidance system compatible with both GPS and GLONASS. The system is common to a number of other cruise missiles including the Kh-101 and the 3M-14 Kalibr and, notably, is reliant on some Western components.[10] It is important to say that Russia during planning the operation acquired significant numbers of the key components and reengineered or developed

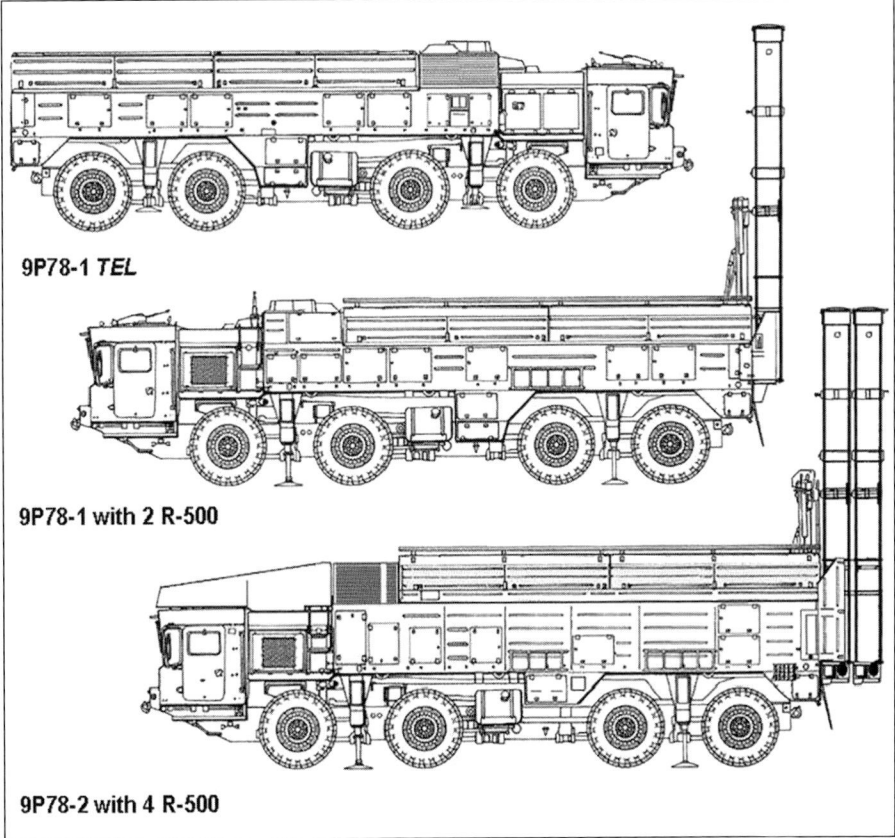

Figure 2-14: 9P78-a and 9P78 launchers with R-500 cruise missiles.

Figure 2-15: R-500 cruise missile.

their own solutions so the statement that it greatly depends on Western technology is not true.

Cruise missiles launched from the Iskander rely on low observability and low-altitude flight paths to evade air and missile defenses. By contrast, the 9M723 variants rely on a combination of speed, a quasi-ballistic trajectory, and penetration aids. With exhaust discharge speeds of roughly 2.5km/s (comparable to a space-shuttle booster), the 9M723 is powerful enough to fly on a quasi-ballistic trajectory that allows it to use aerodynamic drag to maneuver without sacrificing either range or speed to an unacceptable degree. The ability to travel on a quasi-ballistic trajectory represents a significant challenge, both because the missile can spend a longer part of its trajectory under the horizon of air defense radar, and because at altitudes of 40km the missile flies above the intercept envelope of most air defense systems, such as the PAC-3, but below the envelope of ballistic missile defense interceptors.

OPERATIONAL-TACTICAL MISSILE SYSTEMS

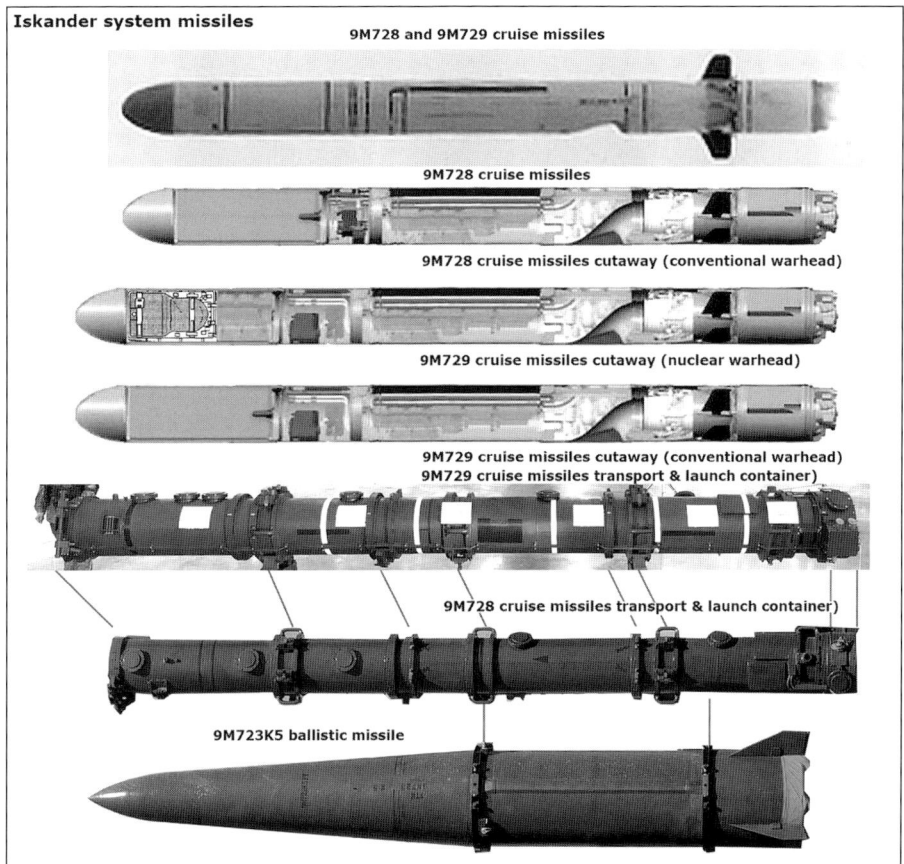

Figure 2-16: Iskander system missiles.

Some variants of the 9M723 missile are equipped with the 9B999 decoy which fits into six canisters at the base of the warhead (Figure 2-17). Some decoys can emit thermal signatures and some are equipped with jammers to counter active seekers. The decoys may also present an enhanced radar signature to spoof ground-based radar. The inclusion of these decoys is somewhat surprising, given Russian claims that the Iskander is capable of maneuvering at high terminal phase speeds of 2.1km/s. One might consider the inclusion of decoys overkill, especially given the age of the S-300 variants and Buk-M1 employed by Ukraine. Employing decoys may mean that the 9M723 is less maneuverable in its terminal phase. Moreover, given that the missile is subject to aerodynamic drag if fired on a quasi-ballistic trajectory, it may be slower in terminal phase than a purely ballistic missile with a comparable range. Ukraine also hopes that the NASAMS AD system may be more effective in intercepting Iskanders but technically it is not likely.

In addition to terminal phase maneuvers, the 9M723 is capable of conducting boost-phase maneuvers. This is simply where the missile

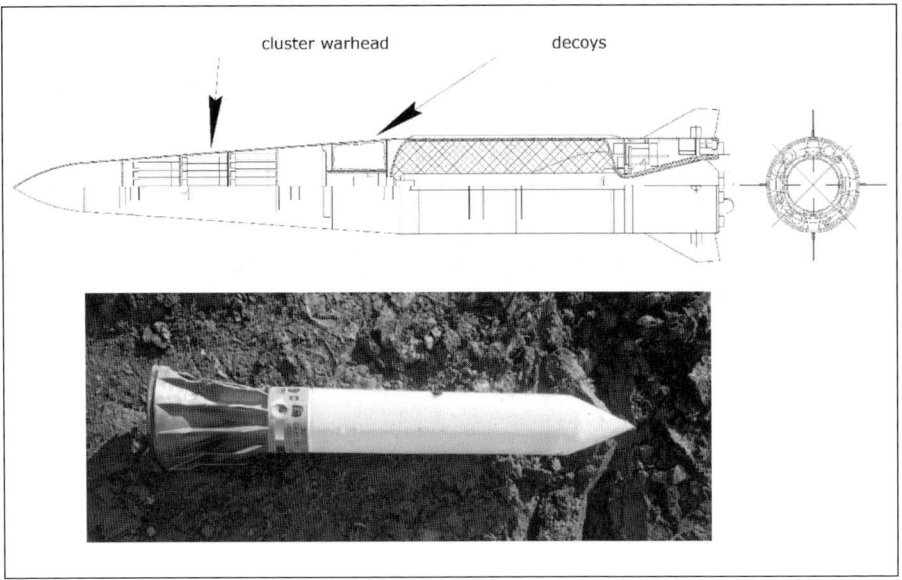

Figure 2-17: 9M723K with 9B999 "dart"-type decoy (according to Russian sources).

conducts rapid and extreme maneuvers shortly after launch to try to limit an opponent's ability to locate the launch site.

Overall, the attention paid to the survivability of Iskander missiles indicates that the design was concerned with the West's ability to conduct long-range precision strikes against the 9P78-1 TELs, as well as interceptions of the missiles themselves. Given their importance to Russia's concept of escalation management and in strikes against an enemy's critical infrastructure in the opening phases of a war, this focus is understandable.

Iskander represents a significant capability for the Russian armed forces. They are designed to perform tactical-operational strikes and have been employed to attack an array of targets in Ukraine. Furthermore, their role in supporting Russia's non-strategic nuclear arsenal means that they are not only a war shaping capability, but also potentially critical to strategies for war termination. At a strategic level, the system is likely to be central to any Russian attempt at escalation management and war termination through either targeting of critical infrastructure across Europe with conventional precision strikes or the threat of nonstrategic nuclear weapons use.

That said, the Iskander also has important battlefield functions. When appropriate intelligence is available, the Iskander has demonstrated a capacity to responsively strike key targets, which will be a critical consideration for NATO forces operating in congested theaters such as the Baltic states. Command posts, key logistical nodes, and apparently even some tactical capabilities may be considered appropriate targets for the Iskander (Figures 2-18, 2-19).

OPERATIONAL-TACTICAL MISSILE SYSTEMS

Figure 2-18: Russian Iskanders during the operation in Ukraine: 9M723 (top) and 9M728 (bottom). (*Source*: RIA and anna-news.info)

On the Ukrainian side, there was an attempt to develop the domestic SRBM namded Hrim (Grom/Sapsan) which would be equivalent to Iskander in some aspects. Once in service the Grom could replace an older Tochka-U with a range of 120km and is currently the main Ukrainian Army's ground-attack missile. It is also planned that the Grom ballistic missile will be offered to export customers. The lack of funding prior to the war and destruction of the manufacturing and design facilities effectively halted the project. It is believed and widely publicized in pro-Ukrainian networks that the prototype was used against the Russian base Novofedorivka in Crimea, but this is just one of many rumors (Figure 2-20).

Figure 2-19: Launch, midflight and immediate impact sequencies. (*Source*: topcor.ru, modified by author)

Figure 2-20: Prototype (mock-up) of the Ukrainian answer to the Russian Iskander named Grom. Recently there are some reports that one unit was able to launch a missile against a Russian target. Ukraine has the technical base and some remnants of production facilities to further develop this system. (*Source*: Wikimedia)

Chapter 3

MLRS

A multiple rocket launcher (MRL) is defined as a type of rocket artillery system that contains multiple launchers which are fixed to a single platform, and launches its rocket ordnance in a fashion similar to a volley gun. Rockets are self-propelled in flight and have different capabilities than conventional artillery shells, such as longer effective range, lower recoil, typically considerably higher payload than a similarly sized gun artillery platform, or even carrying multiple warheads.

Older unguided rocket artillery systems are inaccurate and slow to reload compared with gun artillery. A multiple rocket launcher helps compensate for this with its ability to launch multiple rockets in rapid succession, which, coupled with the large kill zone of each warhead, can easily deliver saturation fire over a target area. Modern rockets can use GPS or inertial guidance to combine the advantages of rockets with the higher accuracy of precision-guided munitions.

The first self-propelled multiple rocket launcher, and the most famous, was the Soviet BM-13 Katyusha (Figure 3-1 top and middle), first used during the Second World War and exported to Soviet allies afterwards. It was a simple system in which a rack of launch rails was mounted on the back of a truck. This set the template for modern multiple rocket launchers. The Germans began using a towed six-tube multiple rocket launcher during the Second World War, the Nebelwerfer (Figure 3-1 bottom).

There are two main types of multiple rocket launchers:[1]

- With steel tubes attached to the launcher vehicle, with options to be reloaded with rockets manually or semi-automatically. This was the most usual type until the twenty-first century. It is more convenient for battlefield usage because it does not require special tools to reload modules and test them before using them on launchers as with other types. All Russian MLRS are of this type (Figure 3-2).

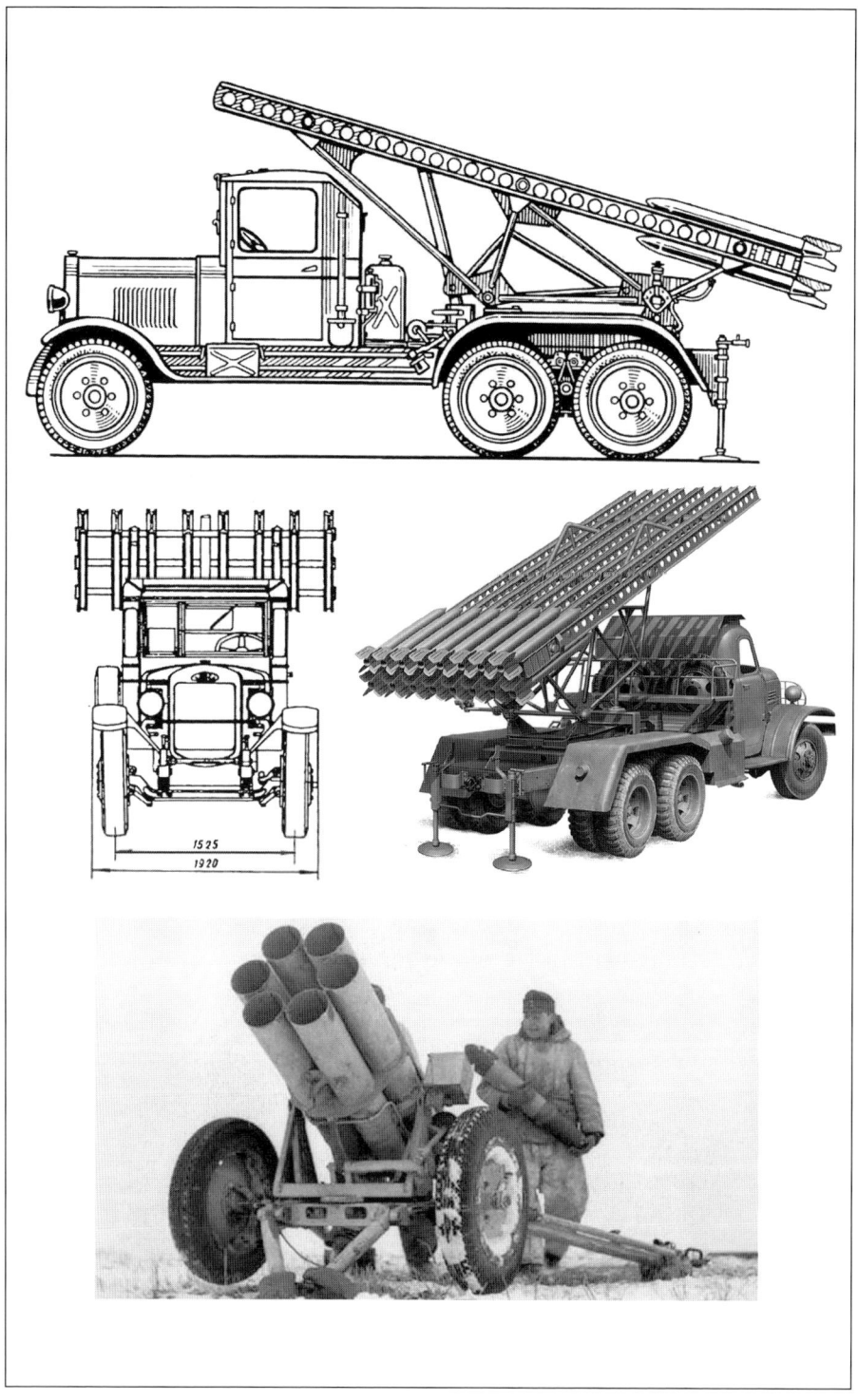

Figure 3-1: BM-13 Katyusha (top and middle) and Nebelwerfer (bottom).

Figure 3-2: The Russian trinity: BM-21 Grad (top); BM-27 Uragan (middle); BM-30 Smerch (bottom).

- With container modules that can be removed from the launcher and quickly replaced with same or different types of rockets and calibers. They are usually reloaded at the factory or within specially equipped army workshops. These are more modern types of weapons as they are not necessarily related to just one type of rocket and give more options to commanders on field to deal with different tactical situations using different types of rockets or to quickly reload. These are US-made M270 and HIMARS (Figure 3-3).

Figure 3-3: M270 (top); M142 HIMARS (bottom). (*Source*: US Army and Lockheed Martin)

Multiple rocker launcher fire can be highly destructive. For example, the very first combat application of BM-13 Katyusha launchers on 14 July 1941, when seven launchers unleashed fire on the railway station in the town of Orsha. The fire obliterated German trains and devastated morale. Enemy formation on the open field as shown is particularly vulnerable to this kind of attacks.

According to some analysts, MLRS are still unable to properly engage reverse slope positions in mountain warfare because it is more difficult to determine the trajectory compared with that of a howitzer by adding or removing propellant increments. An approach to lessen this limit is the addition of drag rings to the rocket nose. The increased drag slows the rocket down relative to a clean configuration and creates a less flat trajectory. Pre-packaged munitions do not offer this option but some MLRS types with individually loaded rockets do.

Recently, there has been a trend toward improvised launchers using helicopter or aircraft mounted pods or individual launch tubes from the MLRS in a combination of few tubes. As a platform, pickup trucks are often used. It is called a "poor man's MLRS." It is evident that some Ukrainian workshops are building these types of improvised launchers.

Design of any MLRS requires in-depth multi-disciplinary calculations for both launcher component (launching tubes, elevation and azimuth mechanisms, stress and strain, gas and thermodynamics, interior and exterior ballistics, etc.) as well as the transport component such as chassis, stabilization, mobility, etc. Even during the design of make-up launchers based on the pickup trucks, the serious stress which includes forces and momentums has to be taken in consideration. Figures 3-4 and 3-5 present the dynamics involved in a typical truck-based launcher.

Survivability in the battlefield may include the ballistic protection from the typical artillery fragments, but majority of the launchers are lightly armored and rely on the mobility – to get to the firing position and be ready to launch in the shortest period of time and to leave the position even faster to avoid the enemy counterbattery fire.

Beside the devastating effect that MLRS can deliver on the target, it is also known for scattering. This means, if one makes a batch of projectiles according to the same drawings and specifications, and launch them from the same launcher, from the same starting position, with the same sighting devices, then at the target these rockets will spread with different points of impact. This phenomenon is caused by deviations of projectile parameters from nominal values lying within tolerance and is called technical dispersion. The projectile trajectories in this case form a bundle (or sheaf) of trajectories emanating from one point.

The dispersion of the points of impact of rocket and artillery shells obeys the normal distribution law, while the points of impact are located on a plane within an ellipse, called the dispersion ellipse. The center of the ellipse is the

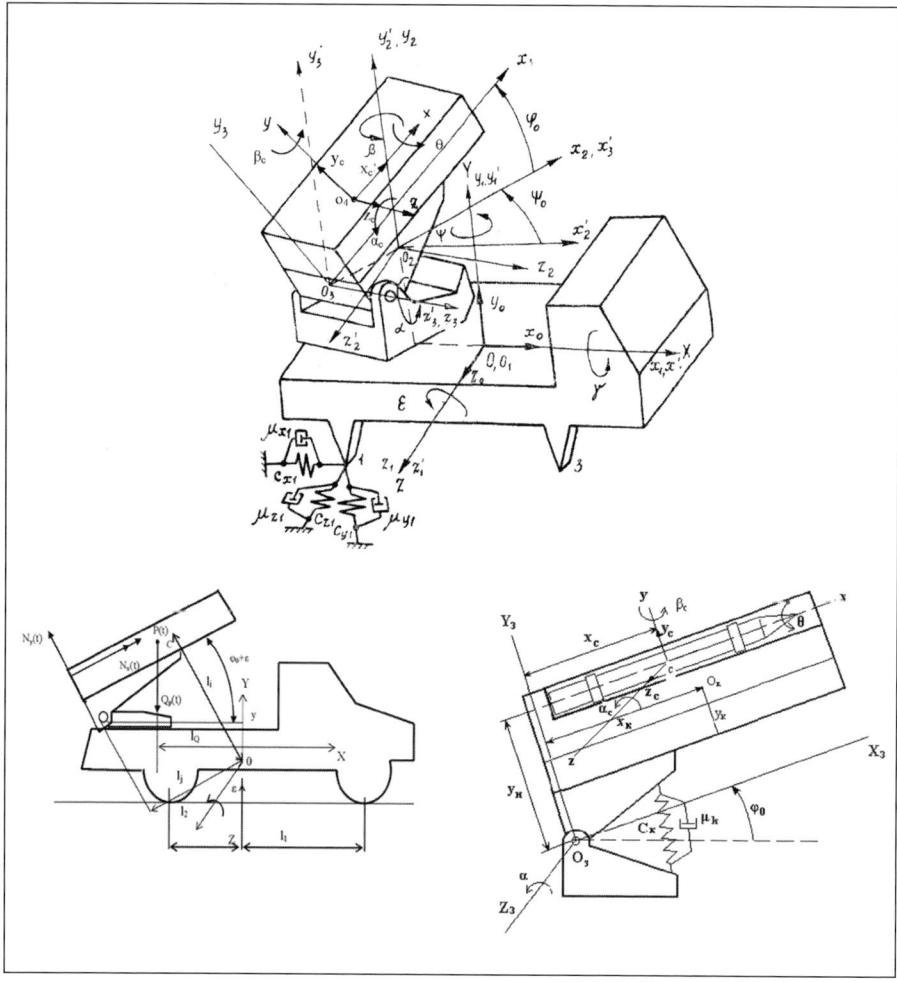

Figure 3-4: MLRS engineering complexity: generalized design scheme of the reactive system (top); automotive section design scheme (left); launcher component design scheme (right). (*Source*: Bogomilov, *Osnovaniya Ustroistva i Raschet Reaktivnih Sistem*)

same as the scattering center (or grouping center). Numerous firings have shown that the correlations between dispersion in range and dispersion in direction are insignificant and, without a large error, deviations in range and direction can be considered independent. Scattering in the direction (lateral scattering) is characterized by the probable lateral deviation B6 (Figure 3-6).

Dispersion is a measure for the deviation of the rocket's trajectory from the trajectory of some standard rocket, called nominal trajectory. For a rocket, dispersion arises from three different sources: events that occur at launching, events during burning after launching, and events after burning. For rockets, most of the dispersion arises during the burning period after launching. This is predicted theoretically and is confirmed by experience.[2]

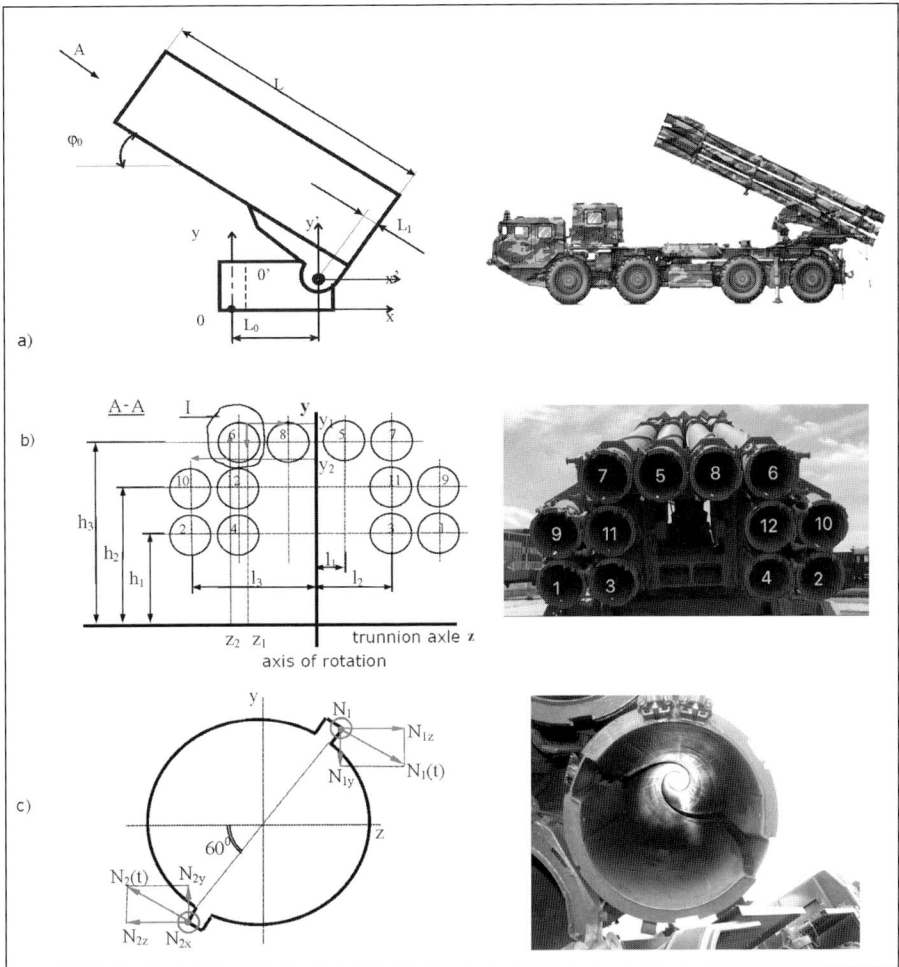

Figure 3-5: BM-30 Smerch basis for calculations: a) rocket launcher section; b) launcher tubes with the sequence launch number for a full salvo; c) launch tube groove. (*Source*: Bogomilov, *Osnovaniya Ustroistva i Raschet Reaktivnih Sistem*)

Scattering in direction or lateral scatter, or directional scattering is determined mainly by the angle between the theoretical firing plane and the perturbed position of the velocity vector of the center of mass of the projectile at the end of the active part of the trajectory.

The lateral deflection of an individual projectile can be seen in Figure 3-7.

The parameters that induce dispersion of the rocket's trajectory are:[3]

- The propellant mass and composition inaccuracy,
- The rocket's total mass, axial and lateral moments of inertia, and resultant centre of gravity inaccuracies,

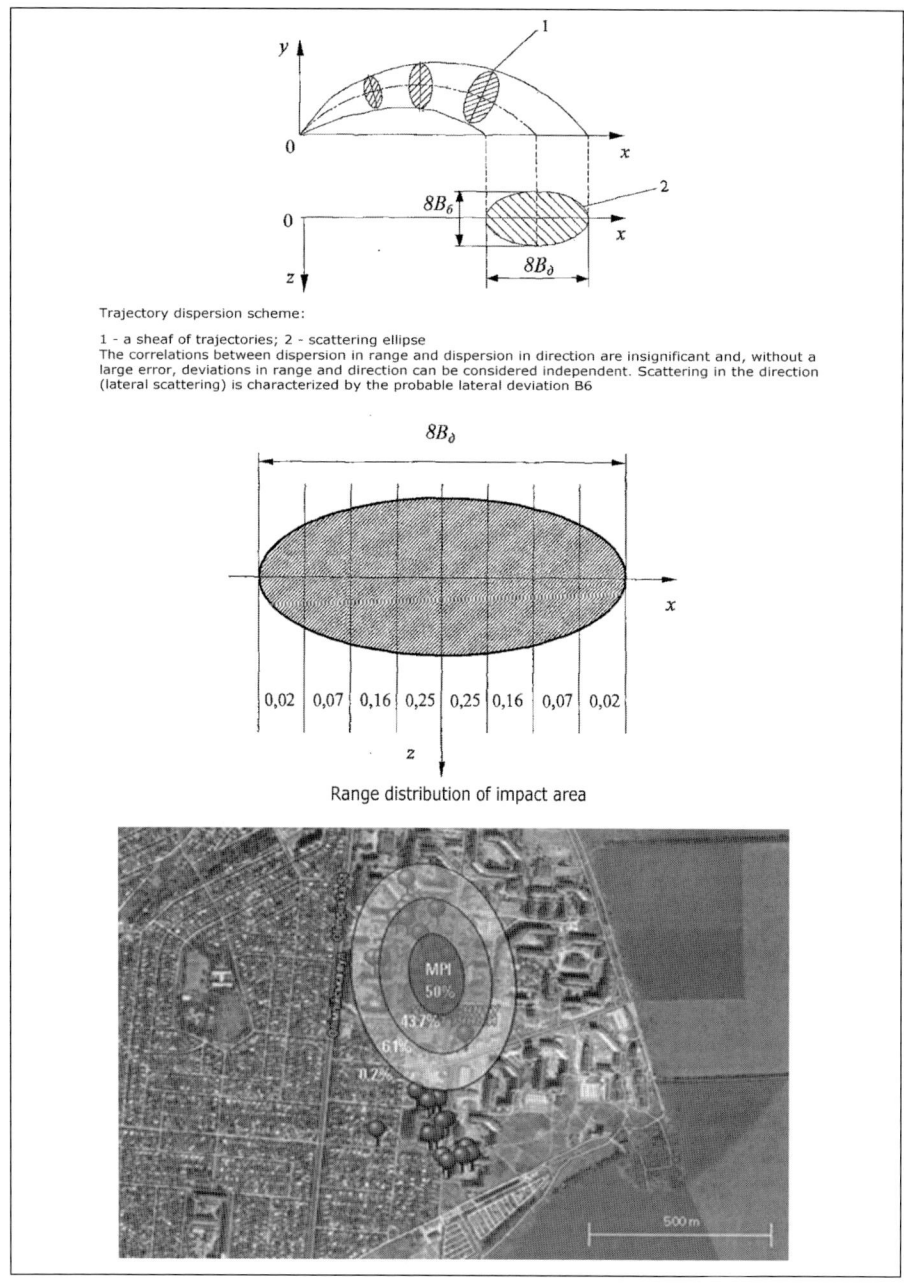

Figure 3-6: Scattering diagram (top); range distribution of impact points (middle); (*Source*: A.P. Orlov, *Osnovi ustroustva i funkcionirovaniya snaryadov RSZO*); probable error for a 122mm rocket fired from a BM-21 Grad at a range of 20km (bottom). (*Source*: ARES). These figures have been overlaid on a real-world example of BM-21 CEP. The map shows select, verified impact locations and approximate scale of an MLRS attack in Mariupol (bottom). (*Source*: Human Rights Watch, 2015)

- Launcher deflection,
- The thrust force of the rocket engine: because of the tolerance in rocket motor design, propellant properties, and manufacturing,
- Thrust and fin misalignments: it is an important source of dispersion in the case of unguided rockets,
- Atmospheric disturbances such as wind profile, tailwind, crosswind, and gusts, variation in atmospheric density,
- Rocket characteristics, such as aerodynamic coefficients which are previously calculated or measured in wind tunnels.

All these parameters differ from their nominal value and will generate errors derived from measurement, manufacturing, or modelling. These sources of error are all mutually independent. Thus, the composite errors are just their combination.

Without getting into the complicated mathematical analysis which is beyond the scope of this book, it can be concluded that the scattering of the unguided MLRS rockets is something that makes these weapons area-type weapons. To improve accuracy, the introduction of the guided (or corrected) trajectory rockets provided these systems with much more accuracy to precisely engage a point type of targets.

Modern MLRS can use modern land navigation (especially satellite navigation such as GPS or GLONASS) for quick and accurate positioning. The accurate determination of the battery position previously required such an extent of effort that making a dispersed operation of the battery was at times impractical. MLRS with GPS can have their launchers dispersed and fire from dispersed positions at a single target, just as previously multiple batteries were often united on one target area.

To improve accuracy and reduce the scattering, precision-guided munitions have been introduced. Guidance principles such as GPS or GLONASS satellite navigation, inertial navigation systems, and semi-active laser seekers are used for this. This improves dispersion from a CEP of hundreds of meters at dozens of kilometers range to just a few meters and largely independent of the range of the round (except for INS, as INS navigation creates a small dispersion that's about proportional to range). This in turn made great increases of rocket (or missile) ranges useful; previously dispersion had made rockets too inefficient and often too dangerous to friendly troops at long ranges. Long-range missiles often fly a higher quasi-ballistic trajectory than shorter ranged rockets and thus pose a deconfliction challenge, as they might collide with friendly aircraft in the air even though this probability is low (Figure 3-7).

Conceptually, the number of launching tubes for MLRS made by the Soviet Union and Russia vary from 40 x 122mm tubes at BM-21 Grad to

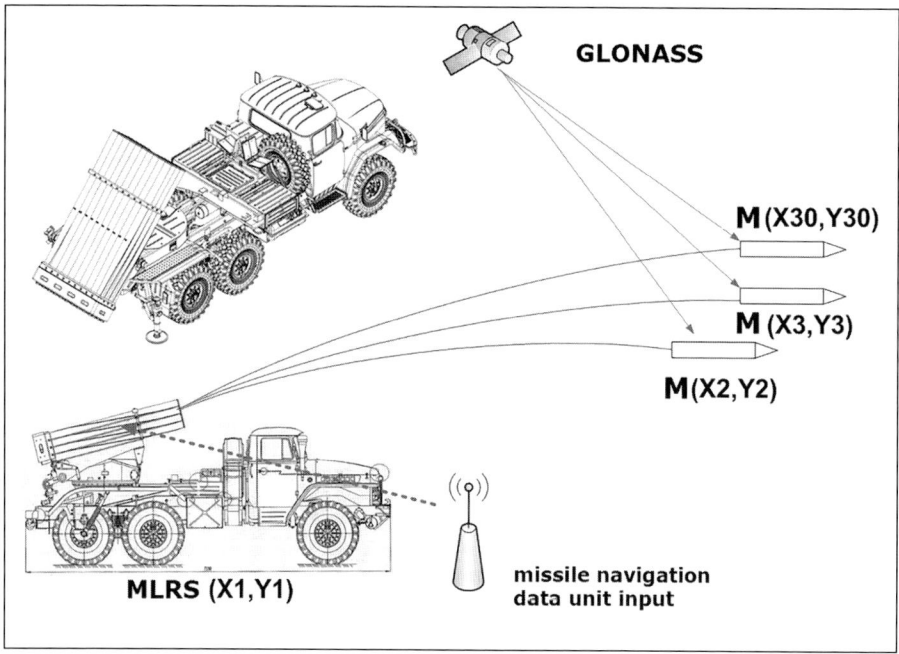

Figure 3-7: BM-21 GLONASS satellite data input. (*Source*: Author's archive)

12 x 300mm tubes in BM-30 Smerch. There are numerous variations, and the newer system has slightly less tubes than the original one.

BM-21 (9K51) Grad

The BM-21 Grad is the most common rocket artillery system in use on both sides of the Ukrainian conflict. There is no theater of operation in which this ubiquitous system is not applied and, even in the shadow of the most powerful and heavier systems as well as the "wonder weapons" delivered from the West, the BM-21 is still the backbone and the workhorse of the Russian and Ukrainian artillery units. The origins of this system lie deep in the past.

Russia was a pioneer of modern rocketry and fielded its first military rocket in 1817. Since then, in the second half of the 1800s, the proliferation of rifling, breechloading, and advances in metallurgy increased the capability of conventional guns and they soon eclipsed rockets in importance as an artillery weapon.

Rocketry underwent a renaissance in the 1920s and 1930s. In the Soviet Union, the Gas Dynamics Laboratory (GDL) was formed at the end of the 1920s and concentrated on the research and development of solid-fuel rockets. A separate organization, the Group for the Study of Jet Propulsion (GIRD), was later established, focused on liquid propellant systems.

The GDL and the Moscow-based arm of the GIRD were merged into the Jet Propulsion Scientific Research Institute (RNII) in 1933.

The introduction of new solid-fuel propellants gave impetus to a number of improved Russian military rockets and launch platforms. Among these and most relevant to the history of Soviet and Russian multiple rocket launchers were the fin-stabilized 82mm RS-82 and 132mm RS-132 air-to-ground rockets.

Development of ground based MRLs by the RNII can be documented as early as 1936. In 1938, one of the projects undertaken by Scientific Research Institute-3 (NII-3) was a truck-mounted launcher for 132mm M-13 rockets. In 1939, two more prototypes followed using the three-axle ZiS-6 chassis that had somewhat better cross-country performance. The first ZiS-6-based prototype used a transverse-mounted launcher, but with traverse and elevation mechanisms and a slightly different arrangement of launching rails.

The second prototype, the MU-2, had the launcher mounted parallel to the long axis of the truck that, in combination with the use of jacks, made for a much more stable launch platform. In addition, a longer and redesigned type of launch rail further improved accuracy and enabled the launch rail to be loaded from the back, which made reloading easier. Each rail carried two rockets, one on top of the rail and the other below. The launcher had simple traverse and elevation controls, a conventional artillery sight mounted on the left of the launcher, and a firing device mounted inside the cab. Armored shutters protected the cab windows. This established the basic configuration that almost all subsequent Russian and Soviet MRLs would follow. It was renamed the BM-13 but is much better known as "Katyusha."

The military acceptance decree was signed just hours before the German invasion and the Soviets decided to focus on the production of the BM-13. Since then USSR and later Russia has become a world leader in MLRS technology.

On 30 May 1960, the resolution of the Council of Ministers addressing the development of a new divisional multiple-launch rocket system named BM-21[4] "Grad"[5] was issued. The idea of the designers was to make a new system that could replace existing launchers in the Soviet inventory with a similar purpose system but much more powerful – to be able to deliver a massive firepower and saturate the target area with a high-explosive rockets (Figures 3-8 to 3-10).

The Russian nickname "Hail" is an appropriate moniker for a weapon system that can launch up to forty 122mm rockets in some 20 seconds, at ranges of up to 20km. Designed to deliver its munitions over an area rather than a point target, the Grad is not a high-precision weapon; at a range of 20km, when a full salvo of forty rockets is fired, the lethal area extends

BM-21 combat vehicle on a modified Ural-375D truck chassis schematics:
A - artillery part of the combat vehicle; B - chassis;
1 - lifting mechanism; 2 - sights; 3 - rotary mechanism; 4 - tubular guide; 5 - cradle; 6 - base; 7 - spare parts box; 8 - front frame; 9 - spare wheel; 10 - air intake; 11 - radio station antenna; 12 - current distributor; 13 - searchlight; 14 - muffler guard

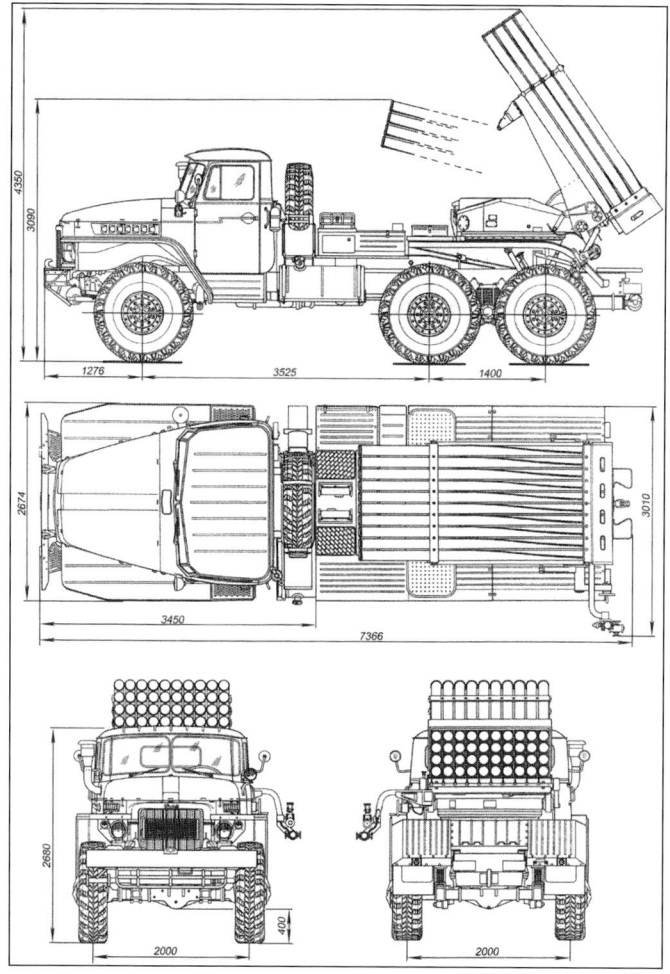

Above: Figure 3-8: BM-21 major components. (*Source*: Author's archive)

Left: Figure 3-9: BM-21 dimensions. (*Source*: Author's archive)

Drawing of the BM-21-1 combat vehicle (index 2B17) on a modified truck chassis of the Ural-4320 series. 1 - chassis; 2 - artillery part.

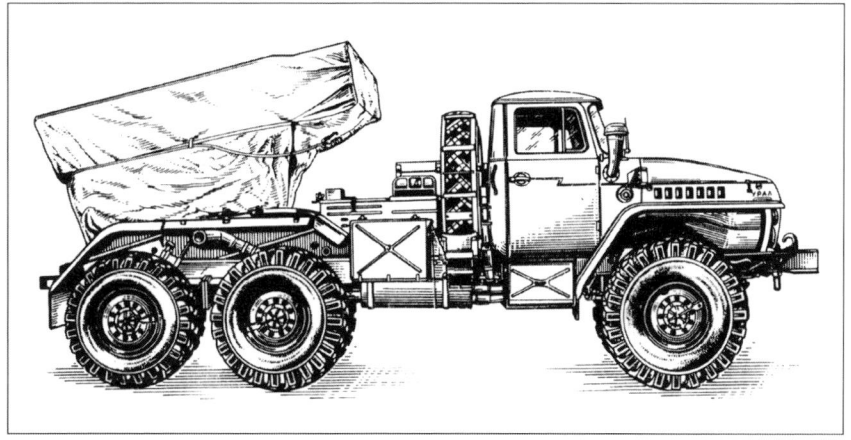

Drawing of the BM-21-1 combat vehicle (index 2B17) on a modified truck chassis of the Ural-4320 series in the marching position.

Figure 3-10: BM-21-1 on Ural 4320 chassis. (*Source*: Author's archive)

up to 600m x 600m. When the rockets impact, they produce a substantial fragmentation effect. The multiple instances of its use in populated areas across the world has resulted in significant numbers of civilian casualties. In addition to the human cost of using Grads in populated areas, there has been devastating damage to civilian objects including residential buildings, businesses, and critical infrastructure.

The system got official designation 9K51 from GRAU. Research institute 147 was appointed the leading executor of the system (since March 1966 Research institute 147 has often changed its name; the latest name – State Research-and-Production Enterprise "Splav" – was given to it in 1992); The work was split between the "Design Bureau No. 203" responsible for the launcher; Research institute No. 6 responsible for a solid-fuel propelled rocket; and "Design Bureau No. 47" responsible for the warheads.

The BM-21 wasn't a direct successor to the famous BM-13 Katyusha rocket launchers. This is rather the much-improved BM-14 launcher. Munitions used by the BM-21 are frequently and incorrectly referred to as Katyusha rockets. The BM-21 was first introduced into service in 1963. The general dimensions are shown in Figure 3-9.

Conceptually, the BM-21 is a vehicle-mounted, multiple-barrel rocket launcher. The BM-21 was designed and manufactured in Tula. The weapon system has since been widely copied throughout the world. The typical barrel configuration consists of four rows of ten launching tubes, meaning that each BM-21 can carry and launch up to forty rockets. When firing its entire complement, a rocket is launched every 0.5 seconds, meaning that it takes a single BM-21 about 20 seconds to launch its full load of rockets.[6] When the rockets impact the target area, they deliver a blast and fragmentation. After firing, it takes approximately 10 minutes to completely reload the BM-21 launcher. The original BM-21 had a maximum range of 20.4km, but modern versions have seen this range increased to 40km (Figure 3-12).

The self-propelled mounting BM-21 consists of an artillery part and chassis. The original launch vehicle was a Ural-375D 6x6 truck chassis. In 1976, the Ural-375D launch vehicle was replaced by the newer and more powerful Ural-4320 6x6 truck (Figure 3-10). Each BM-21 is supported by a 9T450 re-supply truck with sixty additional rockets. Being mounted on 6x6 trucks gives the BM-21 notable cross-country mobility, which is especially useful after firing, when the launchers must move quickly to avoid counterbattery fire. This "shoot-and-scoot" behaviour is typical for self-propelled MLRS.

The artillery part serves for directing the launcher and igniting the rocket motors. The artillery part consists of forty tubular guides, forming a so-called package: four rows of ten tubes in each (Figure 3-11). The launching tube is also used for rocket transportation. The tube caliber is 122.4mm, and it is 3m long. Pointing of the tubes package in vertical and horizontal planes is performed with the help of electric drive. Originally the Grad had the only high-explosive rocket 9M22. The first developed rocket was 2,870mm long and weighed 66kg.

The very first recorded combat use was during the Soviet-Chinese border dispute regarding the Damyansk Island. Chinese border units, numbering few infantry, and armored battalions attacked the Soviet positions defended only by border troops. Soviet command decided to bring BM-21 launchers and within a few minutes, the advancing Chinese units were

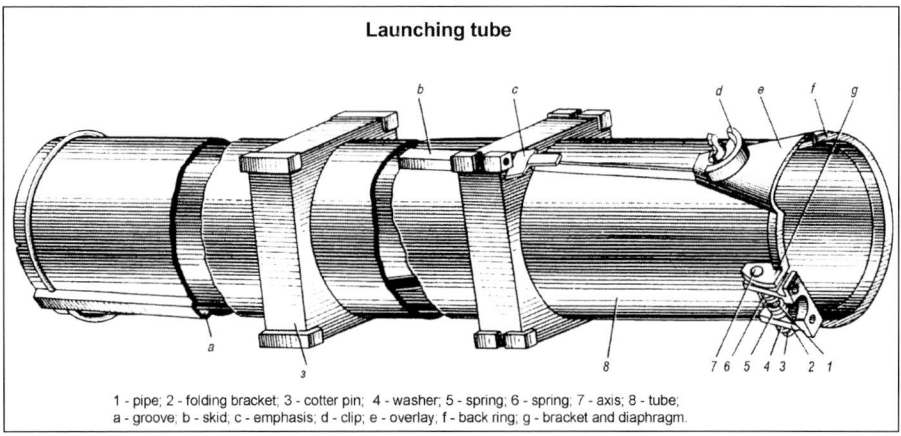

Figure 3-11: BM-21-1 launching tube. (*Source*: Author's archive)

literally annihilated. Since then, BM-21 type systems have been used by many armies and irregular forces, and deployed for various purposes and configurations, manifesting in any number of launch vehicles, or even individual launch tubes, used at the same time.

The Tornado-G (Figure 3-12) is Russia's newest updated version of the BM-21. The launcher vehicle is referred to as 2B17. Even though it looks remarkably like the BM-21 Grad, it has numerous improvements. Rockets of this new system have improved range and more powerful warheads. The Tornado-G is also fitted with automatic positioning, navigation, aiming, and laying systems. Development of these artillery rocket systems commenced in the 1990s. It was first revealed in 1998. However, due to funding problems the first order for thirty-six units was not placed until 2011. The first production systems were delivered to the Russian Army in 2012 and entered service during the same year. It was planned that by 2020 the Tornado-G would have completely replaced the aging BM-21 in service with the Russian Army. However, this did not happen for financial reasons. The aging Grad systems are still widely used by the Russian military, while the Tornado-G is used only in limited numbers. This artillery rocket system is in action in Ukraine.

Rockets have the same dimensions. A standard rocket weighs 70kg. The Tornado-G rockets are fitted with cluster warheads with self-guided multi-purpose submunitions. These have a range of 30km and can be used against enemy infantry and armored vehicles. These submunitions penetrate 60–100mm of rolled steel armor. Also, there are newly developed rockets with HE-FRAG warheads. These have a range of up to 40km. The Tornado-G is also compatible with all previous Grad rockets. Some sources claim that the new Tornado-G rockets have a maximum range of 90–100km, however, this was not confirmed at the time of writing.

Figure 3-12: Tornado-G (top); automated CV 2B17-1 (bottom). (*Source*: Armeiski sbornik)

The vehicle is fitted with a modern fire-control system. The launcher is aimed without the crew leaving the vehicle. The crew was reduced from three to two soldiers.

This artillery rocket system has a brief redeployment time. The Tornado-G can launch a full salvo and leave the firing position before the rockets hit the ground. When the first rockets hit the target the launcher vehicle may be already located 4–5km away from its original firing position.

The launcher vehicle is based on Ural-4320 6x6 army truck.

Reload rockets are carried by escorting trucks. Reloading is performed manually by the crew within 7 minutes. Reloading usually takes place remotely from the firing position to avoid the enemy counterbattery fire.

After the dissolving of the Soviet Union, Ukraine inherited a large number of BM-21 launchers and these still form the backbone of the Ukrainian MLRS artillery. It is estimated that no less than 184 pieces were available before the war started in 2022. The Ukrainians have also developed their own modifications.

The first attempt to modernize MLRS was made in 2001 by the "Morozov Kharkov Design Bureau" and the "Kharkov Special Machines Plant" began the development of the BM-21K project. It proposed to keep the existing artillery unit and missiles, but transfer them to the Ukrainian KrAZ-260 chassis. It also provided for the renewal of communications and fire control.

The work on the BM-21K dragged on. The design was completed in a few years, but testing and refinement continued until 2008. The upgraded Grad showed the required level of performance and coped with the tests, but was not recommended for adoption.

Due to the failure of the BM-21K project, the development of new variants of the MLRS began. In 2007–8, the same enterprises began to create a promising system called "Bastion-01." In this project, it was planned to combine all the advantages of existing weapons and a new chassis.

The KrAZ-01 truck was chosen as the basis for the Bastion-6322 MLRS, shortly before that it was accepted for supply to the Ukrainian Army. This is a three-axle all-wheel-drive vehicle with an engine capacity of at least 300hp and sufficiently high characteristics of carrying capacity and cross-country ability. It was proposed to transfer the standard equipment of the Grad to it with virtually no changes. Only individual devices were introduced, while the launcher and other products remained the same.

The Bastion-02 combat vehicle was also developed on the extended KrAZ-6322 chassis. Additional space on the cargo platform, between the cockpit and the launcher, was used to accommodate the so-called fast reload systems. An additional forty rockets are placed in special mobile clips, which simplifies the preparation for a new salvo.

The first prototype of "Bastion-01" was built in 2009 at the Shepetovsky repair plant and soon went for testing. Later they made a model "02."

The equipment coped with the checks and was recommended for adoption. However, a mass series could not be established. Despite the simplicity of production, in a few years no more than eight to twelve machines of two modifications were manufactured. In the middle of the tenth year, the release of "Bastions" (Figure 3-13 top) ceased.

Simultaneously with the Bastion, another modification of the Grad was created at the KMDB on a new chassis – BM-21U (Verba). The goals of the project were again to replace the chassis and upgrade the means of communication and control, while the artillery unit was not affected. This should take into account the negative experience of the previous project, BM-21K.

The Ukrainians also tried to equip launchers with a control computer, to which are connected means of communication, navigation, and topographic location, as well as guidance mechanisms. A remote control is also provided.

In reality, Ukrainian modernization didn't provide armed forces with a successful alterative to the BM-21 on a large scale. Various options for the modernization of existing "Grads" and other combat vehicles were developed, public statements were made, and even orders were issued for adoption. However, the true results did not justify the expectations. As a result, for twenty years of work, the army received only a few combat vehicles. As a result of the Russian attacks on the military infrastructure which builds and repairs equipment, it is highly doubtful that Ukraine in near future will be able to produce or even maintain equipment.

The attrition losses forced NATO to send former Warsaw Pact BM-21s as well as modifications such as the former Czechoslovakian RM-70 (Figure 3-13 bottom).

The RM-70 was developed in Czechoslovakia as a successor to the RM-51, achieving initial operational capability with its army in 1972. The launcher was produced in Dubnica-nad-Váhom (Slovakia).

The RM-70 replaced the Ural-375D 6x6 truck by a Tatra T813 "Kolos" 8x8 truck as carrier platform. The new carrier vehicle provides enough space for carrying forty additional 122mm rockets pack for reload. Nevertheless, RM-70 performance remains near the same as Grad even in terms of the vehicle's speed and range. This rocket launcher can fire both individual rounds and volleys. It is designed for concentrated fire coverage of large areas (up to 3 hectares in one volley) by high-explosive fragmentation shells. The fire is robust with almost 256kg of explosives used in one volley of forty rockets. The rockets used are either the original Soviet 9M22 and 9M28, or locally developed models. These are the JROF with a range of 20.75km, the JROF-K with a range of 11km, the "Trnovnik" with sixty-three HEAT-bomblets and a range of 17.5km, the "Kuš" with five PPMI-S1 anti-personnel mines or the "Krizhna-R" with four PTMI-D anti-tank mines and a range of 19.45km.

Both Russian and Ukrainian military forces organize the BM-21 into batteries of four or six systems, so as to ensure that a devastating amount of

Figure 3-13: Ukrainian Bastion-3 (top); RM-70 (bottom). (*Source*: Wikimedia)

fire can be brought to bear in a very short period of time. Six launch vehicles can fire 240 rockets in approximately 20 seconds. It is common practice to use several launchers to attack the same broad target area.

BM-21 are notorious for their devastating effects on the battlefield and even more so when used against civilian targets. During the heavy clashes, both in 2014 and recently, the Ukrainian side used these launchers to attack civilian objects especially in and around Donetsk. As the Russians steadily advanced in Lugansk and Donbas, some Ukrainian batteries deliberately opened fire on the civilian objects to inflict numerous casualties. One of the primary goals of the Russian counterbattery fire is to neutralize these launchers and, more or less, the majority of Ukrainian BM-21s have either been destroyed by artillery fire or by air attacks (Figure 3-15).

When the BM-21 launches multiple rockets, these are launched some 0.5 seconds apart. As the launcher is vehicle-mounted, each launch causes the vehicle suspension to compress and rebound. The suspension movement causes fluctuations to the angle of the launching tubes, and subsequently greater inaccuracies in the delivery of the rockets. This means that rockets launched later in the salvo are likely to be less precise than those launched at the beginning.[7]

With rocket artillery, meteorological conditions play a more significant role in determining accuracy and precision than with most other weapon systems, for example, wind may contribute an error ratio of some 2 percent at ranges of 20km. This is the equivalent of an error of 400m from the desired impact point at a range of 20km. Rocket artillery is also affected by a number of errors that do not affect other explosive weapon systems, such as tip-off due to launcher motion, and transverse wind during the boost phase of the rocket.[8]

Due to these factors, rockets launched from an MLRS of a design such as the BM-21 will typically be among the least accurate or precise explosive weapon systems commonly employed. When firing a 122mm BM-21 rocket at a range of 20km, for example, a sample probable error in deflection is 160m, and a sample probable error in range is 300m, representing ideal conditions.[9]

There are hundreds of videos and thousands of photos showing BM-21s firing on both sides (Figures 3-14 to 3-15).

The BM-21 has been involved in the war in Ukraine almost since day one. This has been the situation not just since 24 February 2022 when the Russian attack started, but rather from 2014 when Ukrainian government forces used Grads in the attacks against the separatists' positions in the Donbas and Lugansk regions. The separatists' forces were able to capture some launchers and used them against the former owners. Ammunitions were taken from the government warehouses and later supplied from Russia. One of the most notorious engagements of the BM-21, which entered history as one of the bloodiest artillery barrages in modern times, happened on 11 July 2014 near Zelenopillya in Donbas region. A column from the Ukrainian 24th and 72nd Mechanized Brigades and 79th Airmobile Brigade was struck by an intense artillery barrage near Zelenopillya. The attack lasted less than 3 minutes, with Ukraine's Defense Ministry admitting to nineteen killed and ninety-three wounded in the attack, though other sources claimed up to thirty-six fatalities. No figures were released on the number of vehicles lost, but a survivor reported on social media that a battalion of 79th Airmobile Brigade had been almost wiped out. The full scale of the devastation was extensively manifested when four Ural-4320 trucks full of troops were struck. The direct hits tore apart bodies scattering them all around.

Figure 3-14: Simultaneous launch by two Russian BM-21s (marked with the letter Z). The launcher on the right is a modernized BM-21-1 and that on the left is the older BM-21 (top). (*Source*: Author's archive); a Russian BM-21-1 that has seen heavy engagements – the stars marked on the side represent destroyed Ukrainian vehicles (six). The BM-21-1 can deliver precise hits in contrast to the older BM-21 (bottom). (*Source*: Author's archive)

Figure 3-15: A still from a Russian surveillance drone: a group of Ukrainian soldiers caught in a BM-21 volley (top and middle); a Ukrainian Bastion blown up by a mine (bottom). (*Source*: Author's archive)

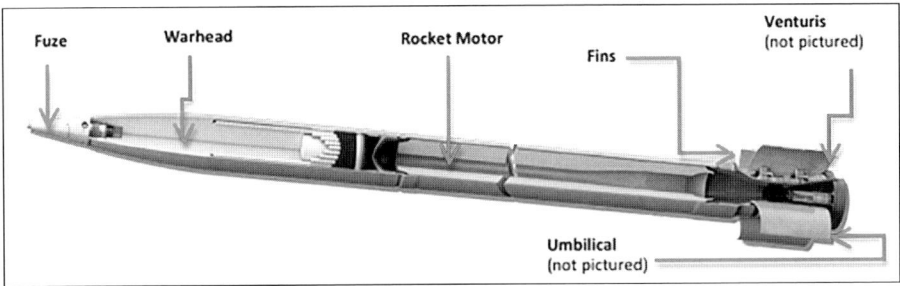

Figure 3-16: BM-21 rocket components.

122mm Rockets

The business end of this system is an unguided rocket (Figure 3-16). It is a fin-spin stabilized solid-fuel rocket motor propelled projectile. In its simplest form, a rocket motor consists of a tube in which solid fuel is burned, with an opening at one end. The escaping gases cause an equal and opposite reaction on the closed end of the tube, propelling the rocket forwards. Thrust is generated by channelling the rapidly expanding gases from the burning rocket fuel through one or more nozzles (venturi). The 122mm rockets for the BM-21 have seven venturis at the rear of the rocket motor. Unlike a missile, an unguided rocket does not adjust its trajectory in flight to precisely strike the target. As such, once the BM-21 has fired an unguided rocket, there is no way to alter its course.

The Fuze

The high-explosive fragmentation (HE-FRAG) warheads are usually fitted with MRV series impact fuzes. These are both relatively simple and cheap to manufacture, and they function reliably. An impact fuze will only detonate the warhead when it strikes the target, and is armed in flight, typically some 150–400m after launch. Many fuzes in use with 122mm HE-FRAG rockets will offer three settings: quick, short delay, and long delay. The fuze has three primary roles: to ensure safe handling of the rocket during storage, loading, transport, and launch; to only arm itself a safe distance from the launcher when fired; and to ensure the warhead functions at the correct time (Figure 3-17).

Warheads

The warheads for 122mm rockets fired by the BM-21 are located towards the front of the munition, behind the fuze, and immediately in front of the rocket motor. The warheads are robust enough to withstand normal handling stresses, and the forces produced by firing. However, it is important to note that these stresses are much lower than for some other weapon systems, such as artillery guns.

For the HE-FRAG rockets that are most commonly fired by the Grad, the steel warhead has an internal matrix of lines scored into it to produce

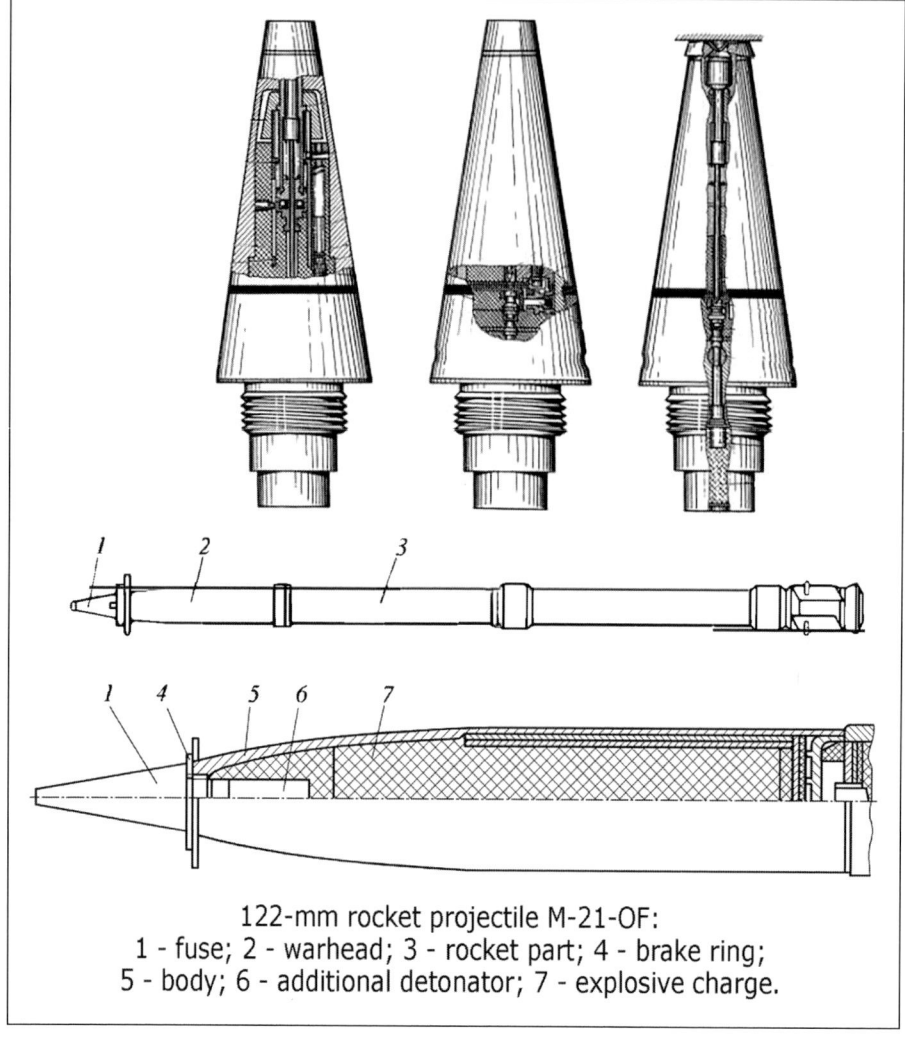

Figure 3-17: BM-21 fuze (top row): inert position (left); striking pin position (middle); impact compression position (right); BM-21 rocket concept and the warhead (middle and bottom).

the desired pattern of fragmentation (Figure 3-17). In addition to a variety of high-explosive warheads, a wide range of other munition types are also produced for BM-21-type 122 MBRLs, including cargo (cluster), illumination, radio-frequency jammer, chemical, and incendiary examples.

The Rocket Motor
The 122mm rocket motor consists of a body surrounding solid rocket fuel. The rocket motor has a relatively short burn time of approximately 3 seconds. Despite the short burn time, the Grad produces a lot of visible

exhaust, tending to make launch sites readily detectable. In addition to the exhaust, and depending on the location of firing, the launch typically generates a cloud of dust and debris upon launch, increasing the visual signature. It is near impossible to disguise the launch of 122mm rockets, so the launch site remains vulnerable to threats such as counterbattery artillery fire.

122mm rockets do not have the capability to burn only part of their rocket fuel; therefore, the only way to adjust the range of the rockets is by altering the angle of the launcher. A rocket fired at a low angle will generally travel further than a rocket fired at a high angle. The remaining rocket fuel burns, or deflagrates, on impact, which may contribute to human injuries and infrastructure damage. The burning can last tens of seconds and creates a hot cloud of toxic fumes while also being capable of igniting flammable objects in the surrounding area.

The primary function of the venturi nozzles is to channel and vent the hot propellant gases from the high-pressure combustion chamber of the rocket motor to the open air. This produces thrust, which overcomes the initial inertia, and accelerates the rocket to maximum velocity. Some rockets have a single venturi, and some have multiple. The Grad has seven venturis, all located at the rear of the rocket motor.

The Fin Stabilizers
In order to achieve aerodynamic stability, a rocket uses tail stabilizers – fins and spins axially. The Grad uses a combination of both these methods. The primary method of providing aerodynamic stability is by four wrap-around fins at the rear. When the rocket is launched, it also begins to spin at a relatively slow speed. The spring-loaded fins are wrapped around the rear of the rocket, and held in place by a thin strap, which is burnt through when the rocket is launched. As the rear of the rocket leaves the launch tube, the springs push the fins into place, and stabilize the rocket in flight (Figure 3-18).

Grad Rockets
The seven main HE-FRAG rocket types as well few non-lethal rockets for smoke and RF frequency jamming:

9M22
The 9M22 is a fin-stabilized rocket with a steel high-explosive fragmentation (HE-FRAG) warhead. The 9N51 warhead contains 6.4kg of TGAF-5 explosive fill, and generates some 3,920 pre-fragmented fragments. The warhead is manufactured with internal scoring designed to fragment into 1,640 fragments, each weighing 2.4g. The warhead is double-skinned, with the outer skin only lightly scored, in order to avoid damaging its structural integrity during launch. The outer skin is designed to produce an additional

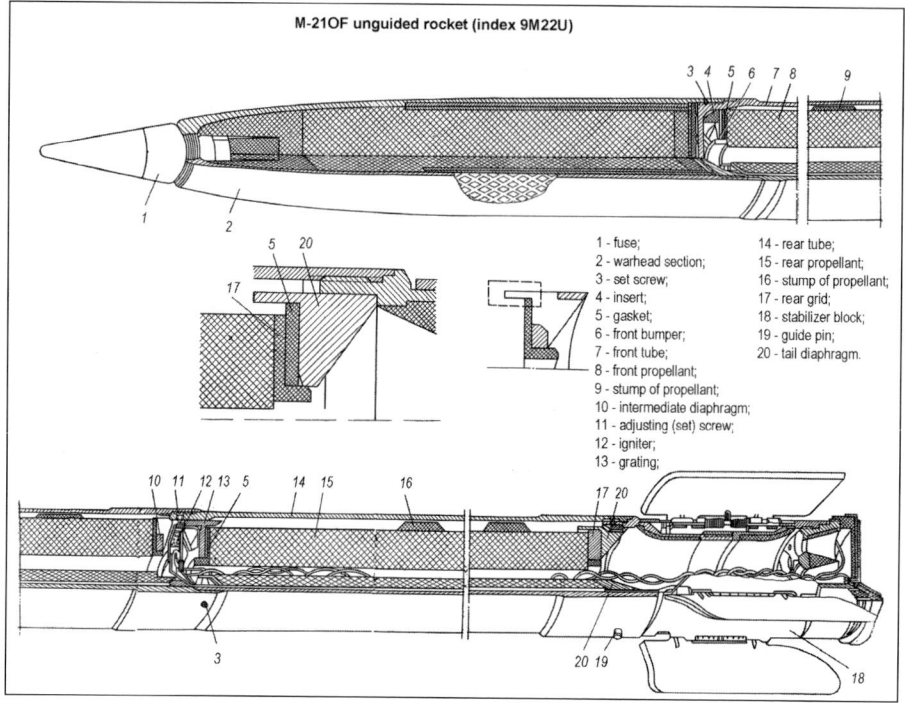

Figure 3-18: M-21OF unguided rocket.

2,280 fragments, each weighing 2.9g. The rocket motor contains 20.5kg of a double-base solid propellant. The range of fire is 5–20.4km.

9M22M

The 9M22M rocket can be fired from both the Grad, and from the single-tube launcher designated the 9P132. It is somewhat shorter than the 9M22 and weighs 46kg. The warhead has a total weight of 18.4kg and contains 6.58kg of TGAF-5. Its maximum range is just under 11km, but an extended range variant, fitted with an additional rocket motor, known as the 9M22MD was developed to fire out to 15km.

9M22U (BM-21OF)

The 9M22U rocket is one of the most encountered types of 122mm rocket fired by the BM-21 and many of its variants, copies, and derivatives (Figure 3-18). The "U" model features an updated rocket motor and a warhead with TGAF-5 (later A-IX-2) explosive fill. It is 2,870mm long and weighs 66.6kg. The 9M22U is one of the most used in Ukraine on both sides. The warhead weights 18.4kg consists of 1,640 pre-formed fragments (2.4g each) and partially pre-fragmented shell with approximately 2,280 fragments (2.9g each). The maximum range is 20.1km.

9M28F

The 9M28F is an interim rocket introduced in the 1970s. It has a more powerful rocket motor and features a more efficient HE-FRAG warhead with pre-formed fragments, designated the 9N55. The 9M28F has a total length of 2,270mm, and weighs 56.5kg. The 9N55 warhead weighs 21kg and contains 5.9kg of A-IX-2 explosive fill. Its maximum range is some 15km. It consists of 1,000 pre-formed fragments (5.5g each) and partially pre-fragmented shell yielding approximately 2,440 fragments (3g each).

9M53F

The primary difference between the 9M53F and the previous 9M22U rocket is the warhead. The 9M53F features a warhead that separates from the rocket motor over the target. The warhead is stabilized by a parachute and is equipped with the 9E260 multi-function fuze. This fuze can operate as an impact fuze, or as a proximity fuze set to activate the warhead at a pre-set height of a few metres above the ground. When detonated, the 26kg warhead produces 2,450 pre-formed fragments that impact in a roughly circular pattern, owing to the vertical position of the warhead. The 9M53F weighs 70kg with a length of 3,037mm. The range is 5,000–20,500m.

9M521

The 9M521 has a range of 40,000m, which is almost twice that of the original base model 9M22 rocket. The warhead weighs 21kg. The total weight of the complete projectile is 66kg. The manufacturer claims that the warhead is twice as effective as the 9M22U warhead against standard targets. The warhead consists of about 1,000 pre-formed fragments (5.5g each) and partially pre-fragmented shell yielding 2,440 fragments (average 3g each).

9M522

On the enhanced 9M522 rocket, much like the 9M53F, the warhead separates from the rocket motor and descends onto the target under a small parachute. The 25kg warhead is claimed to be six times more effective than that of the standard 9M22U HE-FRAG. The total rocket weight is 70kg, 3,037mm length, and the maximum range is 37,500m, which is close to double that of the 9M53F. The warhead consists of 1,800 smaller fragments (0.78g each), 690 larger fragments (5.5g each), and partially pre-fragmented shell with 1,210 fragments (7.5g each).

The following are also rockets that can be launched from the BM-21 but they are of very limited use, if any, in Ukraine:

- 9M218 is a high-explosive anti-tank rocket,
- 9M43 is a smoke-generating rocket,
- 9M519 is a RF jamming rocket.

BM-27 (9K57) URAGAN

The BM-27 Uragan[10] MLRS was developed in the early 1970s. The official GRAU designation is 9K57. The Uragan entered service with the Soviet Army in 1975. Currently it is in service with at least ten countries, including Russia. The Uragan was the largest and most powerful system of its type in service until the late 1980s, when the Smerch was introduced. This artillery rocket system saw combat during the Soviet war in Afghanistan, both Russian wars in Chechnya and the Russia-Georgia War. Recently it saw combat during a military conflict in Ukraine on both sides. After achieving independence, Ukraine retained about seventy systems. Combat losses and breakdowns decimated this system.

The launching vehicle of the Uragan MLRS is designated as the 9P140. It has sixteen launching tubes for 220mm rockets. Launch tubes are arranged in three banks, with the lower two banks having six tubes each and the upper bank having four tubes. The launcher is mounted on a turntable at the rear with powered elevation from 0 to +55° and powered traverse of 30° left and right (Figure 3-19). A standard rocket is 4.8m long and weighs 280kg (Figure 3-20). The warhead weight is 90–100 kg, depending on the rocket type. This system can fire training, HE-FRAG, chemical, incendiary, thermobaric, and cluster rockets with scatterable anti-tank or anti-personnel mines. These are used for remote minefield laying. It can also fire leaflet dispensing rockets but that is not common. The BM-27 fires single rockets or full salvos. A full salvo of one launcher covers an area of 4.3 hectares. The maximum range of fire is up to 34km.

A crew of four can prepare the system for firing within 3 minutes. It might take up to 12 minutes if the position is unprepared. After launch, the vehicle departs the firing position within 3 minutes. Rockets can be launched directly from the cab or remotely from the launch vehicle, via a 60m long cable.

The Uragan uses the chassis of a ZiL-135LMP 8x8 heavy high-mobility vehicle (Figure 3-19). It is powered by two ZiL-375 petrol engines, developing 180hp each. The engines are located behind the cab. Each engine is mated to its own five-speed gearbox and is driving four wheels on each side. The vehicle has two gearboxes. There were also two transfer cases and special synchronizers to control all of these mechanisms and deliver power to the wheels. The design with two engines was overly complicated, not reliable, and troublesome to service. However, back in the 1970s the Soviets had no suitable engine for this vehicle. The Uragan has a fiberglass cab, equipped with NBC protection system. The vehicle is fitted with a central tire inflation system, which improves mobility over difficult terrain, such as mud, sand, and snow. It has a climatic operational range from -40°C to +50°C. This MLRS can be airlifted by Il-76, An-22, or An-124 military transport aircraft.

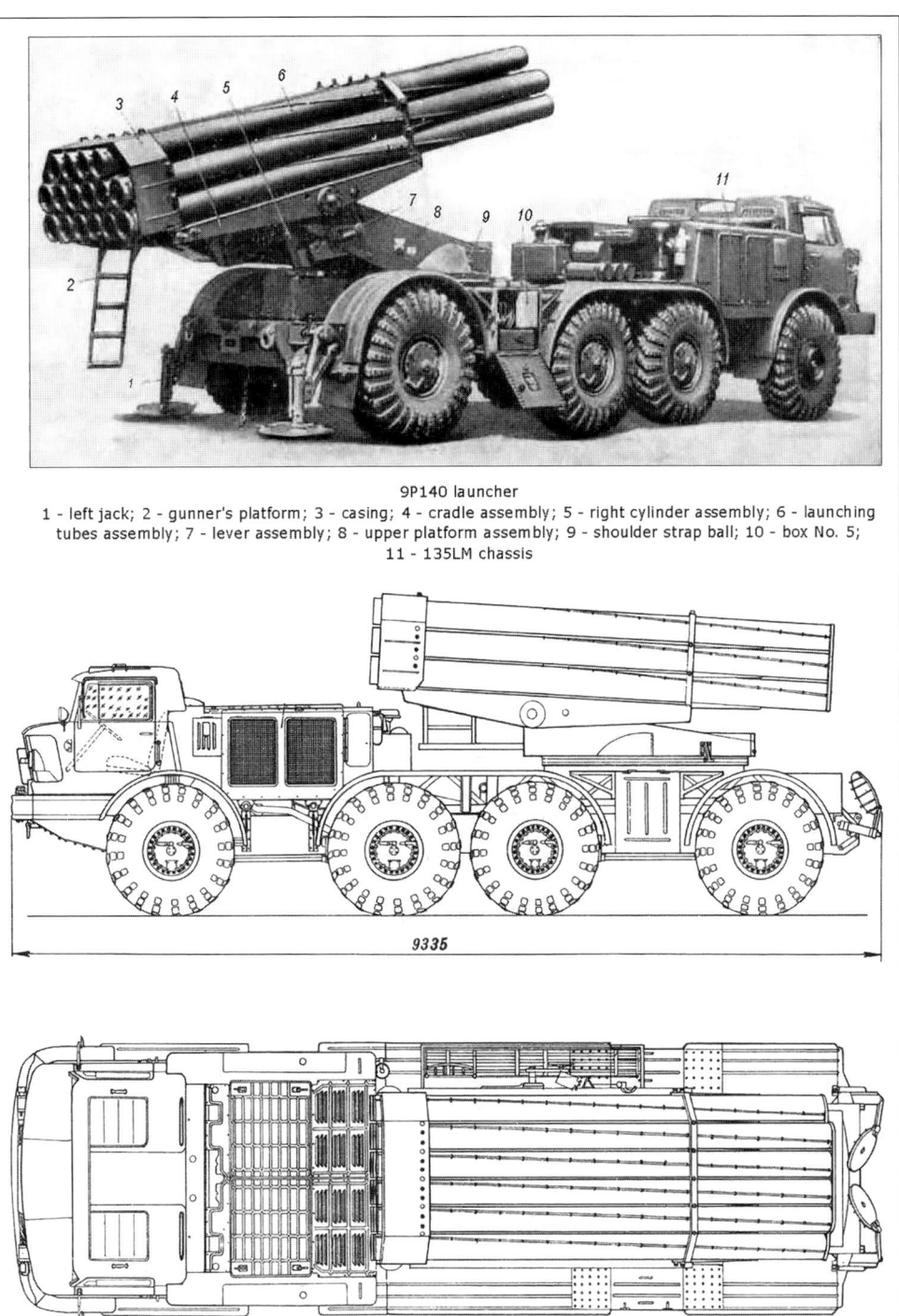

9P140 launcher
1 - left jack; 2 - gunner's platform; 3 - casing; 4 - cradle assembly; 5 - right cylinder assembly; 6 - launching tubes assembly; 7 - lever assembly; 8 - upper platform assembly; 9 - shoulder strap ball; 10 - box No. 5; 11 - 135LM chassis

Figure 3-19: BM-27 Uragan components (top); BM-27 Uragan dimensions (middle and bottom).

The Uragan launcher is supported by a 9T452 reloading vehicle. The reloading vehicle is also based on the same ZiL-135LMP 8x8 chassis and has a crew of two. It is fitted with a crane and carries a full set of sixteen reload rockets. The full launcher pack is reloaded within 15–20 minutes. Reloading usually takes place remotely from the firing position, to avoid counterbattery fire.

A full salvo of sixteen rockets can be fired in 20 seconds and can engage targets within a range of 35km. The most common rockets in use are the 9M27F (HE-FRAG) and 9M27K (cluster) (Figures 3-21 to 3-24).

The 9M27K-1 is intended to carry a 90kg container for thirty 9N210 anti-material bomblets (Figure 3-23). The 9M27K-2 has a container for 24 PGMDM/PTM-1 anti-tank mines and 9M27K-3 has a container for 312 PFM-1 anti-personnel mines. The 9M59 carries nine PTM-3 directional charge bottom attack anti-tank mines.

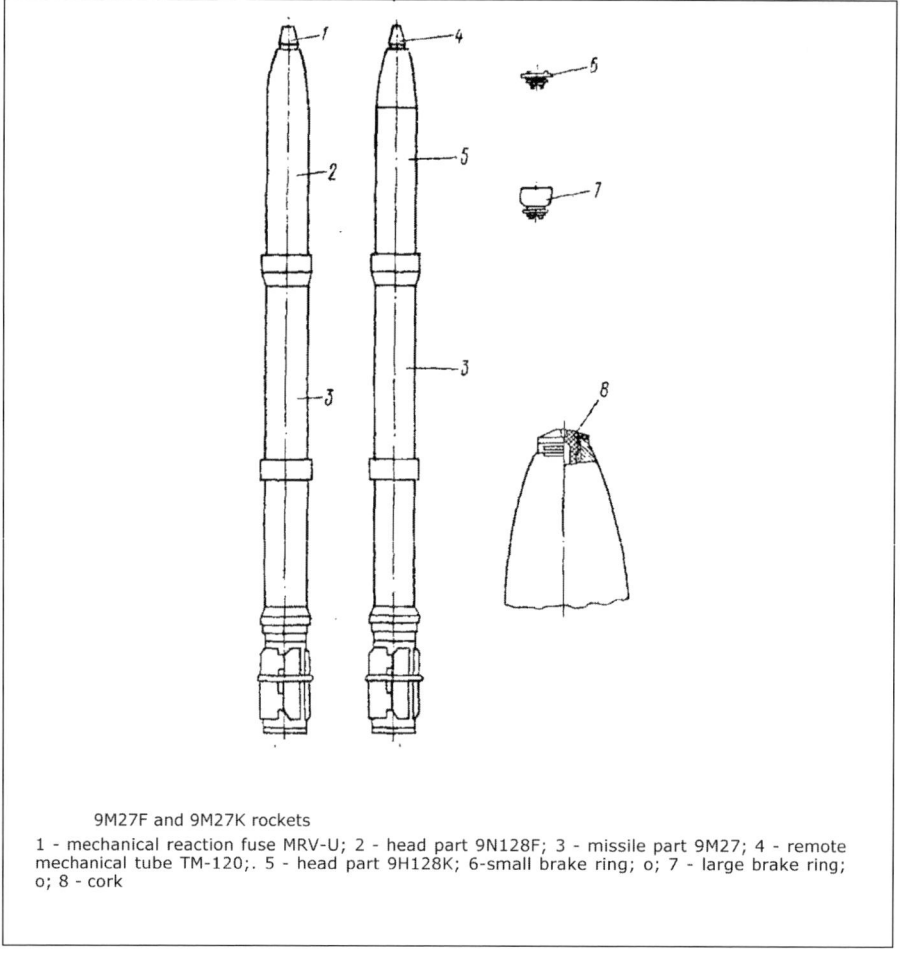

9M27F and 9M27K rockets
1 - mechanical reaction fuse MRV-U; 2 - head part 9N128F; 3 - missile part 9M27; 4 - remote mechanical tube TM-120;. 5 - head part 9H128K; 6-small brake ring; o; 7 - large brake ring; o; 8 - cork

Figure 3-20: 9M27F (left) and 9M27K (right).

Figure 3-21: 9M27F, 9M27K-1, 2, 3, and 9M59 warheads.

The high-explosive projectile's action is as follows: on the command "Start" (pushing the button labeled as "Pusk" from the impulse sensor of the combat vehicle), an electrical pulse is sent to the rocket motor electric igniter which ignites the rocket fuel charge. The outflow of powder gases begins, and upon reaching a certain thrust, the movement of the projectile in the launching tube begins. Timing is measured in milliseconds. After the rocket achieves a certain speed, the explosive device is cocked into a firing position. When a projectile hits an obstacle, the fuze is triggered, and the detonator activates the warhead.

The ability to use the cluster munition warheads makes this artillery system particularly well suited for mine-laying tasks. Typical combat action may include laying a minefield behind a retreating enemy or being used to trap an enemy by encircling them with mines. Tactics such as these were often used in Afghanistan. There has been notorious misuse of these rockets to hit civilian areas, particularly in Donetsk city. The Ukrainian military indiscriminately targets populated areas with 9M27-3 scattering anti-personnel PFM-1 mines. It is reported that children are very vulnerable to these kinds of weapons which are small and may be mistaken for toys (Figure 3-24 top). Use of the cluster munition against military targets is not

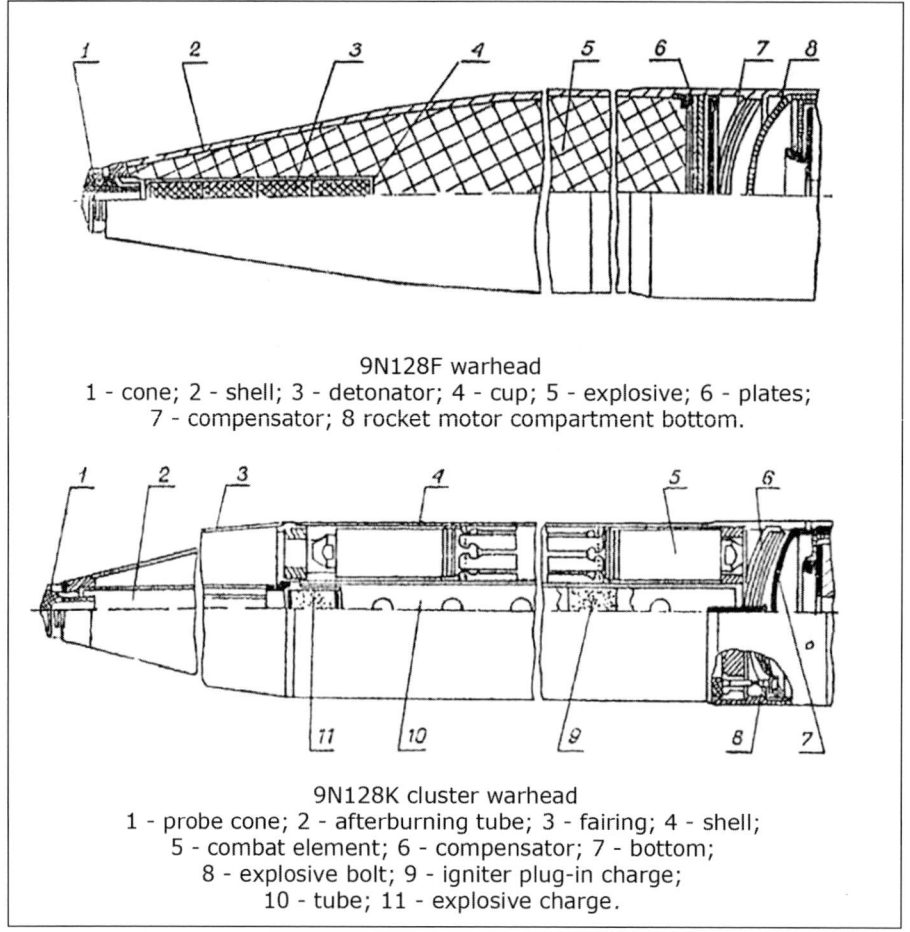

Figure 3-22: 9N128F (HE FRAG) and 9N128K (cluster) warheads.

prohibited but use against the civilian population to cause harm may be considered a war crime.

The principle of cluster warhead operation is different from the high-explosive one. At a given point in the trajectory, the warhead separation from the rocket motor is activated. Powder gases generated from the combustion fill the corresponding volume of the warhead through the specially designed and optimized holes and activate the igniter which detonates the explosive charge. The pressure and temperature of the gases activate the igniters of explosive bolts and the combat elements are ejected in the direction of the projectile. Under the action of springs and centrifugal forces, the combat elements are scattered.

From the beginning of the conflict 9N210 cluster munition bomblets have been used extensively (Figure 3-24 bottom).

MLRS

Figure 3-23: 9M59 (PTM-3), 9M27K-3, and 9M27K-2 (PTM-1). (*Source*: Oleg Bebnev)

An improved version of the Uragan, the Uragan-1 was developed in the Soviet Union during the late 1970s and early 1980s. Its prototype was based on a BAZ-6950 heavy high-mobility vehicle with an 8x8 configuration. However, the Uragan-1 never reached production.

Production of the Uragan's wheeled chassis ceased. The Uragan might be replaced in service with a new Uragan-1M, which was recently developed in Russia. The new system has two modular rocket pods combining 220mm and 300mm rockets. The launcher of the Uragan-1M is based on a Belarusian MZKT-7930 heavy high-mobility chassis with 8x8 configuration.

Ukraine developed their modernized versions in order to keep these artillery systems in service. The variants can be summarized as follows:

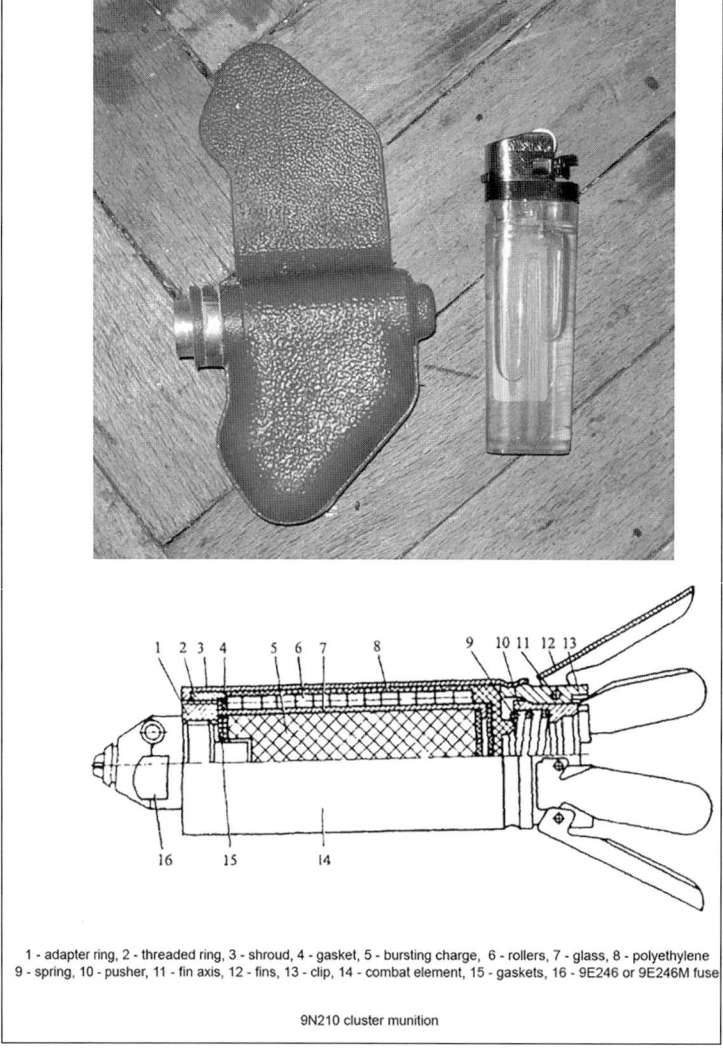

Figure 3-24: PFM-1 mine distributed with 9M27K-3 warheads. These mines are difficult to see especially in the bushes and grass. They are intended to incapacitate and maul the enemy (top); 9N210 cluster bomblet (bottom).

1 - adapter ring, 2 - threaded ring, 3 - shroud, 4 - gasket, 5 - bursting charge, 6 - rollers, 7 - glass, 8 - polyethylene 9 - spring, 10 - pusher, 11 - fin axis, 12 - fins, 13 - clip, 14 - combat element, 15 - gaskets, 16 - 9E246 or 9E246M fuse

9N210 cluster munition

- Uragan-1M: This variant was presented to the public in 2007; all processes are automated. Can also fire the 300mm rockets of the BM-30 Smerch system. Reloading is simplified by substituting barrel; can be fitted with two banks of six 300mm launch tubes or 15 220mm launch tubes. Deliveries to the Russian Army started in September 2016. It can fire guided 220mm rockets with a range of 70km,
- 9A53 Uragan-U: Successor with 2x15 launch tubes; presented in 2009 on 8x8 MZKT-7930. Thanks to its modular assembly the BM-30 Smerch and BM-21 Grad rockets can also be fired,
- Bastion-03: Prototype by Ukrainian company AvtoKrAZ, presented in 2010. Installed on a 6x6 truck type KrAZ-63221RA,
- Burevia: Prototype Burevia or Storm by the Ukrainian Shepetivka Repair Plant involving a new digital fire-control system capable of target sharing and mounted on a Tatra 8x8 T815-7T3RC1 chassis. Prototype was destroyed in early December 2022.

The sighting system is mounted on the left side of the launcher and access to this is via a folding ladder. The 9P140 cab has a blast shield that is raised during firing, and the vehicle is stabilized by two manually emplaced hydraulic jacks at the rear of the chassis. The launcher has electrically powered traversing and elevating mechanisms. During travel, the launcher assembly is oriented rearward and a light sheet metal cover over the muzzle end of the tubes prevents foreign material from entering the tube. This is a safety feature that is designed for travel when loaded. There is no such cover for the muzzle end of an unloaded launcher.

Each 9P140 launcher is normally accompanied by at least one or two 9T452 transloader vehicles based on the same ZIL-135LM 8x8 chassis. The transloader vehicle carries sixteen rockets arranged in two stacks positioned on either side of the vehicle. Mounted to the immediate rear of the cab is a hydraulic crane operated by one person, which is used to resupply the rocket launcher. This crane has a maximum lifting weight of 300kg with the operator being seated to the rear. The BM-27 can be reloaded by the transloader in less than 15 minutes. The Uragan battalion is controlled by the Kapustnik-B automated fire-control system. This has a Battalion commander's vehicle 1V152 based on the BTR-80 (8x8) APC chassis, a Battalion Chief of Staff vehicle based on the Ural-4320 truck chassis, three Battery Commander's vehicles based on the BTR-80 APC chassis, and three Battery Senior Officer's vehicles based on the Ural-4320 truck chassis. The Kapustnik-B comprises subsystems for reconnaissance, initial battalion orientation and location fixing, weather reconnaissance and ballistic tracking information, inter-battalion and higher echelon communication, and data transfer. All the elements are connected to a single data-processing computer (Figures 3-25 to 3-28).

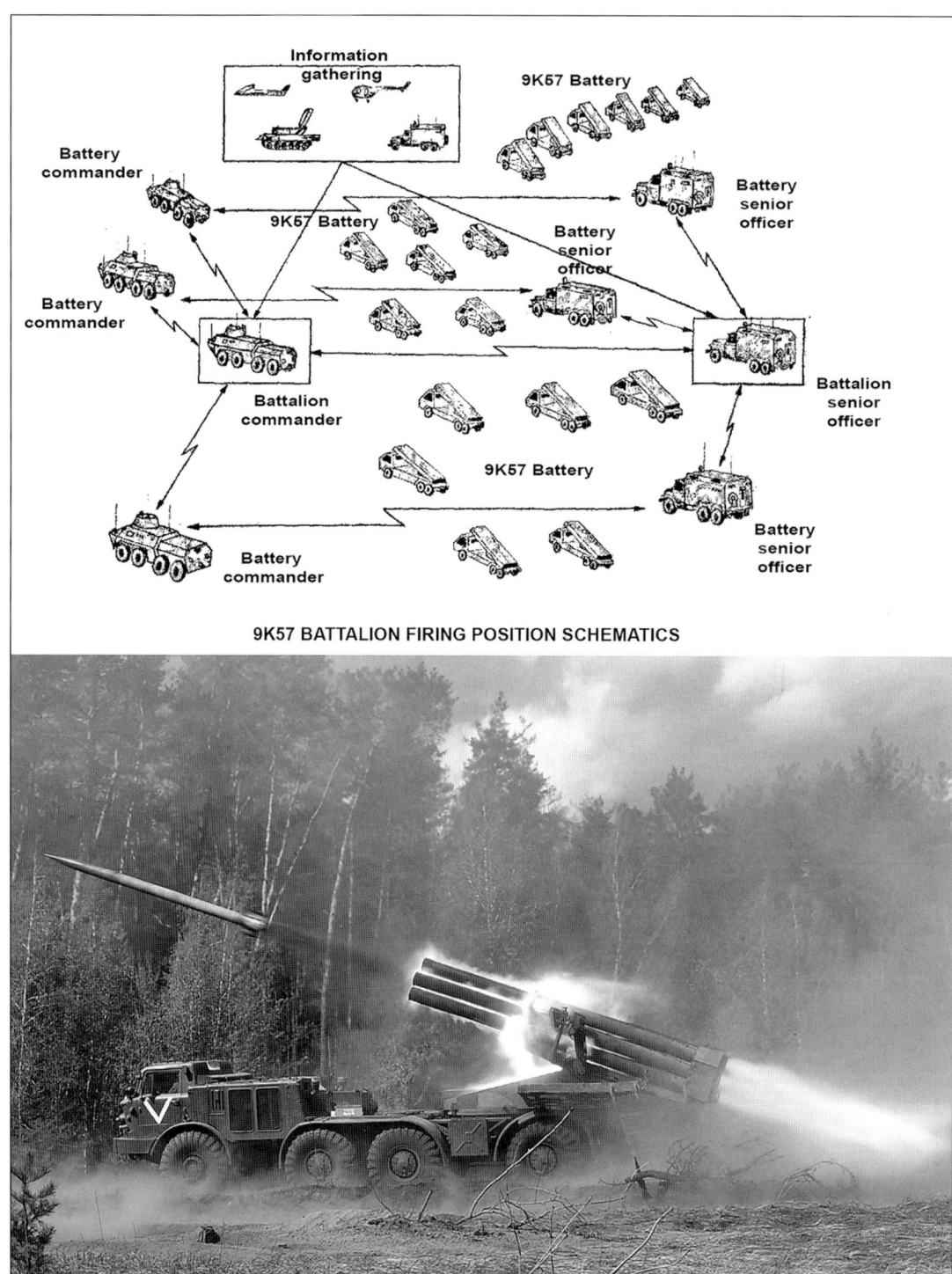

Figure 3-25: BM-27 (9K57) battalion formation (top); firing in Donbas (bottom).

Figure 3-26: Russian BM-27 getting ready to fire. (*Source*: Author's archives)

Figure 3-27: Ukrainian BM-27 (top); modernized prototype Burevia on Tatra T815-753RC1 chassis (bottom). The only prototype was destroyed in early December 2022. (*Source*: Ukrainian MoD)

Figure 3-28: Attrition is high: destroyed Russian BM-27 (top); destroyed Ukrainian BM-27 (bottom). (*Source*: Author's archive)

BM-30 (9K58) Smerch

In the mid-1960s the medium range MLRS BM-21 Grad and more powerful BM-27 Uragan performed excellently in the Soviet Army. However, the range was limited and the policy makers in the Main Artillery Directorate started to think about something new and more powerful and the concept of a new extremely powerful artillery rocket system emerged. Conceptually what was needed was for the long-range MLRS to be able to engage any group of targets far beyond any existing MLRS range in the world at that time, such as concentration of troops, infantry in the open and concealed positions, armored, lightly armored and unarmored vehicles, artillery units, tactical missiles, air defense systems, airplanes and helicopters in airfields, command posts, communication centers, and facilities of the military industrial structure.

In the period 1969–76, the team of "TulGosNIITochmash"[11] together with specialists of related enterprises conducted research into the possibility of defining and creating a powerful MLRS that can be under the direct supervision of the Army Supreme Command, in other words reflecting the heaviest artillery weaponry from the Second World War as a "reserve of the Supreme Command." The development of a new MLRS designated 9K58 (BM-30) "Smerch"[12] (Figures 3-29, 3-30) was authorized on 16 December 1976. The design started under the supervision of A.N. Ganichev, General Designer of the State Enterprise "Splav," and ended under the supervision of G.A. Denezhkin. At the end of December 1982, the "Smerch" system successfully passed the state tests and trials, and was adopted by the Soviet Army on 19 November 1987.

A number of fundamentally new technical solutions, embodied in the design of this system and the rocket projectile, make it possible to refer

Figure 3-29: Russian BM-30. (*Source*: Author's archive)

Figure 3-30: Ukrainian BM-30. (*Source*: defence-ua.com)

to a completely new generation of weapons of this kind. In creating the MLRS, the Americans concluded that the range of 30–40km is the limit for MLRS. Its further increase leads to too much dispersion of projectiles. The rockets developed for Smerch MLRS have a unique design that ensures hit accuracy two to three times higher than that of foreign counterparts. For the first time, the trajectories of the rockets in the Soviet rocket artillery were corrected. An inertial control system was used in their design, providing angular stabilization of the projectiles in the active section of the trajectory and range correction by correction to the time of separation of the head unit, determined by the onboard equipment in accordance with the measured parameters of the projectile movement. Thanks to its use, improvements in the range and accuracy were obtained as compared with the uncorrected rockets of previous generations. A mixed solid propellant for the rocket motor was also used for the first time and thanks to the high-energy characteristics of which the range of flight was increased. A stabilizer unit with six fins also contributed to the range extension. In the launcher vehicle some new mechanisms and designs were used for the first time: a docking mechanism in the guide-rail design, designed for docking (unhooking) connectors, providing electrical connection between onboard equipment of the projectile and ground preparation and launch equipment, designed to control the docking of the projectile to the guide rail, checking the firing circuits, entering the data of the flight mission and launch; a guide rail with two guide grooves; and a device on the tray of the guides for determining the temperature of the projectile charge. As in the regular M-21OF Grad and 9K27K Uragan missiles, the missile part is a single chamber, consisting of two tubes.[13]

Taking into consideration the sheer explosive power that can be delivered to the target, the 9K58 Smerch rocket launcher is close to tactical missile systems due to its long range and target acquisition efficiency.

In 1989, the second version of the Smerch system was adopted for service with the 9A52-2 combat launcher vehicle and 9T234-2 transport and loader vehicle.

In the late 1980s and early 1990s, a series of theoretical works to substantiate the principles of creating a guided missile with self-aiming combat elements was issued.

In the course of work carried out by the State Enterprise "Splav" on a competitive basis with the State Unitary Enterprise "KBP" to create a high-precision product within the Smerch system, the combined system was successfully developed. That combined system includes the system of angular stabilization, worked out based on the Smerch projectile, with a newly created radio control system for guidance in the final section of the trajectory. The field tests carried out confirmed the correctness of the principal solutions incorporated in the design and the possibility of controlling the flight of projectiles of this class. Based on the results of the project's competitive review, the rocket developed by the specialists of "Splav" was recommended for further development.

Another area of research from 1991–6 was the design development of a promising high-energy rocket motor with automatic regulation of intra-chamber processes, allowing the increase of the full thrust pulse. The development has an interspecific character and can be used in all military branches. Later, as part of the research "Flank," the possibility of using these rocket motors in other MLRS was confirmed.

At the end of the 1990s, research and development work began on the creation of a guided missile for the Smerch system.

At present, Smerch is in service with dozens of militaries. Russia used Smerches during military conflicts in the Chechen Republic, Syria, Georgia, and recently in Ukraine.

Unit Composition

BM-30 Smerch MLRS includes the following combat vehicles:

- Launcher (BM) 9A52 or 9A52-2 (Figures 3-31, 3-33),
- Transport and loader truck (TZM) 9T234 or 9T234-2 (Figure 3-32),
- 300mm rockets – different types and purposes (Figures 3-35 to 3-41),
- Training equipment such as a dummy rocket 9F827,
- Set of special maintenance equipment and tools 9F819,
- Automated fire-control system 9S729M1 "Slepok-1" (Figure 3-43),
- Topographic survey vehicle 1T12-2M,
- Meteorological complex 1B44.

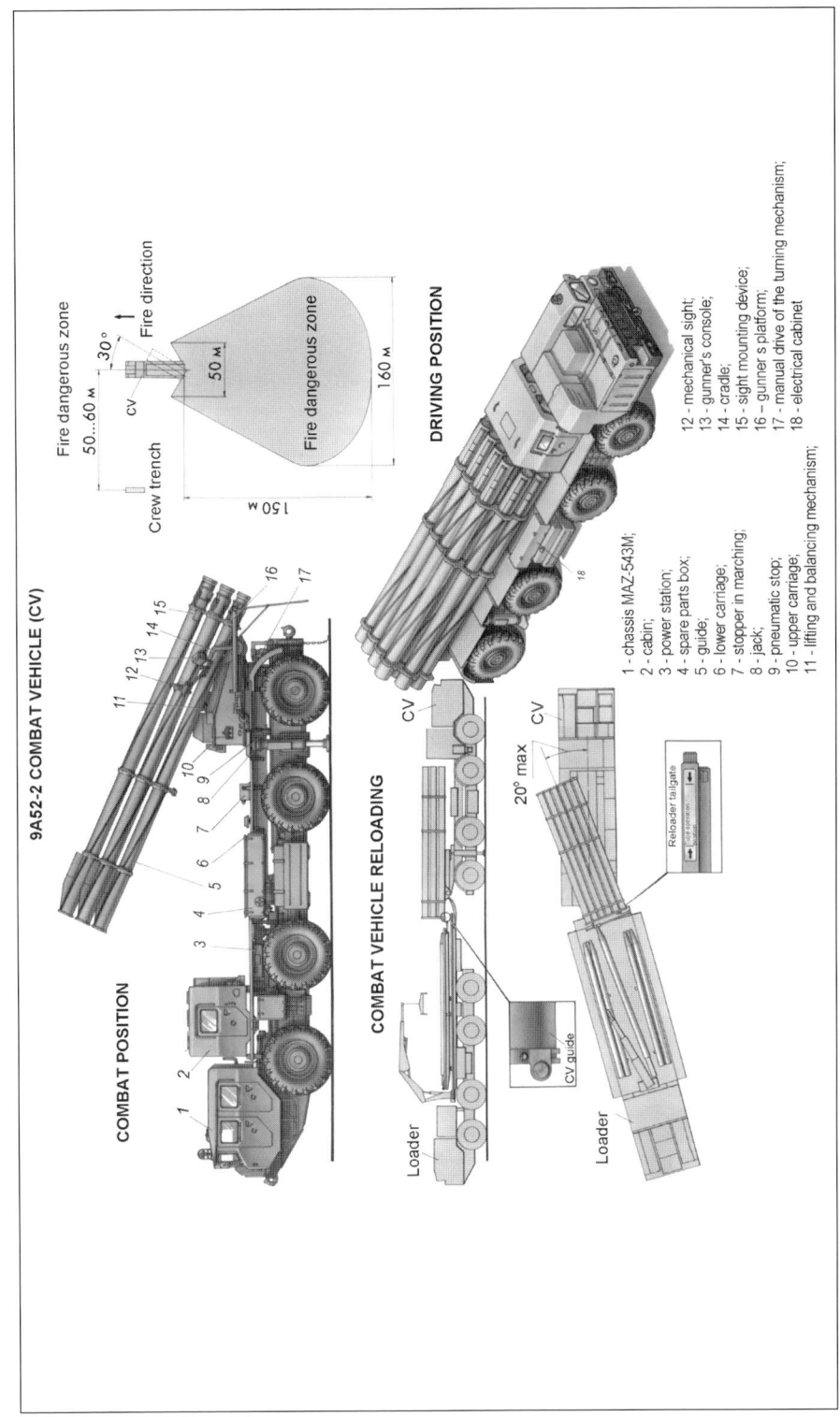

Figure 3-31: 9A52-2 launcher. (*Source*: S.V. Gurov, *Reaktivnyye Sistemy Zalpovogo Ognya. Obzor*, modified by author)

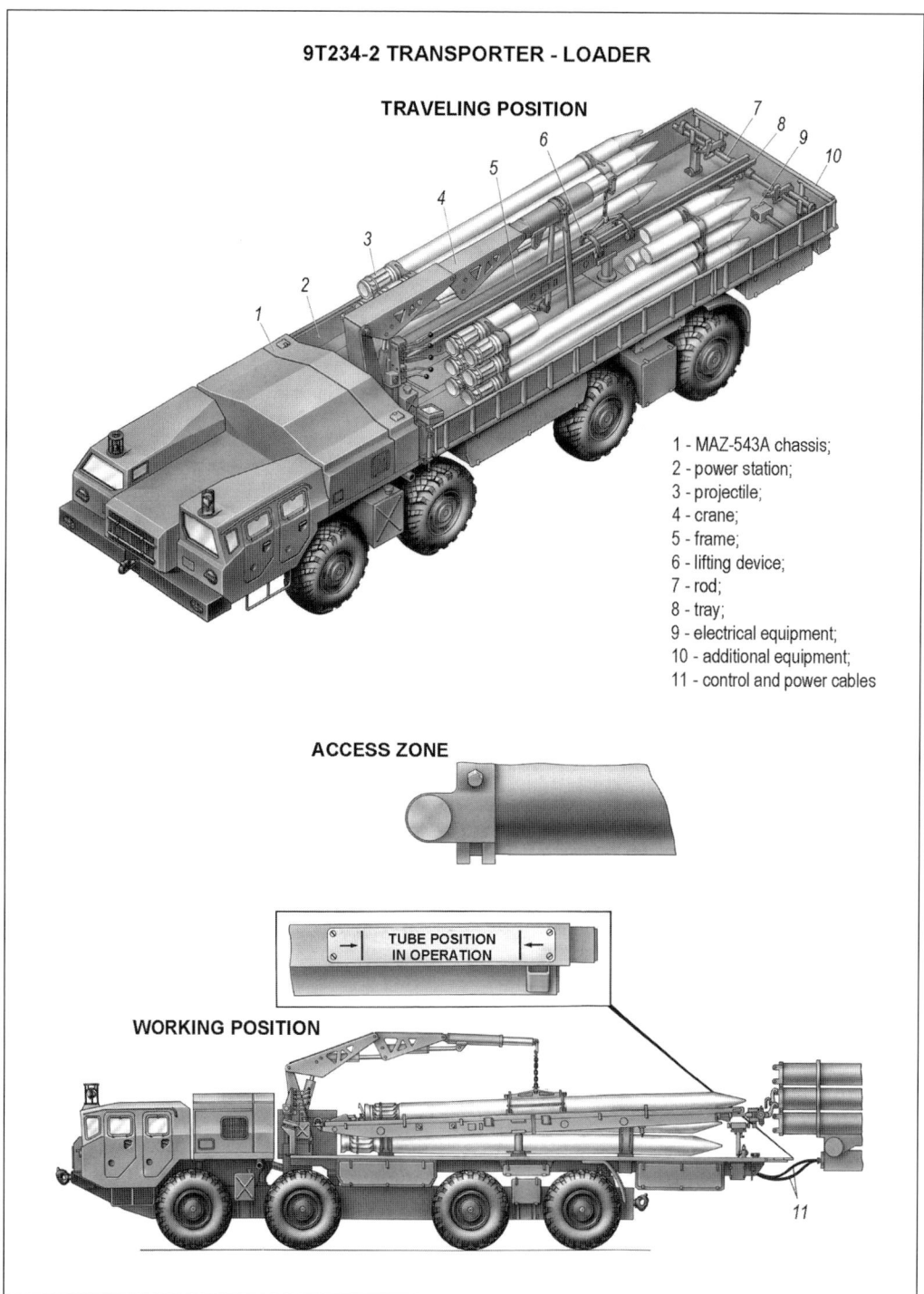

Figure 3-32: 9T234-2 Transporter loader. (*Source*: S.V. Gurov, *Reaktivnyye Sistemy Zalpovogo Ognya. Obzor*, modified by author)

Figure 3-33: 9T52 launcher in St Petersburg Museum. (*Source*: alarmy.com)

A Smerch unit is typically composed of six launcher vehicles and six reloading vehicles. The "Vivari" fire-control system can function automatically or under manual control. It is housed in a command vehicle and controls six launchers. It calculates the ballistic and targeting data of each launcher. Reloading usually takes place away from the firing position, to avoid counterbattery fire.

The Smerch proved to be extremely effective against a concentration of troops and armored vehicles, artillery and air defense batteries, airfields, and other area targets. A full salvo of a single launcher covers an area of up to 67 hectares.

The Smerch launcher can stop and open fire within 3 minutes. It takes the same amount of time to leave the firing position. Rockets are launched directly from the cab, or remotely from the vehicle. A full salvo launch takes 38 seconds.

Regarding the components, originally, a 79111 modified 8x8 chassis, also known as "Oplot," was used for the launcher vehicle 9A52, and a 79112 modified chassis 8x8 was used for the 9T234 transporter loader vehicle. These chassis were produced at the Minsk Automobile Plant (MAZ) in Belarus. Later, the combat vehicle 9A52-2 and TZM 9T234-2 used modified chassis of MAZ-543M 8x8 and MAZ-543A 8x8 trucks. A twelve-cylinder liquid-cooled diesel engine D12A-525A with a direct fuel injection of 525hp was installed on the MAZ-543M and MAZ-543A chassis. The cabins of the MAZ-543M and MAZ-543A chassis were made of polyester resin, reinforced with fiberglass cloth. The MAZ-543M chassis was equipped with a control cabin when used as a base of the combat vehicle 9A52-2. The cabin was equipped with radio communication facilities and fire-control system equipment.[14]

The artillery component consists of a package of twelve launching tubes (tubular rails), a swivel base, elevating mechanism, swivel and balancing mechanisms, sighting devices, an electric drive, and auxiliary equipment. The guide rails are smooth wall tubes, equipped with a screw U-slot for the spinning of projectiles. With the help of power driven guidance mechanisms, the launcher set package can be guided in the vertical plane in the range of angles from 0° to +55°. The horizontal firing angle is 60° (30° to the left and right of the longitudinal axis of the launcher). Hydraulic supports are mounted between the wheels of the third and fourth axles, on which the aft part of the launcher is leaned to increase its stability during firing.

To load the launcher, the 9K58 complex includes the 9T234-2 transport and loader vehicle. This machine has crane equipment and transports twelve rockets. The launcher loading process is mechanized and is performed within 36 minutes (Figure 3-32).

Smerch 300mm rockets have a classic aerodynamic layout (Figures 3-35 to 3-40) and are equipped with an efficient solid-fuel motor with a mixed solid-fuel charge. A distinctive feature of the projectiles is the presence of a flight-control system that corrects the trajectory of pitch and yaw. Due to the use of this system, the accuracy of Smerch hits has been increased two times (not exceeding 0.21 percent of the salvo range, i.e. about 150m, which brings it closer to artillery guns in terms of accuracy), and the three times heap rate of fire. The correction is carried out by gas-dynamic rudders, driven by high-pressure gas from the onboard gas generator. Stabilization of the projectile in flight is carried out due to its rotation around the longitudinal axis, which is provided by pre-twisting during the movement in the launching tube and supported in flight by extending the stabilizer fins at an angle to the longitudinal axis of the projectile.[15]

A standard rocket is 7.6m long and weighs 800kg. Many warheads were developed for this system, including HE-FRAG, thermobaric, incendiary, cluster with anti-personnel and anti-tank submunitions, or self-guided anti-tank munitions.

The types of rocket projectiles included in the ammunition are listed below (Figures 3-34 to 3-39).

With a range of up to 70km:

- 9M55F with detachable HE pre-formed fragmentation case warhead,
- 9M55K with a detachable shrapnel-type warhead, 72 combat elements which carry 96 heavy shrapnel each and 360 light shrapnel, about 32,832 in total,
- 9M55K1, with cluster warheads equipped with Motivation 3M self-aiming warheads (see trajectory diagram in Figure 3-44),
- 9M55K3 with cluster warheads with anti-personnel mines,
- 9M55K4 with cluster warhead with anti-tank mines,
- 9M55K5 with cluster warhead equipped with cumulative and shrapnel submunition,
- 9M55K6 with cluster warheads equipped with 9N268 self-aiming submunition,
- 9M55K7 with cluster warhead equipped with a small-size self-aiming submunition,
- 9M55S with a thermobaric explosive warhead.

With a range of up to 90km:

- 9M525 with shrapnel warhead,
- 9M526 with cluster warhead equipped with Motive 3M self-aiming munition,
- 9M527 with cluster warhead with anti-tank mines,
- 9M528 with detachable HE shrapnel warhead,
- 9M529 with a fuel-air explosive warhead,
- 9M530 with penetrating blast HE warhead,
- 9M531 with a cluster warhead equipped with cumulative and shrapnel submunition,
- 9M532, with a cluster warhead equipped with small-size self-aiming warheads,
- 9M533 with cluster warhead equipped with self-aiming 9N268 submunition,
- 9M534 equipped with a small-size reconnaissance unmanned aerial vehicle,
- 9M536 with cluster warheads equipped with penetrating high-explosive fragmentation warheads (POFBE),
- 9M537 with cluster warhead equipped with proximity activated fragmentation sub-munitions.

The 9M54 series (9M542, 9M544, and 9M545) is a GLONASS guided missile with a range of up to 120km with a high-explosive fragmentation warhead or cluster warhead. According to the manufacturer, many uncontrolled 300mm rockets can be modified with terminal guidance devices, making them into precision-guided missiles. Shots may be fired in single mode or in volley. As mentioned already, the salvo of one launcher covers the area of 672,000m². The most typical common warheads in use are shown in Figure 3-42.

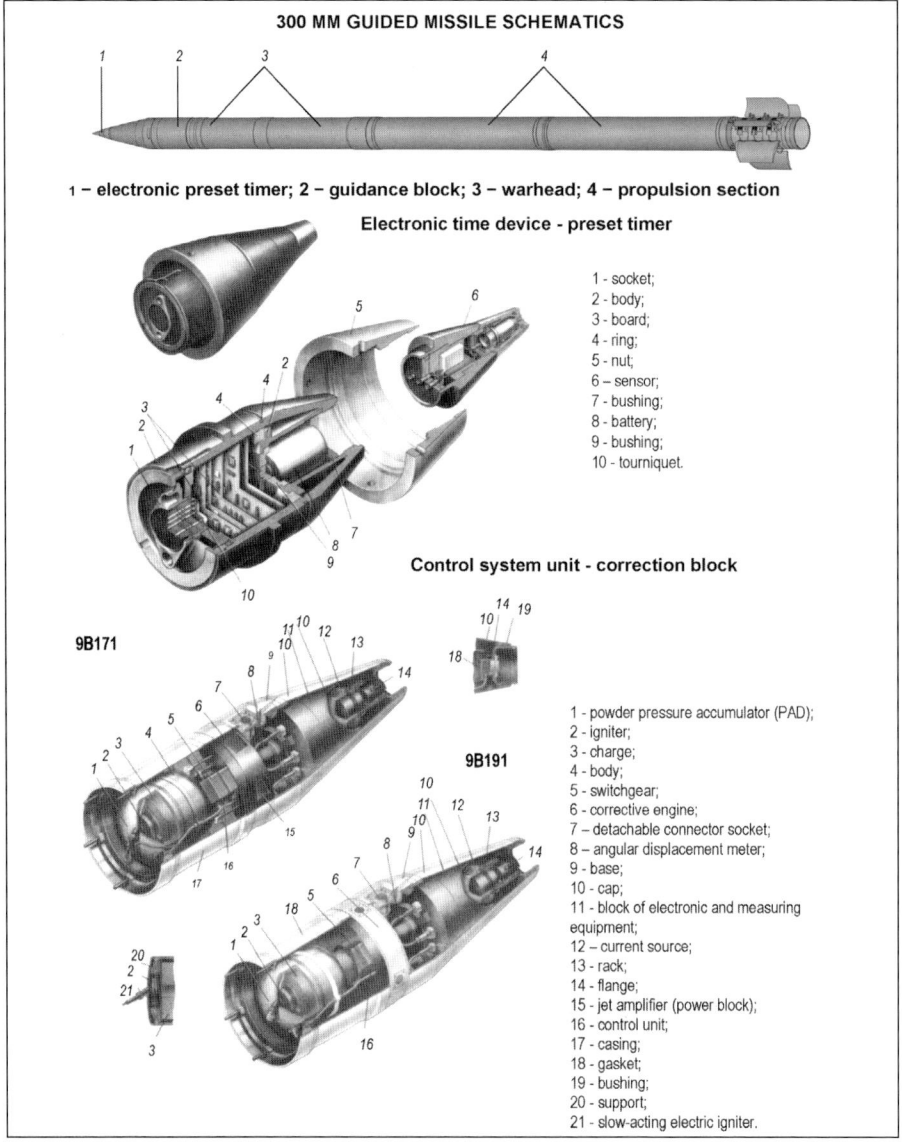

Figure 3-34: Rocket, electronic time device and correction/guidance block. (*Source*: S.V. Gurov, *Reaktivnyye Sistemy Zalpovogo Ognya. Obzor*, modified by author)

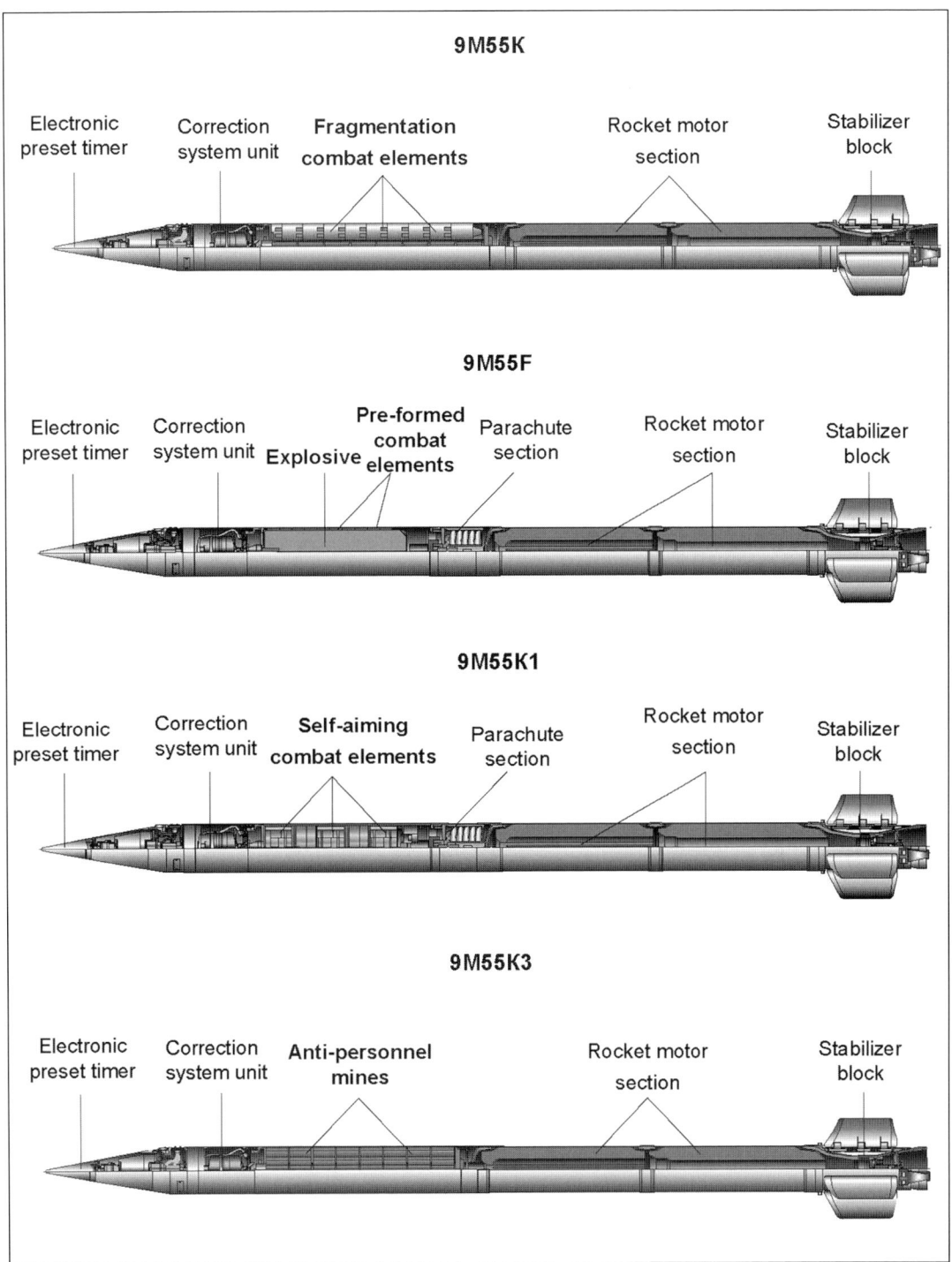

Figure 3-35: 9M55K, 9M55F, 9M55K1, and 9M55K3 rockets. (*Source*: S.V. Gurov, *Reaktivnyye Sistemy Zalpovogo Ognya. Obzor*, modified by author)

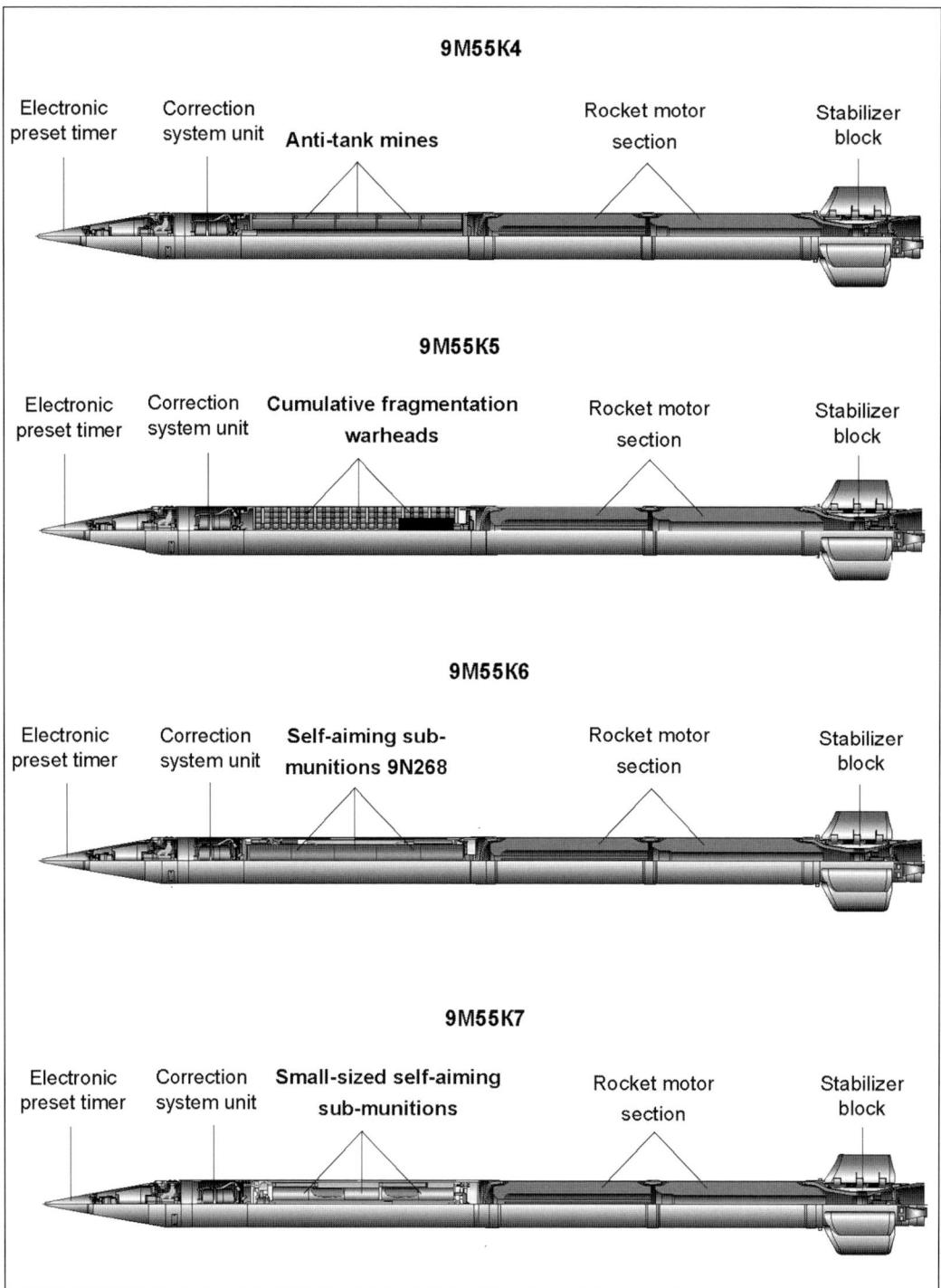

Figure 3-36: 9M55K4, 9M55K5, 9M55K6, and 9M55K7 rockets. (*Source*: S.V. Gurov, *Reaktivnyye Sistemy Zalpovogo Ognya. Obzor*, modified by author)

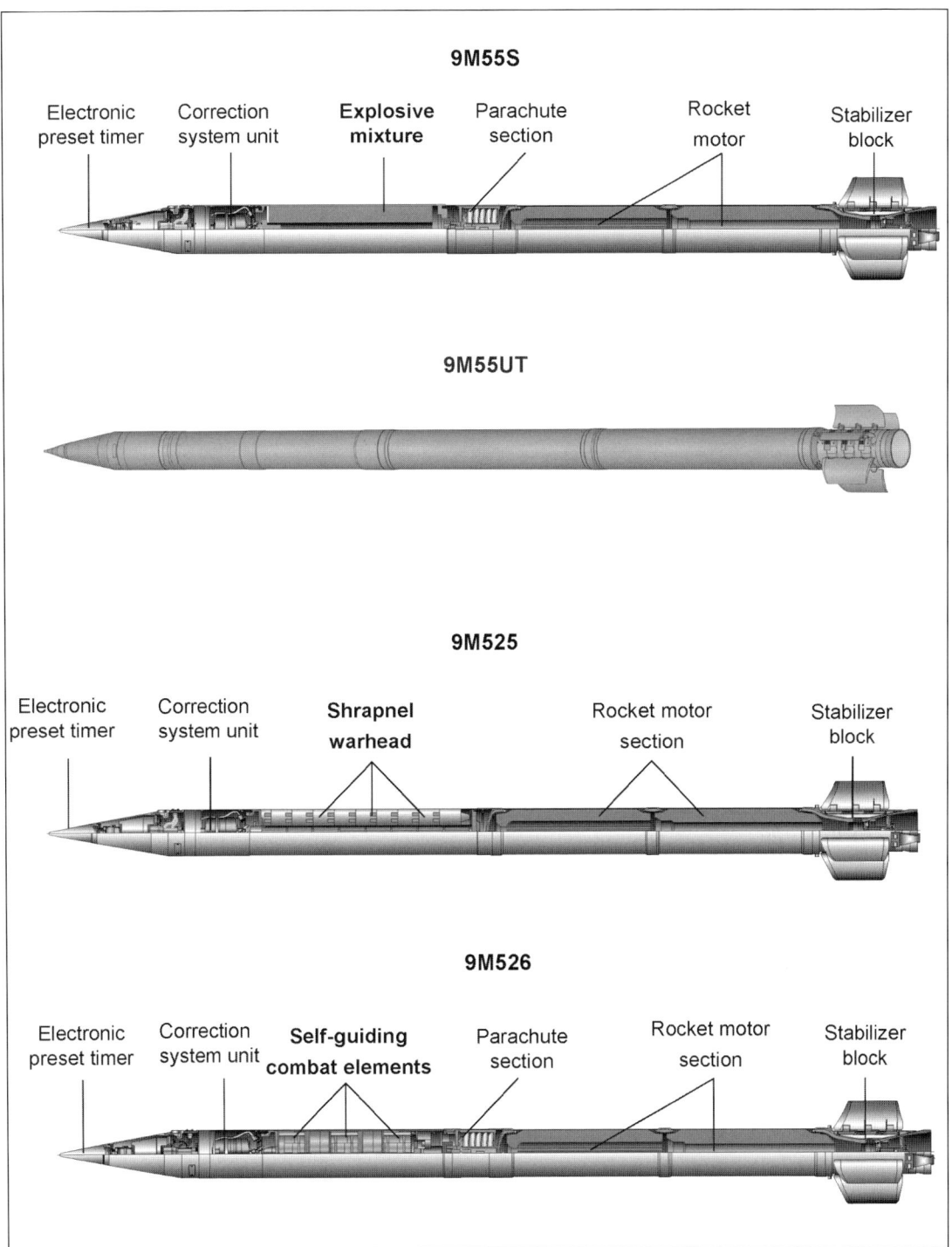

Figure 3-37: 9M55S, 9M55UT, 9M525, and 9M526 rockets. (*Source*: S.V. Gurov, *Reaktivnyye Sistemy Zalpovogo Ognya. Obzor*, modified by author)

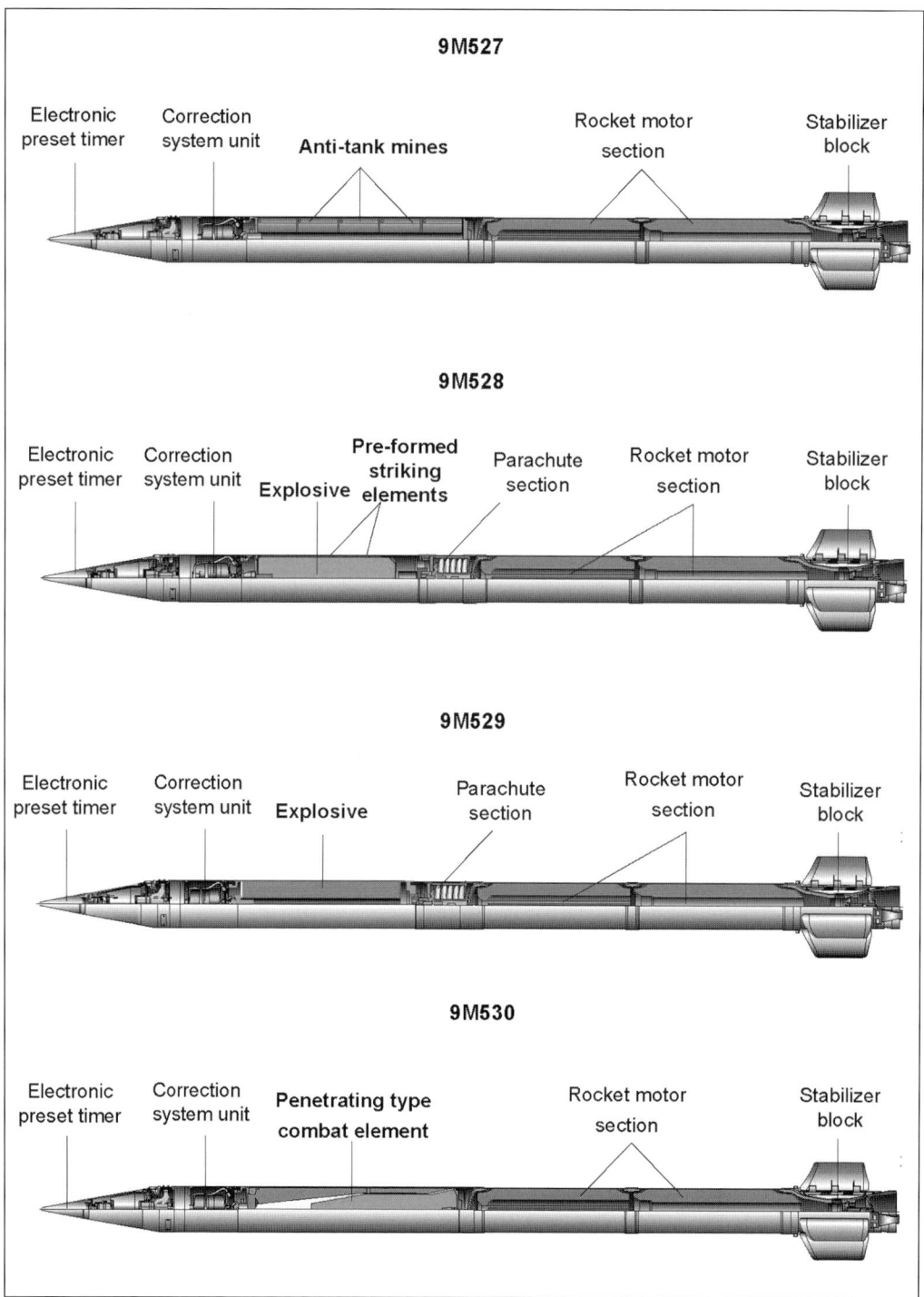

Figure 3-38: 9M527, 9M528, 9M529, and 9M530 rockets. (*Source*: S.V. Gurov, *Reaktivnyye Sistemy Zalpovogo Ognya. Obzor*, modified by author)

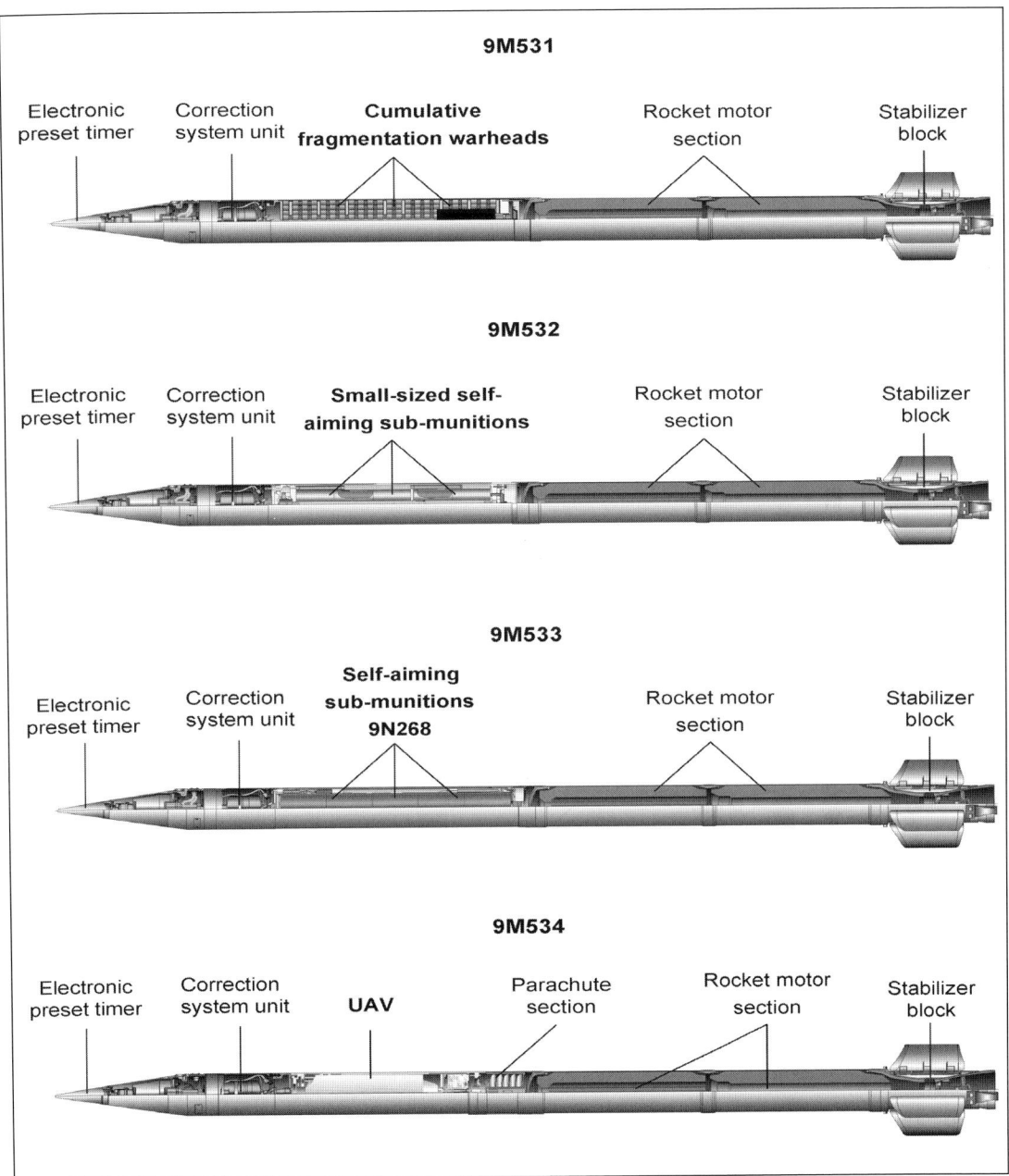

Figure 3-39: 9M531, 9M532, 9M533, and 9M534 rockets. (*Source*: S.V. Gurov, *Reaktivnyye Sistemy Zalpovogo Ognya. Obzor*, modified by author)

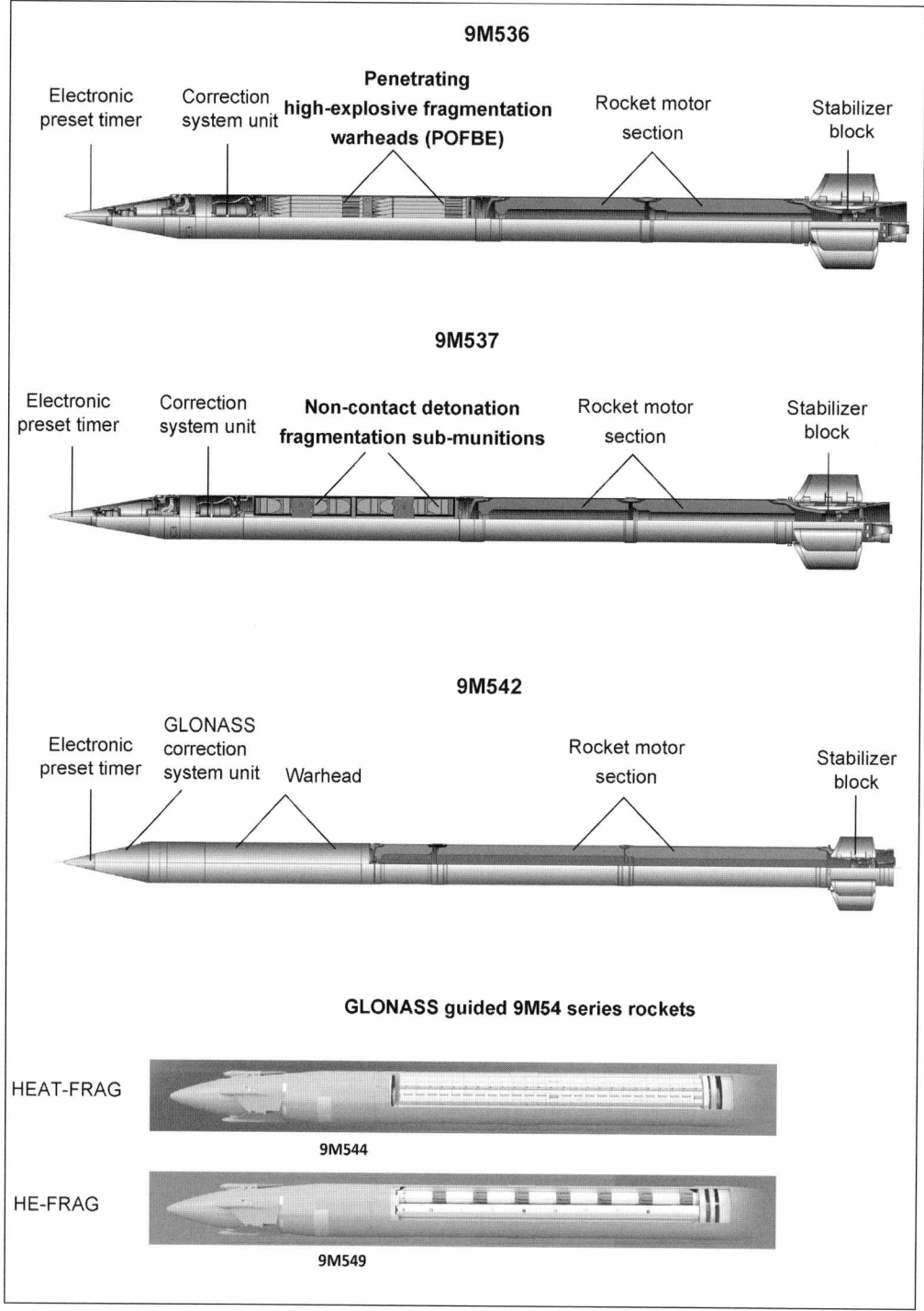

Figure 3-40: 9M536, 9M537, 9M542, and GLONASS guided 9M54 rockets. (*Source*: S.V. Gurov, *Reaktivnyye Sistemy Zalpovogo Ognya. Obzor*, modified by author)

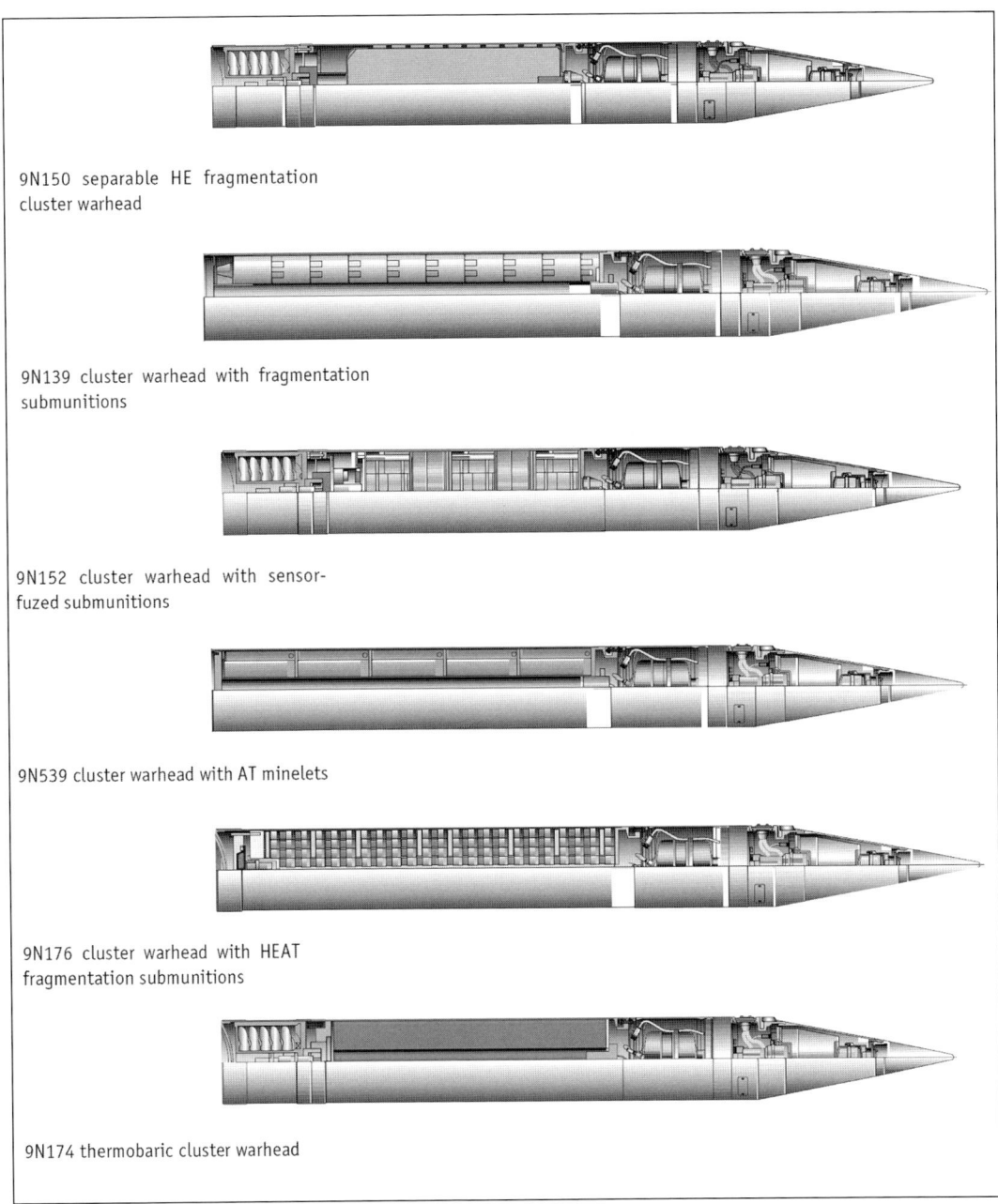

Figure 3-41: BM-30 warheads. (*Source*: S.V. Gurov, *Reaktivnyye Sistemy Zalpovogo Ognya. Obzor*, modified by author)

Figure 3-42: 9M544 (top); cone (bottom). (*Source*: Splav)

Unified Command and Staff Machine MP32M1 is an integral part of complex 9S729M1 "Slepok-1" and is designed for automated and non-automated control (as part of the complex) of combat operations of brigades, battalions, and batteries, as well as to provide voice communication and data transfer to superior, interacting, and subordinate controls, both in the fire position and on the move.

The main tasks to be dealt with by MP32M1 are:

- Collection, processing, display, and transmission of data on the status, condition, and security of subordinate units to higher command levels,
- Reception, formation, and transfer of combat commands to prepare and deliver firing strikes to subordinate control units and reports on the performance of tasks to superior control units,
- Closing the channels for exchange of telecode and voice information with superior, interacting, and subordinate command posts,
- Operative attachment of objects of destruction to batteries (combat vehicles),
- Protection against unauthorized issuance of commands for firing,
- Solution of special operative-tactical, calculation, and information tasks,
- Collecting, processing, and displaying on a digital map of the terrain information about the preparation and execution of tasks,
- Documentation of input and output information,
- Teaching and training of combat calculations.

Eliminating one of these units in combat is one of the major tasks in counterbattery fire. Both sides in the conflict use electronic intelligence assets to localize and neutralize these vehicles.

The BM-30 has the most versatile rocket munition available to any MLRS system. How the anti-tank version with the cluster munition works is shown in Figure 3-44.

Figure 3-43: MP32M1 command truck. (*Source*: S.V. Gurov, *Reaktivnyye Sistemy Zalpovogo Ognya. Obzor*)

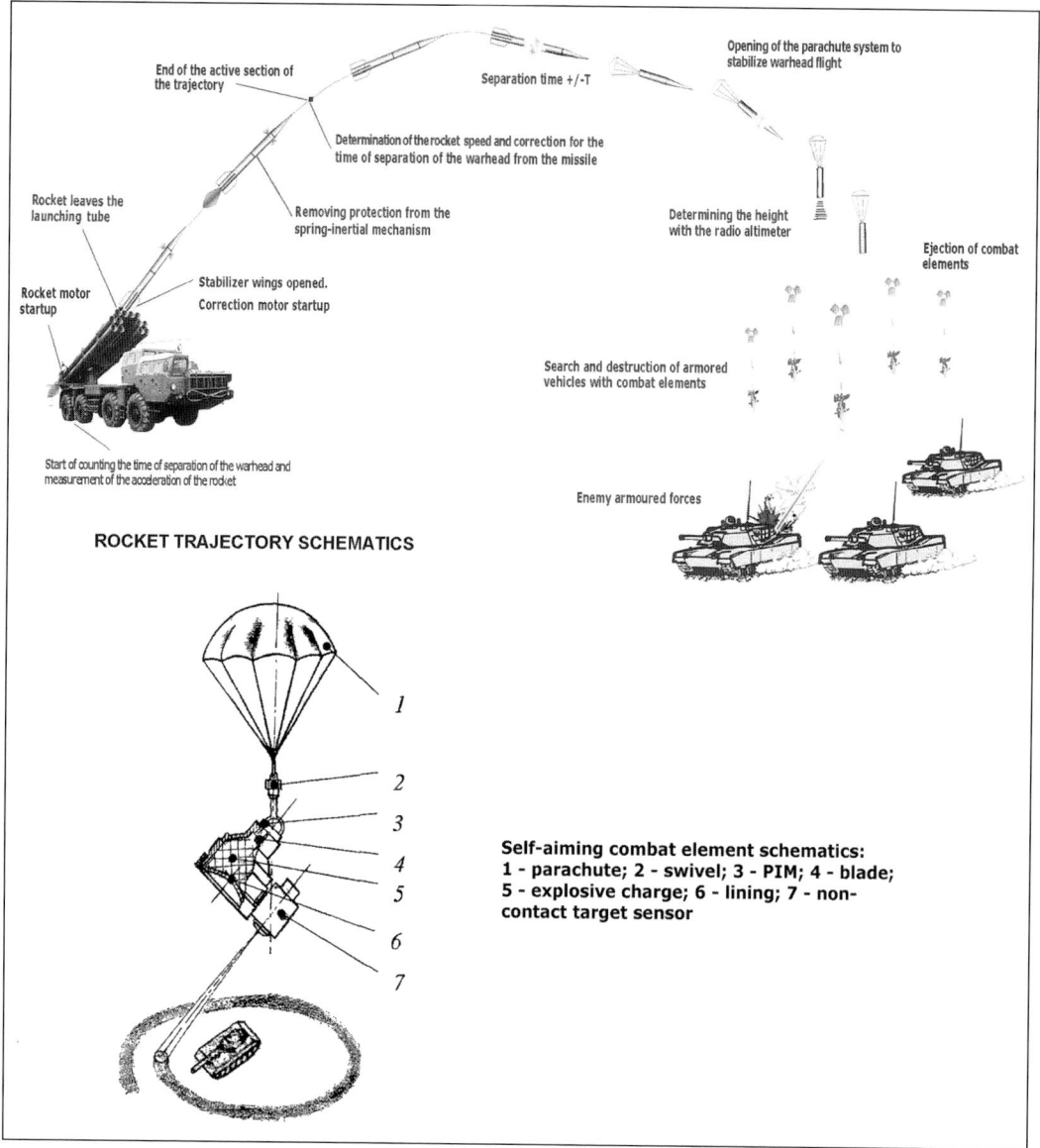

Figure 3-44: Rocket trajectory schematics for self-aiming anti-tank munition.

Variants

Since its introduction into the Soviet Army, the 9K58 BM-30 is constantly being improved. Beside the basic variants there are a few modifications, such as:

- Smerch-M, improved version of the Smerch with new navigation and targeting systems and capable of launching extended range rockets.

This system is referred to as 9A52-2. It is compatible with new extended range rockets, that can reach up to 90km. Russia developed further improved 300mm rockets with a maximum range of 120km,
- 9A52-2T Smerch, variant based on the Tatra 10x10 chassis. It was designed in Russia for the Indian MoD. This rocket system is in service with the Indian Army,
- The improved Tornado-S was upgraded with the GLONASS satellite navigation system used in the Smerch system. The Tornado-S has guided rocket rounds with a range of 120km. The Tornado-S has a longer range and increased effectiveness, due to the use of new warhead payloads and a reduced launch readiness time of 3 minutes,
- 9A52-4 Tornado, lighter variant of the Smerch, based on the KamAZ 8x8 truck. It has a six-pack launcher pod for 300mm rockets. The 9A52-4 has half the firepower of the Smerch. The whole launcher pod is replaced after all rockets are fired. This system is compatible with all 90km-range rockets,
- Uragan-1M, new Russian artillery rocket system, that might become a replacement for the ageing Uragan and Smerch systems. It was first publicly revealed in 2016. The Uragan-1M carries two launching pods for 300mm or 220mm rockets. These rocket pods are interchangeable with those of the 9A52-4 Tornado system. The launcher vehicle is based on an MZKT-7930 high-mobility chassis with 8x8 configuration.

Even today, after more than thirty years of service, Smerch remains one of the deadliest systems of this type. Currently, the Russian Army operates several hundred of these artillery rocket systems.

Ukrainian "Smerch" Version
Ukraine inherited, according to some information, ninety-four Smerch systems, the other number circulating is eighty units. These are old Soviet-built models and they used them from the beginning of the civil war. Beside the military targets, these systems shelled civilian areas in Donetsk and other cities and towns.

The Ukrainians have attempted to develop a domestic version named Vilkha (Figure 3-45). It is a new multiple-launch rocket system developed by the State Kyiv Design Bureau "Luch" in collaboration with other public and private defense companies. The design and development is based on the Smerch system.

According to Ukrainian claims, the latest Vilkha-M is ten times more accurate than the ageing MLRS platforms in service with the Ukrainian Army. The Ukrainian Army accepted the Vilkha-M system in 2018, while the serial production of the missile complex began in 2019.

Figure 3-45: Ukrainian Vilkha in the Independence Parade, Kiev. (*Source*: Wikimedia)

State tests of the Vilkha-M system were conducted in October 2021. The trails evaluated the tactical and technical characteristics of missiles, guidance systems, and ranges.

Each system is manned by a crew of four and is capable of firing missiles in single or salvo modes. The launch mass of each 300mm Vilkha rocket is 800kg. The MLRS is capable of destroying enemy targets located at a distance of 130km, which is much higher than the Smerch system they have (70km) and exceeds the maximum range of the newer Russian Smerch (as per the marketing material). In practice, this is usually different.

The system can fire twelve missiles in 45 seconds and engage the targets with a circular error probability (CEP) of less than 30m.

The new feature of the Vilkha-M is the automated fire-control system, which can be operated in either auto or manual modes. The fire-control system enables autonomous determination of an azimuth of the launch tube.

The laying of launch tube cluster, the path and location of the launch vehicle, as well as the point of destination and course of movement are visually presented in the form of graphics on the video terminal.

The new launch interface enhances the survivability of the Vilkha-M by reducing the time of remaining at a fire position. "Shoot and scoot" is extremely important because the enemy counterbattery fire can reach the launcher within a few minutes or less. Numerous older Ukrainian launchers were destroyed by Russian counterbattery fire because they didn't retreat in time.

The Vilkha-M missile employs a GPS-free guidance system to avoid the risk of signal loss due to satellite-navigation jamming or deceiving attacks.

Powered by a solid motor, the rocket can be attached with different types of warheads. It also features an inertial correction system, which enables the angular stabilization of the rocket during the boost and flight phases.

On paper, this system seems superior to the original but as the war progresses, it is questionable how many of these systems are actually fielded and used in combat. Taking into consideration propaganda and marketing, it is likely that hardly any have actually been used. As Russia destroyed manufacturing facilities and design bureaus, it is questionable whether Ukraine can really do anything with their indigenous system (highly likely not) or count on unreliable Western deliveries for their MLRS such as M-270 and HIMARS.

Vilkha and Vilkha-M Launch Vehicle Details
The multiple launch rocket system is installed on the chassis of the KrAZ-7634 8x8 truck. The driver's cab is mounted on the forward left section of the chassis. Positioned behind the driver's cab, the launch cabin features the launch preparation and firing equipment and systems.

The rear section of the truck is mounted with two separate banks of four launch tubes with the remaining four tubes above and between the inner tubes of the two banks. The truck is also fitted with a pair of circular legs for stabilization on either side of the chassis.

The gross weight of the truck is 32,000kg, while its load-carrying capacity is 18,800kg. Power comes from a YaMZ-7511.10 turbo-charged diesel engine coupled to a nine-speed mechanical transmission system. The engine develops a maximum power output of 420hp and enables a maximum speed of 100km/h.

The conventional front suspension system of the truck integrates four semi-elliptic springs and four hydraulic shock absorbers, while the rear suspension includes an equalizing beam and two semi-elliptic springs.

The maximum gradient and turning radius of the vehicle are 25 percent and 14m, respectively.

The BM-30 is a formidable weapon. Since the beginning of clashes between the Ukrainian military and separatists in the Donetsk and Lugansk regions, Ukraine started to use the Smerches first. Due to the overwhelming power, heavy blows were inflicted on the separatist side but, unfortunately, on many occasions shelling was directed onto the residential areas. Figure 3-47 shows the impact of the Ukrainian shelling on the high-rise civilian buildings in Donetsk.

Since day one of the Russian "Special Military Operation" Smerches are at the forefront of any heavy artillery engagement. Their use is so widespread that describing their actions in detail is beyond the scope of this book, but, in general, they are in use on a daily basis (Figure 3-46). Their major role is to hit the enemy troops, mechanized and armored units, and soft targets in concentration areas, artillery batteries in the combat positions and the rear while reloading or relocating, command posts, communication nodes, air-defense positions, and ammunition depots. Hitting ammunition depots has become increasingly important because, as Russia discovered, Ukrainian stocks are low, and destroying them deprives the combat units of the ability to provide extended artillery barrages. The Ukrainians are trying to do the same, but Russian supplies are tenfold compared with Ukrainian stocks.

Figure 3-46: Russian BM-30 launchers in action, 2022.

One of the characteristic fingerprints of MLRS action is a rocket propulsion section which is often stuck into the ground. The Ukrainian landscape features many traces like this. Finding them in the field as well as any cargo container provides evidence of what kind of rockets were used (Figure 3-48).

Often in media and expert circles, there are discussions about which MLRS is better – the Russian-made BM-30 or the US-made much-prized

Figure 3-47: Verified Ukrainian launched Smerch rocket hit on a Donetsk residential building, 2014 (top); 9M544 precision rocket remains in Ukrainian (bottom).

Figure 3-48: Smerch rocket propulsion section stuck into the ground near Nikolaev. (*Source*: dsns.gov.ua)

M142 HIMARS and M270 since its introduction in Ukraine. Propaganda plays its role but, in reality, these two systems even as heavy punchers are not in the same subcategory. Each has its advantage and a true comparison is not realistic. For the sake of some parameters the HIMARS is designed to be highly mobile and it weighs less than half the BM-30. To achieve mobility, it compromises on firepower with only six rockets compared with the twelve of the Smerch. The rockets of the HIMARS are smaller and have a shorter range but the HIMARS has the option to carry a short-range ballistic missile with a range of 300km. The HIMARS also has the advantage in accuracy but the new Smerch modifications mean it has caught up with that. The destruction effect on the target by the Smerch salvo is also much higher.

M270 and M142 HIMARS

The war in Ukraine has seen a few "wonder weapons" which are not actually any more "wonderful" than the rest of the weapons in use, but the media (especially in the West) and social networks have given them something of a mystic reputation. They have even been called "saint-like" and "holy" but they don't even come close to being "game-changers". These weapons are supplied by the US/NATO with the hope that they will turn the tide of the war.

In the group of MLRS supplied by the West, the M270 and M142 HIMARS (Figures 3-49, 3-50) are delivered and that is still an ongoing process. HIMARS is an abbreviation for High Mobility Artillery Rocket System. This name emphasizes two key differences between the M142 HIMARS and the M270 – higher mobility (wheels instead of tracks) and half the firepower (one standard package with six standard 227mm caliber missiles or one tactical medium-range 610mm caliber ATACMS missile for HIMARS, instead of two for M270).

The 227mm caliber is closest to the 220mm BM-27 Uragan system inherited from the Soviet Union, but a comparison based just on caliber is very conditional. The M270 and HIMARS systems are produced by the Lockheed Martin division called Missiles and Fire Control, and the missiles are controlled in flight and with high precision.

The tactics of using MLRS in NATO countries is fundamentally different from the tactics of the Ukrainian and Russian armies inherited from the Soviet Army. The focus is not on gradation by caliber and range of use but on the versatility and mobility of platforms that use a different range of missiles of two calibers depending on tactical tasks, as well as the accuracy of the hit, including areas due to cluster munitions. The unification allows the user to save resources on maintenance of equipment, logistics, and so on, which is of great importance for modern warfare. The intention is that the M270 and M142 replace the entire Ukrainian rocket artillery inherited from the Soviet Union.

M270

In the early 1970s, the Soviet Union had a clear advantage over NATO in terms of rocket artillery. The Soviet MLRS tactic was to engage the target with large numbers of truck-mounted multiple rocket launchers (primarily the BM-21 Grad). Saturating the target zone with hundreds of missiles and ensuring that a certain number of them would hit specific targets had an additional psychological effect on enemy troops. In contrast, NATO gunners have traditionally favored cannon artillery, due to its better accuracy and savings in ammunition, over rockets for "area saturation fire" (Figures 3-49, 3-50).

The way this type of weapon was perceived changed after the 1973 Yom Kippur War, during which the MLRS performed well. In the second half of the 1960s, the US Army Missile Forces initiated a program to create a multiple launch rocket and artillery system called MARS (Multiple Artillery Rocket System). In March 1974, the US Army created new requirements for the development of a rocket launcher called the General Support Rocket

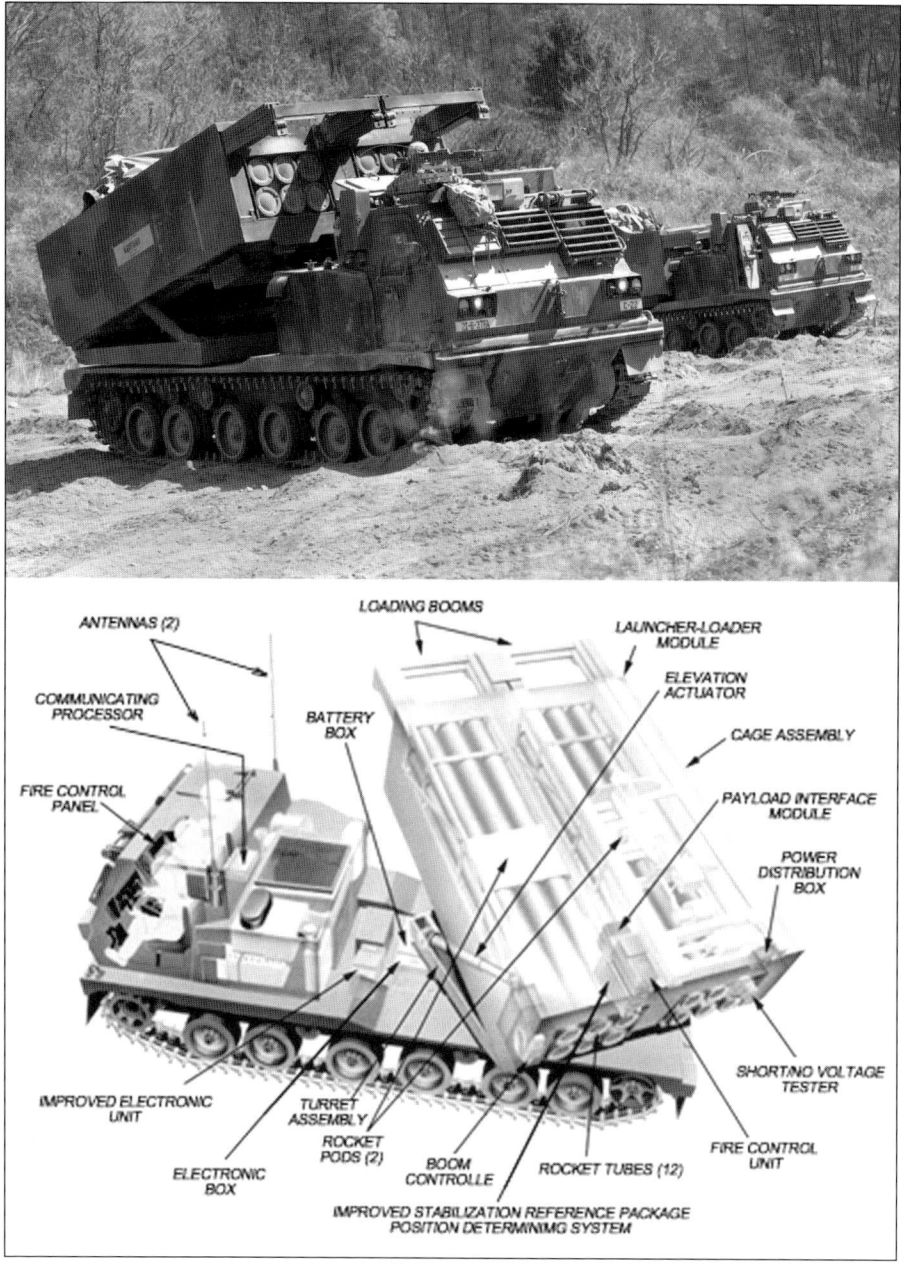

Figure 3-49: US M270 developed to counter Soviet MLRS advantage.

System (GSRS). It was assumed that it would be used to engage the enemy air defense positions and for counterbattery fire, freeing artillery units for direct support of ground forces. At the beginning of 1980, the development program was renamed and received the name MLRS. At this stage, the

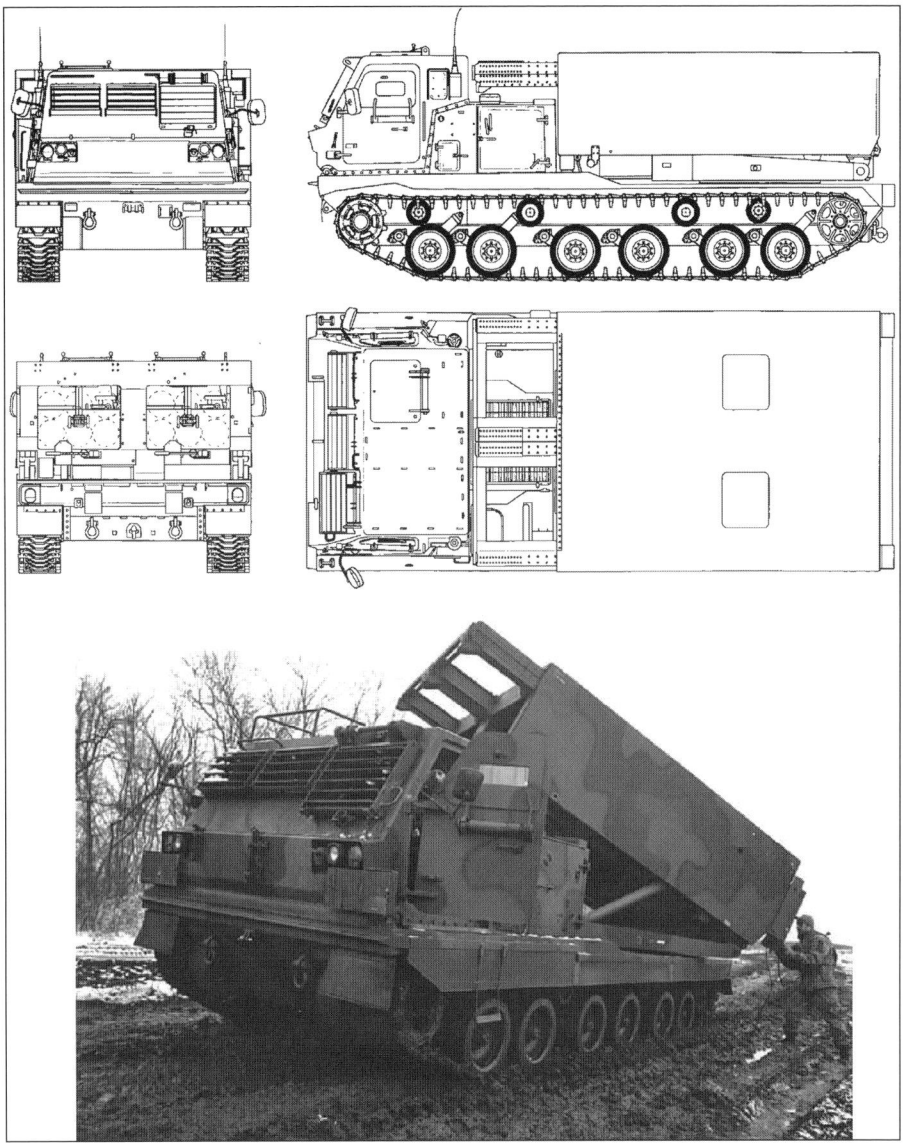

Figure 3-50: M270 launcher.

defense departments and private companies in the UK, Germany, and France joined the program.

The M270 MLRS weapon system is also known under the general name SPLL (Self-Propelled Loading/Launcher) and consists of three main subsystems mounted on one platform: M269 LLM (Loader Launcher Module), electronic fire-control system installed on the M993 transport vehicle, which, in turn, is a derivative of the BMP Bradley chassis.

According to the doctrine of the Cold War, the tactics for using the M270 were that the vehicles were to covertly disperse individually, then, at the right time, move to a firing position, launch missiles, and then immediately withdraw to a reload point, and then move to a new hidden position, and repeat the process again. This tactic, named "shoot and run" or "shoot and scoot," successfully avoided Soviet counterbattery fire. A full salvo of the M270, consisting of 12 M26 rockets, has 7,728 anti-personnel submunitions (bomblets) that can be dispersed over an area of 24 hectares in less than 1 minute like a rain of steel.

An important advantage of this system is the design of the TEL which uses a launch container system with prepacked rockets. The container system allows quick reload of both containers using its own winch installed on the vehicle.

The M270 was accepted into service in 1982. The first combat use occurred on 18 January 1991, during Operation Desert Storm, when the M270 battery fired eight ATACMS missiles at Iraqi air defense positions. In a single engagement, 3 MLRS batteries fired 287 missiles at 24 separate targets in less than 5 minutes, which would have taken an artillery battalion over an hour to fire. In early February 1991, the largest night firing of MLRS in history took place: 312 missiles were fired in 1 volley. Of the 57,000 artillery rounds fired in that war, 6,000 were MLRS rockets and another 32 were ATACMS missiles.

During the NATO aggression in Yugoslavia, it was planned to use MLRS to destroy the positions of the Yugoslav AD, however, Yugoslav intelligence was able to obtain all information related to the MLRS and disperse the AD units in a way that completely neutralized any advantage of the MLRS. Contrary to the Desert Storm experience, in this conflict the effect of MLRS was zero.[16]

During more than forty years, the M270 MLRS has undergone several upgrades and modifications. The current version in production is the M270A2 (third generation with a range of up to 500km using Precision Strike Missile (PrSM)).

The versions comprise:

- M270 – the initial version with a combat load of twelve missiles in two six-seat launch containers,
- M270 IPDS – an interim update designed to allow the use of long-range GPS-enabled ATACMS Block IA missiles until a sufficient number of M270A1 launchers are produced,
- M270A1 – the first major upgrade program. The launcher received improved fire-control and mechanical systems. These improvements made it possible to significantly speed up the firing process of new types of ammunition, including GPS-guided missiles,

- M270B1 – an upgrade for the British Army, similar to the A1, but additionally includes a reinforced armor package for better crew protection against IED attacks,
- M270C1 – an upgrade option proposed by Lockheed Martin using a universal fire-control system such as HIMARS,
- M270D1 – includes a new fire-control system that allows high-precision GPS-guided missiles – GMLRS and ATACMS launch. The upgrade package consists of a new computer, location device, GPS antenna, launch control unit, displays, and remote control,
- MARS2/LRU – European modernization of the M270 with the participation of Germany, Italy, and France,
- M270A2 – a 2019 upgrade program to the US Army variant, which includes the new Common Fire Control System (CFCS) to allow the use of the PrSM.

M142 HIMARS

M142 HIMARS is a baby brother to the M270. The main difference is that it is based on the FMTV wheeled chassis instead of the tracked one (from the Bradley AFV) and carries one pod of six rockets instead of two. As a member of the same family, these pods are interchangeable (Figure 3-51).

The initial development was based on the requirement for a light MLRS as a counterfire asset. The US military also wanted something cheaper and easier to produce than the M270. From the initial idea in 1982, it required longer development time, and the first units were delivered to the US Army in 2001.

The long development process was not accompanied by overinflated costs typical of the US military industrial complex because of the unification of the artillery section. The system was also popular in the Marines and saw use in Afghanistan and the Middle East.

The system was most popular in Ukraine and often featured in the press where the attributes of this "wonder weapon" were discussed.

Without any doubt, it has been proven that it is the most effective MLRS system in Ukrainian use. It has inflicted several heavy blows on the Russian troops hitting the command posts and troop concentration such as on New Year's Eve when six rockets were fired against a school in Makeyevka, Donbas where the intelligence (highly likely NATO) detected the presence of hundreds of Russian troops. Two rockets were downed but the remaining four struck a heavy blow killing more than sixty mobilized Russian soldiers. HIMARS are often used to target civilian buildings and infrastructure such as the one that hit hospitals in Donetsk or the bridge and a dam over the Dnieper in Kherson.

HIMARS can fire almost the same arsenal of rockets used by the M270. M270 and HIMARS are a clear and present danger for the Russians (Figure 3-52).

Figure 3-51: M142 launcher. (*Source*: Ukrainian DoD)

Figure 3-52: Ukrainian M142 firing (top); "kill" marks (bottom). The target coordinates are provided by NATO intelligence. (*Source*: WSJ)

Ammunition

The M270 system can fire all versions of rockets and artillery missiles called MFOM (MLRS Family of Munition) which includes both unguided and guided munition. Munitions are manufactured and used by a number of platforms and countries (Figure 3-53).

Unguided Munition

The major unguided rockets used in M270 are M26 and M28. The following are subcategories (Figure 3-54):

- M26 – a Dual-Purpose Improved Conventional Munitions (DPICM) with 644 M77 submunitions. Its range is 32km. It is worth noting here that this is the same non-conventional weapon, banned, for example, in the European Union, but used by the US Army. One of the results of using such missiles is the abundance of remaining unexploded submunitions, the disposal of which after the war will require enormous resources (plus civilian casualties are inevitable even after the end of the fighting),
- M26A1 – extended range missile to 45km and 518 M85 submunitions (improved version of M77 submunitions),
- M26A2 – a transitional version of the M26A1 with M77 submunitions. Used before the M85 submunition entered service,
- M27 – a completely inert training container, created for LLM loading training by the MLRS crew,
- M28 – a training version of the M26 missile, which uses containers with ballast and smoke marking instead of a payload,
- M28A1 – a version of the M28 with blunt nose and with a reduced range of 9km,
- M28A2 Low Cost Reduced Range Practice Rocket (LCRRPR) with blunt nose. Range reduced to 9km,
- AT2 German M26 variant carrying twenty-eight AT2 anti-tank mines. Range of 15–38km.

Guided Munition

The Guided Multiple Launch Rocket System (GMLRS) has an extended range and has GPS-aided guidance in the inertial navigation system.[17] Flight control is accomplished by four forward-mounted canards driven by electromechanical actuators. GMLRS rockets were introduced in 2005 and can be fired from the M270A1 and M270A2, the European M270A1 variants (British Army M270B1, German Army MARS II, French Army Lance Roquette Unitaire (LRU), Italian Army MLRS Improved (MLRS-I), Finnish Army M270D1), and the lighter M142. The M30 and M31 rockets are, except for their warheads, identical. By December 2021, 50,000 GMLRS rockets

Figure 3-53: Fire-control systems and ammunition. (*Source*: Lockheed Martin)

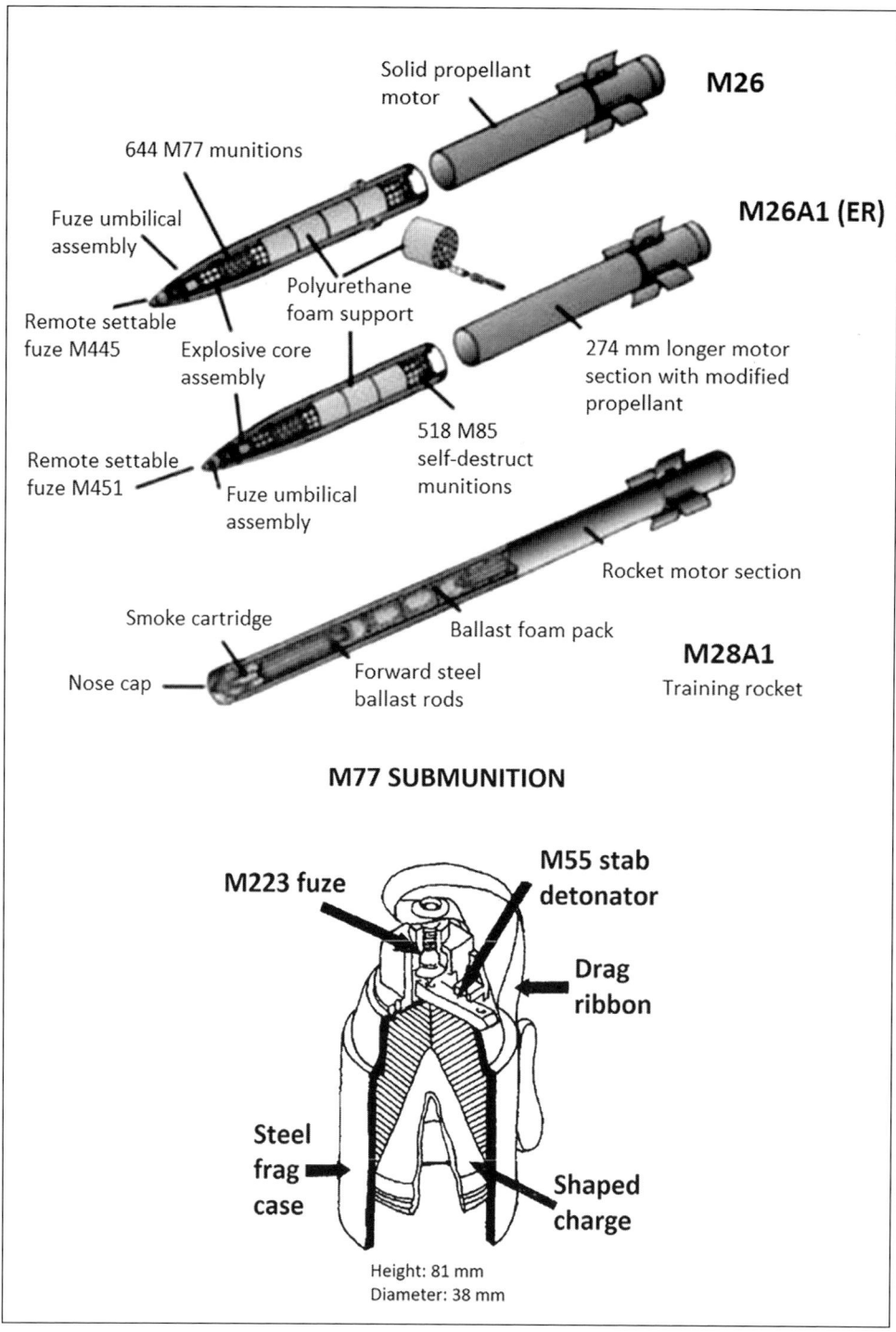

Figure 3-54: M26, M26A1, M28A1 rockets and M77 submunition. (*Source*: Lockheed Martin)

had been produced, with yearly production then exceeding 9,000 rockets. Each rocket pod contains six identical rockets (Figure 3-55). The following are subcategories:

- M30 rockets carrying 404 DPICM M101 submunitions. Range of 15–92km,
- M30A1 rockets with Alternative Warhead. Range of 15–92km. GMLRS rocket that replaces the M30's submunitions with approximately 182,000 pre-formed tungsten fragments for area effects without unexploded ordnance,
- M30A2 rockets with Alternative Warhead. Range of 15–92km. Improved M30A1 with Insensitive Munition Propulsion System (IMPS),
- M31 rockets with 91kg HE unitary warhead. Range of 15–92km. The warhead is produced by General Dynamics and contains 23kg of PBX-109 high explosive in a steel blast-fragmentation case,
- M31A1 rockets with 91kg HE unitary warhead. Range of 15–92km. Improved M31 with new multi-mode fuze that added airburst to the M31's fuze point detonation and delay,
- M31A2 rockets with 91kg HE unitary warhead. Range of 15–92km. Improved M31A1 with Insensitive Munition Propulsion System (IMPS). Only M31 variant in production since 2019,
- M32SMArt – German variant produced by Diehl Defense carrying four SMArt anti-tank submunitions and a new flight software. Developed for MARS II but has not been ordered yet and therefore not in service as of 2019,
- ER GMLRS rockets with extended range of up to 150km. Rockets use a slightly increased rocket motor size, a newly designed body, and tail-driven guidance, while still containing six per pod. It will come in unitary and AW variants. The first successful test flight of a ER GMLRS occurred in March 2021. In 2022 Finland became the first foreign customer to order ER GMLRS.

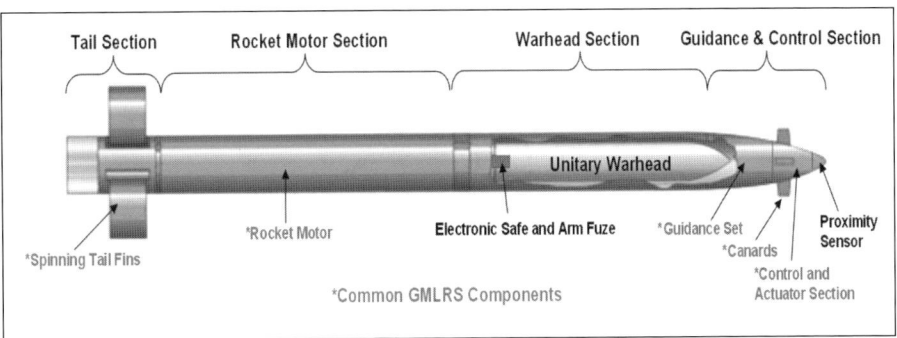

Figure 3-55: Typical guided rocket components.

Ukrainian Hope – ATACMS Long-Range Guided Precision Missiles

At the time of writing this book, there is no firm evidence that the long-range ATACMS series of 610mm caliber surface-to-surface missile with a range of up to 300km missiles was supplied to Ukraine, but there are some rumors (unverified) that some of the of the older production have indeed been "transferred." It is a sensitive point because these missiles can engage targets deep in the Russian territory which may therefore directly involve the US in the proxy war and cause the situation to escalate out of control. There is much debate that Ukraine may use these missiles against pre-determined targets, however, once the missiles are out in the field and under the direct control of the particular unit, it is highly likely that they may attack strategic Russian targets deep in the territory which will provoke a much harder Russian response that will completely change the nature of the war.

Organization and Employment

The M270 crew consists of three members: unit commander, gunner, and driver. It is air transportable but requires the heavier lift such as Boeing C-17 and Lockheed C-5 Galaxy. Reloading time is 4 minutes for the M270 and 3 minutes for the M270A1 which is much faster than the BM-27 or BM-30.

The US military refers to the M270 as the "commander's personal shotgun" or "buckshot on the battlefield." It is also often referred to as the "gypsy van" because crews store additional equipment (camouflage nets, cots, refrigerators, and personal items) on top of the vehicle, as there is not enough space in the launcher itself for items.

The MLRS firing batteries are organized and structured for independent operations. In the US military, the MLRS firing battery consists of a headquarters platoon, an ammunition (ammo) platoon, and three firing platoons. As the Ukrainian crews are trained per US/NATO standards it can be assumed that the organizational structure is the same, but the modes of employment may vary and are dictated by the specific field circumstances. This is how a Ukrainian M270 and HIMARS battery may be organized:[18]

- The battery headquarters (HQ) consists of the commander, 1SG, an NBC NCO, and a vehicle driver. The divisional MLRS battery also has three combat medics and an administrative clerk. The battery headquarters command element (commander and 1SG) and the battery operations center (BOC) provide the necessary C3 and coordination of internal and external administrative and logistical support for the battery. Equipment includes two HMMWVs with secure FM radios,
- The Battery Operations Center BOC is supervised by the operations officer. It is staffed with a fire-direction computer, battery display

operator, five fire-direction specialists, a signal support systems specialist, and, normally, the NBC NCO organic to the battery headquarters. The BOC plans, coordinates, and executes tactical movements, and positioning, maintains situation maps and overlays, and provides tactical fire direction for the battery,
- The Survey Section provides all survey support for the firing platoons under the control of the BOC,
- Logistics Service Section – the battery food service section can draw, prepare, serve, and deliver rations to the battery headquarters, the firing platoons, and the ammunition platoon,
- The supply section draws and issues all classes of supply to the other unit components,
- The battery maintenance section performs organizational automotive maintenance on all battery equipment except radio and electronic equipment. The section is organized and equipped to field on-site unit maintenance teams for equipment repair. It can draw, transport, and issue or install all organizational repair parts for the battery,
- The ammunition platoon comprises a platoon headquarters and three ammo sections. It provides rocket, missile, and small-arms ammunition support to MLRS battery headquarters and the firing platoons,
- The firing platoon headquarters includes a platoon leader, a platoon sergeant, a reconnaissance sergeant, a battery display operator, a radio operator, and two fire-direction specialists. The headquarters conducts platoon reconnaissance, surveillance, and occupation of position and performs all command, control, and logistical coordination functions for the platoon. The platoon may also perform tactical fire direction when required,
- Each firing section includes a section chief, a gunner, and a launcher driver. The firing section is responsible for tactically positioning the launcher for survivability and firing operations. The section performs all technical fire control, operator maintenance, and launcher organizational maintenance.

The "shoot-and-scoot" tactics and NATO intelligence for targeting combined with the wide dispersion of launchers help MLRS avoid detection and minimize vulnerability. Survivability is enhanced by the rapid transmission rate of digital message traffic, secure voice communications, and quick emplacement and displacement. However, they also require more planning and coordination because of competition for terrain. Firing platoon leaders and battery commanders must coordinate with maneuver unit commanders throughout all phases of an operation.

This tactic makes both the M270 and M142 HIMARS a prime target for the Russian counterbattery fire, air attacks as well as for the UAV surveillance and suicide drones. So far, several launchers have been lost, and munition storages destroyed. In any case, the saga of the "wonder weapons" continues.

Quantity has a Quality in Itself[19]

One of the most important questions of the war is which is better: Russian MLRS or US MLRS, and can M270 and HIMARS turn the tide and make Ukraine victorious? Bombastic information about the achievements of the "wonder weapons" pops up on a daily basis in the Western media. The social networks' "troll" and "bot" war is fueling these narratives but, in reality, the situation is far from that described. The war comes down to mathematics and the numbers rule. Let's discuss briefly how "wonder weapons" such as HIMARS may really affect warfare.

Each has its advantages and a true comparison is not realistic. For the sake of some parameters the HIMARS is designed to be highly mobile and weighs less than half of the BM-30. To achieve mobility, it compromises on firepower with only six rockets compared with the twelve of the Smerch. The rockets of the HIMARS are smaller and have a shorter range but the HIMARS has the option to carry a short-range ballistic missile with a range of 300km. The HIMARS also has the advantage in accuracy but the new Smerch modifications have caught up. The destruction effect on the target by the Smerch salvo is also much higher.

One can imagine the role of Ukrainian targeting officers. Their task is to interdict the Russian ammo supply in Ukraine with deep strikes. How much stuff is necessary to hit to succeed?

By now, the Russians are firing something in the order of 50,000 artillery shells daily to maintain their offensive or in defense. Let's abstract this as 152mm shells, the mainstay of their artillery – in actual fact this is a mix of stuff: some are larger calibers, some are smaller but to simplify, one caliber is used. Each one of these shells weighs 43kg. So, 50,000 shells are 2,500 tons – let's round it up to 3,000 tons given that there are also propellant charges with shells. The Russians are bringing into Ukraine, on average, something like 3,000 tons of ammunition per day to replace what they have fired. Let's assume a reduction of one-third of this would cripple Russian combat power (unrealistic).

The Ukrainians would need to destroy 1,000 tons of artillery ammunition every day to impair the Russian war machine. Bear in mind that this ammunition will not be stacked up in one huge ammo dump but dispersed in many smaller dumps to feed formations spread across the front.

How many smaller dumps? The Russians have about 100 BTGs in theater. Let's abstract that into thirty brigades, each with a 100-ton ammo dump feeding its operations. Only about half seem to be active at once, but let's say the active ones can pull ammo from the neighboring dumps.

So, therefore, to cripple the "Special Military Operation," Ukrainians need to find, hit, and destroy ten brigade-sized (100-ton) artillery ammunition dumps every day until the Russians decide to give up … Much easier said than done.

For instance, it's quite easy to disperse those 100 tons into twenty 5-ton truckload positions with adequate standoff so one blowing up won't affect the others. Bear in mind an M31 missile for HIMARS or M270 costs $150,000, and individual 152mm artillery shells probably run under $100.

During the Cold War, NATO had a plan to do this. It was called Air-Land Battle, and it involved "darkening the sky" with thousands of strike aircraft until the Soviet Union ran out of everything.

As of the moment, Ukrainians have less than a hundred long-range rocket and missile launchers, which the Russians are actively hunting down and destroying. Also, they're pretty good at shooting down incoming missiles. Intelligence, no matter how much NATO ELINT information coming every hour into and through the "joint" centers and distributed to the local theaters, isn't very good. Evaluating recent Ukrainian strikes attempting to do exactly this, most seem to have been on known, fixed facilities – and most have been busts. Not every structural fire in the Donbas is a hidden Russian ammo depot going up.

So, no, the Ukrainians aren't going to make the Russians run out of ammunition any time soon.

At the time of writing, HIMARS and M270 missiles are more precise than the older BM27 and BM-30 rockets but Russians are increasing production of the ammunition that has the same precision as the US one. The gap in quality is narrowing quickly. Ukraine will need hundreds of launchers and thousands of very expensive missiles to try to have an advantage but the Western production capacities are limited for the sheer volume of fire, so the opinion of the author is that the M270 and HIMARS launchers will not have any significant influence on the overall outcome of the war.

Improvised Launchers

Battlefield attrition and losses have forced the Ukrainian side to apply some of the makeshift (a "Mad Max" style) launchers utilizing the existing artillery parts of the MLRS or mounting a helicopter unguided missile launcher on the wheeled and tracked platforms. Both Russia and Ukraine have improvised to create maximum impact on the battlefield with their resources.

Figure 3-56: 122mm launching tubes installed on a pickup truck. (*Source*: the3rdforceua)

One of the most common and widely spread improvised launchers includes rocket systems mounted on top of pickup trucks and other light trucks (Figures 3-56, 3-57).

The integration of 122mm launcher tubes on standard civilian vehicles is very easy due to the use of unguided rockets that do not require a

Figure 3-57: Improvised S-8 rocket launcher (top). (*Source*: defence-ua.com); S-8 rocket (bottom). (*Source*: wikiwand)

sophisticated aiming system. Saying this, any local machine or automotive workshop can carry out necessary modifications and install anything from two and up launching tubes. Of course, there is no talk about calculations or any engineering approach including proper design, but rather improvisations based on the available chassis and the launching tubes.

Its simplicity combined with the ability to deliver firepower from a relatively light mobile platform has led to its rapid and widespread adoption.

One of the interesting modifications is a declared use of the captured Russian launchers (from the Ka-52 helicopters). It includes an artillery system using an S-8 rocket launcher system mounted on a Mitsubishi or Toyota pickup truck. Like the 122mm rocket launcher system, the S-8 is a family of unguided rockets.

The S-8 is a rocket weapon that was developed by the Soviet Air Force for use by military aircraft. Saying the source is Ka-52 serves more of a propaganda purpose because the Ukrainian Air Force inherited a large number of these unguided rockets from the Soviet Union. RuAF is also using these.

As the S-8 is an unguided rocket, the launcher can easily be integrated into any civilian platform without using a particular sighting system. Targeting is achieved by simply pointing the launcher in the direction of the target.

A wide variety of warheads is available that includes HEAT-Frag, anti-runway, thermobaric, illumination, and others. Depending on the warhead the maximum range is 2–4.5km. A twenty round rocket pod can be fired in only a few seconds.

Besides the improvised launchers, Poland and Ukraine (WB Group from Poland and UkrOboronProm) were involved in the joint development of the ZRN-01 also named "Stokrotka" (Figure 3-58). The system includes two B8V20 launchers with RS-80P unguided 80mm rockets – the same one used on the Mi-24 helicopter. The missiles are equipped with different time fuzes and different types of warheads depending on the threat (ground or aerial).

The ZRN-01 has a firing range of 7km against ground targets and 4km against aerial targets. A radar system is integrated to detect targets with low effective dispersion surfaces, such as UAVs at a distance of up to 6km.

The system is equipped with the Topaz Automated Fire Control System developed by WB Group. The use of TOPAZ provides the opportunity to optimize the utilization of available artillery fire resources to ensure adequate firepower at the right time and the right place. It appears that the development didn't progress further than the few samples.

The effect of these improvised launchers is below negligible. There is no doubt that they can deliver fire but there is no talk about any precision. Rather, if launched and it hits something, then that is good. It is more like a local terror weapon, rather for intimidation of opponent forces than having any actual impact. It can also be dangerous for the friendly forces because of the lack of sighting equipment and coordination with the proper artillery units.

Freepost Plus RTKE-RGRJ-KTTX
Pen & Sword Books Ltd
47 Church Street
BARNSLEY
S70 2AS

✂ DISCOVER MORE ABOUT PEN & SWORD BOOKS

Pen & Sword Books have over 4000 books currently available, our imprints include; Aviation, Naval, Military, Archaeology, Transport, Frontline, Seaforth and the Battleground series, and we cover all periods of history on land, sea and air.

Can we stay in touch? From time to time we'd like to send you our latest catalogues, promotions and special offers by post. If you would prefer not to receive these, please tick this box. ☐

We also think you'd enjoy some of the latest products and offers by post from our trusted partners: companies operating in the clothing, collectables, food & wine, gardening, gadgets & entertainment, health & beauty, household goods, and home interiors categories. If you would like to receive these by post, please tick this box. ☐

We respect your privacy. We use personal information you provide us with to send you information about our products, maintain records and for marketing purposes. For more information explaining how we use your information please see our privacy policy at www.pen-and-sword.co.uk/privacy. You can opt out of our mailing list at any time via our website or by calling 01226 734222.

Mr/Mrs/Ms ....

Address...

Postcode.......................... Email address..

Website: www.pen-and-sword.co.uk Email: enquiries@pen-and-sword.co.uk
Telephone: 01226 734555   Fax: 01226 734438
Stay in touch: facebook.com/penandswordbooks or follow us on Twitter @penswordbooks

MLRS

Figure 3-58: ZRN-01. (*Source*: WB Group)

Chapter 4

Thermobaric Weapons

If one asks an ordinary soldier at the front line in Ukraine what is the most fearsome weapon that he or she doesn't want to encounter, no doubt many will say that it is the thermobaric one. Against the artillery shells, mortars, and even terrifying barrages of the multiple rocket launchers, the action of the "heavy flamethrowers" (as described by the Russians) is the one that leaves the most devastating effects. Hardly anybody exposed to the direct fire of this weapon has ever lived to tell the tale. But what really is a flamethrower weapon? The name is deceiving – there is nothing similar about it compared with the flamethrowers of the Second World War, which used napalm or the napalm bombs. The so-called "flamethrower" weapons discussed in this chapter work on different principles – volumetric or aerosol bomb and thermobaric effects.

Technological Background

In its most simplified form, the technology behind[1, 2] this weapon lies in the rapid spreading of the specially made mixture in the form of "aerosol" that detonates creating an immense shock wave and temperature. An aerosol bomb, Fuel Air Explosive (FAE) or Fuel Air Bomb, is a weapon whose effect on the detonation of an aerosol or substance distributed as a dust cloud does not depend on an oxidizer being present in the component molecules. A FAE bomb consists of a container with a flammable substance (for example, "ethylene oxide"). Two explosive charges are used as detonators: the first explosion causes the fuel to be distributed as fine particles into the air as an aerosol. Following this, microseconds – milliseconds later the aerosol is detonated, which results in the release of high pressure.

The pressure wave that results from the explosive deflagration is considerably weaker than that of a comparable explosive such as RDX. However, the explosive deflagration occurs almost simultaneously in a large volume of 10–50m diameter. The fuel can penetrate caves, tunnels, or bunkers, which makes this weapon effective when used on "soft" targets or enclosed spaces, unlike conventional explosive charges which only have a limited effect due to their poor pressure effect (Figures 4-1, 4-2).

Furthermore, aerosol bombs have a considerably larger heat effect than conventional explosive charges. Therefore, these bombs are more effective at killing people and at the destruction of other "soft" targets such as unarmored vehicles and other objects that can catch fire easily.

The explosion removes the oxygen from the air, because the explosive composition does not contain its own oxidizer and uses the oxygen present in the air instead. This, however, is not the deadly mechanism present in aerosol bombs. Much more significant is death by suffocation which is what happens when an aerosol bomb is detonated. The reason for this is not the lack of oxygen, but the damage that is done to the lungs through a so-called barotrauma. The negative-pressure phase that occurs after the positive-pressure phase causes an expansion of the air in the lungs, resulting in damage. The properties of an aerosol bomb – long, relatively flat pressure wave with a corresponding distinct "partial vacuum" – as well as the use of atmospheric oxygen are beneficial effects (Figure 4-1).

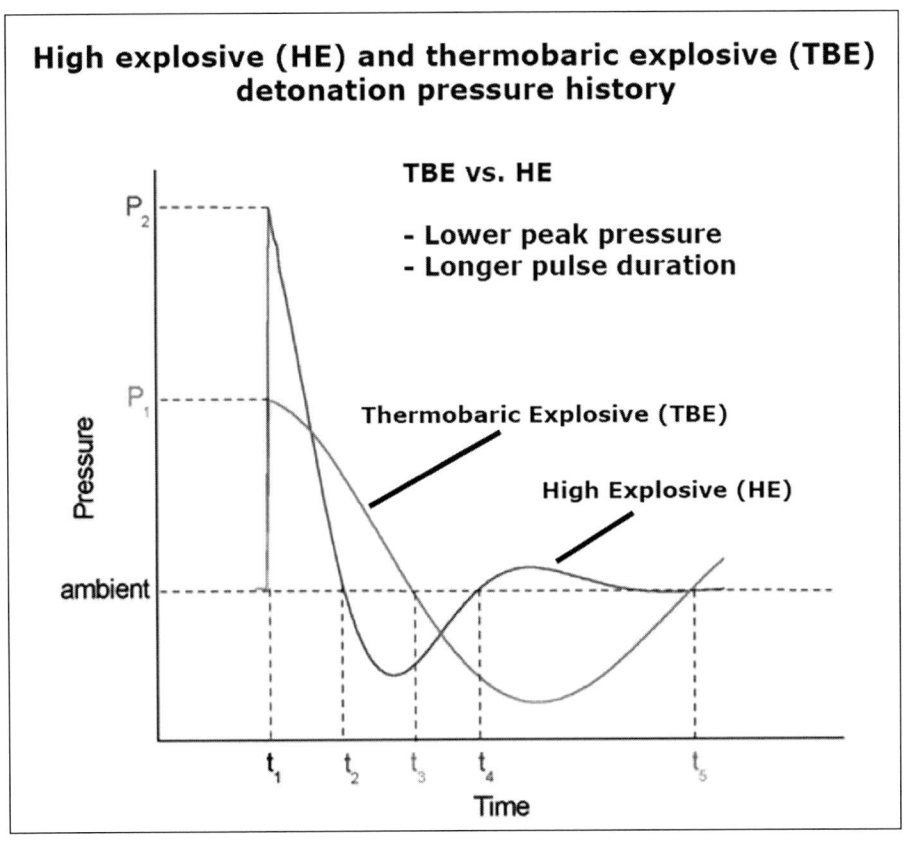

Figure 4-1: Pressure change over time in thermobaric and conventional explosives.

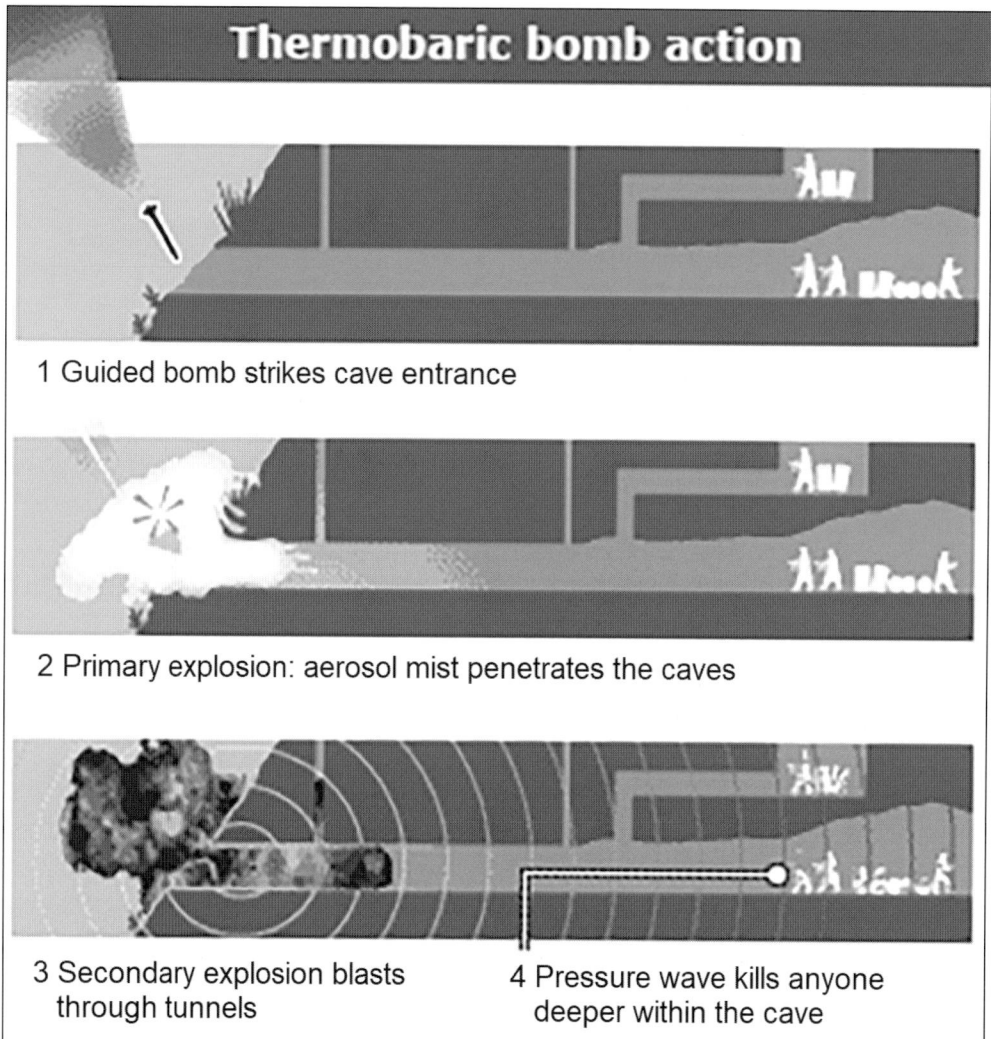

Figure 4-2: Effects of a thermobaric explosion on personnel in a cave or enclosed spaces. (*Source*: Reddit, modified by author)

The first samples of fuel-air explosives or thermobaric weapons were developed in the US in the late 1960s. They were quite small in size and capacity (up to 10 gallons) (Figure 4-3). After the drop, at a relatively low altitude (30–50m), the brake parachute was opened, which provided the bomb with stabilization and velocity most favorable for the sequence of detonation operations (charge explosion and opening of the bomb shell), spraying of the fuel mixture, scattering and subsequent explosion of detonators. A 1.5m-long probe pulls out of the nose of the bomb, which touches the ground and triggers the explosion process.

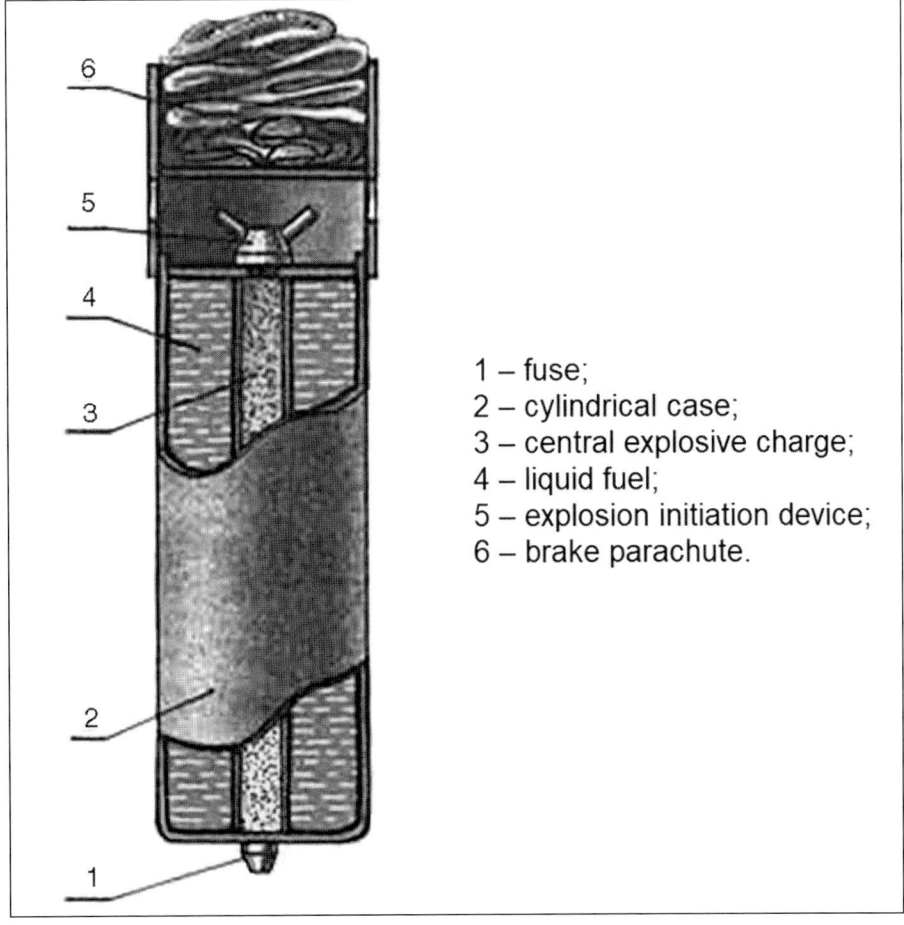

Figure 4-3: Volumetric explosion ammunition. (*Source*: http://army.armor.kiev.ua/hist/obomvzryv.shtml)

1 – fuse;
2 – cylindrical case;
3 – central explosive charge;
4 – liquid fuel;
5 – explosion initiation device;
6 – brake parachute.

Attempts to create larger caliber ammunition failed at the time due to technical difficulties. A workaround, cluster bombs, was found. There were several 32.6kg fuel-air explosive bombs in one cassette. These bombs were distributed over a certain area, thus increasing the size of the cloud. According to the modern classification, such volumetric explosion ammunition is called two-stroke, as its operation is divided into two stages: cloud formation and cloud explosion. Two-stroke ammunition was a qualitative jump in the development of blast ammunition; however, these bombs are not devoid of a number of shortcomings, such as the strong influence of weather conditions on their effectiveness. All this has led to the creation of a weapon with a single-stroke operation scheme, the principal difference being the existence of a single process of fuel-air mixture formation, initiation, and development of an explosive transformation reaction in it. The most wide-spread among single-stroke volumetric explosion munitions is the so-called thermobaric ammunition.

For thermobaric weapons (also known as EBX, Enhanced Blast Explosives), in addition to a conventional explosion, a flammable substance (usually aluminum powder), with little or no oxidizer (for example, oxygen), distributed in the air detonates immediately as a result of the explosion. This post-detonative reaction ("fireball" of aluminum powder with air) usually occurs within milliseconds after the detonation of the high explosive. This causes the effect of the original explosion to be magnified which results in an even larger heat and pressure effect.

The emergence of thermobaric ammunition is connected to the development of special compositions – thermobaric mixtures. As a rule, thermobaric mixtures are paste-like mixtures based on liquid fuel with large negative oxygen balance (for example, isopropyl nitrate), in which a powder of high-brisance explosive substance (for example, hexogen) and fine powder of combustible metal (for example, aluminum) are introduced. Such mixtures can detonate; however, this requires a sufficiently powerful intermediate detonator, and the parameters of detonation are relatively small (detonation velocity of about 5,000–6,000m/s). As a result of the explosive transformation reaction, gaseous products containing non-reacted combustible components are formed behind the detonation front, and metal particles are heated and begin to react with oxidizing components of the explosion products (CO_2 and H_2O).

After the detonation reaches the surface and the container shell is destroyed, the gaseous products begin to expand into the air while being subjected to intense deceleration. Burning metal particles outrun the gaseous products and reach the air where the intensity of their combustion increases significantly. The energy released in this process is used to supply the air shock front parameters and to form a long high-temperature area with an increased thermal effect (Figures 4-4, 4-5). At a later stage, due to the development of turbulent diffusion, the explosion products are mixed with air and the non-reacted combustible components are burned. In this case, energy is released in the "tail" of the shock-wave compression phase and leads to its longer duration.

Volumetric explosion ammunition was used several times in various wars during the period 1980–90. For example, on 6 August 1982, during the war in Lebanon, an Israeli aircraft dropped such a bomb (US-made) on an eight-floor apartment building. The explosion occurred close to the building at the level of the first and second floors. The building was destroyed. About 300 people were killed (most of whom were not in the building, but near the explosion location).

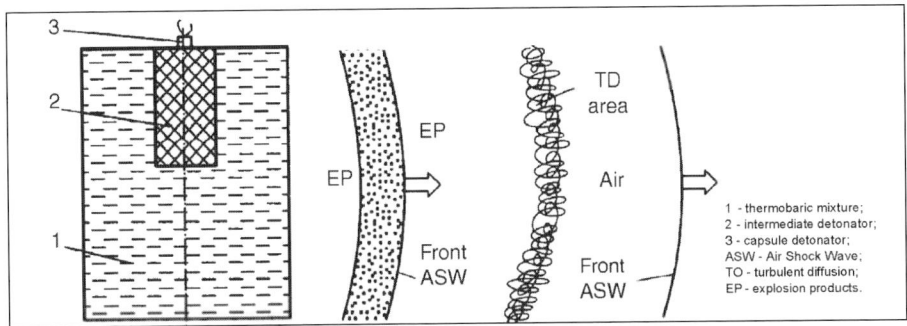

Figure 4-4: Principal scheme of thermobaric ammunition. (*Source*: I. Balagansky, *Damaging Effects of Weapons and Ammunition*)

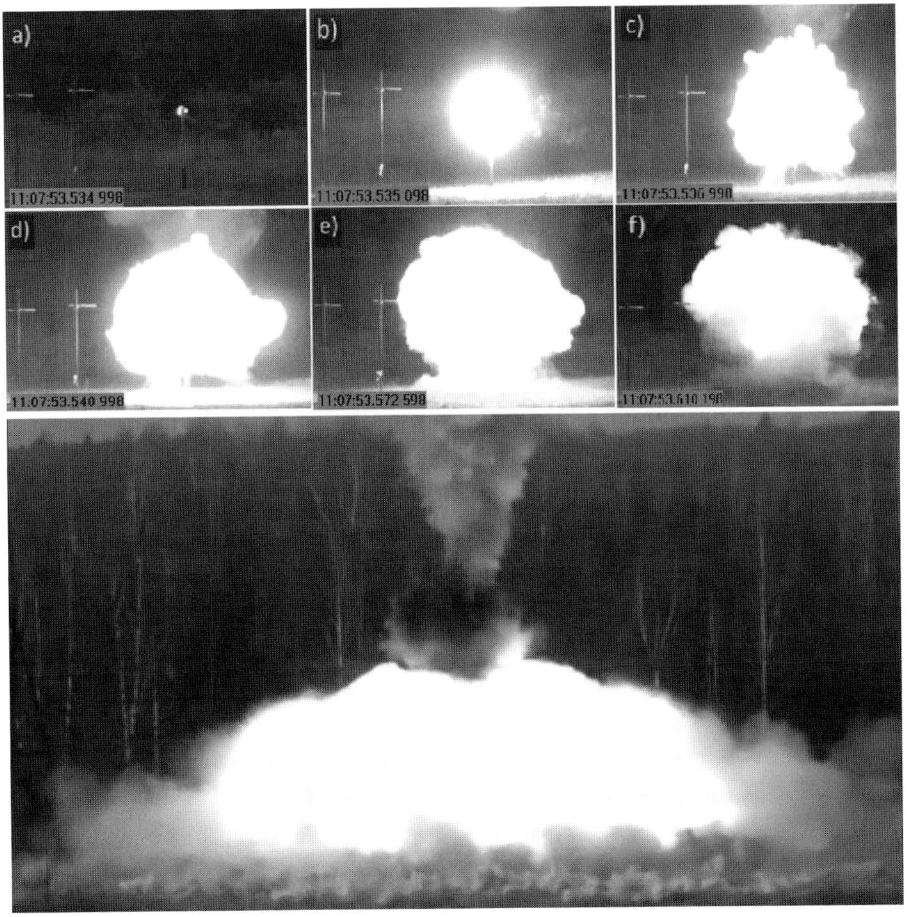

Figure 4-5: Detonation of small thermobaric charge, and formation of the fireball, recorded by high-speed TV camera. (*Source*: D. Simic et al., "Thermobaric Effects of Cast Composite Explosives of Different Charge Masses and Dimensions," *Central European Journal of Energetic Materials*)

The initial pressure wave and the subsequent under pressure follow a phase in which the under pressure resulting from the explosion causes a flux of surrounding air at the centre of the explosion. The released, non-exploded, burning substance is as a result of the under pressure being sucked into where the explosion occurred, and therefore enters all non-air-tight objects (caves, bunker, tunnels) and burns these. Suffocation and internal damage can result for both humans and animals that are located out of the immediate vicinity, for example, in deeper tunnels as a result of the pressure wave, the depletion of oxygen, or the subsequent under pressure.

As discussed above, thermobaric weapons contain monopropellants or secondary explosives and energetic particles. Boron, aluminum, silicon, titanium, magnesium, zirconium, and carbon can be considered to be energetic particles. The main advantage of thermobaric systems is that they release large quantities of heat and pressure, often in amounts larger than for just secondary explosives.

In thermobaric weapons, highly aluminized secondary explosives can be used instead of monopropellants. For example, RDX in combination with a binder and a large quantity of aluminum (fuel rich) can be used.

In thermobaric weapons, first anaerobic detonation occurs within the micro-second timeframe, followed by a post-detonative combustion which is also anaerobic and occurs in the hundredth of a microsecond timeframe. Only then, the post detonative burning occurs, which lasts several milliseconds and generates strong heat radiation even at small shock-wave pressures (approximately 10 bar).

Thermobaric weapons can be used as bombs, unguided rockets or as shoulder launch mobile systems. The first war in which they were used on a larger scale was in Afghanistan. The multiple rocket launcher named TOS-1 Buratino and shoulder launched named RPO-A Shmel[3] were used against Mujahedeen (Figure 4-6).

There are two fields of operation in which thermobaric weapons are superior to other systems: areas of conflict involving caves, tunnels, or other difficult to access areas and deep, confined targets (HDBTs, hard and/or deeply buried targets). For example, during the operation to clear the karez,[4] caves, and sometimes underground structures in kishlaks[5] the Soviets would secure the shaft entrance and then lock and cock a Shmel with a thermobaric round. They would tie two lowering lines on the Shmel and a string on the trigger. Then they would slowly lower the Shmel down the shaft until it was facing a tunnel. They would then pull the trigger string to fire the thermobaric round down the tunnel. It was never determined how many casualties were inflicted using this method.

In August 1999, an ODAB-500 large-caliber volumetric bomb was dropped on the Dagestani village of Tando, where a significant number of

THERMOBARIC WEAPONS

Figure 4-6: RPO Shmel (top); TOS-1 Buratino in Afghanistan (bottom). (*Source*: Russian MoD)

Chechen rebel fighters had gathered. The militants suffered huge losses. In the following days, the mere appearance of a single Su-25 attack aircraft over any settlement forced the militants to hastily leave the village.

Formidable TOS

For the use in MLRS such as Smerch the rocket structurally consists of a head block with the flight-control system, a warhead, and a propulsion system with a solid-propellant rocket motor (see Chapter 3 for details). Although the Smerch system also has thermobaric rockets and is capable of firing the full load of ammunition (twelve missiles) in 20 seconds, the volumetric explosion missiles are fired either by a single missile or at time intervals that allow the previous missile to explode before the next one approaches the explosion zone. The specific model with the thermobaric warhead is 9M55S. The TOS-1A[6] is a MLRS system specifically designed to fire twenty-four rockets and has a different cadence of fire and much shorter range than Smerch.

The missile is divided into three parts as it approaches the target at the downward end of the trajectory: head, combat, and propulsion. At the altitude of 60–70m, the braking parachute is opened, and the radio altimeter is activated. From this point the process is the same way as the aircraft bomb.

The Russian Army also has other volumetric blast weapons, such as S-8DM and S-13D unguided aircraft missiles.

In combat in Donbas and Lugansk the Ukrainian positions are pounded with TOS-1A Solntsepyok (Blazing Sun). It has also been observed that during the urban combat in Mariupol and other cities and towns, Russian and DNR/LNR forces have used shoulder launched Shmel to clear the Ukrainian bunkers and fortifications.

As mentioned, there are a few variants of TOS: TOS-1, TOS-1A, and TOS-2. The idea of a heavy short-range MLRS to launch rockets equipped with incendiary and thermobaric warheads emerged in the late 1970s. The combat system consisting of the combat vehicle, rockets, and loading vehicle was developed in the early 1980s at KBTM in Omsk and was named TOS-1, and remained a secret development for a long time.

The TOS-1 Buratino is intended to engage military personnel, equipment, and buildings, including fortified constructions. The nickname "Buratino" comes from the name of the hero of the Russian retelling of the tale of Pinocchio (by Alexey Tolstoy), reflecting the big "nose" of the launcher (in the original Italian text of Pinocchio). The combat vehicle acts within the combat order of infantry and tanks and can fire thirty rockets. The large mass of the launcher and the need for a high level of protection due to the relatively short range of 3,500m helped determine the use of the chassis of the T-72 main battle tank. The TZM reloading vehicle was built on the chassis of a KrAZ-255B cross-country truck and equipped with a crane for loading/unloading of the launcher. Production of the KrAZ-255B officially stopped in 1994. Therefore, the TZM-T for use with the later Solntsepyok system was created based on the chassis of a T-72A.

In 2003, the improved TOS-1A system Solntsepyok entered service with the range extended to 6km and a better ballistic computer. The number of rockets was reduced to twenty-four (Figure 4-7).

In March 2020, Russia introduced a new rocket for the TOS-1A with a range of 10km, achieved in part by weight and size reductions of a

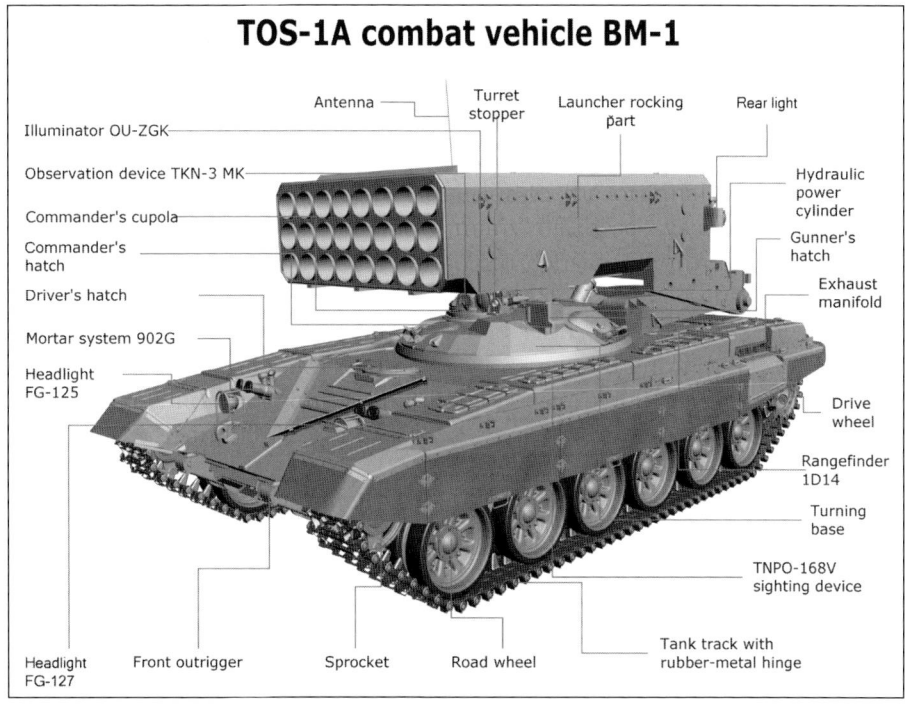

Figure 4-7: TOS-1A general components. (*Source*: btvt.info, modified by author)

new fuel-air explosive mixture in the warhead, while also increasing its power. Minimum range is extended from 400m to 1.6km, so the shorter range M0.1.01.04M rocket will be retained for close-combat environments. In 2018, Russian NBC Protection Troops received thirty TOS-1A Solntsepyok 220mm multiple rocket launchers. One launcher with a full salvo of twenty-four rockets can cover an area of 40,000m^2 meaning that the rocket dispersion on target is significantly reduced from the previous TOS-1.

The main difference is not only in names but in the major components such as chassis (T-72 in TOS-1, T-90 in TOS-1A, and wheeled based on Ural truck in TOS-2), fire-control system, and range. The newly developed TOS-2 Tosochka has also seen the action in Ukraine.

The TOS-1A Solntsepyok system consists of the following items:

- The "combat vehicle" BM-1 (Russian: боевая машина) (Object 634B) based on a modified T-90A chassis and fitted with a rotating launch system for twenty-four unguided thermobaric rockets. All rockets can be launched within 6–12 seconds, individually or in pairs. The launch vehicle is equipped with a fire-control system with a ballistic computer, aiming sight, and 1D14 laser rangefinder (Figure 4-9),

- TZM-T transport and loader vehicle (Russian: транспортно-заряжающая машина) (Object 563). Usually one BM-1 launcher is followed with one or two TZM-T re-supply vehicles. Each vehicle carries 2x12 spare rockets and 400l of fuel for the BM-1 and has a combat weigh of 39t. The TZM-T has a crew of three (Figure 4-11),
- A set of rockets NURS (Russian: неуправляемый реактивный снаряд – unguided rocket) MO.1.01.04 and MO.1.01.04M. These are 3.3m and 3.7m long and weigh 173kg and 217kg respectively (Figure 4-8). The original rocket for the TOS-1A had a range of only 2,700m, but the improved version extends the range to 6,000m. Some sources say its range is 12km. The system was modernized in 2016. Modernized systems with active protection, new engine, and launchers and other improvements were delivered in early 2018. In March 2020, Russia introduced a new rocket with a range of 10km which is now one of the primary rockets used in Ukraine (Figure 4-12).

The newest TOS-2 systems were used for the first time against Ukrainian positions near Kharkov. For the new system, this war is a proving ground.

As already mentioned, while the TOS-1 and TOS-1A were based on the T-72 and T-90 tank chassis, the TOS-2 Is based on a Ural wheeled all-wheel drive chassis to increase mobility.

The new system can be armed with up to twenty-four 220mm rockets, the same used in the TOS-1 and TOS-1A. The rockets are available with smoke-incendiary or fuel-air explosive warheads. They have a maximum range of up to 10km.

Unlike the older TOS-1 and TOS-1A, the TOS-2 is equipped with a digitalized fire-control system, a modern sight, a navigation system, and an electronic protection system from precision-guided weapons (Figure 4-13). The system is also equipped with its own crane, thus it does not need a separate reload vehicle.

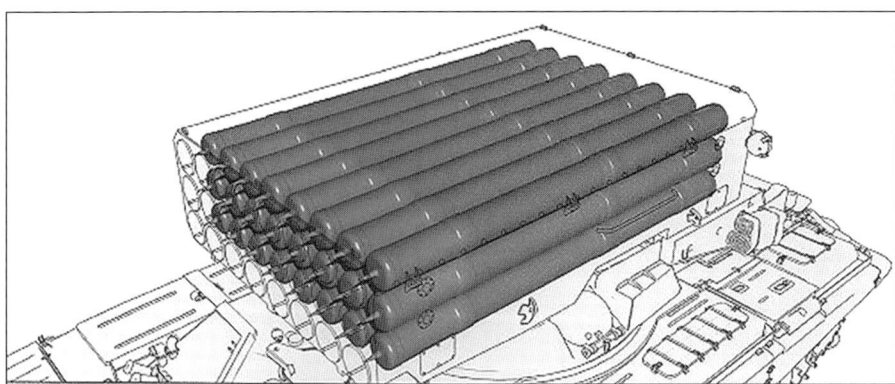

Figure 4-8: Rocket position on the launcher.

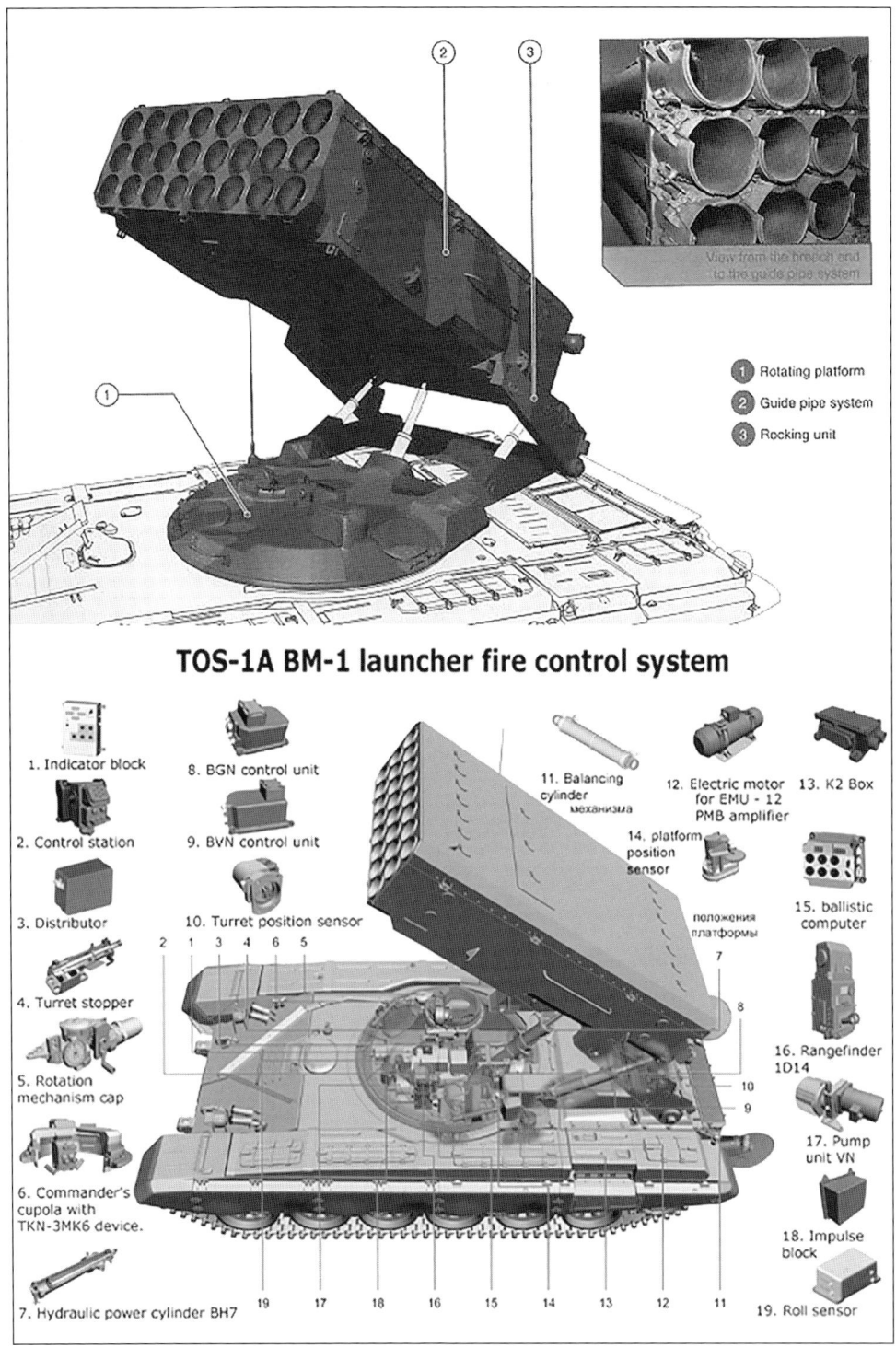

Figure 4-9: Fire-control system. (*Source*: btvt.info, modified by author)

Figure 4-10: TOS-1A with characteristic 'Z' in action. (*Source*: Russian MoD)

Russia has also developed a newer anti-tank-missile firing device, Metis-M1, which launches the thermobaric missile 9M131FM, and this version is designed to be used against structures. The exact composition of the explosive substance contained in the missile is not reported. These missiles are in use against fortifications because of the precise guidance that can put the missile through the "bull's eye." Also, the collateral effect is far less than using the TOS launchers, and the advantage of the range compared with the shoulder launched Shmel is tenfold. These missiles are basically "thermobaric snipers." Russia is also using TBG-29V rocket for RPG-39 which has more destructive power than TBG-7V.

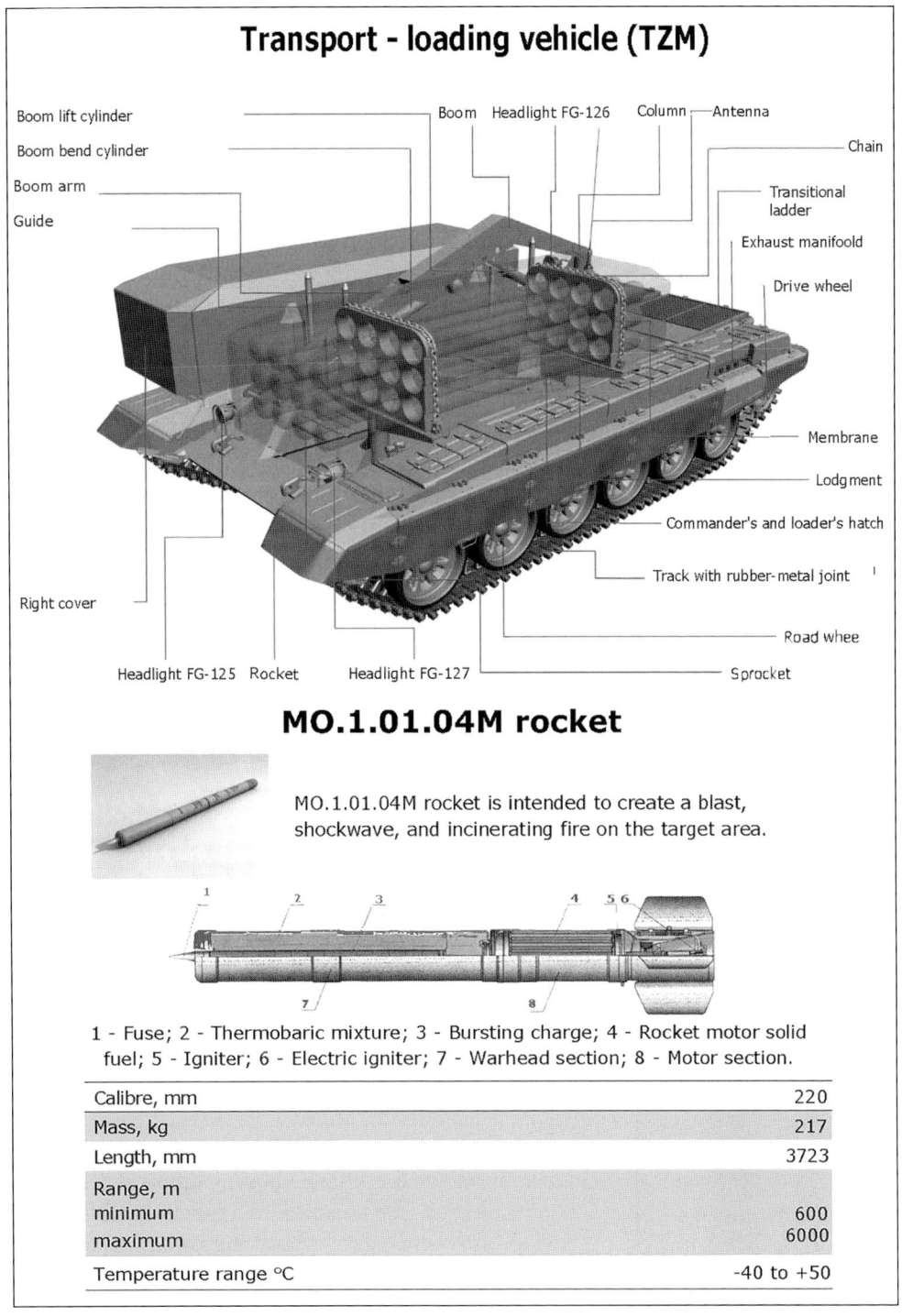

Figure 4-11: TZM-1 (top); MO.1.01.04M rocket cut-out (bottom). (*Source*: btvt.info, modified by author)

Figure 4-12: TZM-1 reloader (top); simultaneous launch of two rockets (bottom). (*Source*: Russian MoD)

The primary injury mechanisms of thermobaric weapons are blast and heat. Secondary injury mechanisms are flying fragments created by interaction of the blast with structures (for example, flying debris) and suffocation through the generation of toxic gases and smoke. The most dangerous and far most effective means of incapacitating the enemy troops in the field and urban fortifications is the primary effect of the shock wave causing damage by enormous compression forces on the body. The effect of various fragments are considerably less as the rocket shell has less

Figure 4-13: TOS-2 Tosochka at the Victory Day parade (top); reloading (bottom). (*Source*: Russian MoD)

fragmentation, but fragments can be created from the surrounding objects that disintegrate under the extreme pressure. Structures such as bunkers and buildings can collapse under the pressure effects and significant numbers of Ukrainian bunkers have been destroyed along with the occupants inside as a result of this effect. The combustion in the immediate vicinity of a thermobaric explosion and fire depletes the use of oxygen making it extremely dangerous for the subject to breathe.

If a regular blast is like an individual touching a high-voltage electrified fence and receiving one very painful but brief zap, then the thermobaric effect feels more like wrapping a hand firmly around the wires and not letting go while the strong electric shock pulsates repeatedly over and over again. This comparison figuratively describes how the extreme violence gets delivered for a longer period of time and wreaks more havoc because of the substantially lengthened time period during which it can stampede through the frail human body. Similarly, the elongated shock wave of a thermobaric explosion smashes against the human lungs for a longer period of time. An explosion can feel like a blow to the chest, a sharp, strong hit that leaves a victim gasping for breath afterward. But there is no firm evidence that thermobaric effect pulls the air out of the lungs.[7]

As one of the goals of the thermobaric explosives is to lengthen the duration of the shock wave, protection against thermobaric weapons is very difficult. Open and enclosed areas do not provide protection against the pressure wave. Even if just a small portion of the shock wave intrudes into an enclosed object such as a bunker, the damage effect is intensified by the shock-wave reflections off the back walls. As the shock waves bounce off the walls of bunkers, or other firm structures, they multiply. When this happens, they increase the total pressure level of the blast exposure. Inside an enclosed space, the long shock wave of a thermobaric explosion can build up to reach the extreme pressure levels of a much larger blast. Each shock wave has a brief time period where the pressure dips down into the negative levels, creating a slight vacuum that sucks some loose material back in toward the direction of the blast multiplying the effect (Figures 4-14, 4-16).

Protection against fragments can be provided by standard body armor and helmets. The thermal heat wave can be minimized using fire-resistant clothing but in practice ordinary troops are not issued with this. It is worth saying that the temperature can reach 1,800+° Centigrade in the vicinity of the rocket explosion and with that sort of temperature even over a short period of time hardly anything can survive. The most important thing to emphasize is that the fabric of enclosed shelters and the reflection walls of structures should be avoided. There is a need for some kind of overpressure release means such as blowout panels and roofs, but in field conditions this is very difficult to achieve. In some Ukrainian positions prepared before the war, there are hardened concrete bunkers fitted with blast doors (such as in Bakhmut). The Ukrainians have tried to prepare themselves by isolating different spaces such as dugouts and bunkers as well as adding blowout panels (according to some reports).

Thermobaric weapons used in the battle for Azovstal in Mariupol, for example, showed that closing access to an underground structure often

Figure 4-14: A salvo of thermobaric rockets destroys everything on a wide front line (top); Azovstal hit by thermobaric rockets (bottom). (*Source*: Russian MoD)

turned against the defenders because shock waves penetrated inside the fortification. The shoulder launched Shmel is often used to hit defenders hiding inside houses and basements with devastating effects for them. There is a perception in the Western media that the "Azovstal fortress" and Azot factory in Severodoneck in which the neo-Nazi Azov Regiment together with the foreign mercenaries and Ukrainian regular forces (such as marines and paratroopers) sheltered waiting for the Russian attack has a vast underground network of tunnels and rooms, which in reality is not true. Nothing is as it is presented in the Western media, rather there is the normal underground infrastructure for the metallurgical plant (which is incidentally modelled on a US plant). Also, the Russians didn't use Shmel to force the defenders out which demanded the close-quarter battle approach but rather attacked the portion of the plant with the underground structures with TOS rockets (Figures 4-14, 4-15).

Urban combat in many villages and towns in Donbas and Lugansk regions requires extensive use of shoulder launched weapons, among them RPO-A. There are numerous videos circulating on social networks showing their use. The experience of storming residential areas and objects (which Ukrainian defenders have often fortified and interconnected through the basements turning them into the makeshift strongpoints) by Russian regular forces, Rosgvardia as well as people's militias from Donetsk and Lugansk, shows that RPOs are irreplaceable in neutralizing the fire points as well as clearing the area. Issues arise if there are civilians among the combatants, with the Ukrainian side on numerous occasions using the civilian population as a human shield. In this situation, the attackers often decide to do classic infantry storming without the use of excessive firepower. Thermobaric weapons are usually only allowed to be used after approval from higher command has been received.

The first massive attack by the Tosochka thermobaric weapons in the Donbas front is said to have occurred near Novomykhailovka and Lyman. In Figure 4-16 the massive shockwaves that the thermobaric rounds cause can clearly be seen, with multiple explosions occurring at once during the attack. The phenomenon which thermobaric weapons are especially prone to produce is called a condensation cloud, or "Wilson cloud." A sufficiently large explosion in high-humidity conditions like those that appear to be seen in this picture will cause a drop in density in the air around it, which in turn temporarily cools the air and causes some of the water vapor therein to condense. This creates the ominous bubble-like clouds seen in Figure 4-16 bottom.

On the Ukrainian side, there are some very limited quantities of Shmel and TBG-7 thermobaric rounds for RPG-7 (remnants from the Soviet Union) but they are insignificant and the question is their operability. Ukraine

THERMOBARIC WEAPONS

Figure 4-15: Chechen special forces 'Akhmat' about to fire a RPG-29 with a TBG-29V thermobaric rocket (top); Ukrainian soldiers killed by the same rocket being fired in the picture above (middle); horrific photo of burned Ukrainian marines after thermobaric rockets fired on Azovstal in Mariupol (bottom). (*Source*: Russian MoD and author)

Figure 4-16: Probably the first use of Tosochka in combat. Stills from a drone video show Tosochka obliterating a Ukrainian position among buildings. (*Source*: Russian MoD)

doesn't have anything like TOS systems domestically manufactured which is a significant handicap for them and there is nothing similar in the Western arsenals that can be sent to Ukraine. Regarding thermobaric weapons, Russia absolutely dominates on the battlefield. According to some unverified data, Ukrainians captured seven launchers, although this is highly questionable. There is only evidence of one captured launcher with a full load of rockets, but the circumstances of this are unknown so most likely the system can't be used against the previous owners (Figure 4-17).

After these first attacks, multiple claims have emerged that deem Russia's use of the TOS-1A as a war crime. There are no specific international laws

THERMOBARIC WEAPONS

Figure 4-17: At the beginning of the war, while Russian troops advanced very quickly some of the equipment experienced mechanical breakdowns and had to be abandoned. The Ukrainians were able to capture some of this equipment, such as this TOS-1A. These launchers are not assigned at battery level, but rather one or two per armored battalion. The state of the equipment is unknown as well as whether it was used against the former operators. (*Source*: Ukrainian MoD and author's archive)

that ban the use of these rockets in combat. Common sense and military logic is not to use them against civilian objects or wherever there is a possibility that civilians are present. The politics behind the system's employment, however, do start to become murky if they are pointedly used against established civilian populations. If the ethics of this attack are later to come into question, it wouldn't necessarily be the nature of the weapon that would be at issue, but its employment.

In many former and current military personnel's experience being under artillery fire is at least very scary. In "normal" combat soldiers can engage the enemy. When under indirect fire (mortars, rockets, artillery), there's nothing that anyone can do but just sit there as the rounds creep closer, watching dust rise after each impact, knowing the only thing that can save an individual is a little luck, prayers, and hopefully the inaccuracy of the rounds. In the case of the use of thermobaric weapons, that inaccuracy is greatly reduced and for those exposed to thermobaric fire, hope is sometimes all that is left.

Chapter 5

Guided Missiles

In the opening minutes of the "Special Military Operation," besides the tactical ballistic missiles, Russia employed its cruise missiles.[1] These missiles were launched from deep inside Russian territory from the strategic bombers Tu-160, Tu-95, and Tu-22M as well as from the seaborn platforms (surface ships and submarines) of the Black Sea Fleet.

Missiles were in the air even before the broadcast of President Putin's speech on TV had finished. The impact on the Ukrainian side was heavy: command posts, communication centers, air defense radars, and warehouses to name just a few were hit.

For Western observers, Russian cruise missiles are not well known. They came into focus when Russia employed them against terrorists in Syria. Launched from a few thousand kilometres distance, by the airplanes or light warships in the Caspian Sea, they performed remarkably well, with almost pinpoint precision.

In the ongoing war in Ukraine, some of these missiles were intercepted and downed but a vast majority were able to hit their designated targets with pinpoint accuracy, especially the new missiles developed in the last ten years.

Russia is using old stocks as well as decommissioned nuclear warhead missiles in which the warheads are replaced with ballast to activate and lure Ukrainian air defense.

In some of the downed missiles, as per Western media reports, some commercial components such as chips were found resulting in an avalanche of memes and mocking of Russian technology. In any case memes and insults do not win battles or wars. The use of commercial components (sometimes scornfully described as washing machines parts) should actually concern Western experts because off-the-shelf components are cheap and available and any country or military group may utilize them for their purposes such as building rockets or missiles. The West has spent hundreds of millions of dollars in researching and developing special military components while commercial components may do the same or an even better job than the usually tenfold overpriced military created ones.

Russia uses several types of air and sea-launched missiles. Ukraine employs just a few. In this chapter the most common air launched and seaborn platform-launched cruise and guided missiles are discussed. Also, the R-500 missile in use with the Iskander-M system, which is detailed in Chapter 2.

Kh-22 and 32 Family

The development of cruise missiles in Soviet Union started more or less at the same time as their counterparts in the West. Soviet designers (locally called "constructors") started from much the same baseline as Western designers, and with similar imperatives. The basis of the design was to provide bombers with standoff weapons allowing them to launch from outside the defensive coverage of an opponent. Soviet designs began to diverge strongly from their Western opponents by the mid-1950s, resulting in many successful designs which had and still have no Western equivalents. In this chapter those designs that are widely in use in the Ukrainian conflict are discussed.

The oldest cruise missile in use in Ukraine is Kh-22 (X-22).[2] Initial development of this started in June 1958. The development of the complex was entrusted to the Dubna branch of OKB-155 (now "Raduga" design bureau). The missile was developed in two versions: to destroy point targets (such as individual ships) and area targets (aircraft carrier groups, convoys, and ground targets). The Kh-22 remains in service as the primary armament of the RuAF's Tu-22M3 bombers. While the Tu-95K-22 Bear G was equipped to carry up to three Kh-22s, its progressive retirement has limited use to the Tu-22M fleet. The K-22U guidance system was developed by KB-1 GKRE in three versions – with an autonomous inertial tracker PSI, as well as with active and passive radar seekers (Figures 5-1 to 5-3).

The Kh-22 fuselage consists of four compartments joined together by flange connections. In the forward compartment, there is a guidance block (for the active version – a radar target coordinator of the PG type) or a DISS of a track-meter and control-system units. Behind it, there is a block of proximity and contact fuzes and warheads, fuel-tank compartments, and an energy compartment with dry batteries (ampouled electrolyte was supplied to them at the time of launch and they worked until reaching the nominal mode of the turbogenerator), an APK-22A autopilot, and the tank-system pressurization units. In the tail compartment there are the rudders actuators, a single turbopump unit of the power plant with a maximum flow rate of 80kg/s, and a two-chamber jet motor R201-300 (C5.44) developed by OKB-300 ("Soyuz"). Fuel reserve is 3,000kg.

GUIDED MISSILES

Figure 5-1: Tu-22M3 with Kh-22. (*Source*: Creative Commons)

The Kh-22 is a one-piece design and, unlike other missiles, is delivered fully assembled, without undocking the consoles. The maximum launching weight is 5,900–6,000kg with a maximum warhead weight of 930–950kg.

When firing at point targets, the homing head monitors the target in two planes and issues control signals to the autopilot. When, during tracking, the antenna angle in the vertical plane reaches a predetermined value, a signal is given to transfer the missile into a dive on the target at an angle of 30° to the horizon. On the dive site, control is carried out in the vertical and horizontal planes according to signals from the homing system equipment. The detection range of a cruiser type target by a carrier aircraft is up to 340km, and the range of capture and tracking is 250–270km. Maximum declared range (depending on the particular model and configuration) is up to 600km but optimal and used in practice is up to 400km. With a maximum speed of 4,000km/h it is very difficult for the Ukrainian Air Defense to intercept.

After detachment from the aircraft, self-ignition of the propulsion components occurs, and the missile starts accelerating with a simultaneous climb (depending on the selected program that determines the nature of the missile's flight trajectory set before the detachment). After reaching the set speed, the rocket engine is transferred to the cruising operation mode.

The Kh-22 missile proved to be a very effective anti-ship weapon even without the use of a nuclear warhead. Tests showed that in the event of a naval target being hit with Kh-22, the damage caused could disable an aircraft carrier or cruiser. At an impact speed of 800m/s, the area of the hole

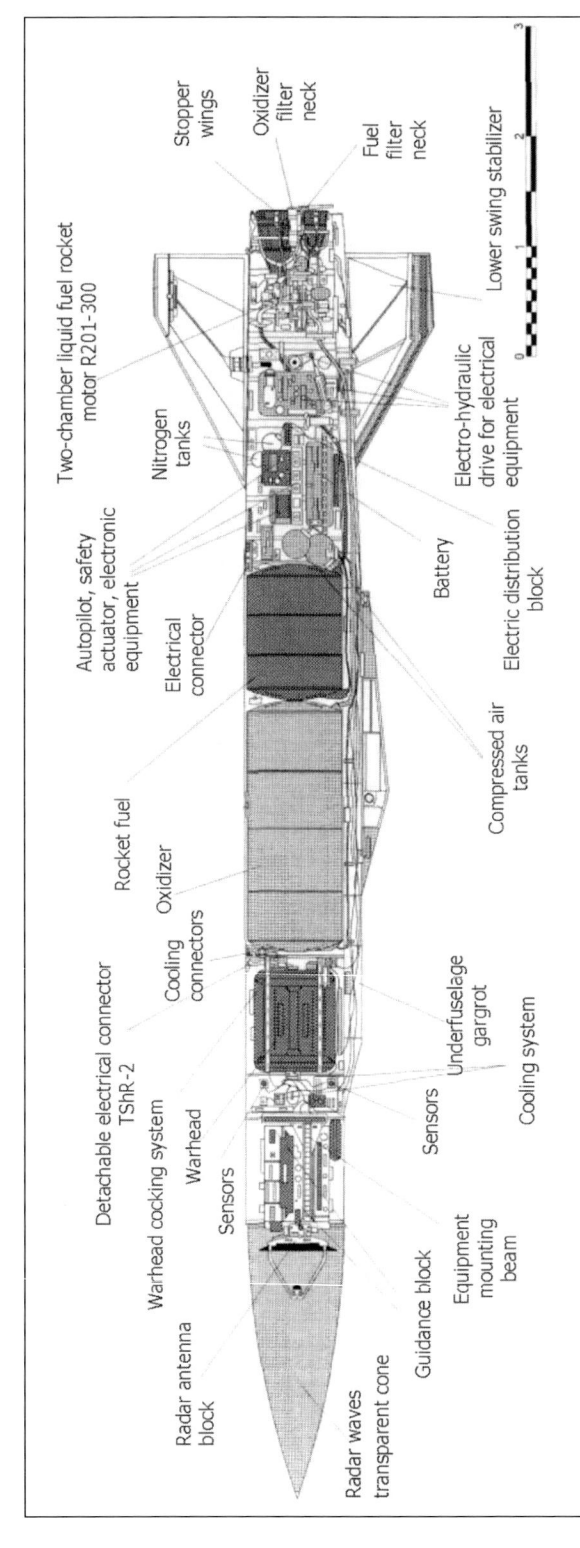

Figure 5-2: Kh-22 cutaway. (Sovetskie I Ruski Krilati Raketi, modified by author)

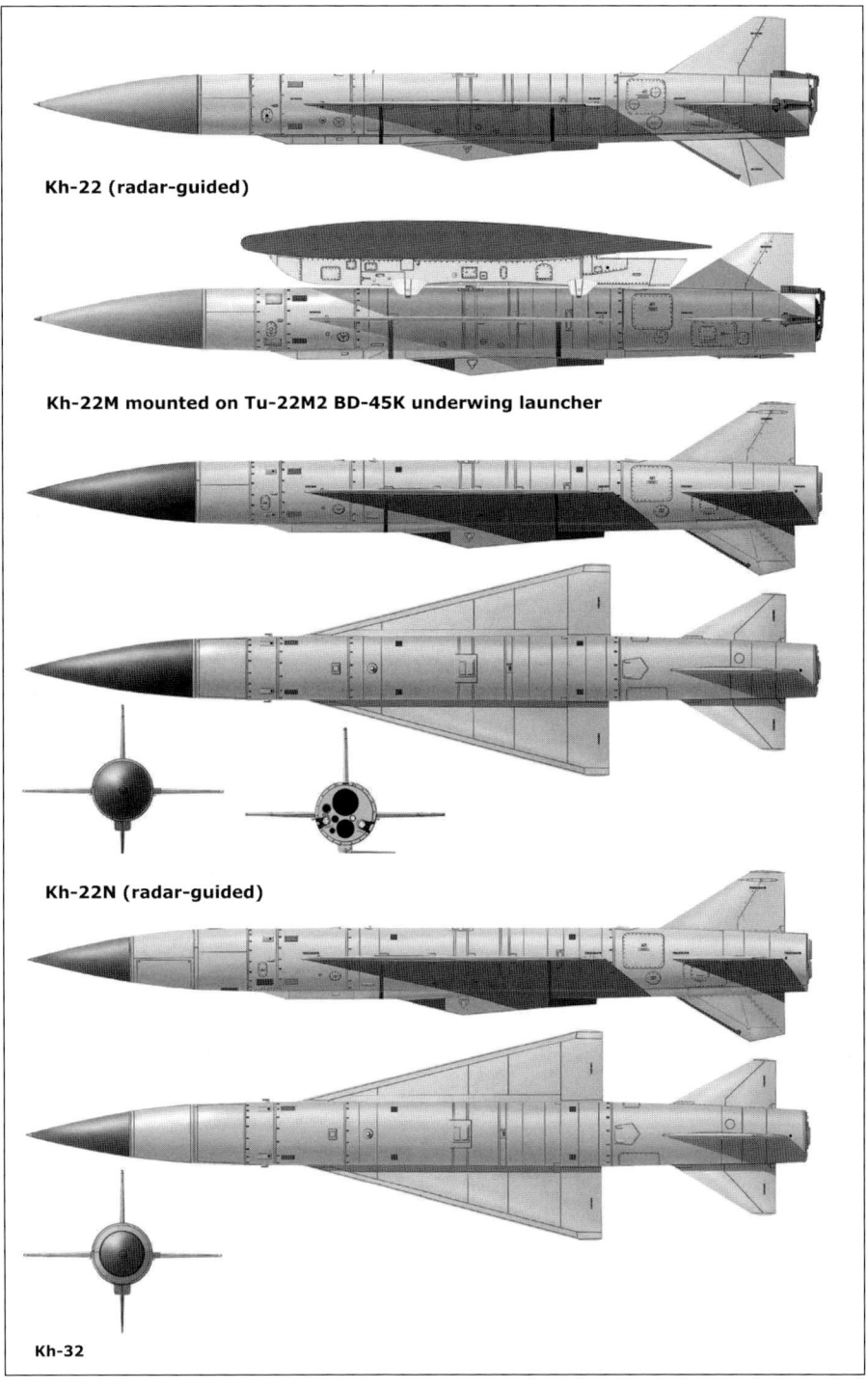

Figure 5-3: Kh-22 and Kh-32 missiles. (*Source*: Sovetskie i Ruski Krilati Raketi, modified by author)

was up to 22m², and the internal compartments were destroyed by a blast and explosion to a depth of 12m.

Of particular interest in the Ukrainian conflict are attacking the ground-based area and point targets inland. For example, when launching Kh-22PSI missile at area targets, the carrier aircraft determines the position of the target using radar and other navigation aids on board the carrier. The onboard equipment of the missile emits electromagnetic waves of a certain frequency in the direction of the target and receives them in the reflected form from the "running" sections of the earth, continuously determining the vector of the true velocity of the missile, which is then integrated over time, the remaining range to the target is continuously determined and the course is held, given from the carrier. At a given distance, the autopilot puts the missile into a dive at the target at an angle of 30°. Activating the warhead occurs at a given height (proximity fuze) or during the impact.

Interestingly, during the joint exercises of the air forces of Russia and Ukraine on 11 August 2000, a pair of Poltava Tu-22M3s completed a 5-hour flight to the north and, together with ten Russian aircraft, attacked targets at the training ground near Novaya Zemlya. Although, due to a long break, only three pilots had previously participated in launches, both target barges were hit.

Two weeks later, on 25 August 2000, the crew of the Ukrainian Tu-22M3 completed an unusual task: providing joint exercises of the air force and air defense at the Arkhalyk training ground, after a long flight, it launched a Kh-22 target missile, successfully intercepted by Su-27 fighters.

The Kh-22s have assumed an exceptional place in both Soviet and Russian aviation and rocket technology – both in terms of the service life of the complex, approaching the sixty year milestone, and versatility of use. Unlike other missiles of its class, whose service was limited to a single type of aircraft (in turn, a special modification of which was created for a specific missile weapon system), Kh-22 was carried with three carrier aircraft – Tu-22K, Tu-22M, and Tu-95K-22.

At the same time, the long service and improvement of the complex could not save it from a significant drawback – low operational suitability associated with the use of liquid-fuel rocket motor. The high performance achieved using liquid-propellant rocket motors brought organic flaws and problems with ensuring the combat readiness of missiles that required equipment with toxic and caustic components – acid and no less harmful fuel.

The Kh-22 is a formidable weapon. Eight variants have been recorded: Kh-22, Kh-22P, Kh-22PSI, Kh-22M, Kh-22MA, Kh-22MP, Kh-22N, and Kh-22NA. A mid-life upgrade for the APK-22 guidance package has also been recently reported. Even a sixty-year-old design still has a place in the war. It is often underestimated by the Western analyst that Russian use of these weapons is a sign of a lack of modern missiles, but what this view neglects is that Russia has a significant number of these missiles available, and it is a logical decision to use them until the old stocks are exhausted. The considerable punches and damage that these missiles can inflict on the static targets in Ukraine justify their use. Numerous warehouses, as well as the makeshift warehouses and storages in shopping malls and factories, have been hit with total devastation. This is a significant sign that the old stuff can still have a major effect on modern warfare (Figure 5-4).

A further development of the Kh-22 is the Kh-32, which is a significantly enhanced version, includes improved guidance, resistance to jamming, motor, and longer range. The Kh-32 was specially designed to attack US carrier battle groups, as well as various ground targets, and was nicknamed

Figure 5-4: Kh-22 impacts on a Kremenchug factory. (*Source*: Wikimedia and Author's archive)

"the carrier killer." The airplane carrier is Tu-22M3M. Development began in the mid-1980s by the "Raduga" design bureau. After the troublesome 1990s and funding problems, the trials were only completed in 2016, and the missile was officially adopted.

Even though the Kh-32 (Figure 5-3) has identical dimensions to the Kh-22, it has a longer range. Advancements in electronics and guidance systems allowed for a reduction in the size of internal components and an increase in the size of the fuel tank. Warhead weight was reduced from 1,000kg to 500kg. It is fitted with a more fuel-efficient motor. All these improvements have allowed its range to be extended significantly.

The maximum range varies from 600–1,000km, depending on the flight profile. Such range allows the Tu-22M3M to approach its target and launch the missile at a standoff range, without entering the AD protected zone. The Kh-32 can reach a top speed of over Mach-4 in its terminal phase.

After launch, this long-range missile was designed to climb to an altitude of 40km and then dive toward the target. Most radars cannot detect and track targets that approach from the top ("the cone of silence"). Alternatively, this missile can perform a lighter dive from the stratosphere and approach the target flying at about 150–200m from the ground. At such extreme altitudes, it cannot be reached by the enemy AD missiles. The previous Kh-22 could only climb to 12–22.5km.

The Kh-32 has a conventional type 500kg warhead. It can also be armed with a nuclear warhead. In comparison with the older Kh-22, Kh-32 is much more accurate than its predecessor.

A baseline version has active radar guidance. The seeker's head has been improved. Some sources suggest that there are versions of this missile with inertial guidance and passive radar guidance, just like the Kh-22 variants.

The new missile is combat tested in Ukraine where it destroyed the targets without even being detected by the AD. Supersonic speed and the top attack made it immune to any countermeasures or interception in numerous instances.

Kh-55 and 101 Family

Beyond any doubt, the Kh-55 (RKV-500) strategic cruise missile and its modified and improved variants are the workhorses of the Russian Air Force strategic aviation and the most common cruise missiles launched by its fleet of Tu-95/Tu-142 and Tu-160 strategic bombers.

The Kh-55 is a subsonic small-sized strategic cruise missile that flies around the terrain at low altitudes and is designed to be used against important strategic targets with previously reconnoitered coordinates.

The missile development started in December 1976 at NPO Raduga under the leadership of General Designer I.S. Seleznev. The requirement was for a long-range precision missile which at the beginning hosted a lot of problems such as low observability (stealth), high aerodynamic quality with a minimum weight, and a large fuel supply with an economical power plant. With the required number of missiles, their placement on the carrier dictated extremely compact forms and made it necessary to fold almost all protruding units – from the wing and plumage to the engine and fuselage ending. As a result, an original fuselage was created with a folding wing and empennage, as well as with a bypass turbojet engine, located inside the fuselage and pulled down before the missile was launched from the aircraft.

What was on the mind of the Soviet designers was the existing US BGM-109 Tomahawk missile. Visually, the Kh-55 family of weapons most closely resembles the early Tomahawk in concept with guidance provided by a TERrain COntour Matching (TERCOM) aided inertial navigation system.

The baseline guidance package is designed around a digital computer running Kalman filter and TERCOM software, with an onboard memory storing a digital map, coupled to a radar altimeter for terrain profiling and a low-drift inertial unit. The Soviets also developed an optical Digital Scene Matching Area Correlator and GPS technology. The cited designation for the Kh-55 guidance package is the Sprut and BSU-55.

As previously mentioned, the carriers of the Kh-55 are strategic bombers – Tu-95MS and Tu-160. Tu-95MS aircraft are distinguished by a modified cockpit, a converted cargo compartment, the installation of more powerful NK-12MP engines, a modified electrical system, a new Obzor-MS radar, and electronic warfare and communications equipment. The crew of the Tu-95MS was reduced to seven people. The crew introduced a new position of navigator-operator, who was responsible for the preparation and launch of missiles.

The need to accommodate a significant supply of fuel for extremely long ranges with limited dimensions led to the organization of the entire Kh-55 fuselage in the form of a tank, inside which the wing, warhead, and other equipment are placed in sealed openings (Figure 5-5). The wing planes are folded into the fuselage, placed one above the other. When released, the planes are at different heights relative to the fuselage horizontal line, fixing with different installation angles, which is why the Kh-55 becomes asymmetric in flight configuration. The tail unit is also foldable, all surfaces such as rudders and the consoles are pivotally broken twice. The keel initially folded to one side, but then the consoles were unified, and another additional hinge appeared on the keel. To reduce the overall length, the tail spinner, which is folded like an accordion, is also retractable.

The engine is extended down under by the squib pusher, after which the opening hatch doors close the opening, maintaining the aerodynamic

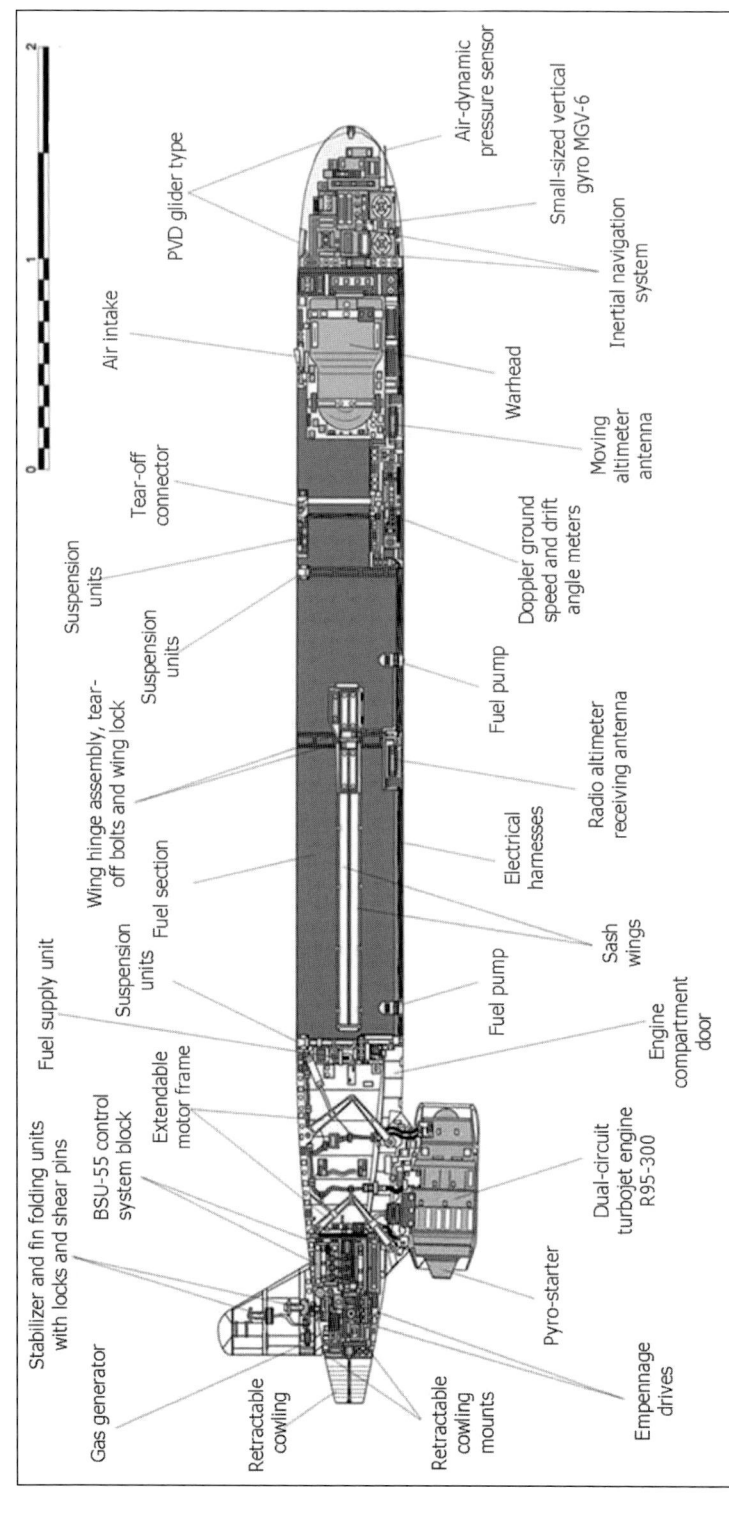

Figure 5-5: Kh-55 cutaway. (*Source*: Sovetskie i Ruski Krilati Raketi, modified by author)

cleanliness of the fuselage. Pyrotechnic pushers also swing open the wing consoles and plumage, and these mechanisms work at high pressures up to 350atm throwing the units out, where they are held by latches.

The double-contour single-shaft turbojet motor R-95-300 is located on a retractable ventral pylon. The low-pressure compressor is a two-stage fan, the high-pressure compressor is a seven-stage axial compressor. The R-95-300 was created taking into account a fairly wide flight range characteristic of cruise missiles, with the ability to maneuver in altitude and speed. The engine is started by a pyrostarter located in the tail spinner of the rotor. In flight, when the engine nacelle is extended, to reduce resistance, the tail spinner of the fuselage is extended (the spinner is extended employing a spring held in a taut state by a nichrome wire, which is burned out by an electric impulse). To carry out the flight program and control, the R-95-300 is equipped with a modern automatic electronic-hydromechanical control system and a built-in electric generator with a power of 4kW. In addition to the usual grades of fuel (aviation kerosene T-1, TS-1, and others), a special synthetic combat fuel T-10 was developed for the R-95-300. T-10 is a high-calorie and toxic compound; it was with this fuel that the maximum characteristics of the rocket were achieved. A feature of the T-10 is its high fluidity, which requires particularly careful sealing of the entire missile fuel system (Figure 5-6).

Concerning the assembly of the missile, the Soviets (and now Russians) put a great deal of emphasis on its manufacturability, which is necessary for mass production. Stories that Russia is not capable of mass production have often appeared in the Western media but are not true. The missile, assembled from separate units, had to have the proper strength, rigidity, and linkage of the joined compartments, ensuring the required cleanliness and accuracy of contours – according to the technical conditions, the latter in the Kh-55 is measured in fractions of a millimeter. It was necessary to establish the production of separate interchangeable compartments, assembled in parallel and going to the general assembly of the fuselage. The fully welded construction, which replaced the usual heavy-weight schemes with flanged joints on bolts and studs, provides a much greater weight reduction but also requires a specific assembly technology.

The Kh-55 fuselage is formed by frames that carry units and equipment and provide docking of the hull compartments. Facilitating the construction, the frames are made of complex shapes, with very high thin-walled ribs and walls. Providing specified contours with numerous transitions in the thickness of the sides and walls, the frames are made by precision stamping, followed by complex milling and boring on CNC machines and machining centers. The main and most difficult problem is the welding of large structural parts. The fuselage is completely welded from AMG-6 alloy. The welding may have a negative side effect such as the warping of

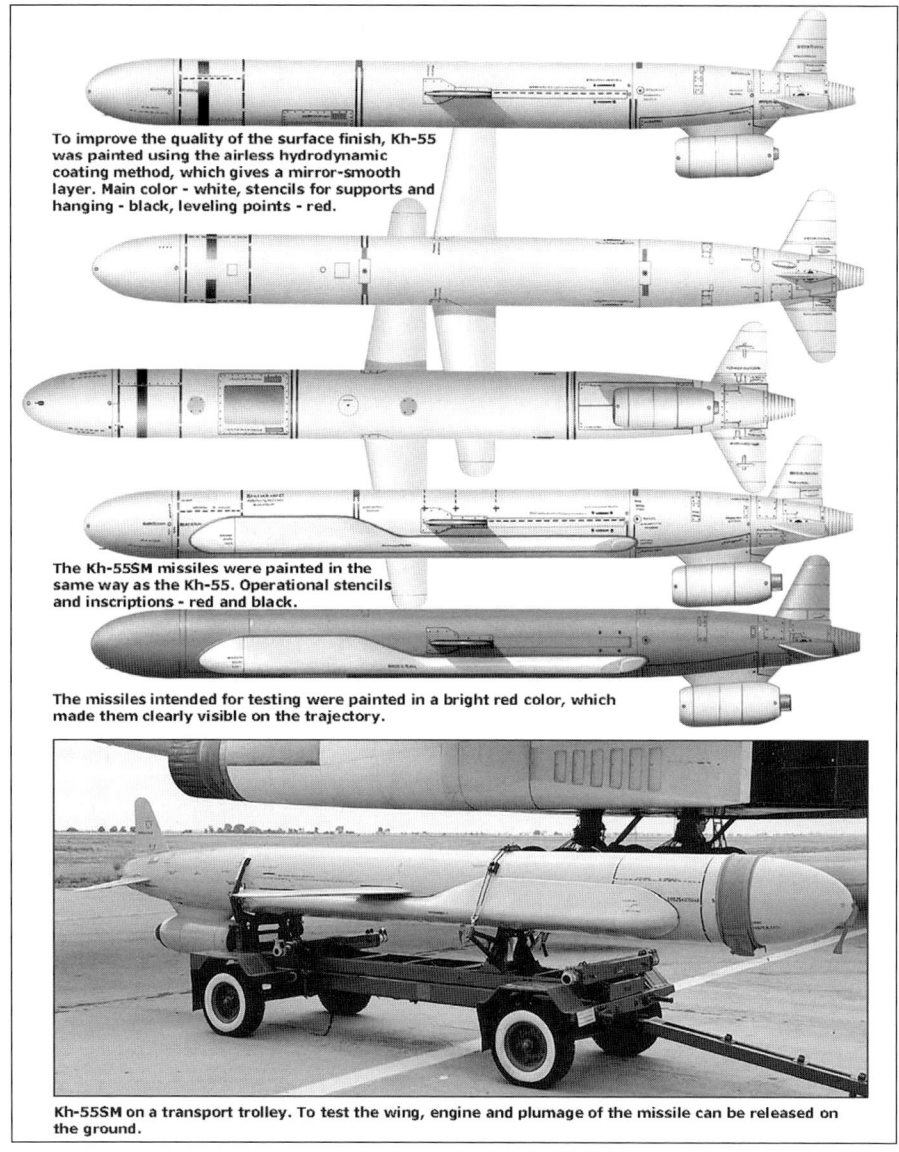

Figure 5-6: Kh-55 missiles of different modifications. (*Source*: Sovetskie i Ruski Krilati Raketi, modified by author)

the structure due to residual internal stresses during heating. Observing the given contours, the fuselage elements are subjected to thermal calibration, which removes the deformations. To avoid "leashes," welded units are placed in thick-walled steel sleeves with electric heating, where they are tempered.

The design of the missile implemented reduces radar and thermal visibility. Due to the small midsection and the cleanliness of the contours, the missile has a minimum RCS, which makes it difficult to detect by air defense systems. The hull surface does not have sharp edges, the engine is covered by the fuselage, and structural and radio-absorbing materials are widely used. The "skin" of the nose of the fuselage, wings, and engine section is made of special electro-magnetic waves absorbing materials based on an organosilicon composite.

The missile guidance system is one of the significant differences between this cruise missile and the previous Soviet-designed air launched cruise missiles. The missile uses an inertial guidance system with location correction based on the terrain. A digital map of the area is entered into the onboard computer before launch. The control system ensures a long autonomous flight regardless of the length, weather conditions, etc. The conventional autopilot on the Kh-55 was replaced by the BSU-55 electronic onboard control system, which works out a given flight program with the missile stabilizing along three axes, maintaining the speed and altitude conditions and the ability to perform specified maneuvers to evade interception. The main mode is the passage of the route at extremely low altitudes (50–100m) with enveloping the terrain, at a speed of the order of 0.5–0.7-Mach. This condition makes it very difficult for Ukrainian AD to intercept Kh-55 and so far the percentage of downed missiles is very small in comparison with the launched one.

The first generation of Kh-55s appeared in three configurations, entering service in 1984. The "Izdeliye 120" Kh-55 was air launched from the Tu-95MS using an MKU-6-5 rotary launcher and external pylons. The air launched Kh-55 was followed by the improved "Izdeliye 124" Kh-55OK, which was supplanted in production by the most capable "Izdeliye 125" Kh-55SM subtype in 1987 (Figures 5-7 to 5-9).

The Kh-55SM design aimed to further extend the striking range of the basic missile, cited at 2,500km. This was achieved by adding a pair of conformal fuselage fuel tanks, which increased launch weight to 1,700kg, but increased cruise range to 3,000km with a 200kT warhead fitted.

A conventional derivative of the Kh-55 is designated as Kh-555. A lightweight medium and shorter ranging derivative weapon, the Kh-65SD and Kh-65SE, has been actively marketed since the 1990s. A further development is "Izdeliye 111" or Kh-101 (Figure 5-10) with conventional warhead and Kh-102 with a nuclear warhead which was developed as a replacement for the Kh-55SM in the late 1990s. This missile weighs some 2,200–2,400kg, the weight of the conventional warhead is 400–450kg. The Kh-101 has a maximum range of 4,500–5,500km and a variable flight profile at minimum altitudes ranging from 30–70m, a cruising speed of 190–200m/s, and a maximum speed of 250–270m/s. The missile is equipped with an electro-optical system for correcting the flight trajectory and with a TV guidance system for terminal guidance. The reports say that is re-targetable

Figure 5-7: Kh-55SM. (*Source*: Sovetskie i Ruski Krilati Raketi, modified by author)

and can be re-routed to alternative targets during the flight. The accuracy is increased with CEP 10–20m.

Interestingly, production of the Kh-55 started in March 1978 at the Kharkov Aviation Industrial Association (HAPO). Ukraine retained the full Kh-55 production documentation but following independence nothing was done to equip the domestic air force or to develop the Ukrainian version. There are indications that the documentation was sold to third parties.

GUIDED MISSILES

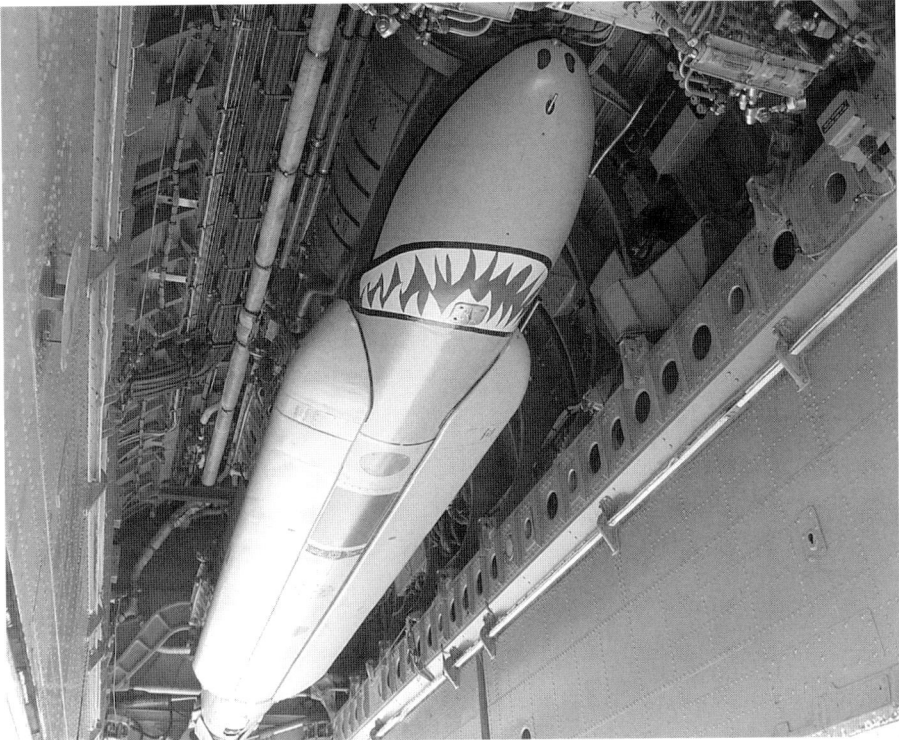

Figure 5-8: Kh-55SM in a Tu-95MS bomb bay. (*Source*: Sovetskie i Ruski Krilati Raketi)

After the collapse of the USSR, most of the Kh-55 missiles and their carrier aircraft remained outside of Russia, in particular, in Kazakhstan and Ukraine, where there were, respectively, forty Tu-95MS in Semipalatinsk, twenty-five in Uzin, and twenty-one Tu-160 in Priluki. Together with the aircraft, about 1,068 Kh-55 missiles remained at the Ukrainian bases. It was possible to reach an agreement with Kazakhstan quite quickly, exchanging heavy bombers for fighters and attack aircraft proposed by the Russian side. By 19 February 1994, all TU-95MS were transferred to the Far East airfields, where they were equipped with the 182nd and 79th bomber regiments. Negotiations with Ukraine dragged on for a long time. Ultimately, the Ukrainian side transferred three Tu-95MS and eight Tu-160s, which flew to Engel's base in February 2000, on account of debts for gas.

During the war, Russian forces extensively targeted the Kharkov facility and it was put out of use. Russian bombers usually flew far away from the Ukrainian border, often above the Caspian Sea, from where they launched missiles. NATO EW assets are constantly tracking these bombers and can in a relatively timely fashion indicate to the Ukrainian side that the bombers are in the air.

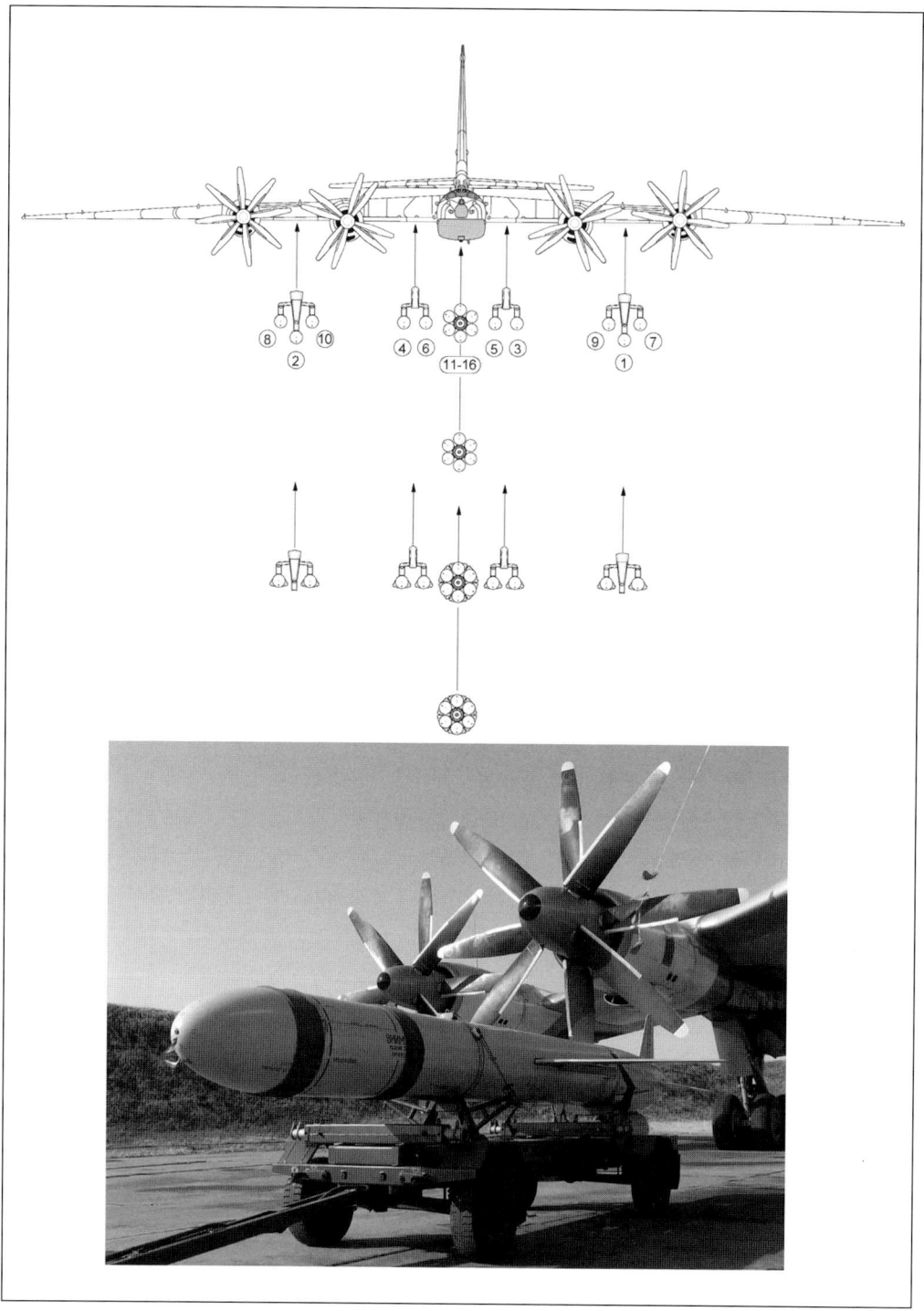

Figure 5-9: Kh-55 and Kh-555 hanging points (top); before loading on Tu-95M (bottom). (*Source*: Sovetskie i Ruski Krilati Raketi, modified by author)

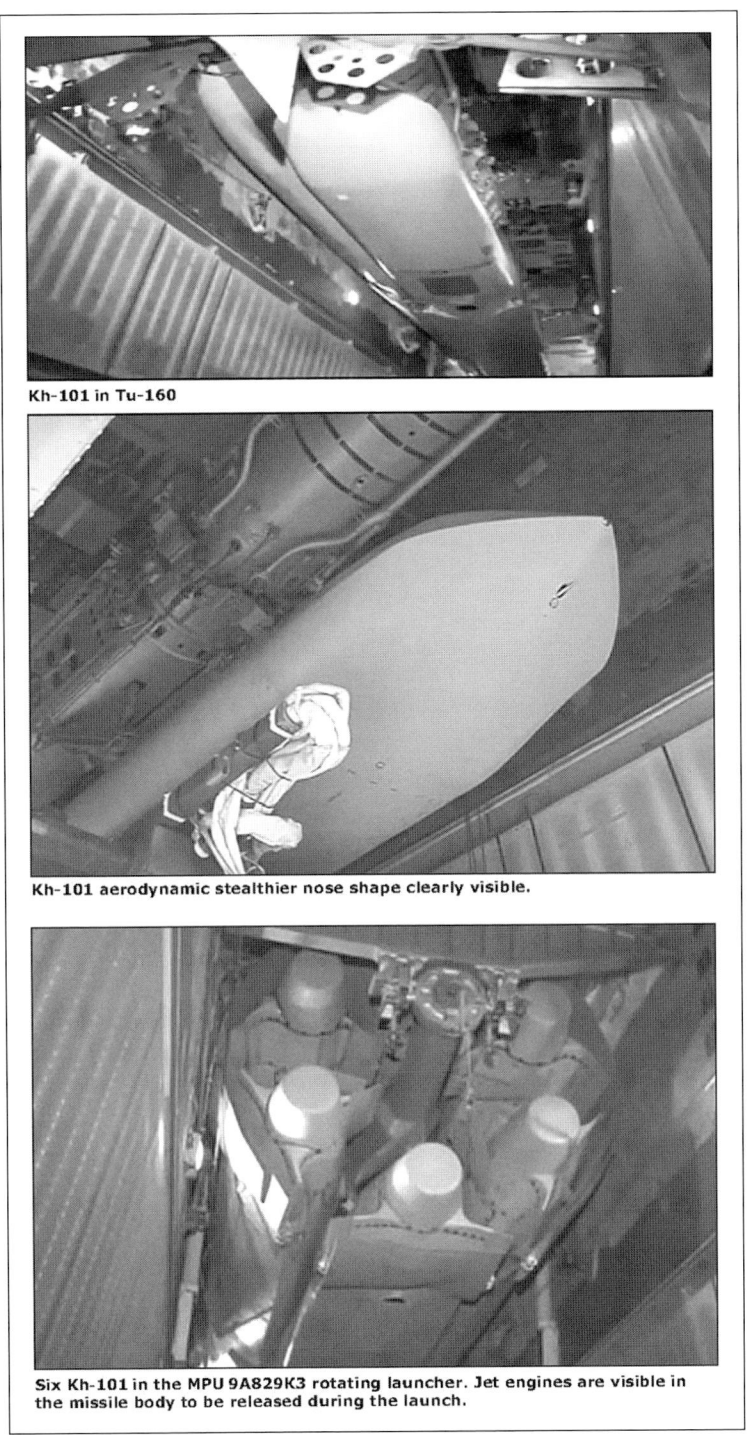

Figure 5-10: Kh-101 on Tu-160. (*Source*: Sovetskie i Ruski Krilati Raketi, modified by author)

Kh-59

The Kh-59 missile comprises a family of long-range air-to-surface guided missiles with an active radar homing head that is designed to engage a wide range of radar contrast surface targets at any time, and in any weather conditions. Its primary purpose was the anti-ship role but it has evolved into a multi-role missile. The main developer is MKB "Raduga" (Figure 5-11).

The Kh-59MK2 multi-purpose missile is a modification of the Kh-59MK designed to destroy a wide range of stationary ground targets with known location coordinates, including those without radar, infrared, and optical contrast to the surrounding background making it optimal for the ground target attacks.

The Kh-59MK missile is tailless and equipped with a cruciform delta wing. Compared with the older Kh-59M, it has a new control system and motor. Replacing the launch booster with an additional fuel tank has made it possible to significantly increase the range.

The maximum firing range against large-ship targets is 285km, and for small (patrol boat) targets it is 145km.

The Kh-59MK anti-ship missile system is equipped with an ARGS-59E active radar homing head, which, in combination with a modern anti-jamming control system and a powerful warhead, means it can perform complex flight trajectories bypassing AD zones with an all-angle approach to the target (Figure 5-12).

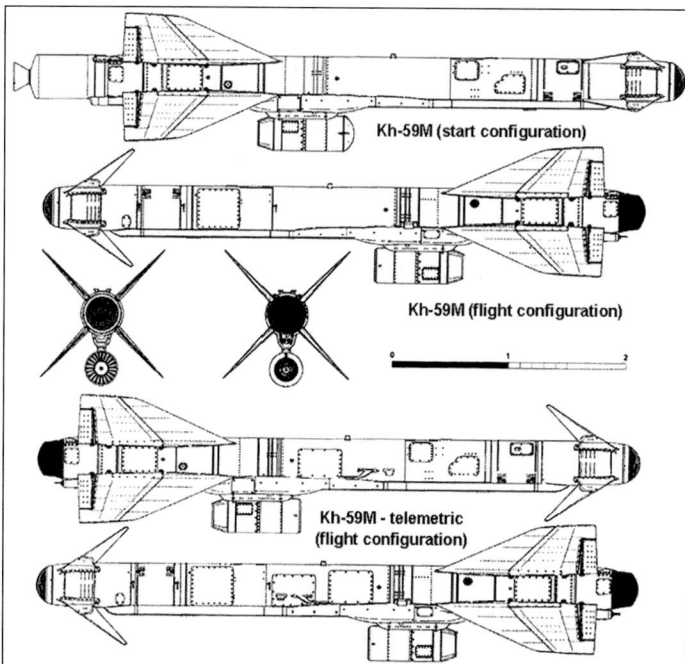

Figure 5-11: Kh-59M. (*Source*: Sovetskie aviacionie raketi vozduh-zemlya)

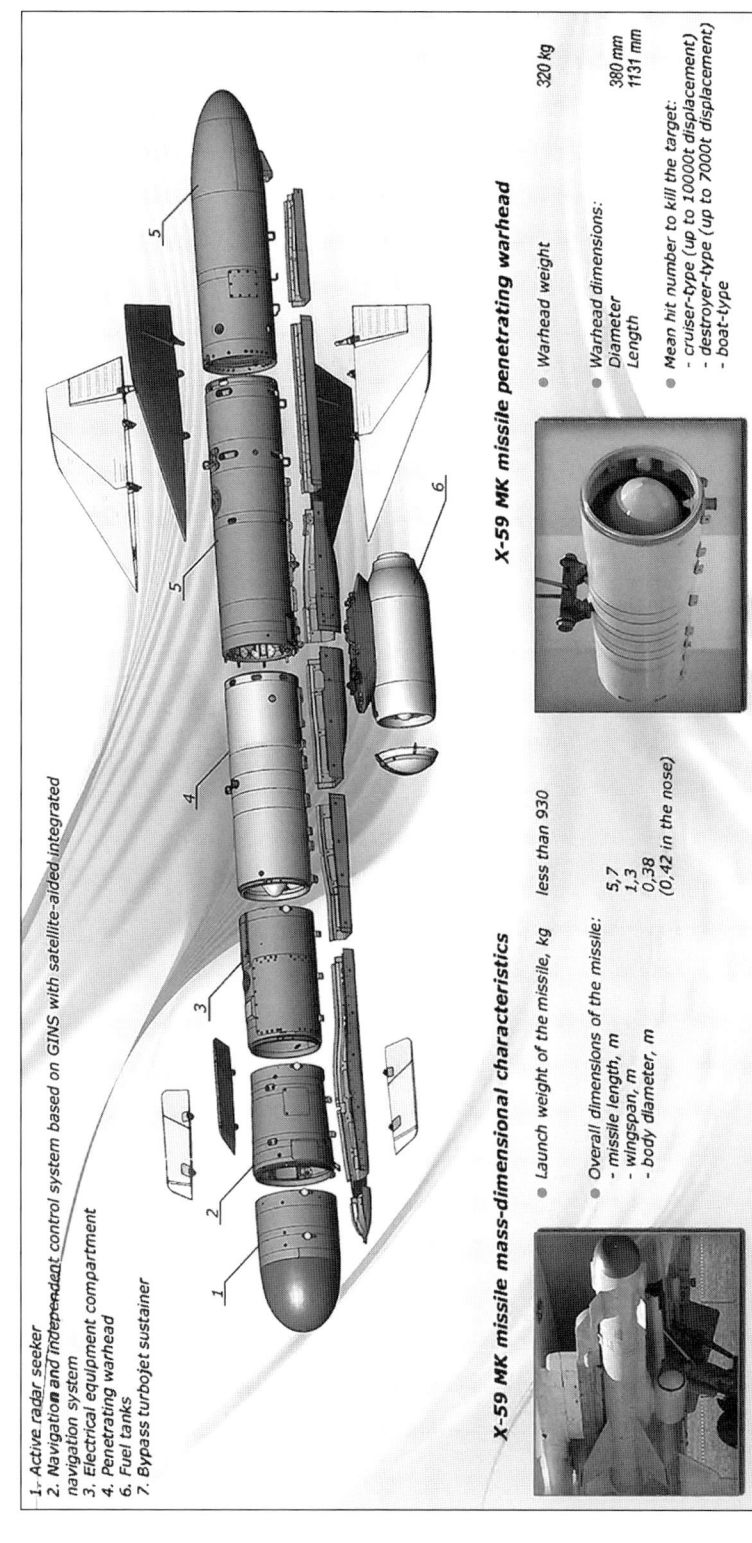

Figure 5-12: Kh-59MK improved range. (*Source*: MKB Raduga and KTRV Tactical Missiles Corporation)

The Kh-59MK2 missile differs from the Kh-59MK in the correlation-optical homing head, which provides autonomous recognition of the area adjacent to the target. It is equipped with a navigation and automatic control system based on a strap-down inertial navigation system and supplemented by a satellite correction unit. The Kh-59MK (Kh-59MK2) missile-control systems include the A-079E radio altimeter. The low-altitude flight route to the target is specified in the flight task. At the same time, the height of the missile's flight above the surface (depending on the terrain) is 50–300m, which makes it extremely difficult to intercept. The final homing system provides a CEP of 3–5m.

The PrBCh (320kg HE) warhead has a fuze with a time delay enabling activation after the missile penetrates the target. The missile can also be

Figure 5-13: Kh-59 debris after hitting the target. (*Source*: Author's archive)

equipped with a 283kg cluster warhead with fragmentation and shaped charge submunitions.

Both the Kh-59MK and Kh-59MK2 missiles are equipped with a highly efficient 36MT turbojet engine. The 36MT (TRDD-50AT) engine was developed by the Omsk Engine Design Bureau and produced by NPO Saturn.

The turbojet engine 36MT is a double-contour, two-shaft, with coaxial shafts of low and high-pressure cascades of pylon design. The combustion chamber is an annular semi-loop with a rotating nozzle. The high-pressure cascade is an axial compressor and a single-stage axial turbine, the low-pressure cascade is a single-stage fan with wide-chord blades and a single-stage axial turbine.

The engine operates in a wide flight range with the ability to maneuver at altitude (0.2–11km) and speed (up to 1,100km/h).

The great advantage of this missile is that it can be launched by almost all fighters and attack airplanes in the Russian inventory making it a universal air-to-surface missile. As a consequence, it is in wide use in Ukraine (Figure 5-13).

3M-14E and 3M-54 "Kalibr"

The 3M-14E "Kalibr"[3] high-precision cruise missile (the improved version of 3M-14) is intended to destroy stationary land and sea targets in all weather conditions, day and night, in intense enemy air defense fire and electronic countermeasures. Typical targets for the 3M-14E missiles are command and control centres, weapons, ammunition and fuel depots, airfields, port facilities, and infrastructure objects such as bridges, powerplants, etc. The complex also has an underwater version for engaging targets such as submarines.

It is one of the most versatile missile systems in the Russian inventory and can be launched in all three media – ground launched, sea and underwater launched, and air launched (Figure 5-14).

Figure 5-14: 3M-14E (top and bottom left); 3M-54 (top and bottom right). (*Source*: TASS)

These configurations are:

- Anti-ship missiles 3M-54E, 3M-54E1 (can be used against ground targets),
- High-precision cruise missiles for destroying ground targets 3M-14E, and
- Anti-submarine missiles 91RET2 ("Kalibr-NKE") and 91RE1 ("Kalibr-PLE").

3M-14E missiles in various configurations are included in:

- Submarine-launched missile system "Kalibr-PLE,"
- Surface ships launched "Kalibr-NKE,"
- Ground launched mobile missile system "Kalibr-M," and
- Airborne missile system "Kalibr-A."

An export version of these systems is designated "Club."

The different-purpose missiles and launching system with the single universal control system makes it possible to vary the ammunition payload of missiles on different platforms depending on the task and the specific combat situation.

For the underwater submarine launch, the missiles of the Kalibr-PLE complex are launched from regular 533mm torpedo tubes from a depth of 30–40m. Black Sea diesel-electric submarines of Project 877 (Kilo class) regularly perform underwater launches against Ukrainian targets (Figures 5-15, 5-16).

Surface ships that use Kalibr-NKE are equipped with vertical 3C-14E launchers or tilting ZS-14PE launchers. The 3M-14E missile of the Kalibr-NKE complex is distinguished by the presence of a special transport and launch tube and is designated 3M-14TE. These missiles can be launched from corvettes and frigates (the Black Sea Fleet has currently available two Grigorovich-class frigates and four Buyan-M corvettes) and even the small patrol boats (Figures 5-17, 5-19).

The air launched 3M-14AE missile from the Kalibr-A system is part of the armament of the Su-35 attack aircraft (up to 3 units) and is planned to arm the MiG-35 fighter. The 3M-14AE does not have a starting motor and is placed in a transport and launch container and the launch is carried out after being dropped from the carrier aircraft (Figure 5-18).

One interesting universal module named "Club-K" is a container missile weapon system designed to destroy surface and ground targets with 3M-54TE, 3M-54TE1, and 3M-14TE cruise missiles. The Club-K complex can be implemented with coastal defense units, surface ships of various classes, and railway and automobile platforms. The technical means of the complex are placed in a standard 40ft sea container.

GUIDED MISSILES

Figure 5-15: Kalibr loading into the submarine of Projekt 877 (Kilo class).

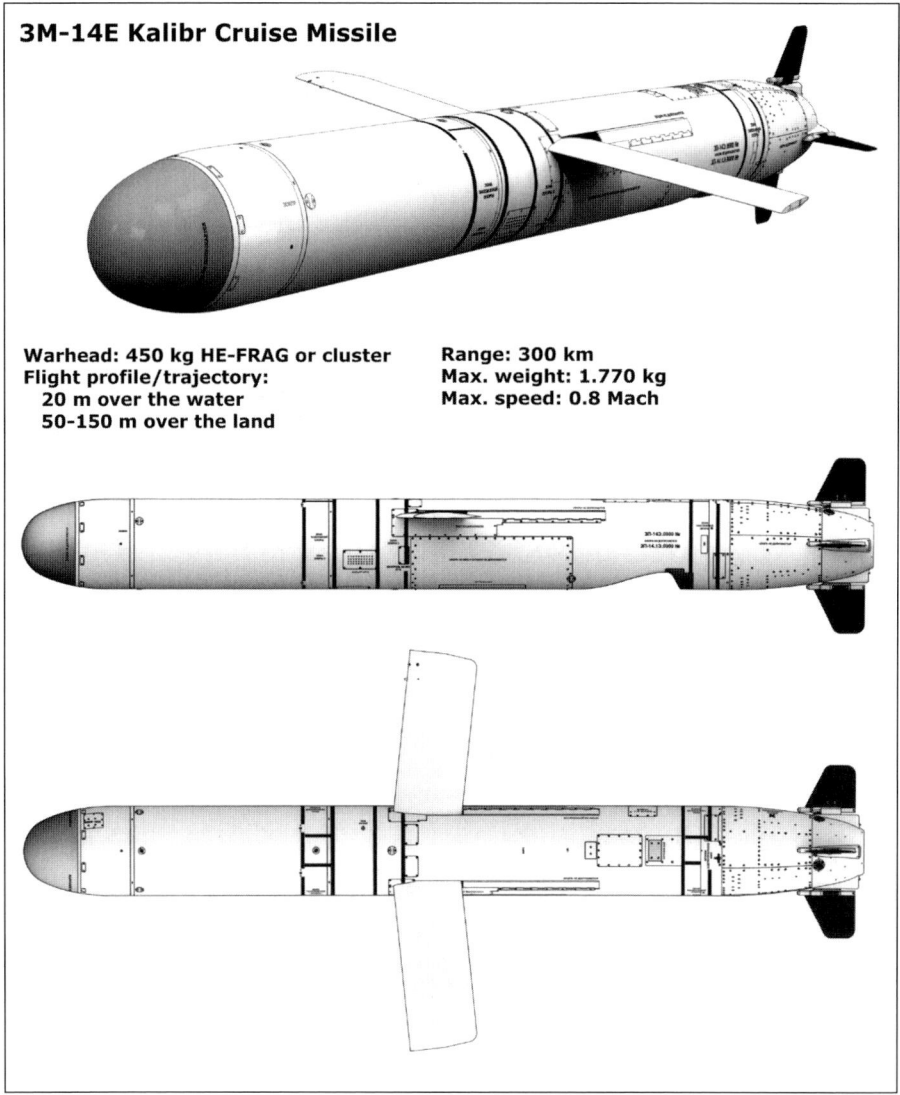

Figure 5-16: 3M-14E.

Functionally, the Club-K complex consists of a universal launch module, a combat control module, and a power supply and life support module. The universal launch module is designed to prepare and launch missiles from transport and launch containers by lifting the launcher for four missiles. These standard sea containers can be easily disguised with ordinary containers meaning that the module can be put on any size of the ship that can accommodate the necessary space.

The 3M-14E cruise missile of the Kalibr-PLE, Kalibr-NKE, and Kalibr-M complexes is equipped with a starting solid-propellant motor in the tail

Figure 5-17: 3M-14 in the vertical launcher (top); launch from the light patrol boat of 2163 class (bottom). (*Source*: Zvezda telekanal)

section of which lattice-type stabilizers are located. The turbofan engine TRDD-50B ("Product 37," 37-01E) is a small-sized double-contour turbojet disposable, unified for all missiles of the Kalibr complexes, developed by the Omsk Engine Design Bureau and produced by NPO Saturn.

The 3M-14E missile is equipped with a combined guidance system. Missile control in flight is completely autonomous. The onboard control system is built based on the AB-40E autonomous inertial navigation system (developed by State Research Institute of Instrument Engineering). The missile control system includes a RVE-B type radio altimeter (developed by

Figure 5-18: Air launched 3M-14E. (*Source*: still from YouTube)

UPKB "Detal") and a satellite navigation system signal receiver (GLONASS or GPS). The radio altimeter provides flight in the terrain envelope mode by accurately maintaining the flight altitude: over the sea – no more than 20m; overland – from 50–150m (reduced to 20m when approaching the target).

The flight of missiles takes place along a predetermined trajectory, following intelligence data regarding the position of the target and the availability of air defense systems. The missiles are capable of penetrating the zones of an advanced enemy air defense system, which is ensured by extremely low flight altitudes (enveloping the terrain) and autonomy of guidance in the "electromagnetic silence" mode in the main area. Correction of the missile's flight trajectory on the marching segment is carried out according to the data of the satellite navigation subsystem and the terrain correction subsystem. The principle of operation of the latter is based on a comparison of the terrain of a particular area where the missile is located with reference maps of the terrain along the route of its flight, previously stored in the memory of the onboard control system. Navigation is carried out along a complex trajectory.

Guidance in the final section of the trajectory is carried out with the help of an anti-interference active radar homing head ARGS-14E, which effectively highlights low-profile small targets against the background of

Figure 5-19: Kalibr a moment before impact on an Odesa warehouse (top). (*Source*: still from CCTV); destroyed hotel in Odesa that housed foreign "volunteers." Hundreds perished upon impact (bottom). (*Source*: Author's archive)

the underlying surface. The ARGS-14E homing head with a diameter of 514mm and a weight of 40kg was developed at OAO NPP Radar MMS (St Petersburg) and has a viewing angle in azimuth ±45°, in elevation from +10° to -20°. The detection range of a typical target is about 20km. Exceptional maneuverability allows bringing the missile to the target with high accuracy. What makes these missiles extremely hard to intercept is the supersonic terminal speed of Mach-2.9 (3,550km/h). The major Ukrainian point defense such as Stinger or Igla MANPADS are powerless in this stage. Even most modern Western short- and medium-range AD systems such as NASAMS and IRIS-T are not able to engage these missiles in the terminal stage.

The 3M-14E missile is equipped with a powerful 450kg high-explosive warhead with an air blast option. A variant of a missile with a cluster warhead equipped with fragmentation, high-explosive, or cumulative submunitions for the striking area and extended targets has been developed.

According to published data, the range of the missile, depending on the type of combat equipment, is up to 2,600km.

The 3M-54E and 3M-54E1 anti-ship missiles have an almost identical basic configuration and are unified as much as possible. As previously mentioned, it can be used in the ground target attack modes. The missiles are made according to the normal aerodynamic scheme with a drop-down trapezoidal wing with a span of 3.1m (Figure 5-20).

After the launch of the 3M-54E/3M-54E1 missile and a climb of about 150m, the booster is separated, the air intake is opened, the second-stage turbojet engine is launched and the wings open, then the missile descends to a height of 15–20m above the sea surface. On the march section of the trajectory, the missile flies at transonic speed under the control of the inertial system according to the target designation data entered into its memory before launch. To reduce the probability of interception of 3M-54E/3M-54E1 missiles, the onboard control system can launch the missile at the target from a given direction along the optimal trajectory, bypassing the obstacles and enemy AD. In addition, when attacking large surface targets, a salvo launch of several missiles can be carried out, which will reach the target from different directions.

The Ukrainian media has presented one of the downed missiles and claimed that the Russians don't have anymore of the "regular" Kalibr missiles, so are forced to use the anti-ship one. This couldn't be further from the truth.

Kalibr missiles are in use almost on a daily basis in the Ukrainian conflict. In the media, even a new term has been forged for the destruction level named "target Calibration." The level of damage caused is significant, especially when hitting infrastructure targets and this greatly affects Ukrainian supplies. From time-to-time the Ukrainians may intercept some of them (often published in the range of up to 90 percent) but these numbers are greatly exaggerated. The level of damage compared with the number of the so-called downed missiles simply does not tally. Certainly, it may be accepted that so far the Ukrainian air defense can intercept about 10 percent of most of the typical missile attack waves. The Ukrainians are trying to concentrate the modern Western AD system around Kiev and some critical industrial and

Figure 5-20: 3M-54 Kalibr (top); remains of the downed missile (bottom). (*Source*: Author's archive and Ukrainian MoD)

infrastructure locations but even those systems are not capable of stopping the layered and multi-level attacks by cruise missiles and suicide drones.

When the Kalibr missiles are launched from the seaborne platforms, they are immediately detected by the NATO ELINT equipment and the tracking starts. The Ukrainian side is notified straight away through the joint intelligence teams. This gives the Ukrainian side time to prepare in advance but the targets are impossible to determine so it puts strain on the entire AD in the potential zone of attack. Through these actions NATO is an active participant in the war.

Kh-29 and 38 Family

The Kh-29 is a shorter range (10–30km depending on type) missile family that utilizes a large 320kg warhead. It can use semi-active laser guidance (Kh-29L), infrared (Kh-29D), active radar guidance (Kh-29MP), or passive TV guidance (Kh-29T/TE), and is typically carried by tactical aircraft such as the Su-24, Su-30, Su-34, MiG-29K as well as the Su-25, giving these aircraft an expanded standoff capability (Figure 5-21).

The missile is mostly used against larger targets and infrastructure such as industrial buildings, depots, bridges, reinforced aircraft shelters, and concrete runways. It can also be used against smaller ships.

Visually it is similar to the air-to-air R-60 missile, just bigger because of the large warhead with similar aerodynamic control surfaces. The laser guidance head came from the older Kh-25 and the TV guidance head from the Kh-59. The Kh-29T version has a top speed of 2,200km/h.

The Ukrainians use these missiles on their Su-25, but the results are currently unknown. Russian tactical bombers use them in much higher numbers. Su-34 for example uses them to target fortified command posts, bunkers, and other high-profile targets.

The latest missile in this category is Kh-38 (Kh-38MA inertial, active radar guidance; KH-38MK-inertial/satellite guidance; Kh-39ML-inertial, semi-active laser guidance, and Kh-38MT-inertial, IR imaging guidance). This model is intended to succeed the Kh-25 and Kh-29 missile families. It can be armed with up to 250kg HE-FRAG, cluster or armor-piercing warheads. The declared operational range is 40km. Visually compared with predecessors, control surfaces have been replaced with longer and narrower fixed ones.

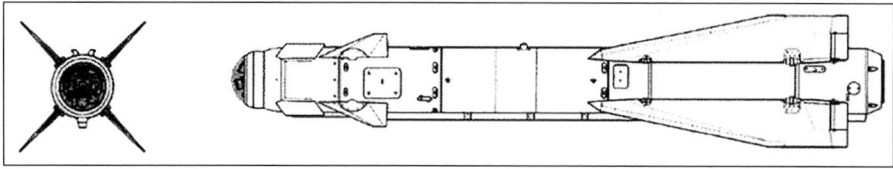

Figure 5-21: Kh-29T TV guided missile.

The latest developments are the Kh-36 Grom-E1, which is a tactical cruise missile with a 120km range and larger warhead, and the Kh-36 Grom-E2, which is a glide bomb with a 50km range. These missiles can be launched by Su-34, Su-57, and MiG-35, as well as the Ka-52K attack helicopters. The first combat use of Kh-38M missiles was in Syria and they are also in use in Ukraine.

P-800 Oniks/Yakhont

The P-800 Oniks (3M55 GRAU index) was first developed in 1993 by NPO Mashinostroyenia (Figure 5-22). In 1999, a ground-launched export version, the Yakhont, and an air-launched version, the Yakhont-M, were developed. Russia fielded its first Oniks missiles in 2002. In 2015, Russia

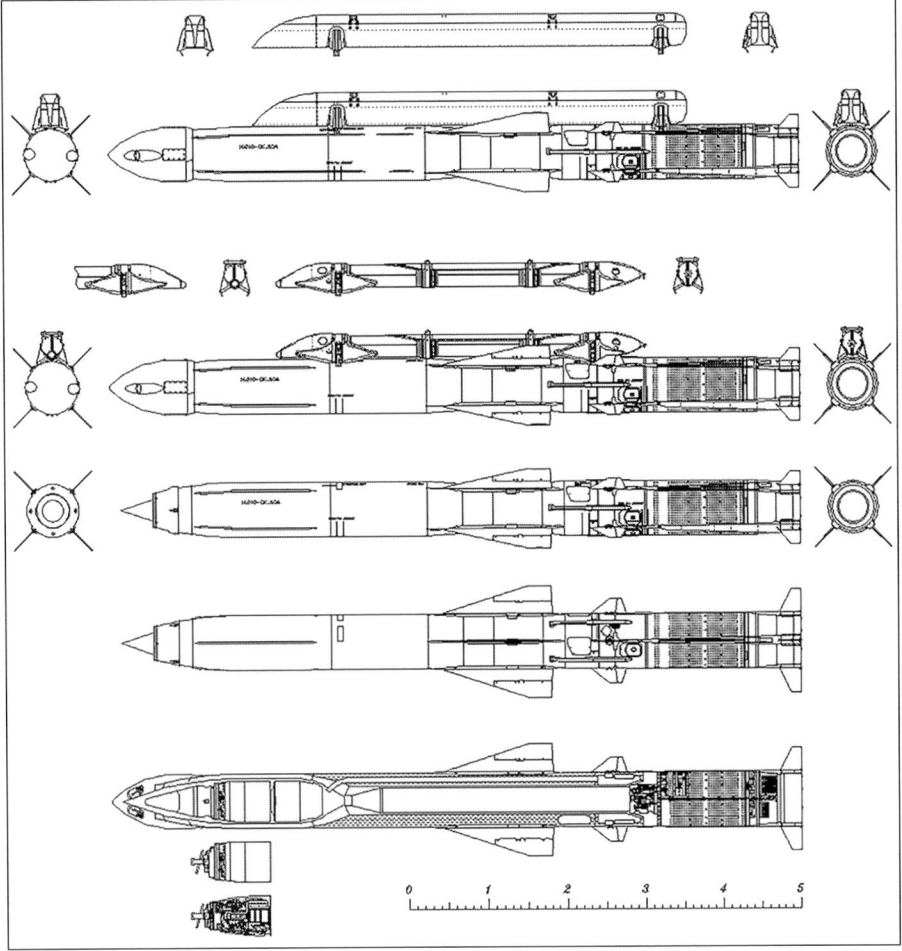

Figure 5-22: For illustration, the Indian PJ-10 Brahmos is very similar in terms of dimensions, shape, propulsion, weight, etc. (*Source*: Nayeem Sheikh blogspot)

began deploying the coastal system named Bastion which utilizes mobile ground launchers. The ship-launched variant is known as the P-800 Oniks. A submarine-launched version is fitted to Yasen-class attack submarines. The Oniks can be ground-launched using two variants of the Bastion launch system: the stationary Bastion-S and the transportable Bastion-P.

The mobile coastal missile system Bastion (Figure 5-23), with unified supersonic anti-ship missile Yakhont, is designed to destroy surface ships of various classes and types from amphibious operations, convoys, aircraft carrier strike groups, as well as single ships and land radio-contrast targets in conditions of intense air defense and electronic countermeasures. One brigade of the Bastion anti-ship missile defense system protects the coast along a length of more than 600km from enemy landing operations, the far frontier of the political and administrative region as part of a single system of its coastal defense. As that, it is permanently assigned to Crimea.

The maximum range is 300km in its higher-altitude trajectory and in a low-altitude trajectory is 120km. After being accelerated by a rocket booster, the missile propels itself with a kerosene-powered ramjet motor. In a typical flight, the missile can reach altitudes of up to 14km and speeds of up to 750m/s (Mach-2.2). When approaching the target, the missile descends to a 10–15m altitude to avoid detection. At low/terminal altitudes, the missile's maximum speed is 680m/s (Mach-2).

The Oniks' anti-ship variant is 8.3m long, while its surface-to-surface variants are slightly longer at 8.6m. All variants have a diameter of 670mm and a launch weight of 3,000kg. The missiles have both an active and

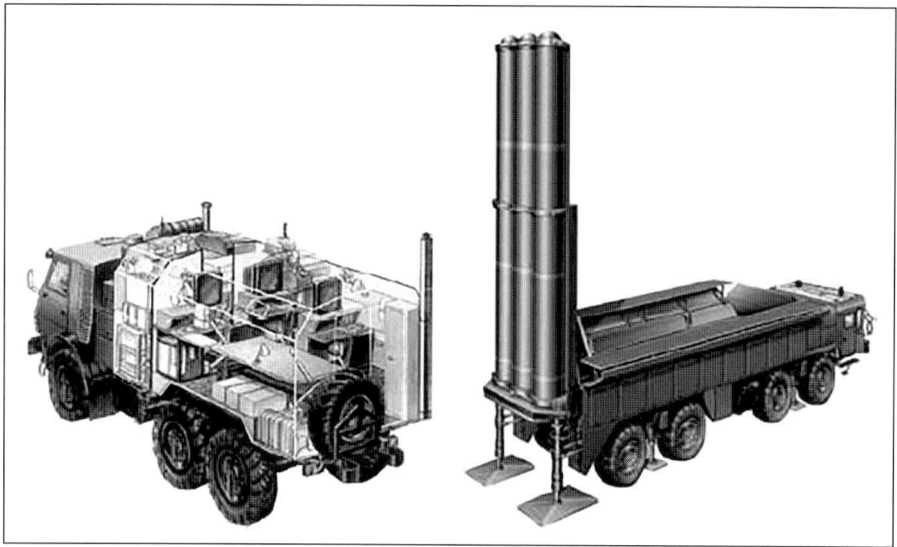

Figure 5-23: Bastion system battery command post (left); Transporter-Erector-Launcher (right). (*Source*: Oruzhie Rossii)

passive inertial navigation system and are equipped with either a 200kg HE or 250kg penetrating warhead. Further modifications involved updating the previous terminal seeker with an active radar seeker and imaging infrared seeker.

The missile is enclosed in a sealed transport and launch container. The dimensions of the missile make it possible to increase the ammunition load of anti-ship missile carriers of the same class by two or three times (Figure 5-24).

Figure 5-24: Bastion launchers. (*Source*: Russian MoD)

In TPK, being completely ready for combat use, the missile leaves the manufacturing plant, and is transported, stored, and installed in the launcher. Without opening the container, the technical condition of the missile and its systems are monitored through a special onboard connector.

The missile in the sealed TPK is self-sufficient and does not need any exterior support or maintenance and requires only connection to the launcher system once installed.

The use of TPK, a wide range of possible launch angles, and a launch scheme that does not require jet gas removal, makes it easy to fit it into the architecture of a significant range of carriers. Moreover, launchers of various designs can be used for this. For example, rack-type launchers that are extremely simple in design, created for small-tonnage ships of the "missile boat and corvette" class, and modular vertical launchers for surface ships of larger displacement – frigates, destroyers, and cruisers. If the complex is installed on a modernized ship, instead of the launch site of the "old" cruise missile, it is possible to install three containers of Yakhont anti-ship missiles. For example, when upgrading the Project 1241 "Tarantula" boat, instead of four P-15 Termit missiles, twelve Yakhont/Oniks anti-ship missiles can be installed.

One combat unit (brigade) can have up to thirty-six anti-ship missiles installed on eighteen self-propelled launchers K-340P. The time to bring the complex into combat readiness from the traveling position is less than 5 minutes. The time of autonomous combat duty without auxiliary means is 24 hours (thirty days with external support units). The launch interval during salvo firing from one launcher is 2 to 5 seconds.

There are some reports that the P-800 was used to target some of the larger Ukrainian Navy ships at the beginning of the war. As the Ukrainian Navy has been effectively destroyed (with some small patrol boats still operational but not worth engaging with an expensive missile), the Russians are using P-800 to attack ground targets. The range from the Crimean Peninsula effectively covers deep into the Ukrainian rear in the Odesa and Nikolaev regions. The CEP of 10m is sufficient enough for stationary targets within the maximum range.

R-360 Neptune

The Ukrainian answer to the Russian air and sea-launched anti-ship missile onslaught is the RK-360MC Neptune with R-360 missile (Figure 5-25). The main developer is the Luch Design Bureau.

It is very similar to the Russian Kh-35 (developed in the Soviet Union but produced in Russia) but has a longer body with more fuel, a larger booster, and some other local modifications. Ukraine had all the technical documentation for the Kh-35 missile and was producing engines and some other components for the Russian Kh-35 missiles. The first examples were reportedly completed and tested in 2016. This version didn't have a guidance system. The declared range is up to 280km and it can be carried and launched from naval, land, and air platforms. The development was completed in 2019, military trials were completed in 2020, and a pre-production system was delivered to the Ukrainian military for testing in 2021. In 2021 the Ukrainian MoD funded the production of a batch of Neptune coastal defense systems. It was planned that eighteen to nineteen launchers would be delivered in 2022.

An exact copy of the Neptune was first observed in 2014, in North Korea. It is locally known as Kumsong 3. Initially, it was thought that the North Koreans had acquired the Russian Kh-35E or Kh-35UE missiles. However, after both technical and intelligence analysis, it appeared that it is not a Russian missile, but is extremely similar to the Ukrainian Neptune. It is unclear how a missile that was under development in Ukraine came to be tested in North Korea even before being tested in Ukraine. One of the explanations could be that Ukraine "contributed" to the development of the North Korean Kumsong 3 anti-ship missile. Ukraine had a large weapons industry but also engaged in intensive black-market trading. They also supplied rocket motors for North Korean ballistic missiles via Russia.

It carries a 145kg HE-FRAG warhead. This missile should be efficient against vessels with a displacement of up to 5,000T, such as corvettes or

Figure 5-25: Neptune missile (main image). (*Source*: Ukrainian MoD); *Moskva* cruiser (inset). (*Source*: Russian MoD).

frigates from the Russian Black Sea Fleet. Theoretically, it can inflict damage even to a cruiser (such as *Moskva*) but wouldn't be sufficient to sink it.

The missile has an inertial navigation system with active radar homing in the terminal stage. The missile flies 10–15m above the surface. In the terminal stage of the flight, it will descend to 3–10m above the surface to overcome AD. This missile is subsonic and because of this it can be intercepted easily, especially by advanced AD systems on Russian ships.

The Ukrainians also developed launchers with control and command units based on a Czech Tatra 8x8 T815-7 series heavy high-mobility chassis. Surveillance radar Mineral-U was specially developed for the Neptune system. It can detect ships at a range of 500–600km. Initially, this radar was planned to be based on the Ukrainian KrAZ-7634.NE chassis, but the KrAZ company reportedly could not deliver the chassis in time and this pushed it back one year behind schedule.

Overall the RK-360MC could be equivalent to a Russian "Bal" coastal defense system, though not as capable. A typical Neptune battery consists of six launchers with a total of twenty-four anti-ship missiles. Launcher vehicles can be located up to 25km from the sea. It takes 15 minutes to prepare it for firing.

Since the beginning of the war, the Russians have meticulously targeted production and development facilities so it is unlikely that this system will be developed and produced in the near future.

Ukrainian propaganda has bragged that the Neptune was responsible for the sinking of the Russian cruiser *Moskva*, but taking into consideration the capabilities of the system, this is highly unlikely. *Moskva* sank rather because of the internal explosion and fire.

Harpoon

The second Ukrainian hope to cripple the Russian Navy is a well-known US-made AGM-84 Harpoon anti-ship missile family. Three major subcategories based on the launching platforms are: RGM-84A (surface-launched), AGM-84A (air-launched), and UGM-84A (submarine-launched) (Figures 5-26, 5-27).

The Harpoon is an all-weather, over-the-horizon, anti-ship missile developed and manufactured by McDonnell Douglas (now Boeing Defense, Space & Security). It is produced in many variants (blocks) and is in use in almost all NATO navies either in surface, submarine, air, or land launch configuration.

The operational range is 139km for the ship-launched Harpoon Block I and Block IC; 124km for the ship-launched Harpoon Block II; and 220km for the air launched Block IC. During the flight, it applies a sea-skimming cruise monitored by a radar altimeter with the active radar terminal homing. The maximum speed of 240m/s (Mach-0.71) means that it is more difficult

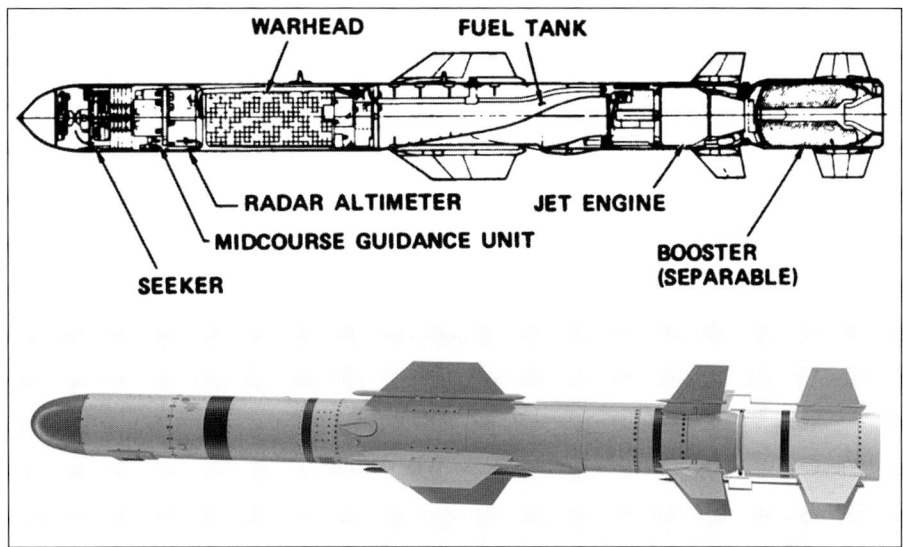

Figure 5-26: RGM-84 Harpoon. (*Source*: Free 3D and Wikimedia)

Figure 5-27: Harpoon ground launcher with four ready-to-fire missiles. (*Source*: USNI)

to detect but the subsonic speed is a great disadvantage because modern Russian ADs can deal with that easily.

Harpoon is a proven weapon both in real combat and through accidents. In real combat it participated in the Iran-Iraq War and sank two Iraqi missile boats in 1980; the US attack on Libya in the Gulf of Sidra when it sank a few patrol boats in 1985; US clashes with Iran when it sank a frigate in 1988, as well as incidents when launched by the US Navy and Danish Navy and the missiles damaged civilian buildings in 1981/82 and an Indian merchant ship in 1988.

Figure 5-28: The victim – Russian tugboat *Vasily Bekh* (top); TB2 Baryaktar video showing the hit. (*Source*: Ukrainian MoD)

For the Ukrainians, the danger of the Russian Black Sea Fleet is constant and after negotiations, NATO decided to supply ground-based launchers. Denmark sent their Harpoons in May 2022, while the Netherlands followed with the missiles. The US decided to supply launchers and missiles in June. NATO ELINT assets actively support the Ukrainian side and transfer all data about Russian ships to the combat units. On 17 June, Ukrainian sources claimed to have sunk the Russian tugboat *Spasatel Vasily Bekh* with two Harpoon missiles. The ship was transporting personnel, weapons, and ammunition to Snake Island. Ukraine's Naval Command said the Russian tugboat had a Tor missile system onboard (Figure 5-28).

Following the sinking of the tugboat, Russia started actively searching for missiles and launchers. It was reported that Harpoon missiles were located in the Odesa warehouse which was promptly attacked by Russian Kalibr missiles. Unknown quantities of missiles and launchers were destroyed. The Russians also claimed that by end of November 2022 they had neutralized two-thirds of all Harpoon launchers.

Kinzhal

The 9-A-7660 (according to some publications Kh-47M) Kinzhal is an Air Launched Hypersonic Ballistic Missile or aeroballistic missile. There are two types of hypersonic weapons: hypersonic glide vehicles (HGV) and hypersonic cruise missiles (HCM). Hypersonic glide vehicles are launched on top of a rocket booster, like those used in Intercontinental Ballistic Missiles (ICBM), which boosts the hypersonic glide vehicle to an altitude below that of the trajectory of a ballistic missile. The weapon is then released, re-enters the upper atmosphere, and glides towards its targets at hypersonic speed, using the aerodynamic lift as it descends. Hypersonic cruise missiles (HCM) are launched similarly to cruise missiles by using a booster rocket in their initial launch phase and then a supersonic-combustion ramjet (scramjet) engine. Once the scramjet ignites, the missile follows a cruise trajectory at a relatively constant speed and altitude. Hypersonic cruise missiles fly at lower altitudes (20–30km) than hypersonic glide vehicles and have a shorter range because they must carry fuel.

Russia has been conducting research on hypersonic technology since the 1980s and is more advanced than any other country in this field. During his public address regarding the new weapons, President Putin claimed that the new missiles (Kinzhal, Tsirkon, and Avangard) flying at a hypersonic speed, ten times faster than the speed of sound, can also maneuver at all phases of their flight trajectory, which also allows them to overcome all current and prospective anti-aircraft and anti-missile defense systems while delivering nuclear and conventional warheads in a range of over 2,000km (Figure 5-29). Russia tested and recently implemented the Kinzhal

(Kh-47M2) and Tsirkon. According to intelligence reports, these weapons are in limited use in the Ukrainian conflict.

Kinzhal (dagger) is a hypersonic short-range ballistic missile launched from a high-speed aircraft. Technically, Kinzhal is not generally characterized as a hypersonic weapon based on some parameters, but is considered hypersonic due to its similarities which feature a maneuverable re-entry vehicle. The Kinzhal weapon-delivery system mates a short-range solid-fuel aeroballistic missile to a modified MiG-31K interceptor jet, to provide a hypersonic medium-range standoff strike (Figure 5-30).

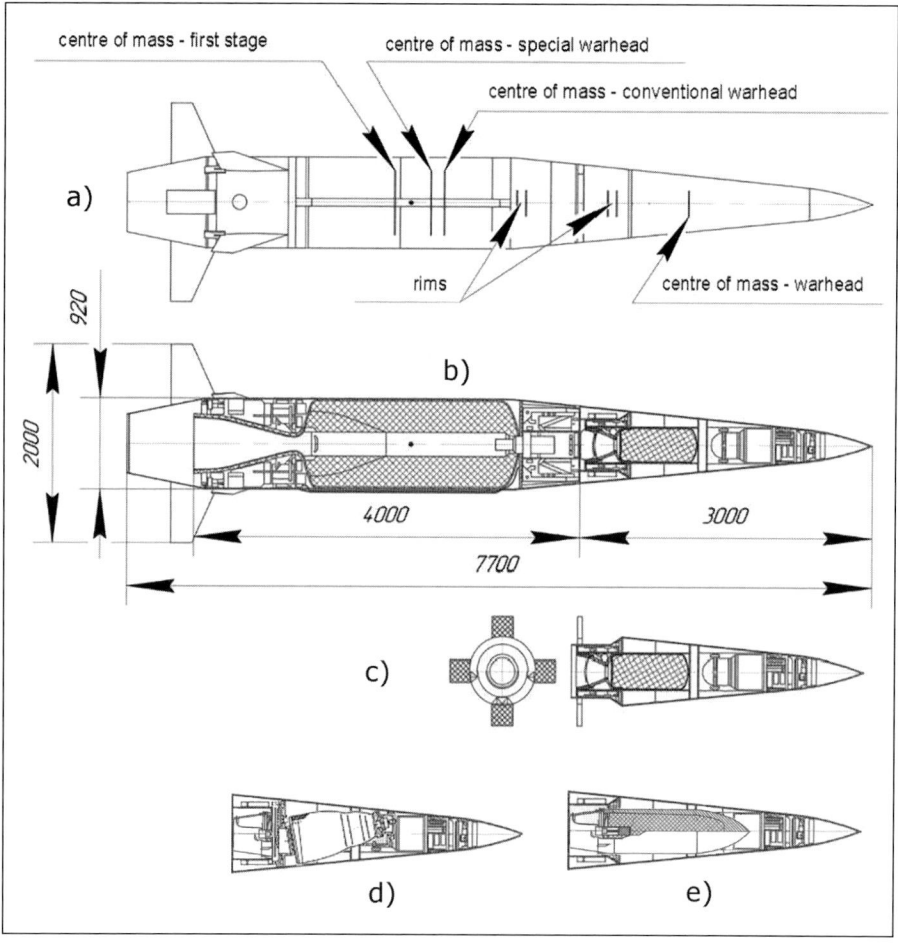

Figure 5-29: Kinzhal overall dimensions, centre of mass distribution, and warheads. At the time of writing, there are no officially published Kinzhal cutaways and the diagrams are solely based on the Iskander ballistic missile dimensions: a) the center of masses diagram; b) the hypothetical hypersonic vehicle attachment; c) a separate hypersonic warhead; d) the conventional warhead; e) the hard penetrator warhead based on the BetAB-500 concrete piercing bomb intended to engage deep underground reinforced bunkers. (*Source*: Topwar, modified by author)

The Kinzhal is reported to be a substantially modified Iskander-M (see Chapter 2) short-range ground-launched ballistic missile using a solid-propellant rocket with small fins for maneuverability.

The Kinzhal hypersonic system consists of the MiG-31K jet carrying the Kinzhal missile to altitudes of about 18km at supersonic speeds. The missile is released and falls probably 30m, ejects a rocket cap that is used to protect the rocket motor during the jet flight, then uses its solid rocket motors to accelerate to hypersonic velocity. Following its launch, Kinzhal quickly accelerates to Mach-4 and is reportedly capable of reaching Mach-10 (Figure 5-31). Some Western analysts criticize these parameters and claim that Russia intentionally misled the West, citing that NATO intelligence has not independently confirmed those parameters and that the maximum speed is in a range of Mach-5. In any case, Kinzhal is a formidable weapon able to target critical NATO infrastructures, such as airfields, command centers, and reinforced weapon storages, and to counter US or Israeli missile defenses, such as THAAD or Arrow.

The MiG-31K interceptor jets can carry/launch one Kinzhal at a time. The MiG-31K aircraft is a high-speed maneuverable interceptor, and because the Iskander-M can maneuver during the terminal phases of flight it is certain that the Kinzhal can as well. Some Russian sources have indicated that the upgraded Tu-22M3 bomber also may carry and launch up to four Kinzhals, although there is some skepticism about whether the bomber is fast enough or flies high enough for this purpose. The range of Kinzhal if carried on the MiG-31K is 2,000km and 3,000km if carried on a Tu-22M3 (based on the carrier's maximum range). This a medium- or intermediate-range system. Russia also conducted MiG-31K air refueling while carrying

Figure 5-30: MiG-31K with air launched hypersonic Kinzhal missile. (*Source*: Wikimedia)

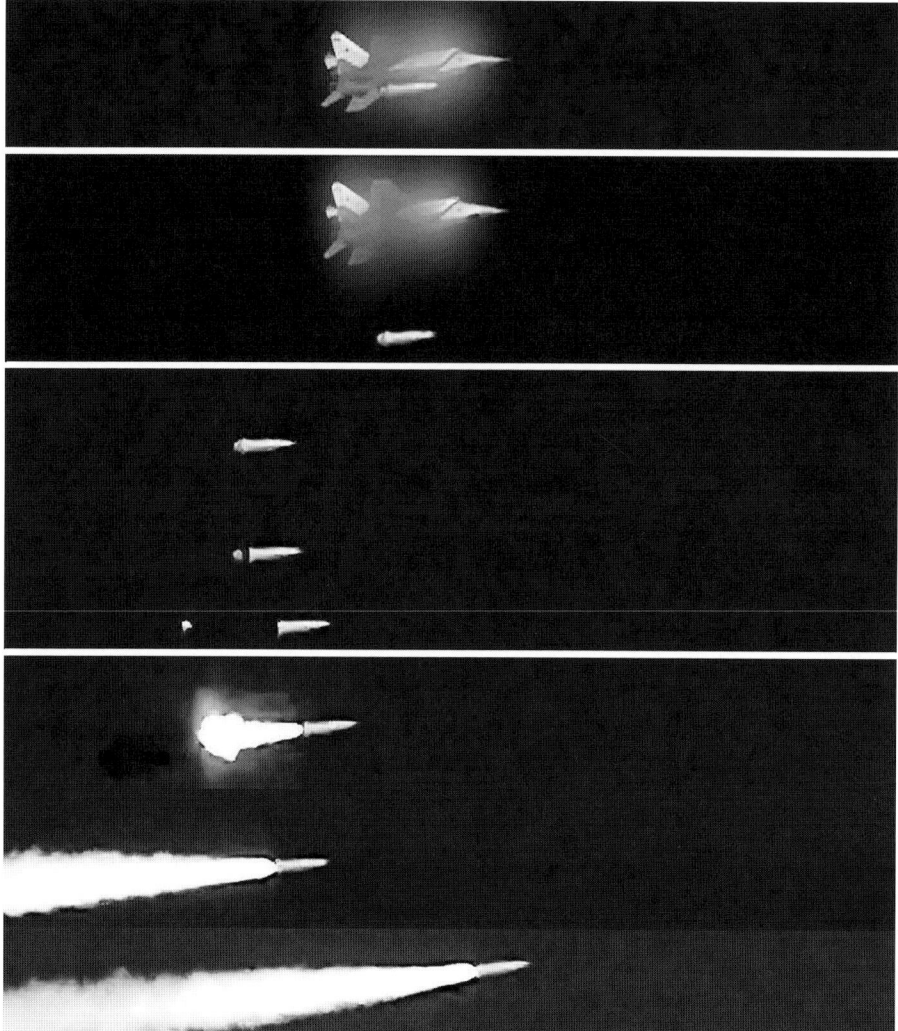

Figure 5-31: MiG-31K Kinzhal launch sequencies. (*Source*: Russian MoD)

the Kinzhal, suggesting the capability to increase the overall range of the delivery system. Some of these MiGs visited Syria and are also located in Belarus for the action against Ukraine or as deterrents to NATO.

According to some reports, Kinzhals are used against reinforced underground ammunition storages and some command centers. There are no official Ukrainian confirmations (yet) but these types of targets are something that Kinzhal is optimized to engage. Some potential new targets may be decision-making centers including high-level government offices and joint NATO/Ukrainian centers (Figure 5-32).

What is important in Kinzhal attacks is that there is no means to counter them, neither in the Ukrainian military nor NATO forces. Once the

Figure 5-32: MiG-31K with Kinzhal missile (insets); hit in the Ukrainian underground ammo depot (main image). (*Source*: Wikimedia and Russian MoD)

missile is launched, it will fly to the designated target and only technical malfunction will prevent it from scoring a hit.

Russia has used Kinzhals to hit Ukrainian underground bunkers and command posts. They have claimed 100 percent hits and destruction. One of the most publicized and at the same time controversial attacks occurred in western Ukraine in early March 2023, when a Kinzhal allegedly struck an underground bunker. The depth of the bunker was more than 50m (some estimates in the media put it at even 80m or even 130m). According to the Russian media, this bunker near Lviv was a strategic command center with mixed NATO and Ukrainian staff. Intelligence estimates are that there were up to 300 personnel in the bunker, 40 of which were high-ranking foreign specialists. The Ukrainian side categorically rejects the Russian claim (as expected). The facts are that there is an underground bunker near Lviv (from the Soviet era), a Kinzhal missile was used for the attack, and many ambulances were observed going to the location afterwards. The subject is very sensitive and the truth is known only to those with the highest security clearances. Perhaps, long after the war has ended, the facts will emerge.

In May 2023 Kinzhals were also used to target Ukrainian Patriot AD batteries, destroying the radars, launchers, and command post. The Ukrainians claim to have shot down all Kinzhals even showing some remnants which are very similar to the concrete-piercing hardened bombshell. However, their claim is baseless because Kinzhals hit their targets and not a single one was shot down. The propaganda war is of the highest intensity and great caution should be exercised when considering claims.

Anti-Radiation Missiles

Anti-radiation missiles are in wide use in suppressing the enemy air defense (SEAD). They were the first ones to be launched against Ukrainian radar sites and in the initial stages of the conflict they destroyed significant numbers of Ukrainian radar equipment, both in AD units and long-range surveillance ones.

The Soviet Union developed a series of anti-radiation missiles. The latest ones are Kh-58 and Kh-31 (which succeeded Kh-58).

Kh-31 and 58

There was a long tradition of development of anti-radar missiles in the Soviet Union. Some of their designs actively participated in the Arab-Israeli War with some successes. The latest versions are the Kh-58 and its successor Kh-31 (Figure 5-33).

The Kh-31P is a supersonic missile with a passive radar homing head designed to destroy the enemy radar. It was developed to counter radars of medium and long-range anti-aircraft missile systems "Patriot" and "Improved HAWK." Some of the differences compared with the previous generations are a longer firing range, high cruising speed, stable targeting in conditions of intense jamming interference, and countermeasures.

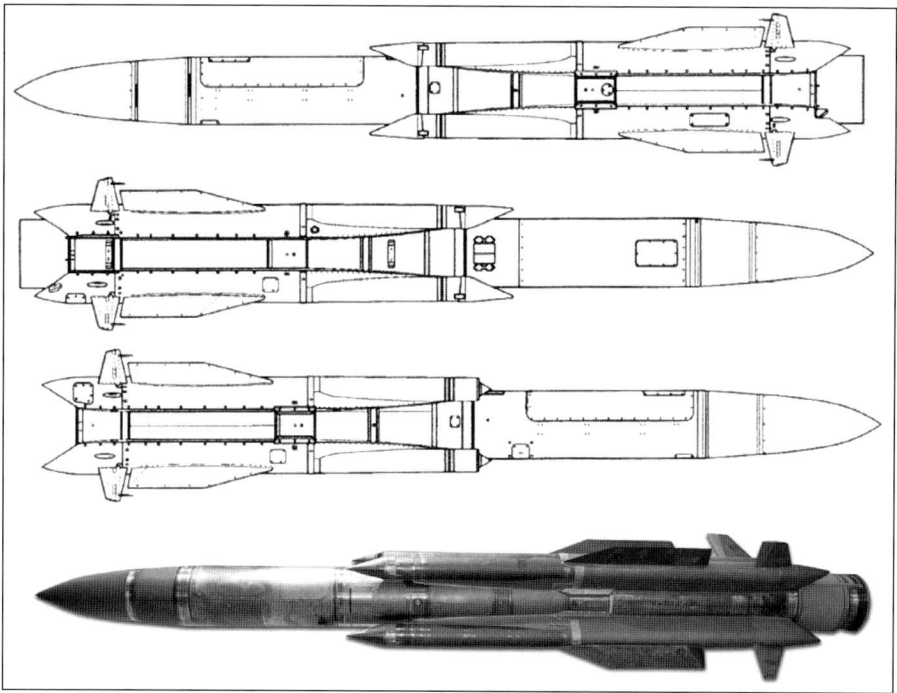

Figure 5-33: Kh-31 anti-radiation missile. (*Source*: Author's archive)

The development of the Kh-31P anti-radar missile began in 1975 at the Zvezda Design Bureau under the leadership of Chief Designer G.I. Khokhlov. It was assumed that the new missile would have a launch range of about 60km, a mass of less than 400kg, a speed of 750m/s, and when launched at 25km from low altitudes would destroy the "Improved HAWK" SAM radar before the missile launched by HAWK reached the airplane. It was planned to strike at the Nike Hercules air defense radar outside the range of the missile defense system. It was planned to equip attack aircraft of the third generation, MiG-27, Su-17M, and Su-24 types, each of which was to carry at least two missiles. To ensure the required average speed for a given mass, it was decided to use a ramjet. To accelerate the rocket to the launch speed of the ramjet, a starting solid-propellant booster was used, which was placed in the combustion chamber of the ramjet.

After almost a decade of development, Kh-31P serial production began in 1987 at the Kaliningrad production association "Strela" (now "Zvezda-Strela" research centre).

The development of the upgraded Kh-31PK missile was carried out by equipping the missile with a non-contact detonation sensor and a warhead of increased efficiency. The tactical Kh-31PK with passive homing heads is designed to effectively destroy radars, including those with antenna devices (up to 15m) placed upwards, operating in continuous and pulsed radiation modes.

The range of the missile, increased to 110km, ensures its effective use, out of enemy air defense missile systems. Due to the high speed, combined with the autonomy of guidance, an advantage is also provided in situations when the launch is made within the ranges of the SAM system.

At present, an improved Kh-31PD missile with an increased flight range of up to 250km is being proposed. In addition, a variant of an air-to-air missile is being developed to combat AWACS aircraft.

The Kh-31P is made according to a normal aerodynamic configuration with an X-shaped arrangement of the wing and rudders. The missile consists of three compartments. Each compartment is a structurally and functionally complete block. On the body in the plane of the bearing surfaces, there are four sides of round supersonic air intakes, closed with conical plugs dropped in flight. The Kh-31P missile is equipped with a high-explosive fragmentation warhead. The modernized Kh-31PD missile is equipped with a multi-purpose cassette, weighing 110kg, of increased blast and fragmentation power.

The 31DPK rocket motor includes air intakes, fuel tanks with a displacement system and fuel dosing equipment, a front device, a combustion chamber with an unregulated supersonic nozzle, and an electro-hydraulic ignition control system.

A solid propellant launch booster is located in the combustion chamber of the propulsion motor, which, after separation of the missile from the carrier aircraft, reliably ensures its acceleration to the launch speed of the propulsion ramjet. After the end of work, the starting accelerator is pushed out by the oncoming airflow. The use of such an integrated propulsion system provides an increase in the average trajectory speed and firing range while reducing the dimensions of the missile. The combustion chamber of a ramjet engine has an air curtain cooling system, which significantly increases the allowable operating time and opens almost unlimited possibilities for rocket modification. The specific fuel consumption during the operation of the ramjet 31DPK is about six times lower than that of the solid propellant rocket motor, and low smoke increases the secrecy of the flight. The original solution provided an independent launch of a missile from a ramjet (usually requiring booster stages), and stable operation at maximum specific impulse. The design of the 31DPK is simple, it is compact and inexpensive to manufacture, but it is highly reliable. And the use of solid fuel in the ramjet simplifies the storage and operation of the rocket. At high speed, the rocket is able to perform maneuvers with high overloads, reaching 10g in tests.

The Kh-31PD guidance system includes an inertial system and a wide-range L-112E passive radar homing head (PRGS) (Figure 5-34).

The Kh-31PD missile can be used in two modes: jointly with target acquisition for auto-tracking of the PGSN on a suspension under the carrier aircraft and in autonomous mode with target acquisition for auto-tracking of the homing head on the missile flight path after launch. The choice of mode is made by the crew of the carrier aircraft, depending on the flight altitude and target detection range. PRGS provides search and capture of a target according to the data of the carrier equipment or autonomously, as well as tracking the target and generating signals for missile guidance. After detecting it, the pilot directs the aircraft to the target and enters the target designation data into the missile. After launch, the missile enters the climb mode according to the program. It moves further upon reaching a certain target sighting angle.

The older Kh-58U missile (which uses a different layout and components) was designed with the same purpose as the Kh-31 series. The missile was designed at the Raduga Design Bureau led by the chief designer I.S. Seleznev. The main carrier of the missiles was a specialized MiG-25BM aircraft. The development of the PRGS-58 homing head and the "Jaguar" aircraft system, which provides detection of radar targets, was entrusted to the Omsk Central Design Bureau of Automation. Under the name of Kh-58U (U for unified) the missile also became part of the armament of the Su-24 and Su-24M. The Kh-58U has an increased flight range and differs from the Kh-58 with a new motor and improved aerodynamic plumage.

Ukraine had some quantities (leftovers from the Soviet period) at the beginning of the war but it cannot be confirmed that any of their Su-24M

Figure 5-34: Kh-31 seeker (top). (*Source*: missiliery.info); destroyed Ukrainian S-300 5N63 fire-control radar (bottom). (*Source*: Russian MoD)

have ever been used by them in combat. There is some evidence that some missiles were sold to the US.

AGM-88 HARM
The AGM-88 HARM (High-speed Anti-Radiation Missile) is a US-made tactical, air-to-surface anti-radiation missile designed to home in on electronic transmissions coming from surface-to-air radar systems. It was designed specifically to detect, attack, and destroy a radar antenna or electromagnetic waves transmitter within the specific bands and with

minimum airplane crew involvement. Guidance is a proportional system that locks and homes in on enemy radar emissions. Constructively it has a fixed antenna and seeker head in the cone. The maximum speed is Mach-2 (Figure 5-35).

The blast-fragmentation type warhead in HARM is designed to destroy enemy radars and vehicles such as command modules. When the missile carrying the warhead reaches a position close to an enemy missile control

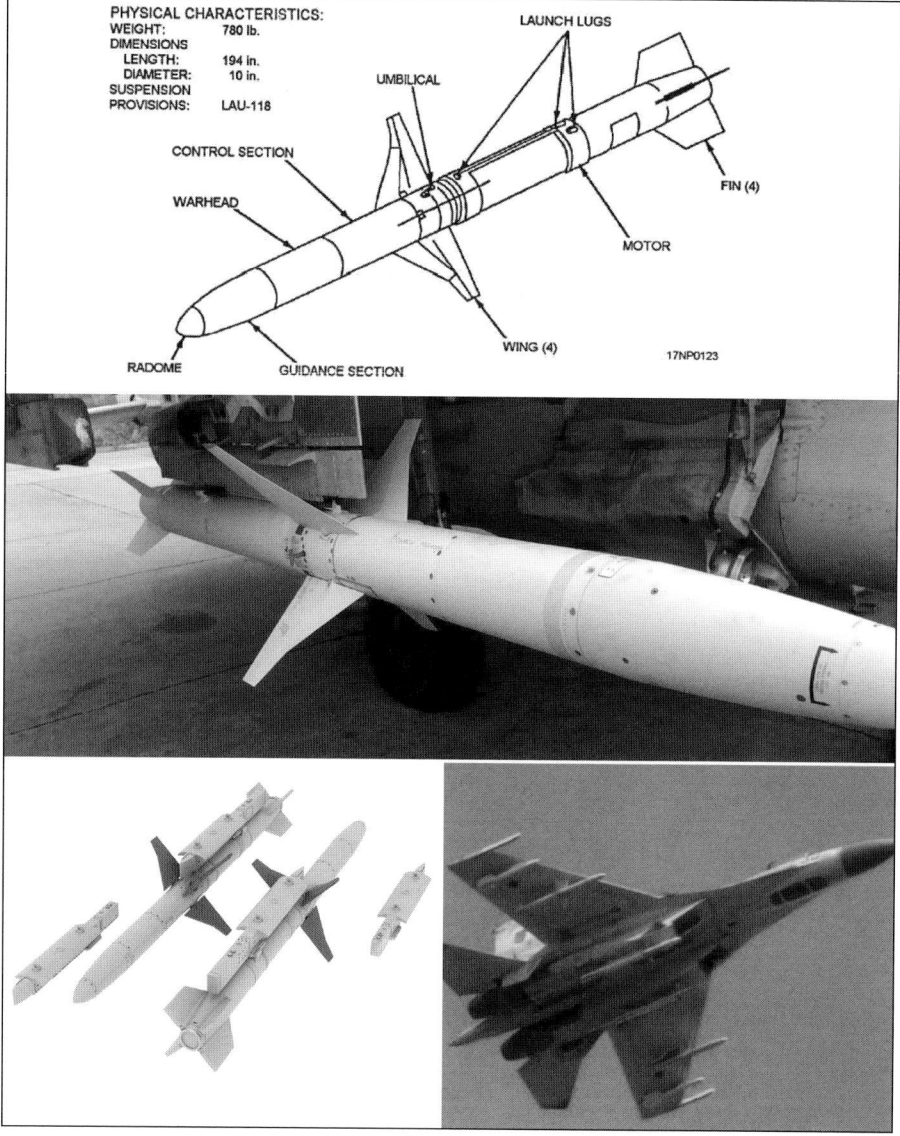

Figure 5-35: AGM-88 HARM (top); Ukrainian HARM launcher adaptor for MigG-29U and Su-27 (middle and bottom). (*Source*: thedrive.com and AGM-88 operation manual)

radar or other target, a pre-scored or pre-made band of metal on the warhead is detonated and pieces of metal are accelerated with high velocity and strike the target. Approximately 30 percent of the energy released by the explosive detonation is used to fragment the case and impart kinetic energy to the fragments. The balance of available energy creates a shock front and blast effects. The fragments overtake and pass through the shock wave after a short distance. The rate at which the velocity of the shock front decreases is generally much greater than the decrease in the velocity of the fragments. The radius of effective fragment damage, although target dependent, thus considerably exceeds the radius of effective blast damage in an air burst. The radar, the guidance station and everything along the way is showered with fragments.

The missile consists of four sections: guidance, warhead, control, and rocket motor. The AGM-88A missile is powered by a Thikol SR113-TC-1 dual-thrust (boost/sustain) low-smoke solid-fuel rocket motor and has a 66kg WDU-21/B blast-fragmentation warhead (25,000 steel fragments) in a WAU-7/B warhead section. The warhead is triggered by an FMU-111/B laser proximity fuze. The seeker of the WGU-2/B guidance section has to be pre-tuned to likely threats at depot-level maintenance, so every base or ship has to store a selection of differently tuned HARM seeker heads. In flight, the AGM-88 is controlled by the WCU-2/B control section using four movable BSU-59/B mid-body fins and stabilized by fixed BSU-60/B tailfins.

The HARM can be used in three different operational modes, known as Pre-Briefed (PB), Target-of-Opportunity (TOO), and Self-Protect (SP). In PB mode, the long range (up to 150km) of the AGM-88 is used to launch the missile on a lofted trajectory towards a known threat. When the HARM reaches lock-on range, and detects the radar emission, it can home in on the target. If the target radar is switched off before a lock can be acquired, the missile destroys itself to avoid possible friendly casualties by the now unguided missile. In SP mode, the aircraft's radar warning receiver is used to detect enemy emissions. The CP-1001B/AWG HARM Command Launch Computer (CLC) then decides which target to attack, transmits the data to the missile, and launches the AGM-88. TOO mode means that the seeker of the AGM-88 itself has detected a target, and the missile can be fired manually if the radar emission is identified as a threat. In SP and TOO modes, the AGM-88 can even be fired at targets behind the launching aircraft, although this of course significantly reduces the missile's range. The AGM-88 missile has an inbuilt inertial system, so that whenever it has acquired a lock once, it will continue towards the target even if the emitter is shut down (although the CEP is larger in this case).

It is known that the US supplied AGM-88 missiles to Ukraine (some of them even dating from the 1990s) and specialists from Raytheon Technologies allegedly helped to adapt HARM for firing from the MiG-29s and Su-27s. An LAU-118/A pylon which is the standard carrier

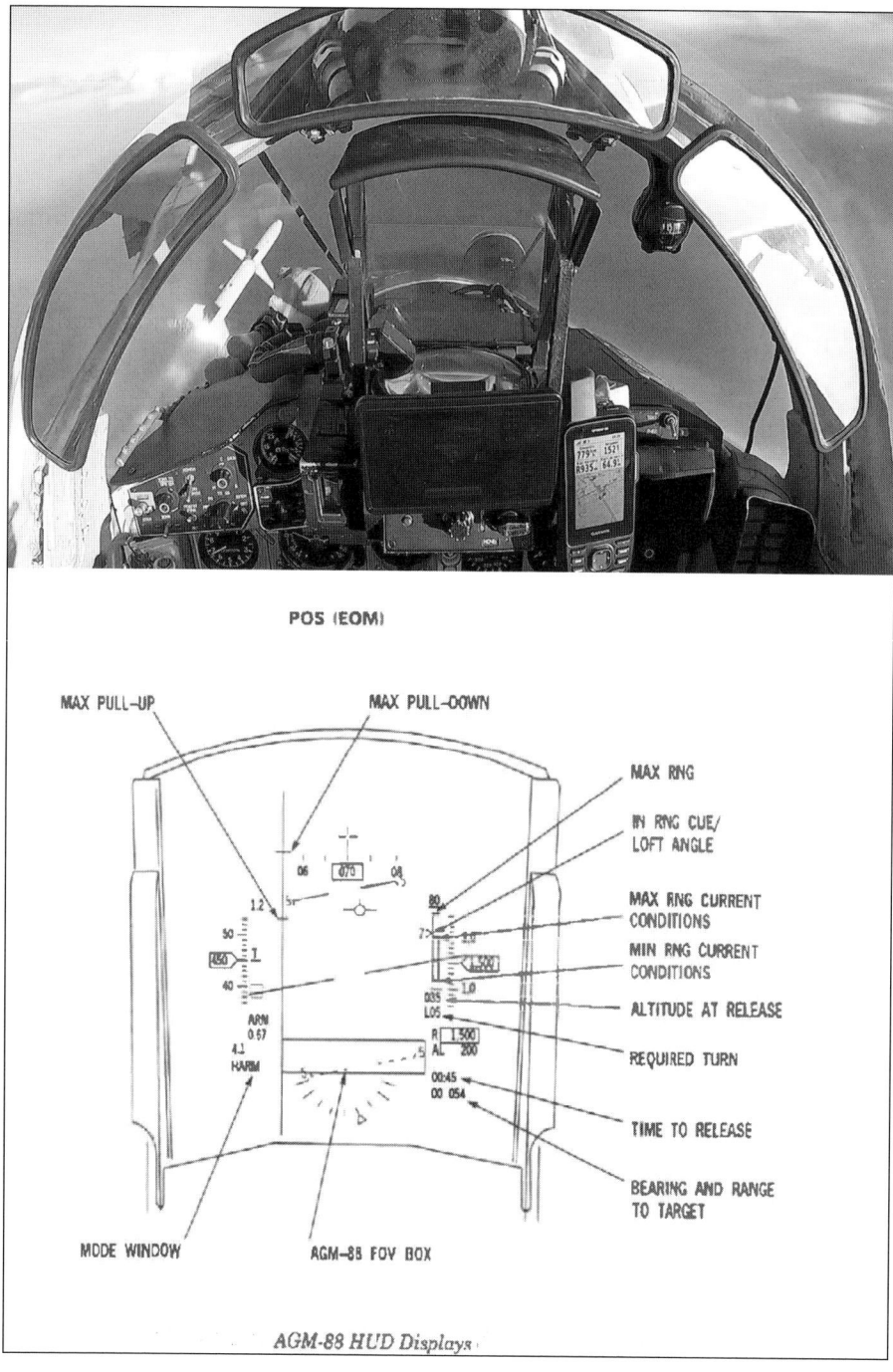

Figure 5-36: Ukrainian MiG-29 HARM launch (top); HUD display for HARM launch on F-16C/D (bottom). Ukrainians are using HARM in target of opportunity mode launching without hood indicator, just as soon as the radar radiation bulb is illuminated. (*Source*: Ukrainian MoD and AGM-88 operation manual)

for a HARM missile is attached to the MiG-29's native pylon with some modifications (Figure 5-35 bottom). During the flight, the AGM-88 HARM is powered by a portable battery attached to the plane. In some airplanes, a cable is stretched from the launcher to the pilot's cabin, and it is connected to a radar radiation sensor and the launch button. The HARM sensor works continuously and is powered by the "external" battery; the launch of the missile occurs immediately after it detects radiation from Russian radars. When it comes to firing the missile, the MiG-29 needs to raise the nose by 20–30° to fire it in an arc trajectory to extend the firing range as much as possible. This is a rather improvised solution but it works. The MiG-29 approaches the radar's expected zone and launches hoping that the missile will lock onto the radar. In a few instances, these missiles scored hits, but the vast majority were downed by Russian AD or diverted and often hit decoys or even metal roofs that reflected electromagnetic radiation (Figures 5-36, 5-37).

One of the tactical applications is to try to "open" the airspace by eliminating Russian radars so the UCAVs and guided missiles can engage the important targets. Russian SHORAD systems have so far been able to intercept a large number of UCAV/UAVs rendering them useless as well

Figure 5-37: Remains of HARM (top); alleged destroyed Russian 9S18M Kupol radar likely not by HARM missile because the antenna was not erected meaning no electromagnetic emission, but still claimed as by Ukrainian HARM in the Western media. (*Source*: t.me/donezkiy and Ukrainian MoD)

as missiles launched by HIMARS. Eliminating SHORADs may create opportunity for larger offensives.

Russian AD and interceptors such as Su-35 are successfully downing Ukrainian MiG-29s in these "quasi-SEAD" attacks.

In the pro-Ukrainian media, AGM-88 has been celebrated as one more "wonder weapon" but in reality the effect is negligible.

Storm Shadow/SCALP

The latest weapon system supplied by the Western allies with high hopes of it being a game changer is a British/French-made Storm Shadow/SCALP air launched missile (Figure 5-38). It is a long-range, deep-strike weapon, intended to engage high-value fixed or stationary targets. It is not known how many have been delivered by the end of May 2023, but anything up to 200 missiles may be considered.

The supplier claims it has the ability to be operated in extreme conditions, with a highly flexible, deep-strike capability based around a sophisticated mission planning system. It also has a low observability (often wrongfully reported by the media as "Stealth").

After launch, the missile, powered by a turbojet engine, descends to a low cruising altitude. Guidance is based on a triple navigation system that uses Inertial Navigation (INS), Global Positioning System (GPS), and Terrain Profile Matching (TERPROM) and Infrared Thermography (IRT). This three-level system provides a high degree of navigational precision. The missile is equipped with an imaging infrared seeker that is activated during the final approach phase. This final phase also requires automatic target recognition algorithms which compare the real scene with the target impact point designated during the mission planning phase.

The missile is equipped with a tandem charge warhead that has two or more stages of detonation, to penetrate reinforced structures. The warhead weight is 450kg and the total missile weight is 1.300kg. During the final phase, it can select the direction and dive angle of attack. The missile is able to engage a variety of targets such as control centers, reinforced aircraft shelters, runways, buildings and bridges, air defense, and ships. Because of this, for Ukrainian planners (and associate NATO advisers) expectations are high, especially with preparations being made for the widely publicized counteroffensive(s).

Storm Shadow can be launched from Tornado, Rafale, Mirage 2000, and in the future Eurofighter and F-35. As Ukraine doesn't have these aircraft, efforts were made by the British/French and Polish teams to design an interim carrier so the missile can be used on the remaining Ukrainian Su-24M bombers. The idea is similar to the application of the AGM-88 anti-radiation missiles on MiG-29 and Su-27 fighters. The Su-24M is just a carrier and it does not have the interface required to operate the missile except a pure

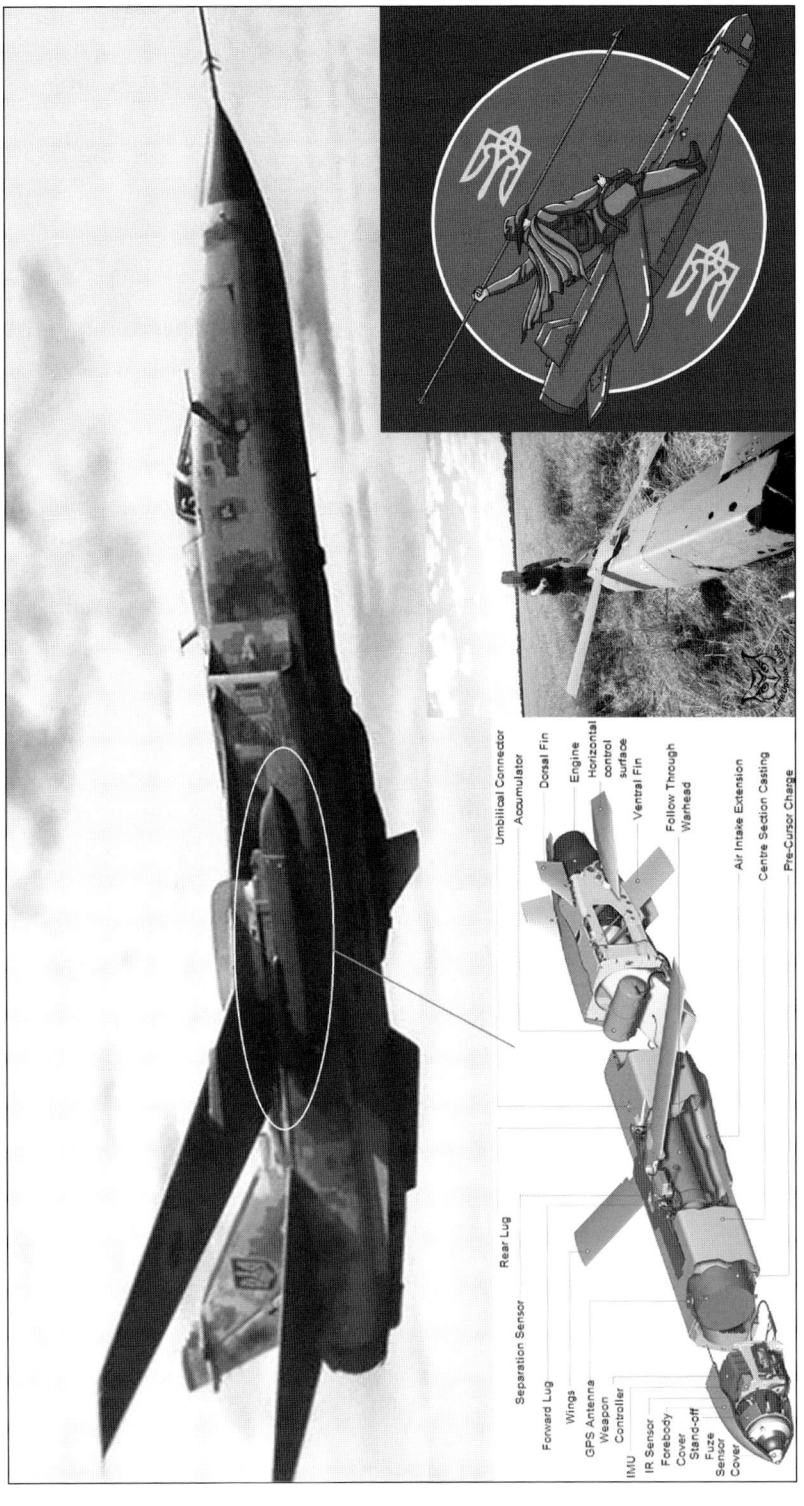

Figure 5-38: Ukrainian Su-24M taking off with attached Storm Shadow, 3D cutaway model, and new logo. Allegedly the photo (a postcard version of which was signed by a British official) was used to pinpoint the location. Consequently, an air attack by Russian forces followed, leading to the destruction of the plane and the stocked missiles.

electrical switch to jettison the missile from the plane at the designated area. The rest is down to the mission planners to load the necessary information for the guidance and that this is executed on the ground.

The Ukrainians have put great faith in this as a game changer, that they can destroy Russian command centers, bases, supply hubs, and especially the Kerch Bridge by launching the missiles from the safe standoff distances without getting into the AD engagement zones. The version they received has a 300km range (an export version) but British Storm Shadows and French SCALPs intended for domestic use will also likely be delivered. Based on the weapon characteristics, there is some merit in the Ukrainians' hope, however, Russia has the most sophisticated and robust AD system in the world and during the first attacks by the end of May 2023, just a few missiles were able to penetrate the AD, and hit some buildings of no military value. The Ukrainian side claims a 100 percent success rate (which is unrealistic). Russian AD claims the interception and destruction of at least twenty Storm Shadows. What is more important, in a few spectacular bombings, Russians were able to destroy the warehouses and Su-24M carriers at the bases as well as the interceptors downing several Su-24M before they were able to launch their missiles. There are also rumors that the combined teams suffered casualties but this information is difficult to verify during the ongoing war. In any case, Storm Shadow is a serious threat and time will tell how effective it may be in Ukraine.

Chapter 6

Surface-to-Air Missiles

Ukraine's battlefield is saturated with a mix of modern and old air defense systems. The air defense weapons in the Ukrainian conflict represent the best ex-Soviet era developments in that field as well as the modern Russian AD systems and Ukrainian "imported" Western systems.

After gaining independence, Ukraine inherited a significant amount of the Soviet air defense systems and among others some of the most modern of that period. On paper, Ukraine was the second best-equipped army regarding air defense in Europe, right behind Russia.

This chapter examines the missiles used by both sides. For greater detail about the Russian systems, development, and tactics please see the author's book *Defending Putin's Empire: Russia's Air Defence System*.

The core of the Ukrainian AD consists of the ex-Soviet systems: long-range S-300PS and S-300V, medium-range Buk-M1, short-range Osa-AKM, Tunguska, Strela-10, and Tor-M as well as the MANPADS such as versions of Igla. From the Western "allies," numerous MANPADS such as the US-made Stinger, British StarStreak, French MISTRAL, Polish Piorun arrived just before the war, and there is ongoing delivery of the modern medium-range NASAMS, IRIS-T, veterans Aspide and HAWK missile systems. In short, there is a mishmash of everything available.

Russia operates many modern systems including the formidable S-400, S-300V4, Buk-M2 and M3, Pantsir-S, Tor-M1 and M2, and MANPADS such as Igla S and Verba.

Long-Range AD Systems

S-300PT/PS/PM
On paper Ukraine inherited about 100 batteries (PT, PS) from the USSR. These batteries were in different states of readiness just prior to the Russian attack. Combat and non-combat losses greatly rendered these batteries non-operational so by November 2022 just a few dozen were left. Lack of maintenance, spare parts, and missiles made this system generally

ineffective. Still, even with that, it is a strong opponent to the RuAF. Russia operates the more modern S-300PM version.

The main combat assets of each battalion include up to four 5P85S/D launchers. The 5P85S/D complex includes the main launcher 5P85S and up to two additional launchers 5P85D. All launchers are mounted on the chassis of four-axle heavy duty off-road vehicle MAZ-543M and carry four transport and launch containers with 5V55 missiles of various modifications.

The main missile of the S-300PS complex is 5V55R (V-500R) with a range of up to 75km (according to some sources, 90km); 5V55KD missiles are also used (Figures 6-1 to 6-4).

The deployment time from marching to combat position is 5 minutes, the transition from standby to combat mode is determined by the time of

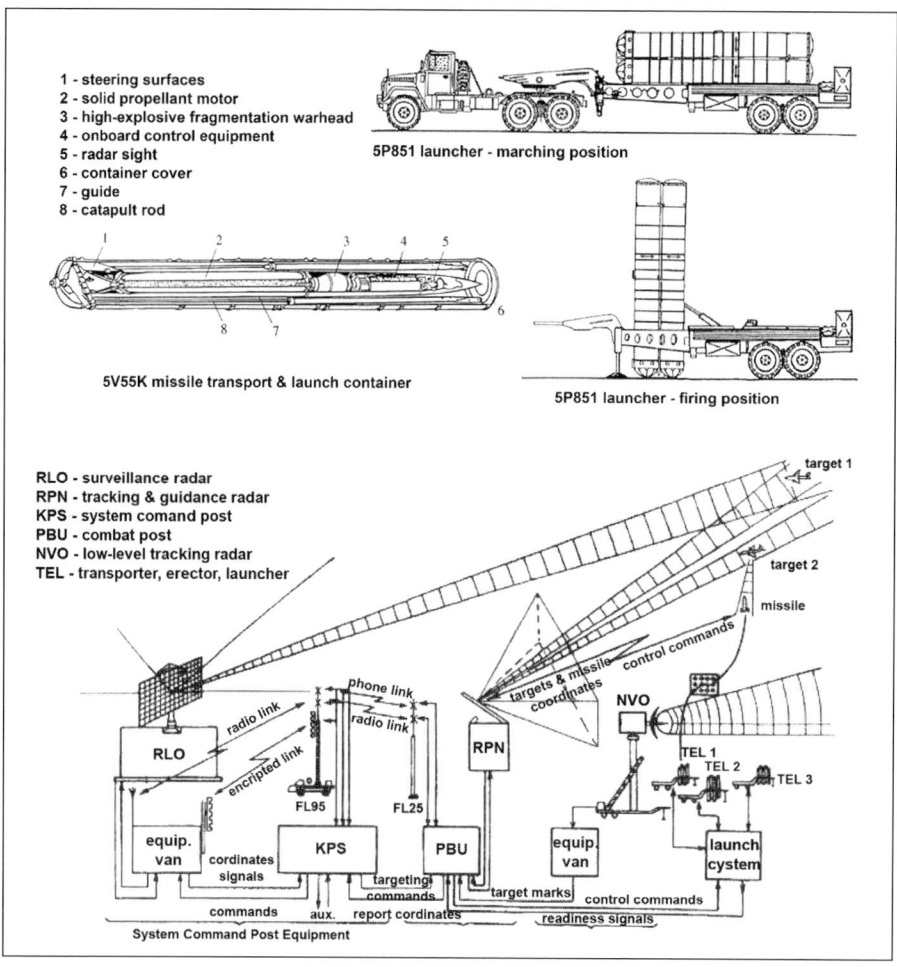

Figure 6-1: 5P851 launcher with 5V55 missile (top); S-300 PS/PM guidance loop (bottom). (*Source*: M. Mihajlović, *Defending Putin's Empire: Russia's Air Defence System* (2023))

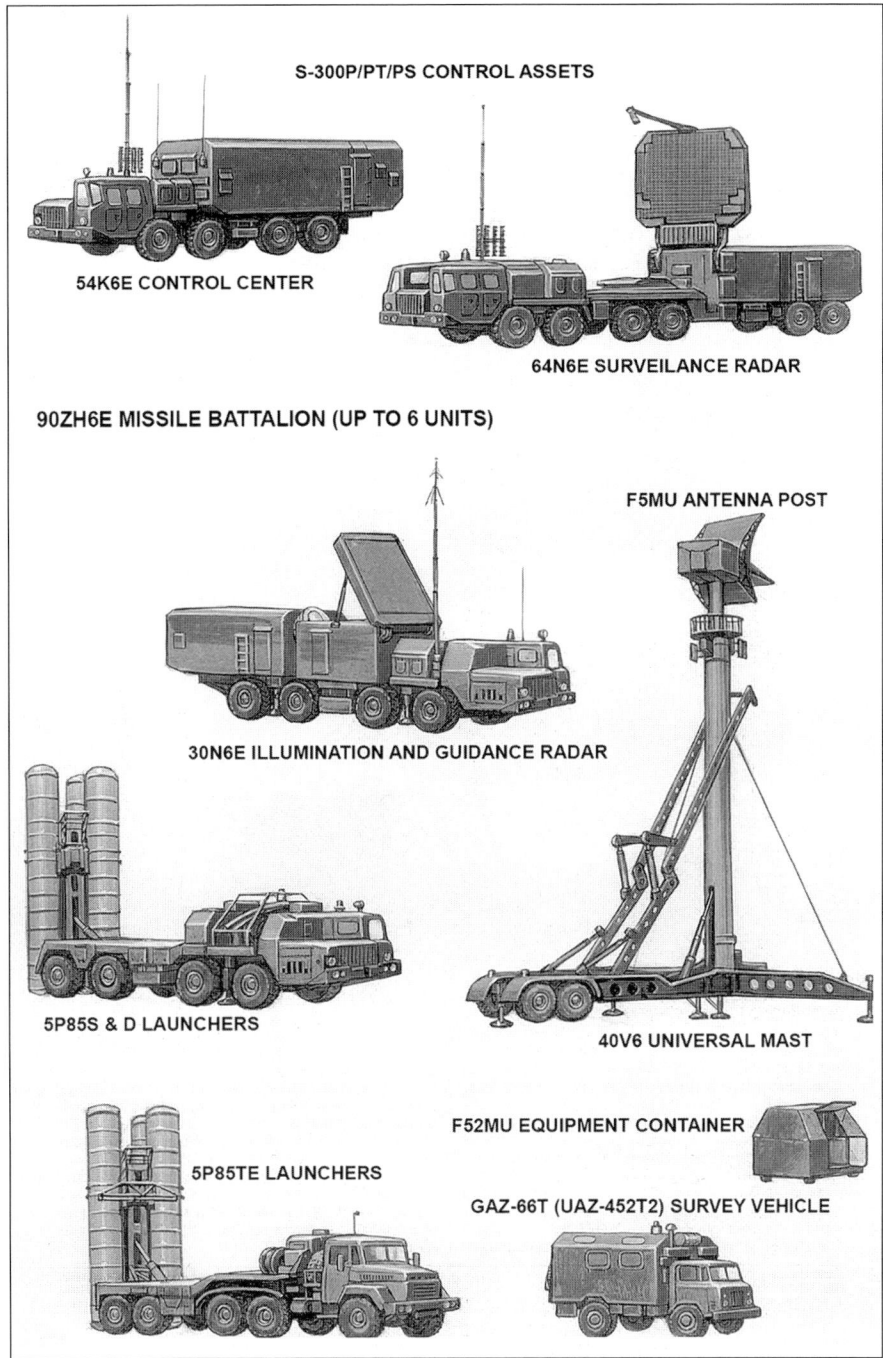

Figure 6-2: S-300 command and control assets. This is the typical battery used on the Ukrainian side. The standard configuration is with four launchers, but the attrition often renders one or two launchers. (*Source*: M. Mihajlović, *Defending Putin's Empire: Russia's Air Defence System* (2023)

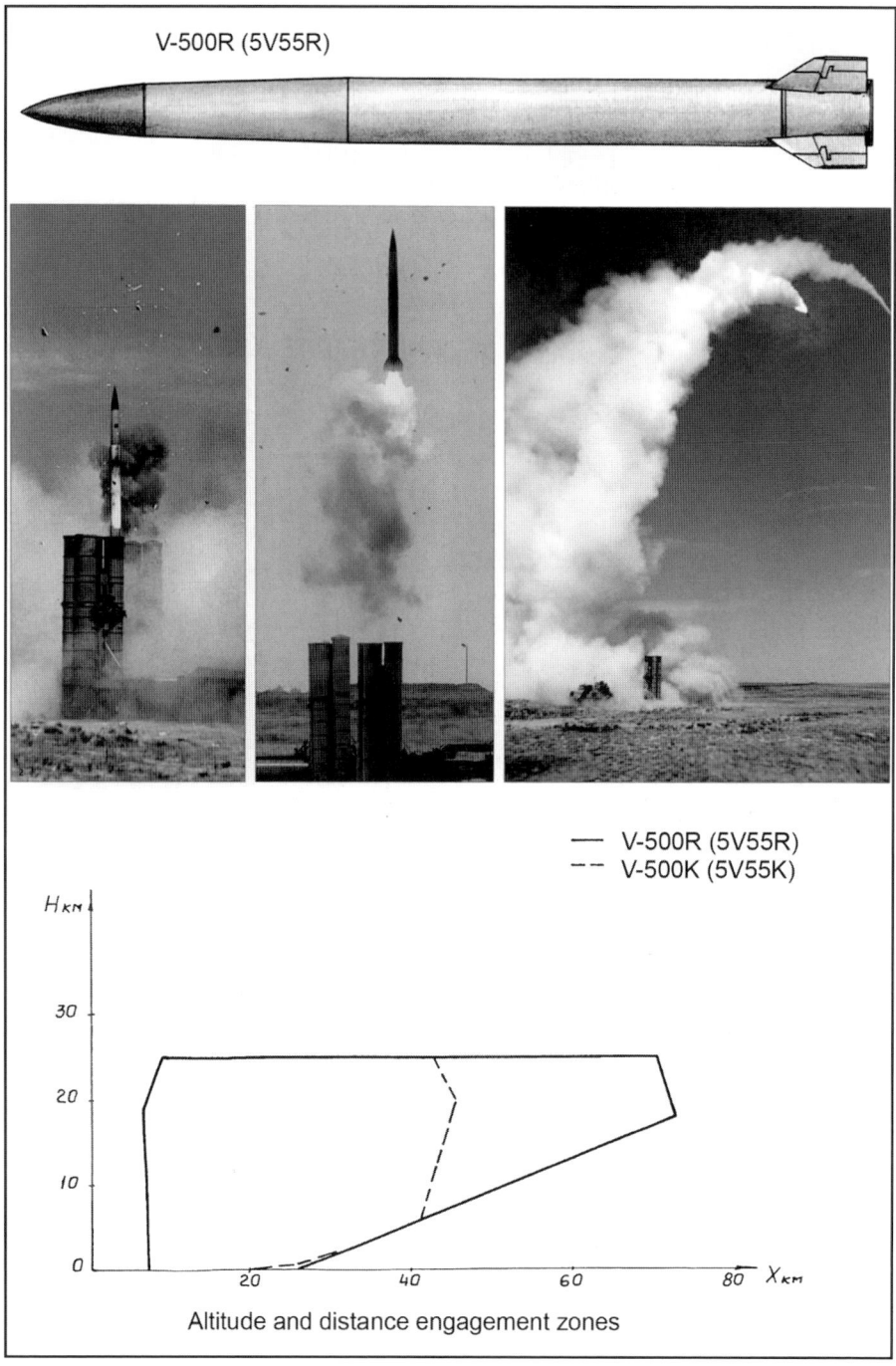

Figure 6-3: 5V55R and 5V55K missiles. The launcher uses a cold start which catapults the missile from the container after which the rocket motor ignites. The optimal target engagement is up to two-thirds of the maximum range. (*Source*: M. Mihajlović, *Defending Putin's Empire: Russia's Air Defence System* (2023))

SURFACE-TO-AIR MISSILES

Figure 6-4: Ukrainian 30N6 with victory marks of destroyed targets that includes a mixture of drones, cruise missiles, and an airplane. These marks are highly likely exaggerated. The system can engage drones and cruise missiles, but this is not its primary role. Ukrainians are known to display false victory numbers (top); destroyed Ukrainian S-300PS battery (bottom). Ukrainian AD was based on the ex-Soviet systems and available ones are multiple decades old, far beyond their shelf life. The attrition reduced the available missile quantities to very low levels and there is no way that any NATO country can supply these in more than symbolic numbers (such as Bulgaria and Greece). The ex-Slovakian S-300PMU system was destroyed before entering the combat. Russia is succeeding in grinding the Ukrainian IADS and it is just a matter of time before the ex-Soviet heritage is eliminated. The danger is that the Western supplies are not even close to being sufficient to close the sky. (*Source*: Author's archive and Russian MoD)

automatic monitoring of the functioning of the complex systems and the output of transmitters to high-voltage mode. All operations are carried out by combat crews from the launching vehicle's cabin and CP.

The rate of fire is 3–5 seconds, and up to six targets can be fired at the same time with twelve missiles when engaging each target with two missiles. There is a mode of shooting at ground targets as well.

S-300V
Conceptually, the S-300V is designed as a multi-channel mobile all-weather AD system. It is equipped with two types of missile to be a ground forces air defense weapon and engage ground- and air-based ballistic missiles, cruise missiles, strategic and tactical aircraft, EW/ECM aircraft, and attack helicopters, under conditions of their mass use, in a complex air and ECM environment, when the protected troops conduct mobile operations (Figure 6-5).

The business end of this system against both operational tactical ballistic missiles and aircraft comprises two types of missiles: 9M82 and 9M83.

The 9A82 TELAR carries two 9M82 SAM/ABMs, and the 9A83 TELAR carries four 9M83 SAM/ABMs. Each TELAR is equipped with a steerable high-gain antenna used to transmit midcourse guidance commands to the missiles and provide continuous wave illumination of the target for the missiles' semi-active radar seekers during the terminal guidance.

The 9M82 ("Type I") and 9M83 ("Type II") missiles are two-stage solid-fuel vertical launch missiles, made according to the aerodynamic scheme "bearing cone" (Figures 6-6, 6-7).

Figure 6-5: Two types of launchers (9A83 and 9A82) and missile-guidance radar 9S32.

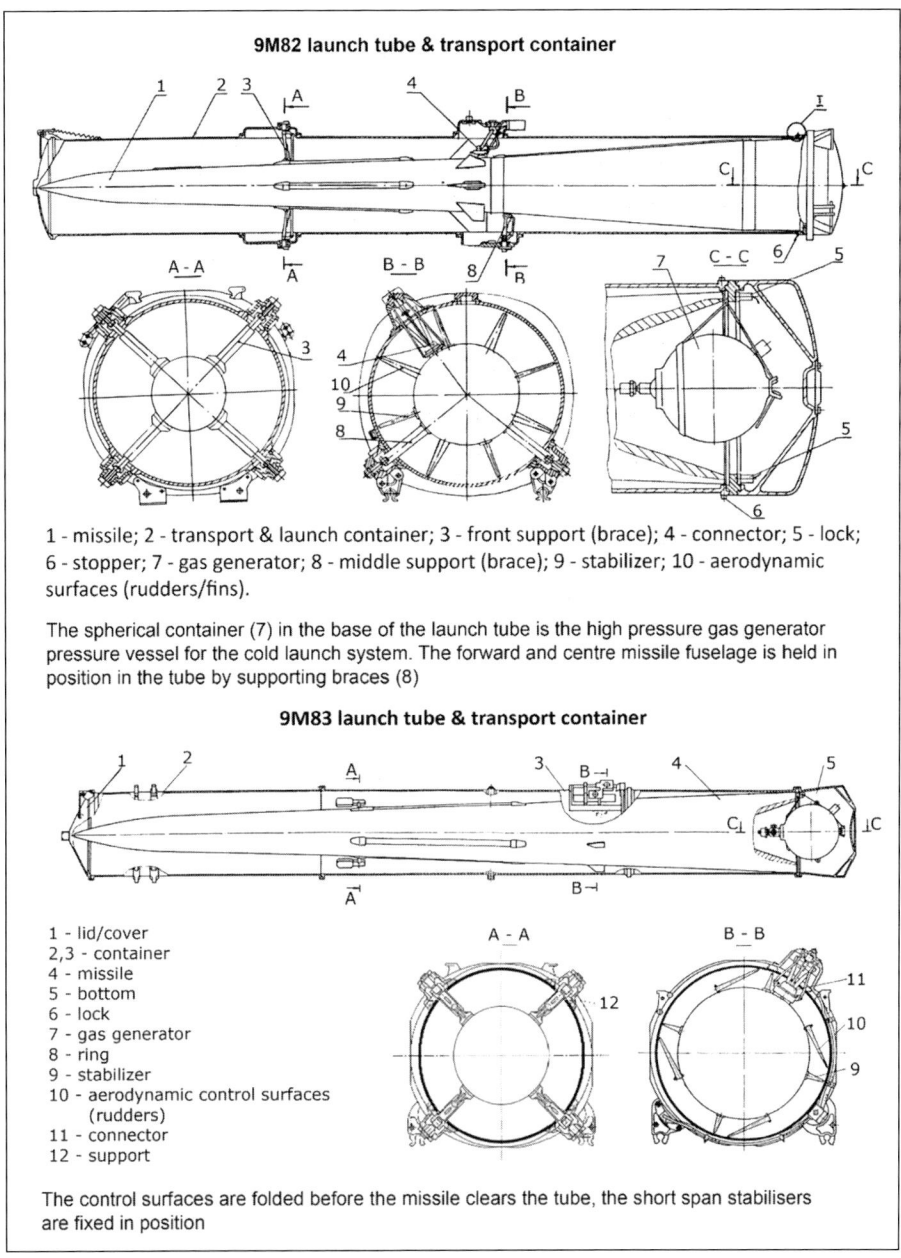

Figure 6-6: 9M82 and 9M83 missiles in TLC (Transport-Launch Container). (*Source*: M. Mihajlović, *Defending Putin's Empire: Russia's Air Defence System* (2023))

The method of guiding missiles is a combined inertial output with semi-active homing in the final part of the flight. As the missile approaches the target, it will perform a rolling maneuver to align the directional warhead with the plane of the target. The proximity fuzed warhead produces a

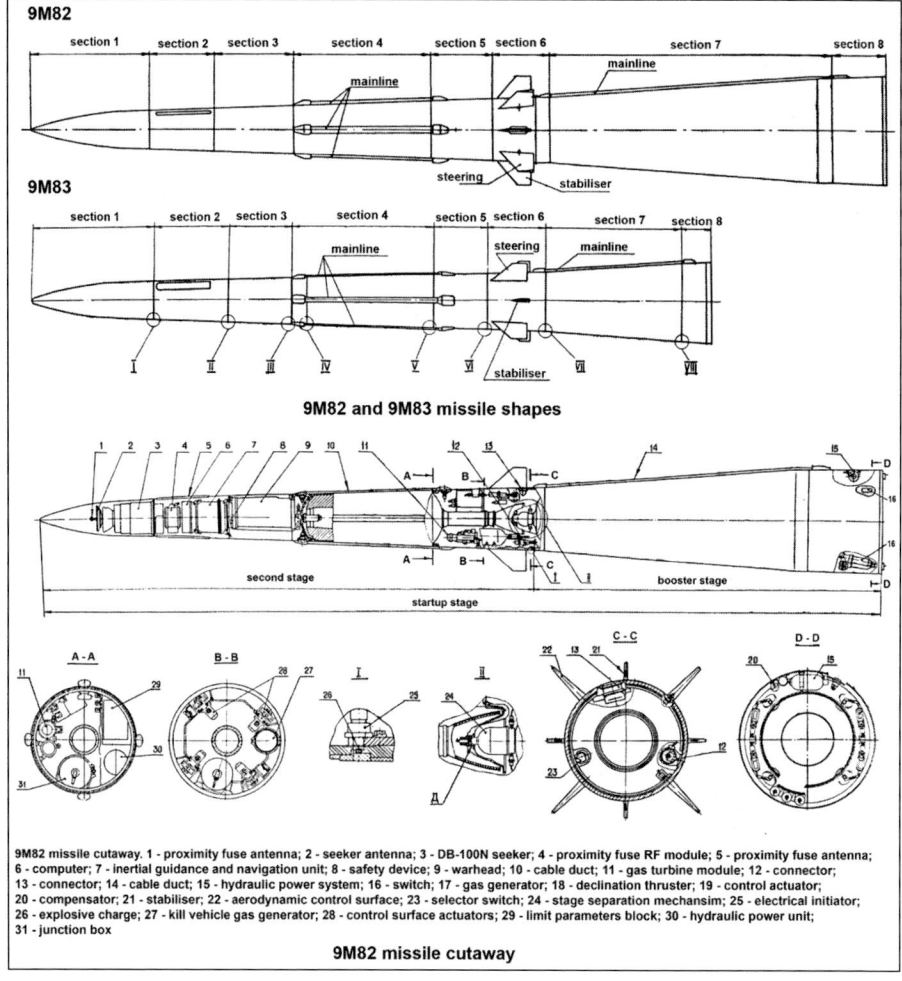

Figure 6-7: 9M82 and 9M83 planner and 9M82 cutaway. (*Source*: M. Mihajlović, *Defending Putin's Empire: Russia's Air Defence System* (2023))

high-velocity stream of fragments in a narrow cone normal to the axis of the missile. The 9M82 Giant missile velocity entering the endgame is ~3.5M (Figure 6-9).

The warhead weighing 150kg is a high-explosive fragmentation-directed action (Figure 6-8). When approaching the target, an additional turn of the missile is made to roll for the appropriate orientation of the warhead and the destruction of the target by a dense stream of heavy fragments (weighing 15g each). The detonation of the warhead is carried out based on the type of target: in the area of the warhead when firing at a ballistic missile (the target is hit with the explosion of its warhead or its removal from the calculated trajectory) and in the area of the center of the glider when firing at aircraft.

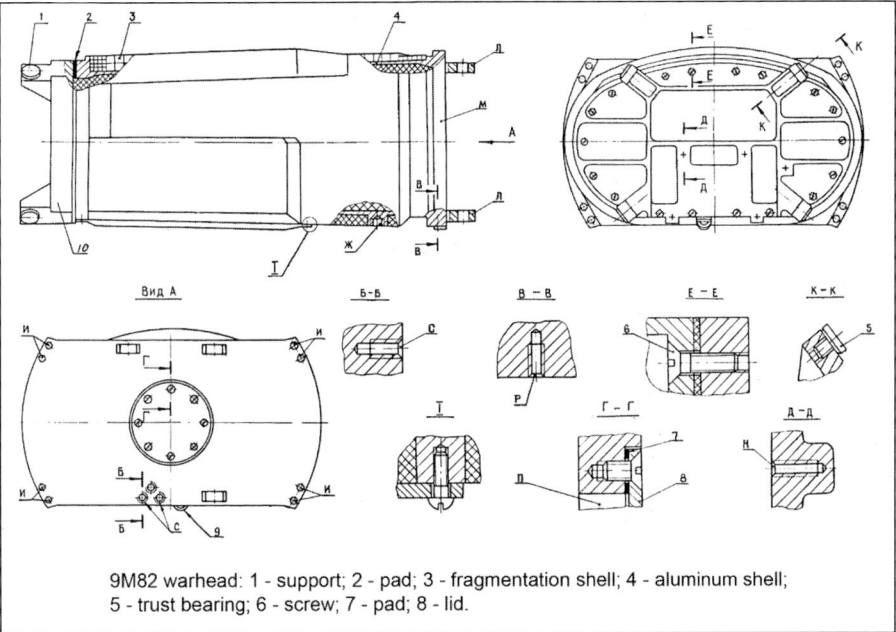

Figure 6-8: 9M82 warhead. (*Source*: M. Mihajlović, *Defending Putin's Empire: Russia's Air Defence System* (2023))

Up to two missiles with one launcher or up to four missiles with two launchers can be guided to each target at the same time.

The 9M82 missile is designed to defeat operational-tactical ballistic missiles at ranges up to 40km, and aeroballistic missiles, aerodynamic targets, including active jamming aircraft at ranges up to 100km.

The 9M83 missile is designed to defeat aerodynamic targets, including maneuvering with an overload of up to 7–8g, ballistic, aeroballistic, and cruise missiles.

The first combat application of this system was in Ukraine where it has been engaged in intercepting the Ukrainian 9M79-1 ballistic missiles launched by OTR-21 Tochka-U. According to the verified information, S-300V was able to intercept almost all missiles. The Russian S-300V also holds the longest AD kill of 217km when two Ukrainian Su-24s were downed.

S-400

This system is the latest addition to the family of operational Russian long-range AD systems. One brigade, comprising up to 8 battalions, can control up to 72 launchers, with a maximum of 384 missiles (Figure 6-11). The missiles are fired by a gas system from the launch tubes up to 30m into the air before the rocket motor ignites, which increases the maximum and decreases the minimum ranges. In April 2015 a successful test firing

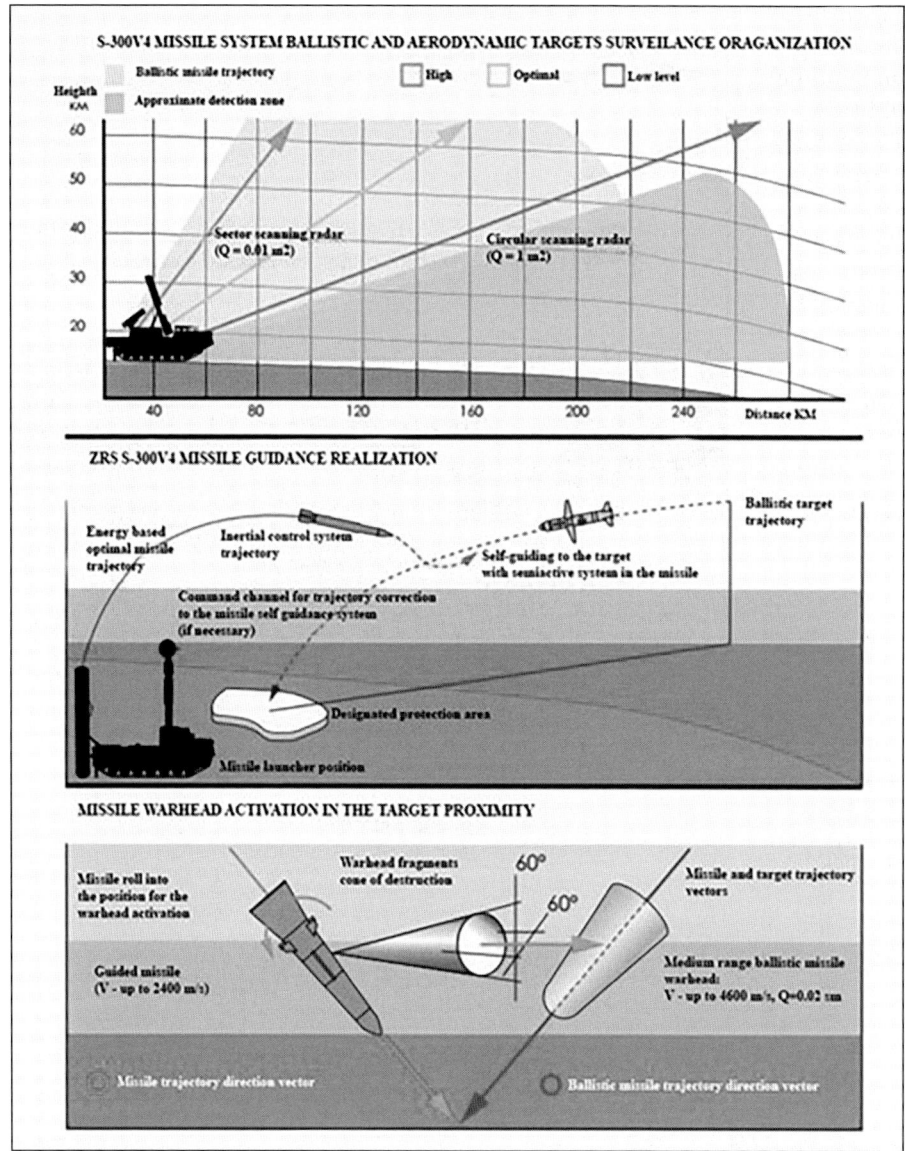

Figure 6-9: S-300V4 surveillance, guidance, and warhead activation. (*Source*: M. Mihajlović, *Defending Putin's Empire: Russia's Air Defence System* (2023))

of the missile was conducted at an airborne target at a range of 400km; TELs carrying the long-range 40N6 may only be able to hold two missiles instead of the typical four due to its larger size. Another test recorded a 9M96 missile using an active radar homing head reaching a height of 56km. All the missiles are equipped with directed explosion warheads, which increases the probability of complete destruction of targets (Figure 6-10).

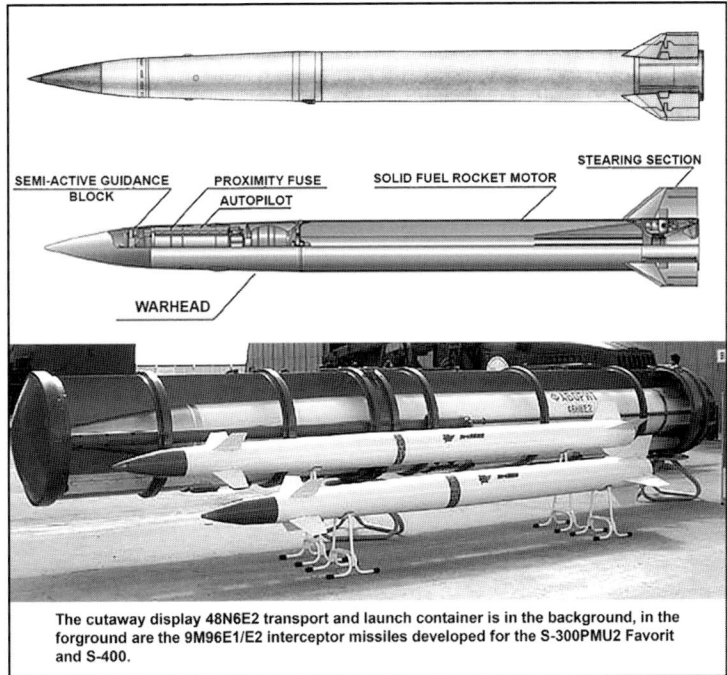

Figure 6-10: 48N6 (top and middle); 9M96E1/E2 (bottom). (The letter 'E' stands for 'export'.) (*Source*: M. Mihajlović, *Defending Putin's Empire: Russia's Air Defence System* (2023))

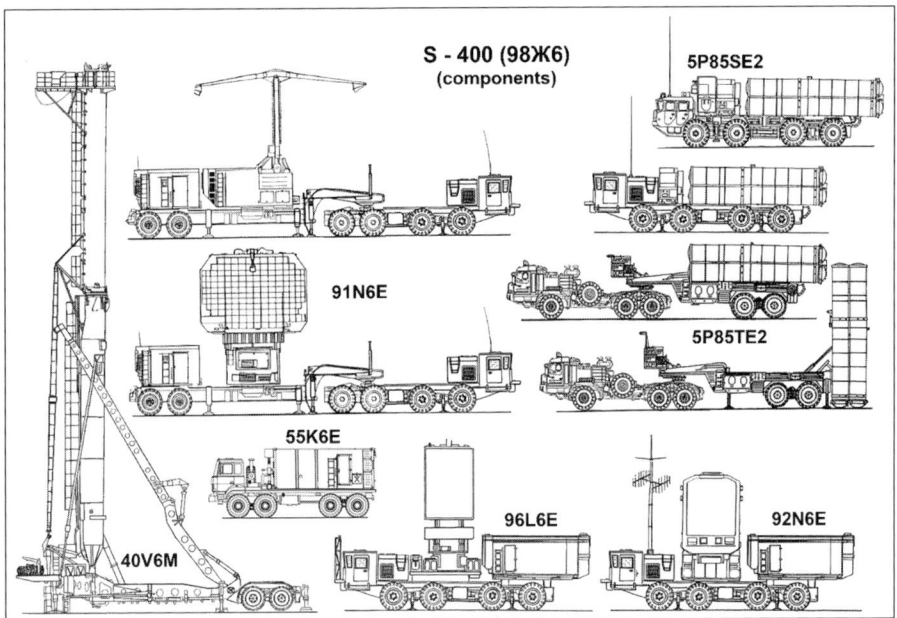

Figure 6-11: S-400 combat unit typical components. (*Source*: M. Mihajlović, *Defending Putin's Empire: Russia's Air Defence System* (2023))

S-400 ammunition includes 48N6M (export designation 48N6E2) and 48N6DM (export 48N6E3) missiles. Those used by the Russians and export missiles have some differences. The 48N6E missile may also be in use. The 48N6E and 48N6E2 missiles are similar to those the Favorit air defense missile system employs (Figure 6-12).

A new 48N6DM has been developed by upgrading the 48N6M. The motor has been enhanced by using a solid propellant grain with higher energetic characteristics offering an opportunity to expand the engagement zone at the outer boundary and to increase the employed engagement zones of ballistic missiles.

Figure 6-12: 40N6E, 40N6E2, 9M96E2, and 9M96E1 missiles. (*Source*: M. Mihajlović, *Defending Putin's Empire: Russia's Air Defence System* (2023))

Upgrade of the missile payload, i.e. a radio fuze with the controlled warhead, has improved the effectiveness of high-speed, small, maneuvering targets, also providing for high probability of initiation of the high-explosive war payload of ballistic targets, including medium-range ballistic missiles flying at up to 4,800m/s.

In the war in Ukraine, a Russian S-400 was able to engage and shoot down a Ukrainian Su-27 fighter at a distance of more than 150km (launched from the Belarus territory and hitting the target over Kiev) in the first combat engagement. It was also engaged in Crimea downing numerous Ukrainian UAVs. At the time of writing, the combat results have not been disclosed by the authorities.

Patriot

The Pentagon announced that it will transfer one MIM-104 Patriot battery to Ukraine in 2023. For the time being, this is far more of a political statement than something of real tactical value.

The MIM-104 is the first US-made fully digital deployable land-based SAM system. It is designed to defend specific strategic objects and areas on the assumption that the US/NATO have quickly gained air superiority. It can operate as part of integrated AD or in stand-alone mode. It can acquire target data and coordinates from multiple sources to create a real-time tactical map which makes it unnecessary to use the radar of the battery in some cases before missile guidance (Figure 6-13).

It is often compared with S-300P/PS but there are fundamental differences and, in general, the expert opinion is that the Patriot is an inferior system. The basic composition of a Patriot battery is essentially different from any previous SAM systems even compared to the most similar S-300PT/PS. The S-300 family is frequently compared with Patriot regardless of the fact that their basic design conceptions are mostly different. Some major differences include:

- 360° missile launch and target-tracking capability are not possible concerning a single Patriot battery. For a single battery the main threat is from a direction not covered by the radar and from that direction a single battery is defenseless and is not able to see and engage any target. Patriot has only 270° missile launch capabilities,
- Patriot is not as mobile as S-300,
- The Patriot has a single radar for target acquisition/search and fire control (missile guidance). It was designed assuming other sources such as other Patriot batteries, AWACS, other static radars, etc. are available to create a picture of the tactical situation.

The Patriot system has four major operational functions: communications, command and control, radar surveillance, and missile guidance. A full Patriot battalion typically consists of six batteries, although this can vary.

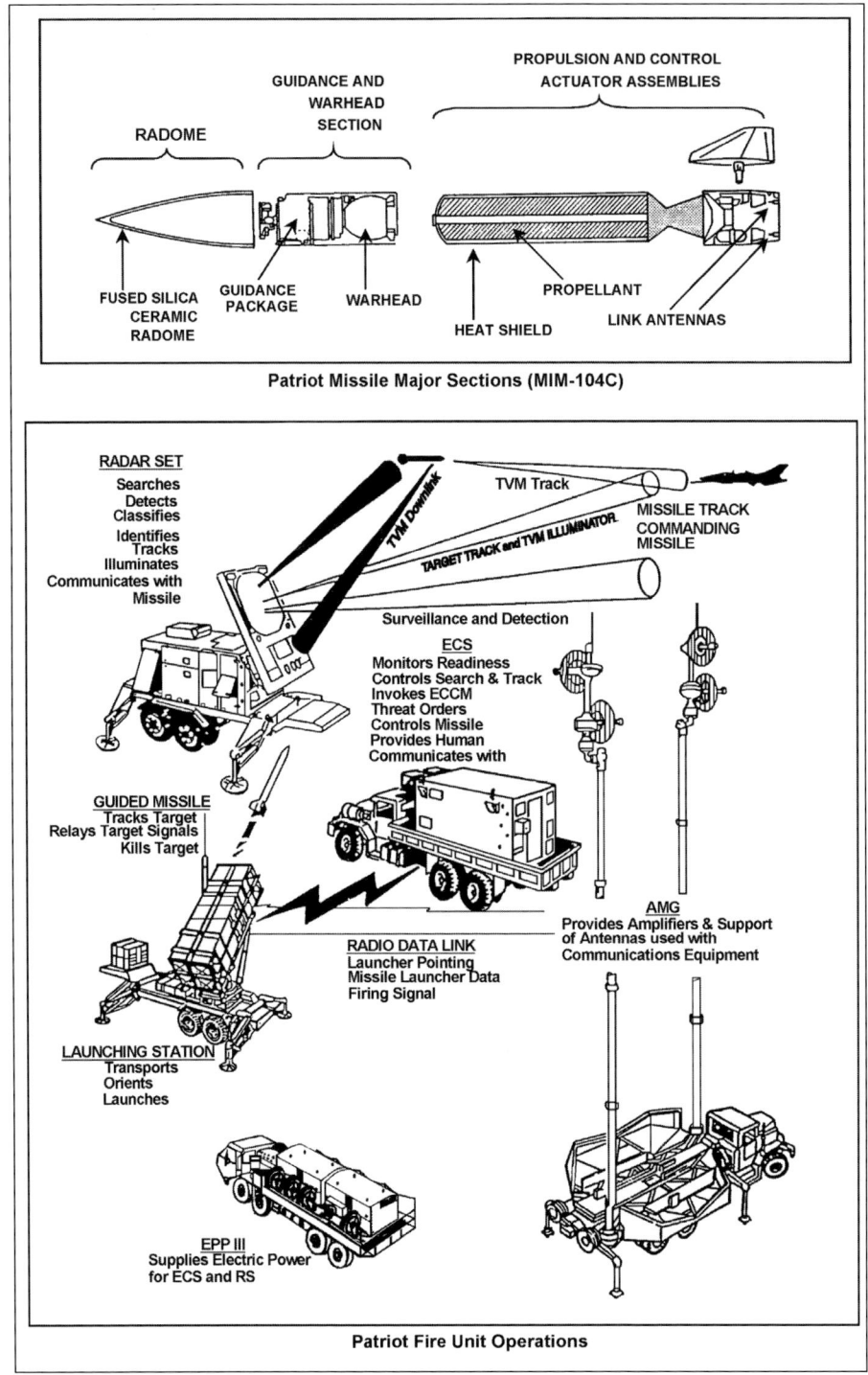

Figure 6-13: Patriot components. (*Source*: FM3-01.11)

The main equipment of a battery comprises:

- Fire control/guidance and command center engagement control station (ECS),
- Target acquisition and fire control radar,
- Missile launchers (launching station-LS) in two sections in total 8 pcs (2x4) vehicles,
- Electric power plant (EPP) with 2x150kW capacity.

The Patriot radar station is not manned meaning that a hit by an anti-radiation missile may disable the radar but not eliminate the crew (another difference between this and the S-300P/PS radar). The radar is placed ahead of the command station meaning that one battery can cover only 270°. The second battery is needed for full coverage. For Ukraine, one battery is very vulnerable because 90° is not covered and from that direction Russian drones or missiles can attack. The radar has ± 45° azimuth limitation for target acquisition and ±55° for target tracking. From the 270° zone only within 90° arcs is it useful for target search and 110° for target tracking.

The launchers are divided into two sections. Half of them can launch missiles to the left and main zone another half to the right and main zone. This is a consequence of the slant angle and hot launch method missile motor starting in the launch container.

According to some information, at the initial stage, Ukraine received at least two Patriot systems (some sources also mention three). One came from the US and one from Germany. It is assumed these are the MIM-104C (PAC-2) and MIM-104F (PAC-3) versions. The MIM104C will use a PAC-2 missile with the capacity to engage Russian ballistic missiles (in theory). The warhead with a dual-mode fuze contains a more powerful explosive and larger fragments designed to place sufficient kinetic energy on the ballistic missile warhead section to achieve a kill. The dual-mode fuze allows the PAC-2 missile to retain anti-aircraft performance and also optimize performance against ballistic missiles. The system software based on the mission selected for the missile sets the fuze mode. The Guidance Enhancement Missile is an improved PAC-2 missile. A "Low Noise Front End" and improved fuze have increased lethality and expanded ballistic-missile engagement volume.

The PAC-3 missile family in MIM-104F is a departure from the original PAC-2 design. While the PAC-2 uses blast-fragmentation warheads, PAC-3 uses hit-to-kill technology to engage the targets. PAC-3 has a higher maneuverability and utilizes a more responsive airframe design and an array of 180 solid-fueled attitude control motors (ACM) mounted in its forward section. The PAC-3 also features an active Ka-band radar seeker for endgame guidance. With its smaller diameter, lighter weight, and newer propulsion system, the PAC-3 can reportedly defend an area seven times greater than the PAC-2.

The PAC-2 has an operational range of 160km, and the PAC-3's operational range is 30km against ballistic missiles. The PAC-3 MSE (Medium Extended Air-Defense System) version has a 60km operational range. These declared characteristics, at least on paper, provide the Ukrainian side with the ability to protect the capital city of Kiev and the surrounding area against Russian ballistic (Iskander), aeroballistic (Kinzhal), and cruise missiles and suicide drones.

What can Patriot achieve in Ukraine? Basically not much, just trying not to be destroyed. It can't work with the existing IADS; it can't communicate with the Soviet-made Ukrainian equipment; it has limited engagement zone and mobility; and it requires a strong maintenance base. As mentioned previously, this donation by the US is a political gesture with next to zero military value without a minimum quantity of at least ten battalions (thirty batteries).

In May 2023 Patriots tried to draw "first blood" against the Russian air raids. It was claimed by Ukrainian sources that they achieved a 100 percent destruction rate of incoming missiles (including hypersonic Kinzhals and Shahid/Geran drones) which is difficult to believe because that percentage is impossible even in the simulations. The truth is that the Patriots (either with the foreign crews or the mixed NATO and Ukrainian crews) tried to engage and launched against the incoming missiles and drones but were targeted and two batteries were hit losing radars and launchers. The crews indiscriminately launched all missiles to avoid secondary explosions after the AD site was hit. Some of those missiles fell in urban areas.

Medium-Range Systems

BUK family

The workhorse of the Ukrainian medium range AD is the Buk-M1 system (Figures 6-14, 6-20). The Russians use much modern versions such as Buk-M1-2, Buk-M2, and Buk-M3 (Figure 6-15).

Visually, in Buk-M1 the notable 9S35 Fire Dome radar housing provides a limited search and acquisition capability, a tracking capability and illumination for terminal guidance of the semi-active homing seekers. It incorporates an IFF interrogator, optical tracker, datalink, and is powered by the TELAR's gas-turbine generator.

The 9K317 Buk M2 introduced the new Tikhomirov NIIP 9S36 passive phased array engagement radar.

The system family uses 9M38M1, 9M317 and 9M317E missiles (Figures 6-16 to 6-19).

Figure 6-14: Ukrainian 9A310 launcher with 9M38M missiles. (*Source*: Ukrainian MoD)

The principal tactical element of the Buk system capable of performing combat missions independently is a battalion. The SAM battalion can perform air defense missions in the interests of combined-arms formations in all types of combat, protect high-value objectives (territories), simultaneously engage up to six aerodynamic targets or six ballistic missiles at a distance of up to 140km, or attack six waterborne or ground targets. As a tactical module, the SAM battalion (regiment) protects an area of about 800–1,200km.

The latest modernization of the Buk family is the 9K317M, or the Buk-M3 "Viking." It is a modernized version of the Buk-M2, features advanced electronic components and a deadly new missile and could be regarded as a completely new system. The Buk-M3 system boasts a new digital computer, high-speed data exchange system, and a tele-thermal imaging target designator instead of the tele-optical trackers used in previous models. A battery of Buk-M3 missiles can track and engage up to thirty-six targets simultaneously, while its advanced 9R31M missile is capable of knocking down all existing flying objects, including highly maneuverable ones, even during active electronic jamming. The Buk-M3 can launch vertically and can engage sea and land targets.

A Buk-M3 missile battery consists of two TELAR 9A317M and one TEL 9A316M vehicles. The TELAR is based on the GM-569 tracked armored chassis and carries six ready-to-fire missiles mounted on a turntable that can traverse a full 360°. The turret of the Buk-M3 TELAR includes fire-control radar at the front and a launcher with six ready-to-fire missiles on top.

The new 9R31M missile is radar guided. The Buk-3M's target-destruction probability has been tested to 0.9999. It can destroy any type of air target

Figure 6-15: Russian 9A317 Buk-M2 TELAR (top); 9A317M Buk-M3 TELAR (bottom). (*Source*: Vitaly Kuzmin and Russian MoD)

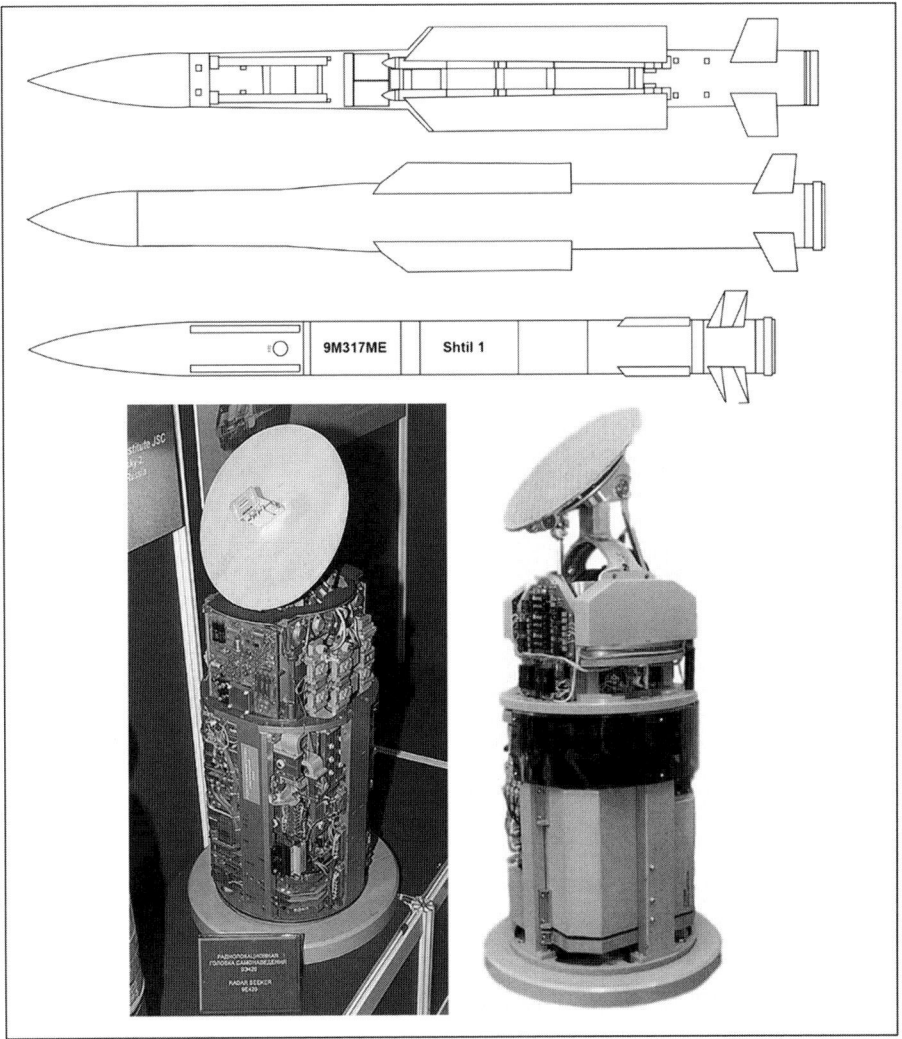

Figure 6-16: Drawings, top to bottom: 9M38M1, 9M317, and 9M317ME Buk surface-to-air missiles comparison; Agat 9E420 digital CW (continuous wave) dual plane monopulse semiactive radar homing seeker for the 9M317 missile. The unique antenna arrangement is inherited from the 3M9/SA-6 series seekers (bottom left); Agat ARGS Slanets monopulse active radar homing seeker for the 9M317 and 9M38M Gadfly missiles (Agat) (bottom right).

from 2.5–70km, with a speed of 3,000m/s at altitudes of 15–35,000m. The missile has been optimized for the interception of low-flying cruise missiles. It includes a high-speed data exchange system and a thermal target imaging designator replacing optical trackers on previous Buk models. The 9M317M missile, stored in container, is fitted with a HE-FRAG warhead.

The missile guidance system is very similar to the missile guidance system applied in the S-300V missile system, which has resulted in a very

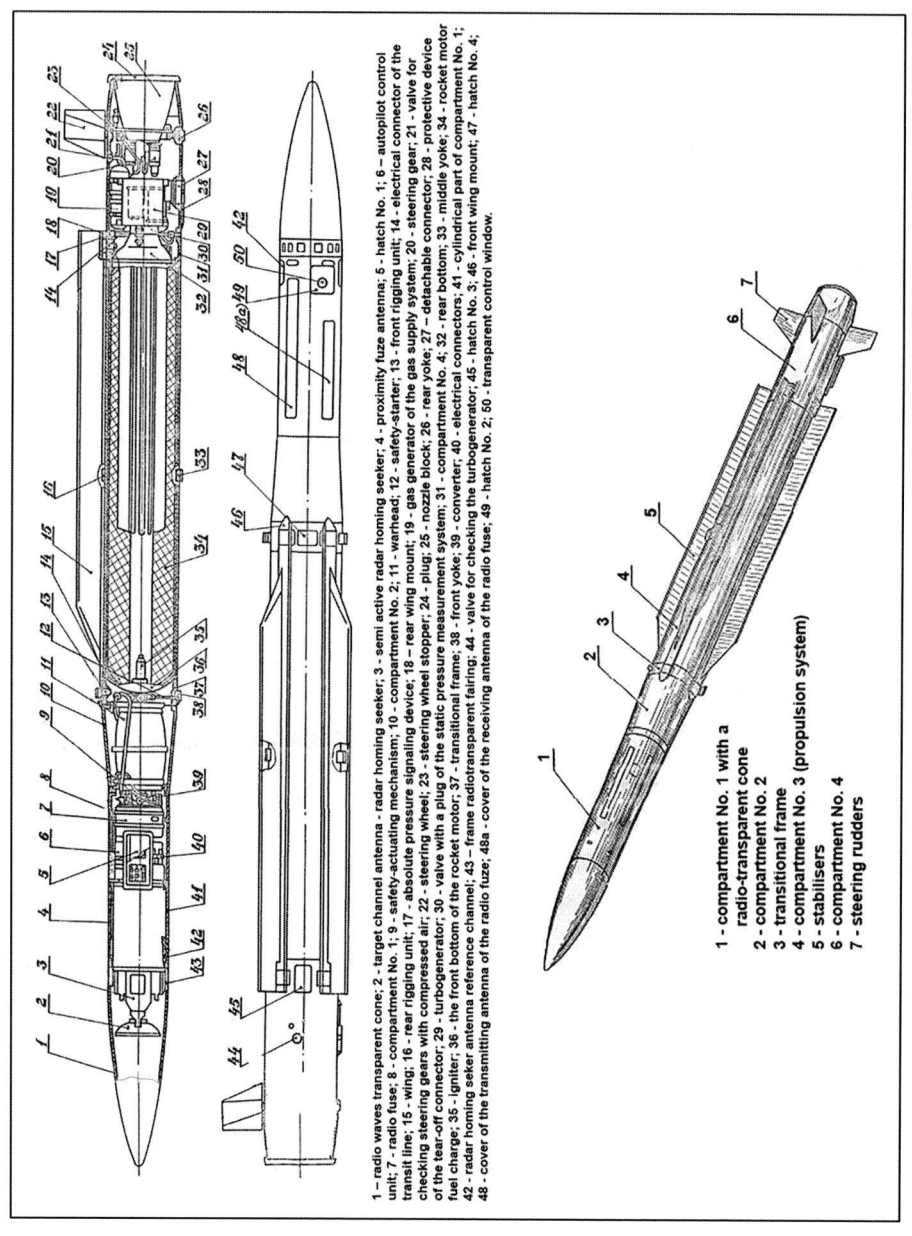

Figure 6-17: 9M38M1 missile. (*Source*: S.N. Elcin, *Raketa 9M38M1 Ustroistvo i funkcionirovanie*, modified by author)

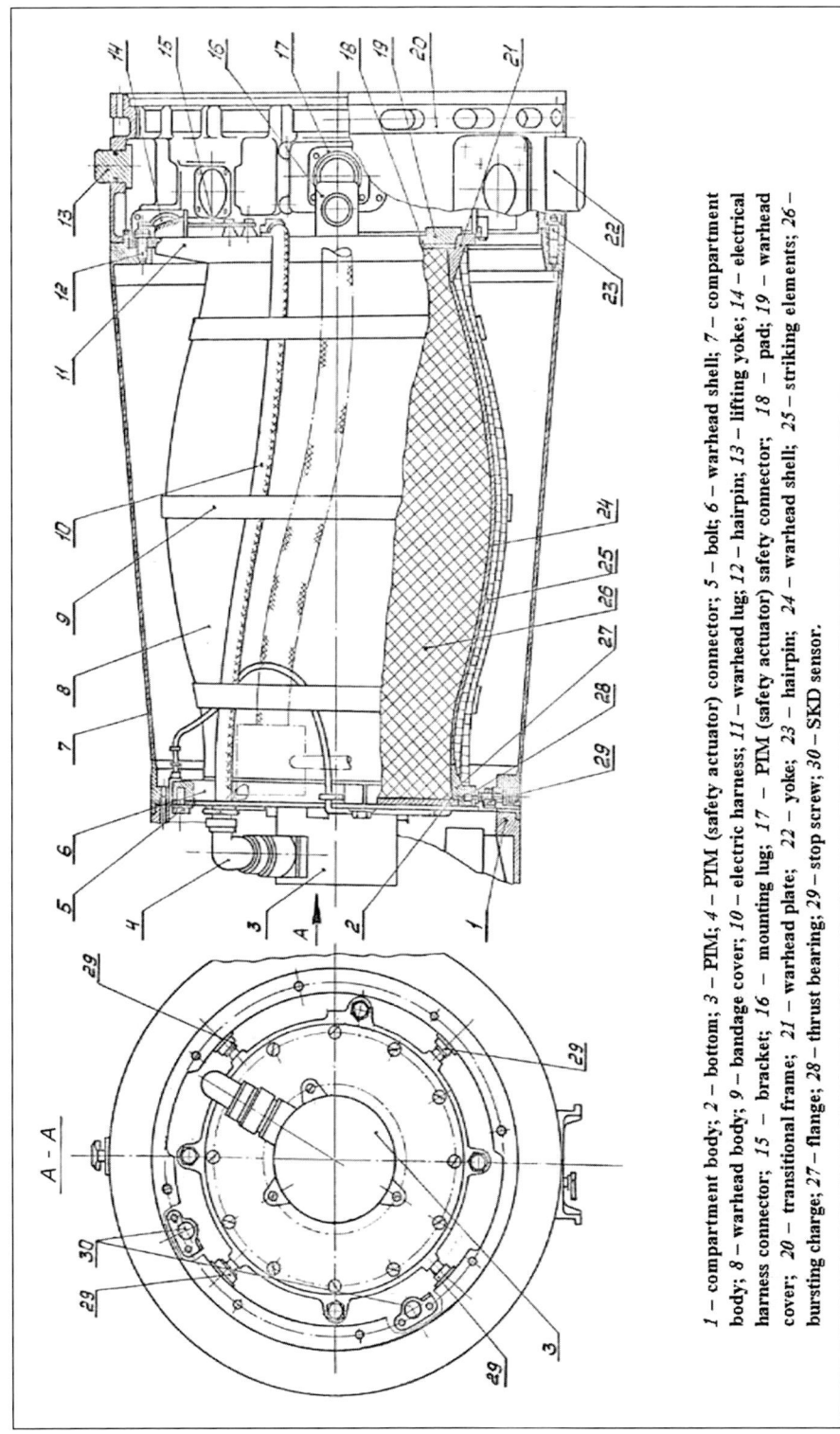

Figure 6-18: 9M38M1 warhead. (*Source*: S.N. Elcin.: *Raketa 9M38M1 Ustroistvo i funkcionirovanie*, modified by author)

1 – compartment body; *2* – bottom; *3* – PIM; *4* – PIM (safety actuator) connector; *5* – bolt; *6* – warhead shell; *7* – compartment body; *8* – warhead body; *9* – bandage cover; *10* – electric harness; *11* – warhead lug; *12* – hairpin; *13* – lifting yoke; *14* – electrical harness connector; *15* – bracket; *16* – mounting lug; *17* – PIM (safety actuator) safety connector; *18* – pad; *19* – warhead cover; *20* – transitional frame; *21* – warhead plate; *22* – yoke; *23* – hairpin; *24* – warhead shell; *25* – striking elements; *26* – bursting charge; *27* – flange; *28* – thrust bearing; *29* – stop screw; *30* – SKD sensor.

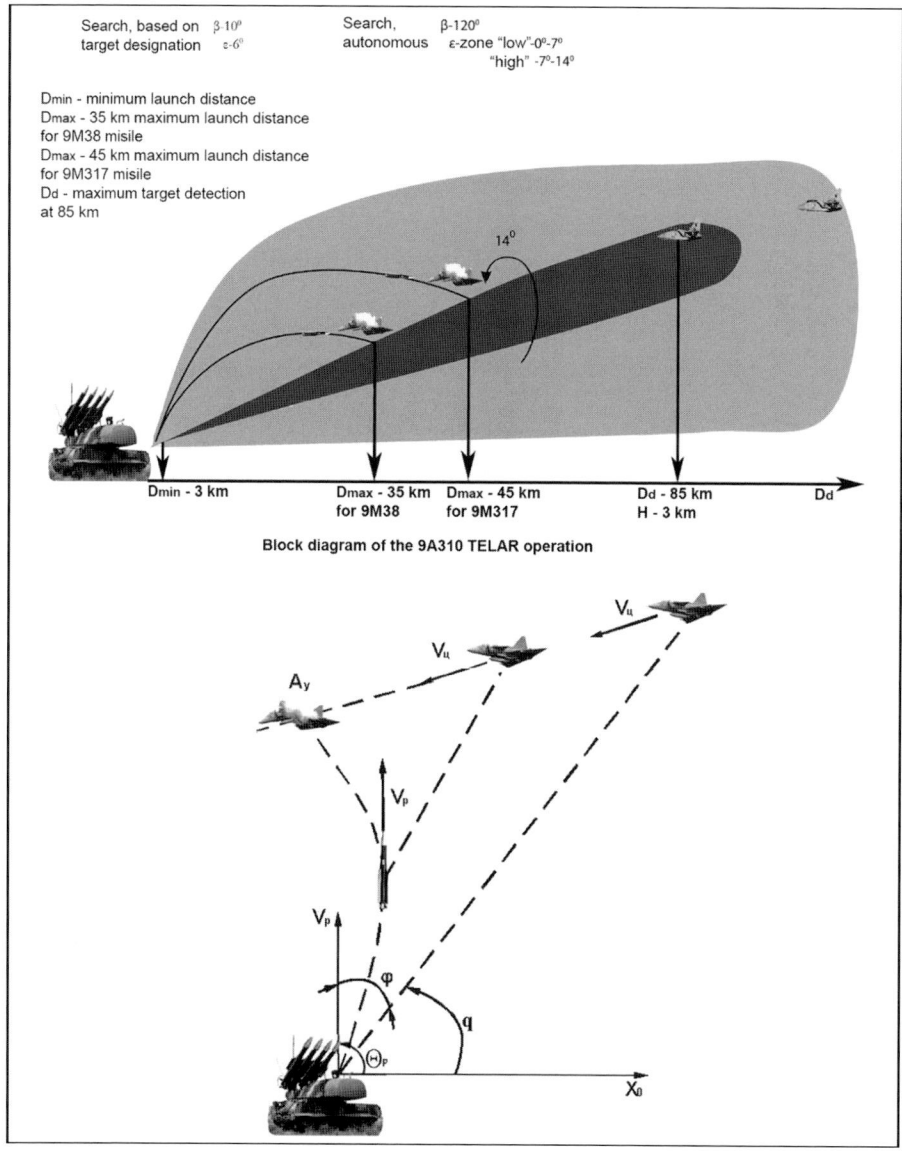

Figure 6-19: 9A310 TELAR interception capabilities (top); missile proportional semi-active command guidance (bottom). (*Source*: Buk manual, modified by author)

interesting modification with the integration of one launcher with 9A383 radar with four 9M83M missiles from the S-300V system.

In this configuration, the 9K17M Buk-M3 battalion can engage aerodynamic targets at distances up to 100km, and ballistic targets at distances up to 40km, with 9M83M missiles, so that the system can also be considered an anti-ballistic system. These targets could be engaged with a maximum of two missiles at a time.

Figure 6-20: A 9M38M missile lost control and hit a residential building in Kiev. A smoke trail is characteristic of this type of missile. Ukraine has older missiles that have occasionally lost guidance or had mechanical problems and as a result have hit residential areas. Nevertheless, in the Western media these are claimed as Russian missiles targeting civilian objects. (*Source*: stills from security camera video/Telegram)

So far, Russian Buk-M3s are credited with at least 4 Ukrainian Su-25s, 5–6 Mi-8/Mi-24s, and more than 100 drones and rocket munition.

Pantsir
The Pantsir-S1 (SA-22 Greyhound) is an air defense gun-missile system designed to protect vital small and big military areas, industrial objects,

and land-forces units and to reinforce the air defense units responsible for the protection of troops and military installations against precision-guided air attack from low and extremely low altitudes. The mobile version of the Pantsir-S1 system includes a combat vehicle (up to six vehicles in a battery), surface-to-air guided missiles, 30mm rounds, a transporter loader vehicle (one per two combat vehicles), and maintenance and training facilities. The Pantsir-S1 is designed by the KBP Instrument Design Bureau of Tula, and is manufactured by the Ulyanovsk Mechanical Plant, Ulyanovsk (Figure 6-21).

The armament of Pantsir-S1 consists of twelve 57E6 surface-to-air guided missiles (Figure 6-21) and two 2A38M automatic guns developed from the two-barreled 30mm GSh-30 gun. It is provided with a multi-range radar capable of detecting aerial targets with an effective surface of dispersion

Figure 6-21: Pantsir-S1 (top); combat operation mode (bottom). The combat value of the system is very high. In January 2023 it was also installed on the rooftops of some of the most important government buildings in Moscow. (*Source*: M. Mihajlović, *Defending Putin's Empire: Russia's Air Defence System* (2023))

of up to 2–3m² at a distance of more than 30km and tracking them down from a distance of over 24km. With its missiles, the Pantsir-S1 can engage tactical aircraft at a maximum range of 20km and altitude of 10km, subsonic cruise missiles at a range of 12km and altitude of 6km, and high-speed air-to-ground missiles at a range of 7km and altitude of 6km. With its gun weapons, the Pantsir-S1 can destroy aerial targets at a maximum range of 4km and a maximum altitude of 3km. The Pantsir-S1 can operate independently or in a formation.

Missiles are arranged into two six-tube groups on the turret. The missile has a bi-caliber body in tandem configuration. The first stage is a booster, providing rapid acceleration within the first 2–3 seconds of flight after it is separated from the sustainer stage (Figure 6-22). The sustainer is the highly agile part of the missile and contains the high-explosive multiple continuous rods and fragmentation warhead, contact and proximity

Figure 6-22: 57E6 missile marching stage (top); Pantsir-S1 with "kill" marks (bottom). (*Source*: M. Mihajlović, *Defending Putin's Empire: Russia's Air Defence System* (2023))

fuzes as well as radio transponder and laser responder to be localized for guidance. The missile is not fitted with a seeker to keep target engagement costs low. Instead, high-precision target and missile tracking are provided via the system's multi-band sensor system and guidance data is submitted via radio link for up to four missiles in flight. Missiles can be fired in at up to four targets but also salvos of two missiles at one target. The missile is believed to have a hit probability of 70–95 percent and have a fifteen-year storage lifetime in its sealed containers. Pantsir-S1 combat vehicles can fire missiles on the move.

The Pantsir-S1 can be mounted on a different truck chassis with a turret that houses the armament, laying drives, sensors, control equipment, and crew. The turret is a modular design and can be installed on multiple platforms.

The Pantsir-S1 fire-control system includes a target acquisition radar and dual waveband tracking radar (1RS2-1), which operates in the UHF and EHF wavebands. Its detection range is 32–36km. This radar tracks both targets and the SAM while in flight. The minimum target RCS for tracking is 2–3cm^2.

The fire-control system has an electro-optic channel with a long-wave thermal imager and an infrared direction finder, including digital signal processing and automatic target tracking. The two independent guidance channels (radar and electro-optic) allow two targets to be engaged simultaneously and four for more recent options. The maximum engagement rate is up to ten to twelve targets per minute.

The specific feature of the Pantsir-S1 system is the combination of multiple-band target acquisition and tracking system in conjunction with a combined missile and gun armament creating a continuous target engagement zone from 5m height and 200m range up to 15km height and 20km range, even without any external support. By design and functionality, the compact combat control system, with the high automation level, is very similar to the combat system of the fighter jet.

Western "Wonder Weapons"

NASAMS

NASAMS[1] is one of the latest "wonder-weapons" in which Ukraine places much hope that it will turn the tide of war and stop RuAF and cruise-missile attacks (Figure 6-23).

Version 1 uses a surface-launched AIM-120 AMRAAM.[2] The upgraded Version 2 can use new datalinks and the latest Version 3 can use AIM-9 Sidewinder and IRIS-T short-range missiles (25km) and AMRAAM-ER extended range missiles (50km). It has also, for the first time, had light air-liftable launchers introduced.

Figure 6-23: NASAMS battery components. (*Source*: Lithuanian DoD)

The AMRAAM missile is fired from a towed launcher with six missile containers.

A typical battalion consists of up to four batteries. A battery includes three launchers each carrying six AIM-120 AMRAAM missiles, one AN/MPQ-64F1 Improved Sentinel radar, one Fire Control/Distribution Center vehicle, and one MSP500 electro-optical camera vehicle.

The Improved Sentinel radar has a broader frequency spectrum, variable rotation speed, and increased capacity to detect and follow targets. The radar platform comes with its own power supply and can be mounted on a variety of vehicles. Each radar can process and distribute the data independently and can be connected via radio links, cable, through Multi Rolle Radio, or through TADKOM.[3]

The MSP500 electro-optical sensor is equipped with a laser rangefinder, TV camera, and thermographic camera. These can be used to fire the missiles passively, which has been successfully tested.

Fire-control/distribution centers can form a network with geographically distributed sensors and use either centralized or distributed data fusion to process radar tracks and form a complete airspace picture for the Tactical Control Officer (TCO). Each command post includes two color displays with a task-based Common Tactical Operation Control (CTOC) interface. The control system can detach itself from the sensors to become less visible.

Operators can switch to a centralized control role by running operation center software (GBADOC). An optional Tactical Control Center (TCC) vehicle, similar to the Batallion Operations Center (BOC) for the HAWK XXI upgrade, includes a third command post that can be used for this role.

The control modules can be mounted on a large variety of vehicles. Each module can automatically determine its position using an electronic northfinder and GPS receiver.

The AMRAAM is one of the most widely used air-to-air missiles in the world, and stockpiles of it are high. As NASAMS uses existing air-to-air missiles such as the AIM-9 Sidewinder, AMRAAM, and AMRAAM-ER, there may be thousands of older missiles in NATO's arsenal that can be fired from a NASAMS battery without change. The AIM-9X variant includes an internal cooling system, eliminating the need for the launch-rail nitrogen supply required by older variants of the missile (Figure 6-24).

NASAMS is a good choice for Ukraine because of the large quantities of missiles that NATO can supply. Older AMRAAM A and B models have been replaced, making available many older missiles that could be sent to Ukraine.

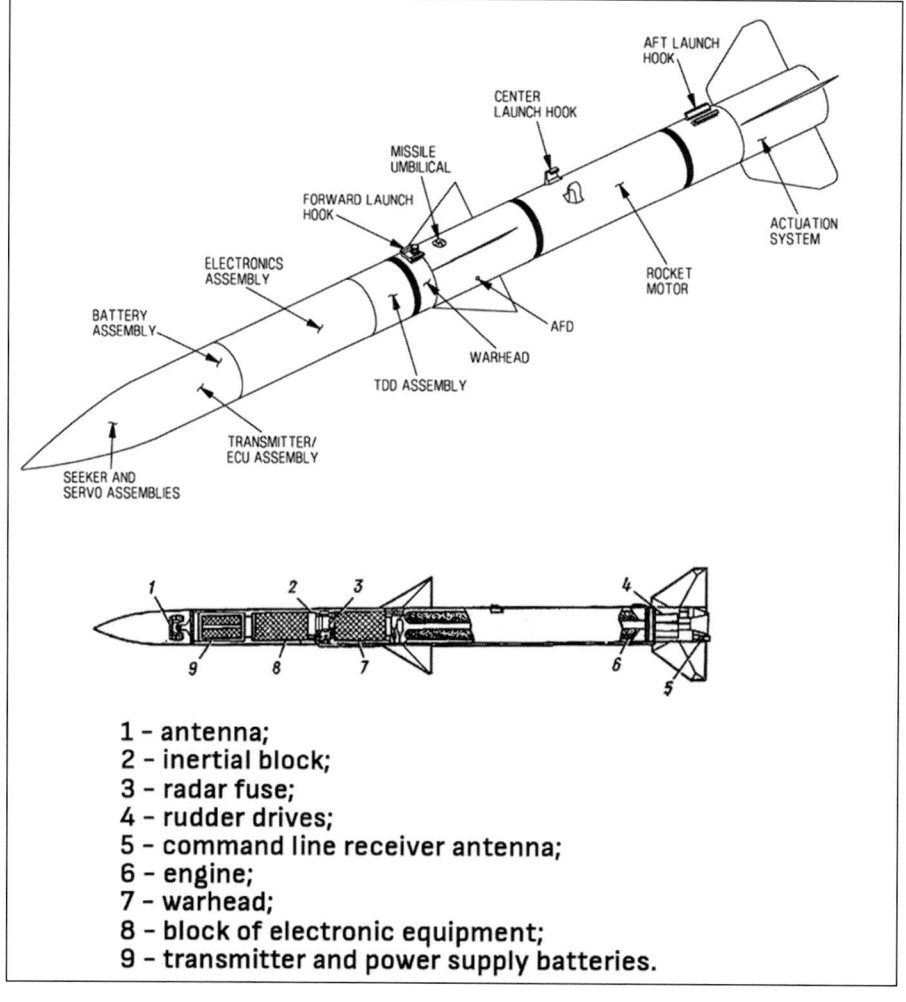

Figure 6-24: AIM-120 AMRAAM missiles. (*Source*: Hughes/Raytheon Technologies)

A disadvantage is that it is not mobile like the Buk-M1. Also, it requires extensive training. Maintenance is an issue and current capacities are not sufficient in terms of both equipment and manpower. A few batteries are not enough to cover all strategic locations and the system will be on the Russian primary hit list. Maintenance requires new capacities. Only time will tell how this system will operate in the enemy air-superior environment. In any case, the few battalions operating are far from "closing the sky" to Russian attacks.

Being a modern system does not guarantee it is failure-free: on 22 November, two AIM-120 missiles slammed into a residential building in Kiev causing civilian casualties. Ukraine blamed this on the Russians, but the debris was easy to identify. The missile likely lost guidance or had a mechanical malfunction. The process is ongoing.

IRIS-T

The second "wonder weapon" that Ukraine expects to turn the tide is the IRIS-T (Figure 6-25 top and middle).[4] It is a medium-range infrared guided missile available in both air-to-air and surface-to-air variants.

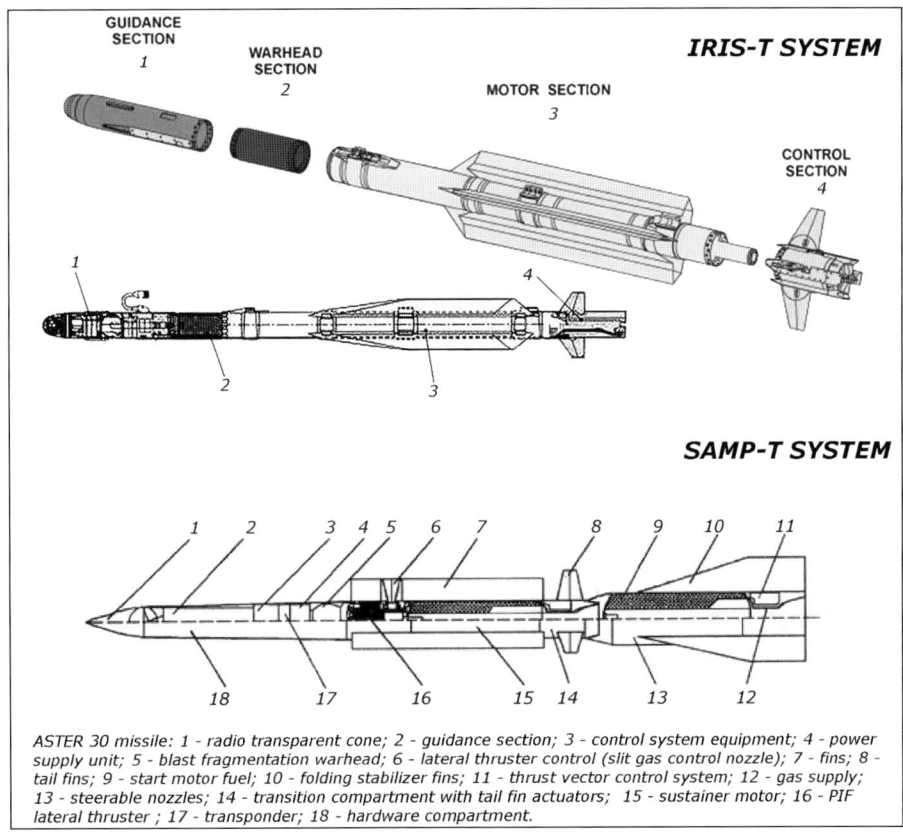

Figure 6-25: IRIS-T missile components (top). (*Source*: Diehl defence); SAMP-T ASTER 30 missile components (bottom).

The missile was developed by a German-led program to develop a short- to medium-range infrared homing air-to-air missile to replace the AIM-9 Sidewinder. Surface-to-air variants came later, with the short-range IRIS-T SLS fielded in 2015, and the medium-range IRIS-T SLM fielded in 2022. One IRIS-T SLM battery consists of three truck-mounted launchers, carrying eight missiles each (with a range of 40km), and a separate command vehicle that can be positioned up to 20km away. The command vehicle integrates multiple radar sources and can launch and track all twenty-four missiles simultaneously. The primary role of IRIS-T SLM in Ukraine is to intercept cruise missiles, including low-flying, stealthy ones.

Visually, the surface-to-air IRIS-T SL has a pointed nose with a jettisonable drag-reducing nose cone. It also has an increased power rocket motor. The missile uses a GPS-aided inertial navigation system with radar datalink for command guidance during the initial approach, while the interference-resistant IR seeker head is activated at the terminal stage.

Two variants are available for Ukraine: the IRIS-T SLS (short-range) with a 12km range and altitude and the IRIS-T SLM (medium-range) with a 40km range at a 20km maximum altitude.

As a new system, it will take time for Ukrainian crews to master it. As with NASAMS, the introduction of a few battalions will not have any significant influence on the war.

SAMP-T

The latest addition to the clusters of the Western medium-range AD systems is a Franco-Italian SAMP-T. The main difference compared with the IRIS-T is declared anti-ballistic tactical missile capability. The MIM-104 Patriot and SAMP-T are two modern systems that Ukraine has (deployed in the Kiev area) that have some capabilities to engage ballistic missiles, at least on paper. It fell in a similar launch system group as IRIS-T because both use container vertical launch. The difference between the Soviet-made S-300P/PS, S-300V and the Tor-M in Ukrainian use is a catapult launch instead of the hot launch startup in the container, as in the IRIS-T and SAMP-T.

The system can track up to 100 targets and engage 10 of them simultaneously based on the priority criteria. A fire-control system is based on a command and control system – an engagement module connected to a multi-function Arabel radar. It uses up to six vertical launchers each fitted with eight, ready-to-fire ASTER 30 missiles. The developer has claimed that the system has 360-degree capabilities (better than the MIM-104 Patriot) and a response time of 10 seconds from each launcher. The rate of fire is eight missiles in 10 seconds from each launcher.

The system is highly automated with a built test-in capability and requires only two crew members to operate the fire-control station. The rest of the unit crew is tasked with support roles. High resistance to countermeasures can be useful against the Russian EW systems. The great advantage compared with the MIM-104 is fast deployment and withdrawal time.

It can be included in the national IADS, but in Ukraine it is used as a stand-alone version because the Western systems are not compatible with the existing IADS. It has the ability to work in stand-alone mode or as an integral part of a wider architecture.

The business end is the ASTER missile (Figure 6-25 bottom). It is a two-stage concept. The solid propellant booster ensures the optimum shaping of the missile's trajectory in the direction of the target and separates a few seconds after the vertical launch. Up to its mid-course, the missile is inertially guided, using refreshed target data transmitted by the engagement module through the multi-function radar. During the homing phase, guidance is achieved by an electromagnetic active seeker.

The ASTER missile (version 15 and 30) combines a large lateral acceleration capability – aerodynamic control, called PAF, with a direct force control using lateral thrusters right at the center of gravity of the kill vehicle, called PIF. This innovative control concept provides the weapon with agility and maneuverability within its whole intercept domain, especially at high altitudes. The operational range, with a maximum speed of 4.5-Mach (declared by the manufacturer), against large targets flying above 3,000m is 120km. The operational range against ballistic missiles is 15km.

The missile combines a proximity fuze and a blast fragmentation warhead. The efficiency of this warhead against ballistic missiles can be proven only in practice. It is highly likely that the Ukrainians are using it against cruise missiles and drones. As of the time of writing, there are no official reports of any attempts to intercept Russian Kinzhals, but that may change. Based on the characteristics, it is not likely that these missiles can intercept hypersonic aeroballistic missiles.

The ASTER 30 SAMP/T is in service with the French and Italian armed forces, and one battery was sent to Ukraine in 2023. One battery can't change anything even if the crew consists of experienced professionals (contractors or volunteers). It is more a form of political support and the opportunity to test the system in real combat conditions.

HAWK

The MIM-23 HAWK (Homing All the Way Killer) is one of the oldest AD systems in use in some NATO and many other countries worldwide (Figure 6-26).[5] It was the best of the medium-range systems when it was introduced in the 1960s and had some successes in the local conflicts, but nowadays, despite many improvements and modifications, it is considered an "old-timer" alongside its Soviet counterpart the S-125. It can still be used but its moment has passed.

The MIM-23B has a 74kg blast-fragmentation warhead, a smaller and improved guidance package, and a new M112 rocket motor. The new warhead produces approximately 14,000 2g fragments that cover a 70° arc. The missile M112 rocket motor has a boost phase of 5 seconds and a sustain phase of 21 seconds. The engagement envelope is 1.5–40km in range at high altitudes and 2.5–20km at low altitudes. The minimum engagement altitude is 60m (it can't engage Russian UAVs or low-flying cruise missiles).

As Ukraine has become an arms dumpster (many Western countries have simply dumped their existing old stocks of the equipment), it has received some batteries but the outcome is not difficult to predict: HAWK is a demanding system, which requires many years of training to master it, is semi-mobile and takes time to deploy, but as it was the main AD system in NATO during the 1970s and 1980s, there are large quantities of the missiles available.

Ukrainian AD is badly damaged and any help is more than welcome so HAWK may find some use, at least for the second or third tier AD units.

For Ukraine, it might be better to bring back the old Soviet S-125 and 2K12 systems because they still have trained crews (even though they may be long-term retired) and they can at least resurrect the old system much more quickly and satisfactorily. The maintenance issues associated with HAWK and Aspide may also be factors.

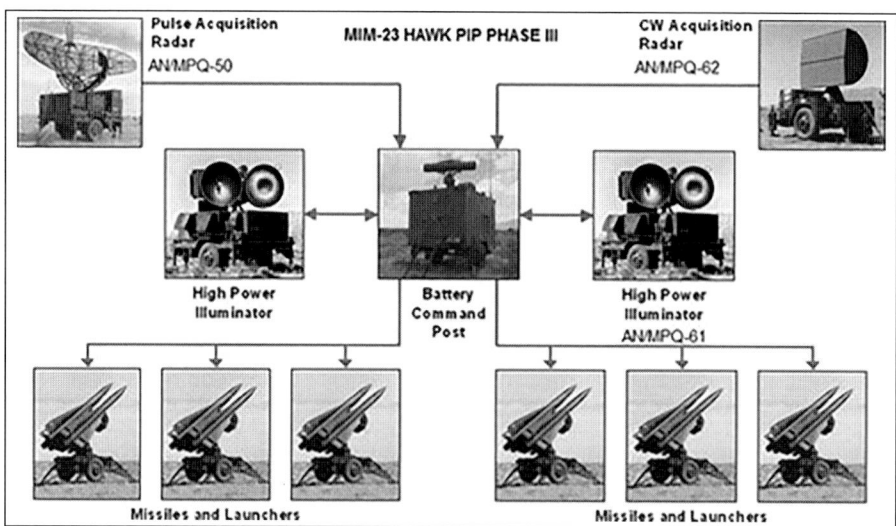

Figure 6-26: The Hawk structure was integrated into one system AN/TSQ-73 called Missile Minder or Hawk-MM. It consists of MPQ-50 Pulse Acquisition Radar, MPQ-48 Improved Continuous Wave Acquisition Radar, TSW-8 Battery Control Central, ICC Information Coordination Central, MSW-11 Platoon Command Post, MPQ-46 High Power Illuminator, MPQ-51 Range Only Radar, and the M192 launcher. (*Source*: armyreckognition.com)

Aspide

One of the older AD systems, Aspide was donated as a gift. Everything that has been said about the application of the HAWK system is true of the Aspide system as well.

Aspide is an Italian medium-range air-to-air and surface-to-air missile. It is provided with a semi-active radar homing seeker. By design, it is very similar to the US AIM-7 Sparrow air-to-air missile, with the same airframe, but uses an inverse monopulse seeker that is far more accurate and much less susceptible to ECM than the original conical scanning version.

The best implementation of the Aspide 2000 missile may be in the modified 2K12 systems which Ukraine is familiar with and has some in the reserve. Czech designers have already modified a 2P25 SA-6 launcher with three Aspide missiles instead of the original used in the SA-6 system. The missile guidance station is also modified.

The key disadvantage of the Aspide missile is that the speed is slower than the original 3M9ME, with a shorter range and maximum altitude. In any case, as it was a gift from Spain that included the training of the operators, perhaps it should be viewed along the lines of "take whatever you can if it is free." The impact of this system in the air war is lower than negligible.[6]

SHORADs

OSA-AKM

The 9K33 Osa SHORAD[7] was designed as a ground forces SAM system on a divisional level with the intention of providing low-level and short-distance air defense for the mechanized and armored units. The requirement was for a fast, mobile, and amphibious system to keep up with the ground forces units. Development was started in the 1960s but took longer than anticipated and some unusual solutions were applied (Figure 6-27).

Figure 6-27: 9K33 OSA-AKM.
(*Source*: Russian MoD)

The 9K33 Osa was designed with one of the most complicated mechanically scanned radar systems ever fitted on a movable platform. The positive thing was that Osa was very resistant to all anti-radiation missiles of the 1980s and 1990s and only AGM-88 HARM in the late 1990s could inflict damage.

In normal operation mode, the target is tracked optically with the target video-tracking camera. Information about the target locations can be transferred through the IADS or individually. By using the TOV the Osa can operate without any radar emission until the launch of the first missile.

The latest improved modification, OSA-AKM, is in use with both sides of the conflict. It uses modified missiles of the 9M33M2/M3 series. These missiles have dual-thrust rocket motors providing a solid range and altitudes for the short-range AD system. The maximal engagement range is 10.3km and up to 5km altitude. In practice, operators use about two-thirds of those declared values (Figure 6-28).

The 9M33M2 missile can engage targets with a maximum speed of 500m/s. With a well-organized information network, the system can successfully engage helicopters, low-flying airplanes, and UAVs.

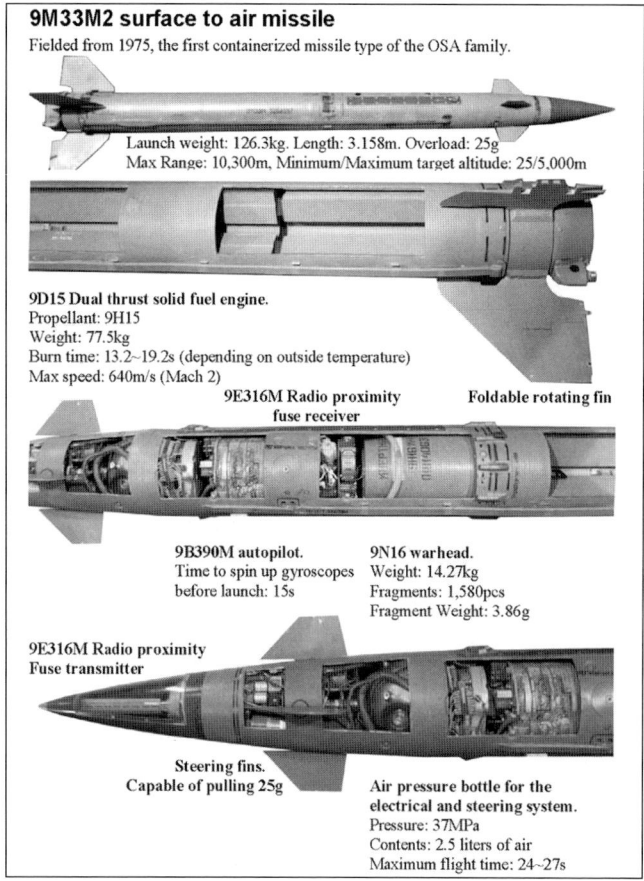

Figure 6-28: 9M33M2 missile. (*Source*: simhq.com)

Ukraine mostly uses the 9K33M2 version, while Russia uses a mix of 9K33M2/M3.

Tor

The 9K330/9K331 Tor missile system (and successive variants) system is a highly mobile rapid reaction SAM built to replace the Osa-AKM system. Like the Osa-AKM, the Tor is a fully self-contained package, with a search radar, a monopulse tracking and engagement radar, and a magazine of Automatic Command-to-Line-Of-Sight (CLOS) guided missiles. The design aims of the Tor were, however, broader than those for the Osa, and not only are low-flying aircraft and helicopters intended targets, but also cruise missiles, standoff missiles, and smart bombs during their terminal flight phase. The Tor SHORAD system is intended to engage and destroy guided munitions targeting the S-300V long-range army AD systems but also command posts, and important infrastructure objects such as powerplants and bridges. In this role, the Tor exceeded assigned tasks in Ukraine downing numerous HIMARS missiles, UAVs, and aircraft. For example, one launcher claimed twelve drones and three helicopters in the first three months of combat. Before the war Ukraine had just six old Tor-M, while Russia has the modern upgraded Tor-M1 and much more modern Tor-M2 (Figure 6-29).

The Tor uses a 9M330/9M331-type missile with an aerodynamic configuration similar to that of the 9M33 used in the Osa system, thus ensuring the necessary continuity of development. Also, during the development of the 9M330, as with other new-generation SAMs, the concept of guaranteed reliability of its maintenance-free operation in the army and navy throughout the entire warranty period was implemented (Figures 6-30, 6-31).

What differentiates Tor from the other SHORADs is the vertical launch of the missile stored in the containers with the help of the catapult and turning to the designated target.

Figure 6-29: 9K331 Tor-M1 (left); damaged Tor-M2 (right). (*Source*: Russian MoD)

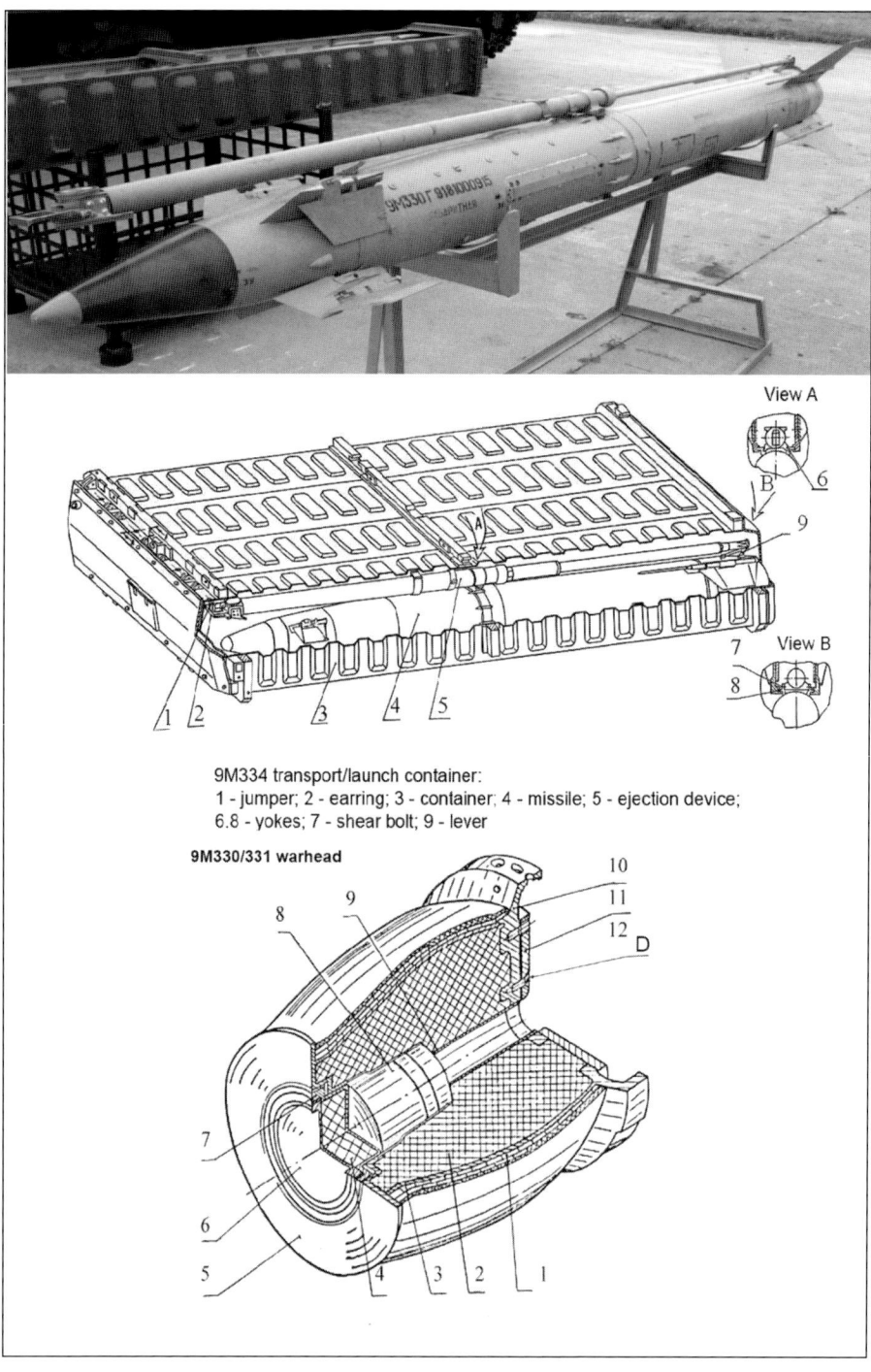

Figure 6-30: 9M330 missile (top); 9M334 transport-launch container (middle); 9M330/331 warhead (bottom). (*Source*: M. Mihajlović, *Jetliner Down: Tor-M1 missile system which downed Ukrainian PS752 flight*)

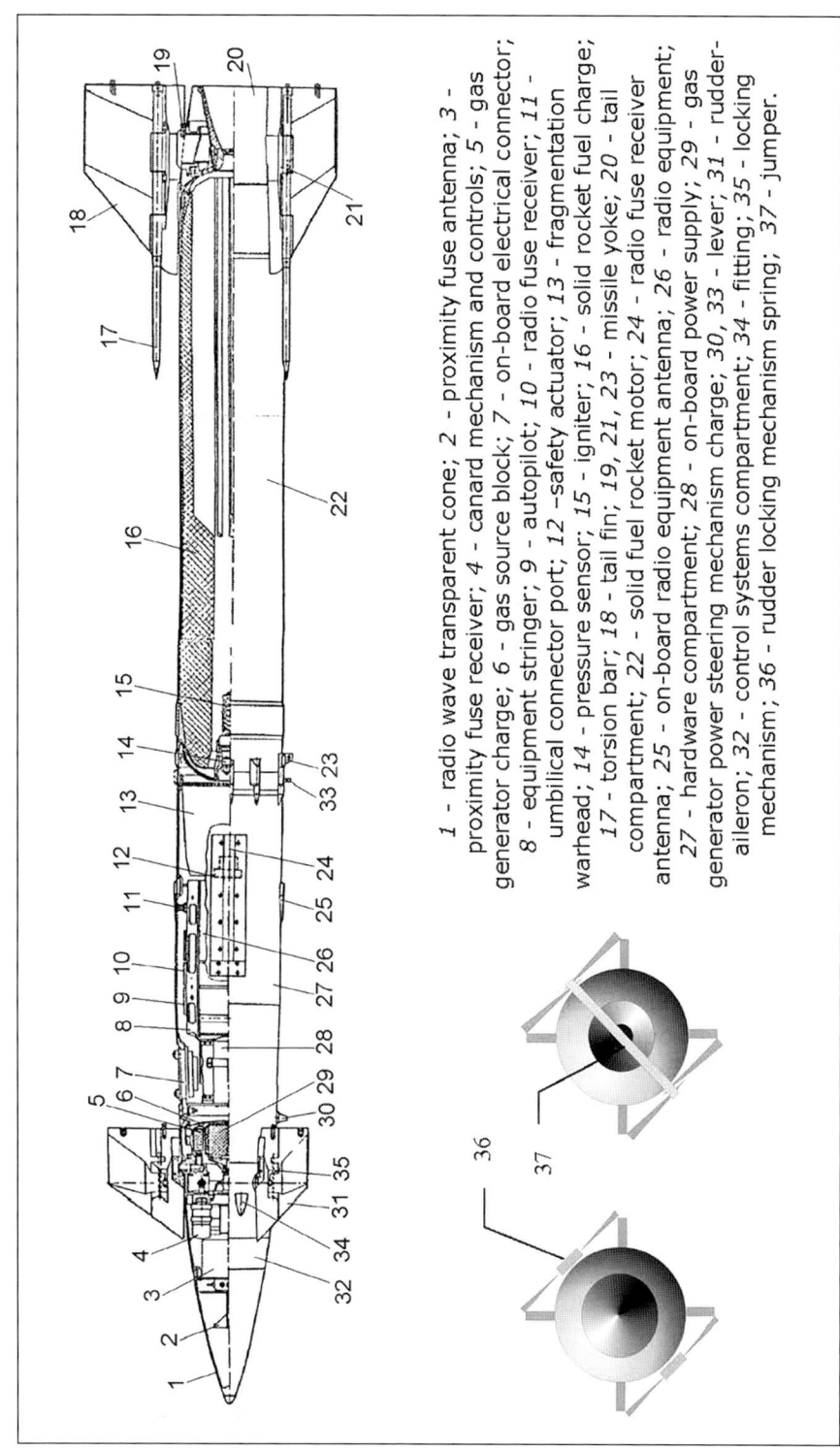

Figure 6-31: 9M331 cutaway. (*Source*: S.N. Elcin, *Raketa 9M331, Ustroistvo i funkcionirovanie*, modified by author)

Tunguska

The 2K22 Tunguska is a point/SHORAD defense gun-missile system designed to replace the ZSU 23/4 Shilka and Strela-10 point defense systems. Target tracking is possible with radar and TV camera. The vehicle has its own target acquisition radar which makes it similar to the 9K33 Osa. The target acquisition radar has an 18km nominal detection range with a minimal 15m altitude search capability.

The main armament of the Tunguska is the eight 9M311M or 9M311-M1-type missiles with radio control guidance. The maximum range is 10km (with 9M311M 8km) and altitude up to 3,500m. The maximum 4km distance (offset) parameter maximal intercepted target speed is 600m/s. During movement, only guns can be used.

The design of the missile is different from any previous Soviet SAM system. The missile has two stages but the second stage is just a "dart." it does not have a rocket motor and it flies by inertia. The burnout speed of the missile is about 900m/s. The first stage is separated just 2 seconds from the launch. The launch weight of the 9M311M is 57kg, with a warhead weight of 9kg.

For point defense this system is optimal and presents a danger for low-flying helicopters. The 30mm cannons can also be used in an infantry support role. Both sides are using them.

Strela-10

The 9K35 Strela-10M is an amphibious tracked system that works in the passive mode, without any radar emission. The missile has an additional selectable IR mode but it is not a dual seeker missile. Before the launch, the operator has to select between the photo contrast or the IR guidance.

The photo-contrast channel (also used by the Strela-1M) does not require cooling and can be used against both incoming and receding targets but is not protected against natural optical interference (heavy clouds with strong contrast, horizon line). The infrared channel requires prior cooling and can be used only against receding targets but it is effective against natural optical interference. As the 9M37 missile uses a PbS detector with IR guidance against an incoming target, it is not possible to perform a lock.

The 9M37 missile weighs 40kg with a 3kg warhead. The missile is equipped with a proximity fuze. The maximal engagement distance is 5km up to 3,500m altitude. Maximal target speed against incoming targets is 415m/s and against receding targets 310m/s.

The vehicle carries four missiles ready to launch and four more inside for reloading. The design is quite interesting in that the carried missile quantity remains only four on the turret. By comparison, the 9K33 Osa system was expected to double the carried quantity from 4x to 8x but only 6x was doable for the AKM. The predecessor of the Strela-10, designated as Strela-1M and based on the wheeled chassis, has not been improved compared with its predecessor system aside from the reloaded quantity being increased and put inside the vehicle.

As well as other SAM systems, the Strela-10M has received many upgrades since its introduction. The 9M37M had only IR/photo-contrast guidance with the 9E47-type guidance section and was replaced with the 9M333 variant which was applied on R-27T/ET (AA-10B/D Alamo) missiles as well. The missile got a laser proximity fuze against targets with a small RCS.

CROTALE

Besides the SAMP-T and Mistral systems, France has also supplied Ukraine with a short-range Crotale system. It is reported that two batteries are operational. The Crotale (rattlesnake) is an all-weather short-range system whose primary role is to engage cruise missiles, helicopters, drones, or low-flying aircraft. The Crotale missile battery consists of launchers with tracking radar and two to eight missile containers and the surveillance radar which is mounted on another vehicle. The modernized Crotale NG incorporates both the launcher and the surveillance radar in one vehicle.

The missile is propelled by a solid-propellant rocket motor and can accelerate to a maximum speed of 2.3-Mach in 2 seconds. The guidance is from the launcher unit utilizing the line-of-sight method. The missile is equipped with the IR proximity fuze which is activated in the proximity of the target.

The surveillance radar and fire-control radar have a range of 20km. The TV guidance has a range of 15km and utilizes regular and IR cameras. The system can follow eight targets simultaneously, and the guidance radar can follow both slow-moving or hovering targets as well as fast-moving targets. This is a good combination for the front-line AD as it can engage surveillance drones as well as fast-flying cruise missiles and tactical aviation. The Crotale can be integrated into the IADS and use information from other systems. In Ukraine, this is not likely because of the issue of compatibility with the existing IADS, but as a stand-alone system it can fulfill the basic tasks.

It is reported that Crotale has successfully engaged and downed a Russian cruise missile.

MANPADS

9K38 Igla and 9K338 Igla-S

These MANPADSs are almost undetectable by reconnaissance equipment, can be employed suddenly and quickly, and are highly accurate. As a result of their massive use, military aircraft cannot dominate airspace altitudes up to 3,500m, where the majority of the close-support attacks against ground targets are performed (Figure 6-32).

This has led to a significant change in air attack tactics and the mass use of relatively low-cost cruise missiles. Engaging the latter requires weapons, the

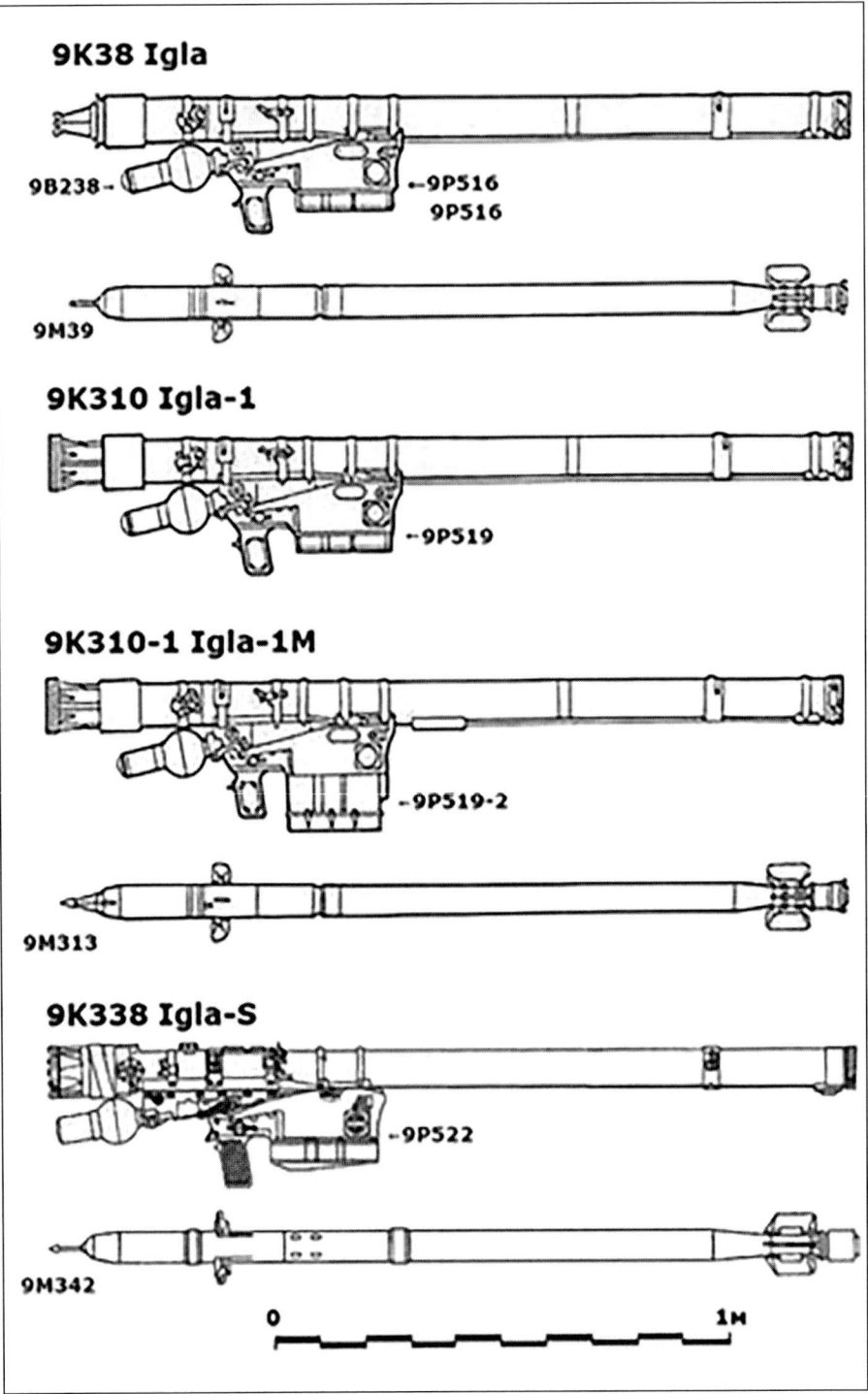

Figure 6-32: 9K38, 9K310, 9K310-1, and 9K338 Igla models. (*Source*: M. Mihajlović, *Defending Putin's Empire: Russia's Air Defence System* (2023))

number of which has exceeded the number of cruise missiles several times, with high-hitting accuracy and of relatively low cost, which can be quickly moved and deployed. The Igla-S can be launched from any unprepared open area, an emplacement, trucks and platforms, even from small bodies/areas of water.

The 9K38 Igla was designed with dual seeker which put the missile into a totally different category in comparison with any other missiles available at that time and not just in the Soviet Union. The system was named after the small spike on the nose of the missile. "Igla" in Russian means "needle." The engagement zone of the Igla is identical to that of Igla-1.

This seeker incorporated sensitivity, vibration- and shock-resistant characteristics that were unique for that time. As with the Igla-1, compressed nitrogen was used to cool the seeker to the working temperature of -200°C.

The Igla-S also differs by having a far heavier warhead both in the explosive weight (2.5kg for the IGLA-S against 1.1kg for the Igla) and the number of fragments, as well as the use of a contact/proximity fuze, operation algorithm of which selects the optimum time of warhead detonation, both in contact and proximity modes. To this end, a laser proximity target sensor was added to the warhead to provide its detonation when the missile flies at a distance of 1.5m from the target. This has considerably increased the killing efficiency against small targets such as cruise missiles and UAV. In turn, the replacement of the existing explosion control actuator with an electric proportional one reduced the drag coefficient of the missile and increased the average missile speed and target engagement range.

A detachable night sight allows the use of the MANPADS at night – provides target detection and identification by the gunner, aiming and target tracking before missile launch. In addition, there is maintenance equipment used periodically to check the system's combat assets.

The Igla-S remains operable under extreme temperature and high-humidity conditions, following sudden changes in ambient temperature and condensed precipitation, after immersion in water, the ascent in an unpressurized aircraft cabin to an altitude of 12km, and after prolonged carriage by any kind of transport, including in automotive and tracked vehicles, on all types of roads and terrain.

The Igla-S development process has incorporated many trends in the evolution of these weapons, in particular, the use of a MANPADS missile as part of the various ground-, sea-, and air-based platforms. This allows light mobile guided missile systems to be built around them. In these installations, missile establishment and firepower of the platform can be significantly increased owing to the small sizes and weight of the missile; on the other hand, the MANPADS has approached short-range air defense systems in terms of their performance and increased range of engagement.

These systems are in heavy use on both sides. The Ukrainians claim to have downed hundreds of Russian UAVs and tens of helicopters and airplanes.

Poland supplied their version of Igla named Piorun which has similar characteristics to the original.

9K333 Verba

The Verba's (Willow)/(SA-25) primary new feature is its multi-spectral optical seeker, using three sensors – ultraviolet, near infrared, and mid-infrared – as opposed to the Igla-S' two. Cross-checking sensors against one another better discriminates between relevant targets and decoys, and decreases the chance of disruption from countermeasures, including lasers that attempt to blind missiles (Figure 6-33).

According to a KBM, the Verba can engage fixed and rotary wing aircraft and "new types of threats" such as UAVs and cruise missiles. The 9K333 can effectively engage aerial targets with low infrared signature. The system can be coupled to an external IFF unit.

The Verba's containerized 9M336 SAM can be integrated into ground- and sea-based short-range air-defense systems. The Verba can also be used by air platforms.

The system is in serial production for the Russian armed forces, with several ground forces and airborne formations having received Verbas since 2014.

In the recent conflict in Ukraine, the Verba has successfully engaged and downed several Ukrainian Su-25s, Mi-8/M-24 helicopters as well as numerous UAVs and loitering munitions.

Stinger

The FIM-92 Stinger is a US MANPADS that operates as an infrared-homing surface-to-air missile. Since entering service in 1981, it has become the standard MANPADS for many NATO and allied countries. Hardly any local conflict or war is conducted without the use of Stinger. Ukraine has been (and still is) supplied with several thousand units by NATO countries (Figure 6-34).

What has been observed in Ukraine is that the majority of the delivered units are beyond their shelf life. Some Ukrainian units have reported malfunction during the launch or inability to acquire even clearly visible

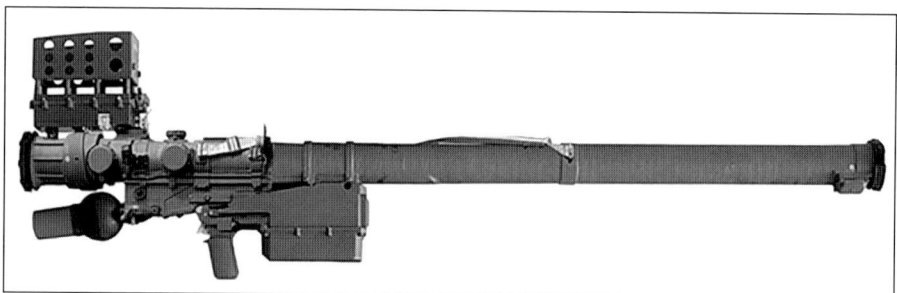

Figure 6-33: 9M333 Verba. (*Source*: imfdb.org)

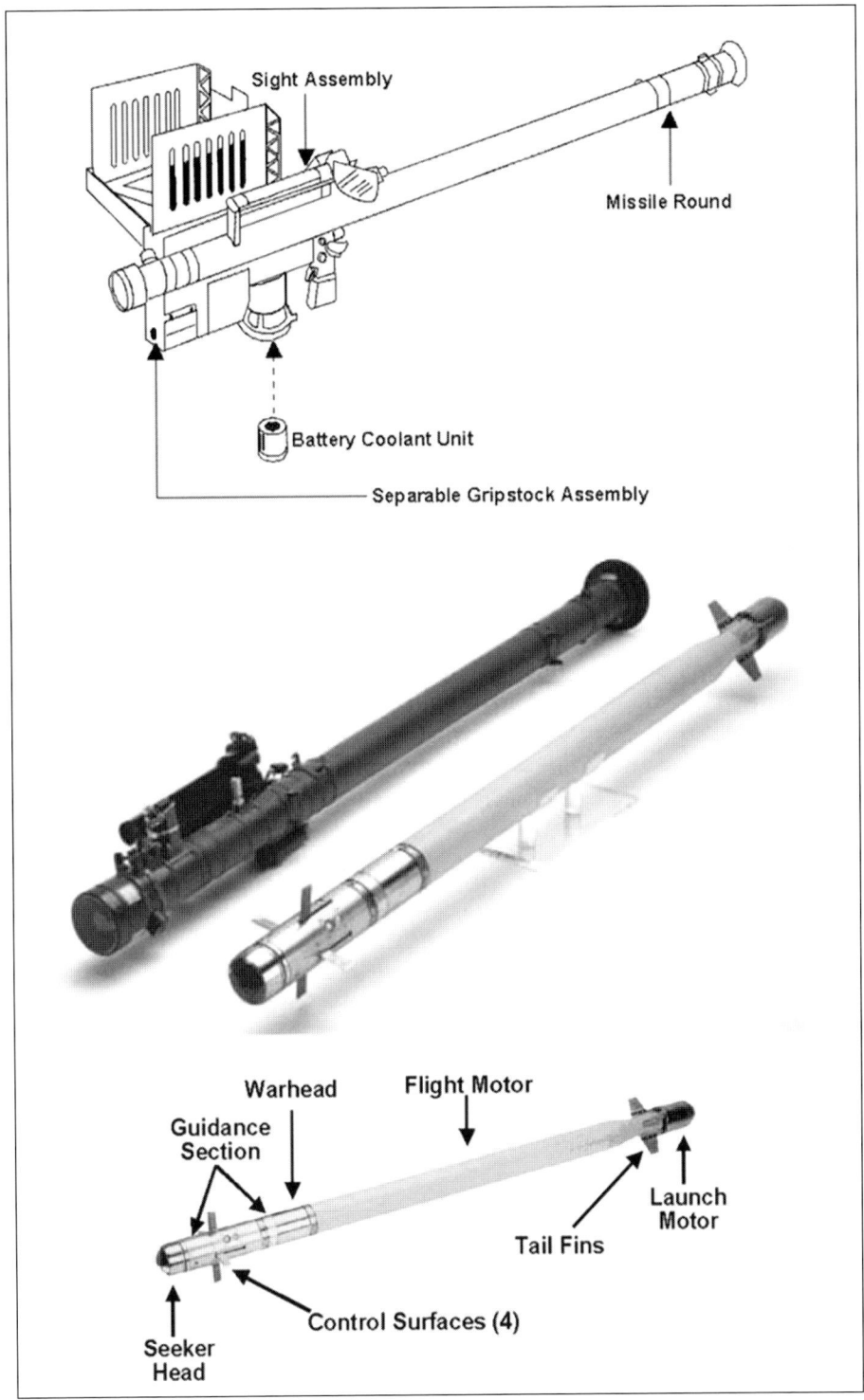

Figure 6-34: FIM-92 Stinger. (*Source*: fas.org and alpa.org)

Figure 6-35: Russian Su-25 tactical fighter with extensive damage caused by the Stinger warhead explosion. (*Source*: still from YouTube)

targets. Despite these setbacks, the Stinger is still a powerful portable AD system and so far has been credited with downing several Russian tactical aircraft and helicopters (Figure 6-35).

The missile is 1.52m long and 70mm in diameter. The missile itself weighs 10.1kg, while the missile with all targeting accessories weighs approximately 15.2kg. It has a targeting range of up to 4,800m and can engage low-altitude enemy threats at up to 3,800m.

The Stinger is launched by a small ejection motor that pushes it a safe distance from the operator before engaging the main two-stage solid-fuel sustainer, which accelerates it to a maximum speed of 750m/s. The warhead contains 1.02kg of HTA-3 explosive with an impact fuze and a self-destruct timer that functions 17 seconds after launch.

Ukraine also uses a US-made Avenger system. The Basic configuration consists of a gyro-stabilized turret with Stinger missiles pods mounted on a modified heavy HMMWV Humvee. The turret has two launcher pods, each capable of firing up to four missiles in rapid succession. Ukraine received more than twenty vehicles, some of which were lost during the failed offensive on the Zaporozhie front.

StarStreak
StarStreak is a British short-range surface-to-air missile that can be used as a MANPADS or in heavier systems. It is also known as StarStreak HVM (High-Velocity Missile). After launch, the missile accelerates to more than

SURFACE-TO-AIR MISSILES

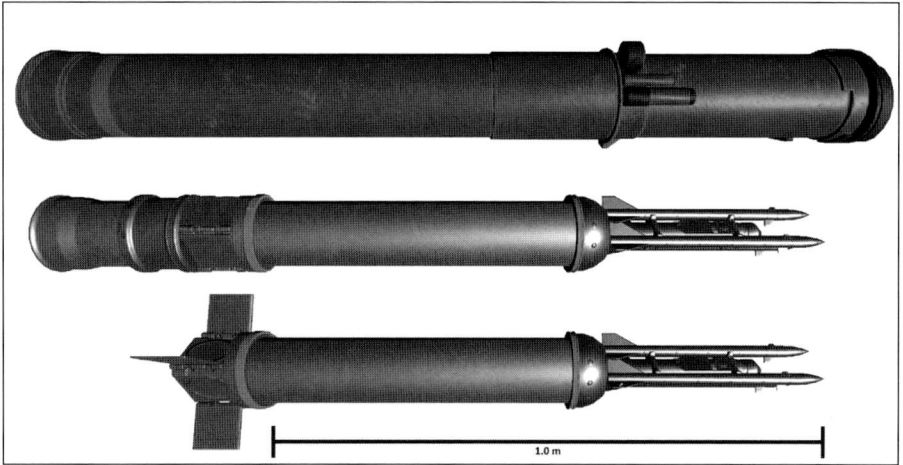

Figure 6-36: StarStreak launcher tube and missile. These launchers are also installed on the Stormer SAM system which provides necessary mobility. Often Russian suicide drones (such as the Lancet) operating behind the front line target these vehicles.

Mach-4 making it the fastest short-range surface-to-air missile in existence. It then launches three laser beam-riding submunitions, increasing the likelihood of a successful hit on the target (Figure 6-36).

The operator tracks the target using the aiming unit's optically stabilized sight. The missile is configured to fire the first-stage rocket motor that launches the missile from the tube but burns out before leaving the tube to protect the operator. The second stage is activated at a safe distance (4m). This rapidly accelerates the missile to a burn-out velocity exceeding Mach-4. As the second stage burns out, three dart sub-munitions are released.

The dart housing is made from a tungsten alloy. The darts are each 396mm long, 22mm in diameter, and weigh 0.9kg. About half the weight of each dart – approximately 450g – is its explosive charge, detonated by a delayed action, impact-activated fuze. Each dart consists of a rotating fore-body, with two canard fins, attached to a non-rotating rear assembly with four fins. The rear assembly of each dart also houses the guidance electronics including a rearwards-facing sensor.

The darts do not home in on laser energy reflected from the target; instead, the aiming unit projects two laser beams that paint a two-dimensional matrix upon the target. The lasers are modulated, and by examining these modulations the sub-munitions sensor can determine the dart's location within the matrix. The dart is then steered to keep it in the center of the matrix. The sub-munitions steer by briefly decelerating the rotating fore-body with a clutch. The front wings then steer the missile in the appropriate direction. The three sub-munitions fly in a formation

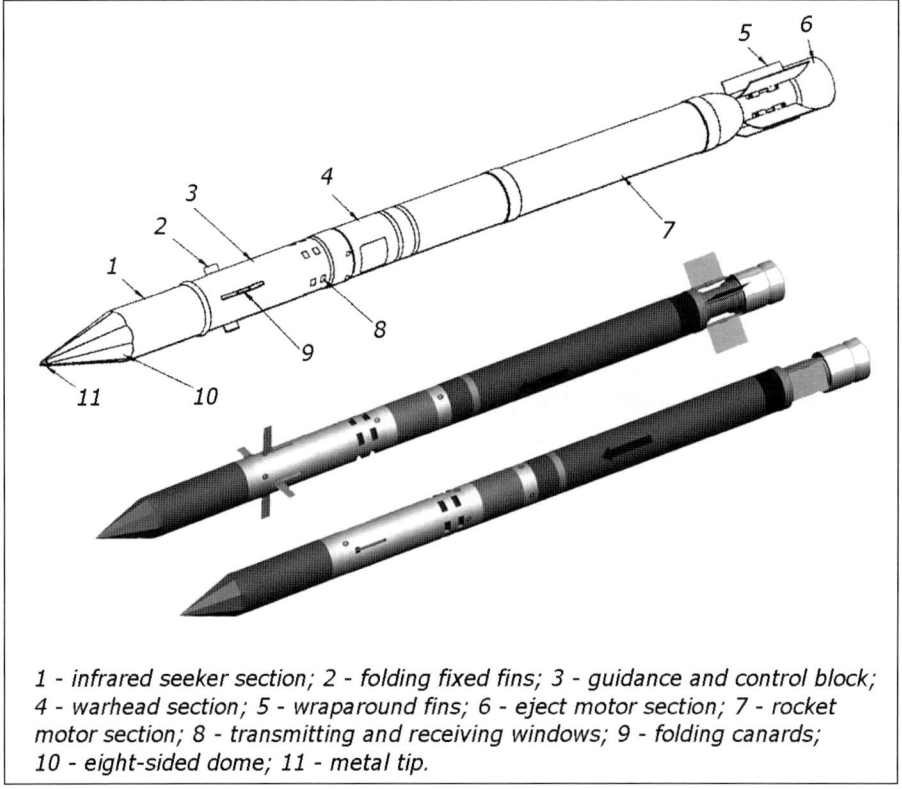

1 - infrared seeker section; 2 - folding fixed fins; 3 - guidance and control block; 4 - warhead section; 5 - wraparound fins; 6 - eject motor section; 7 - rocket motor section; 8 - transmitting and receiving windows; 9 - folding canards; 10 - eight-sided dome; 11 - metal tip.

Figure 6-37: Mistral missile components.

about 1.5m in radius and have enough kinetic energy to maneuver to meet a target evading at 9G at 7km altitude.

On impact with the target, a delayed-action fuze is triggered, allowing the projectile to penetrate the target before the explosive warhead detonates. The tungsten housing is designed to fragment and maximize damage inside the target.

The biggest advantage of this system is that it cannot be jammed by infrared countermeasures or radar/radio countermeasures and cannot be suppressed with anti-radar missiles.

In Ukraine, these missiles are credited with at least one downed helicopter.

Mistral

Mistral is a French-made AD system that can be used from platforms such as vehicles, surface ships, and helicopters, as well as a MANPADS. When used in the MANPADS role it is operated by a crew of two – the commander and the shooter. The missile is optical infrared guided. It uses proportional navigation based on a gyro as a reference instead of the pursuit method in earlier IR-guided MANPADS. The seeker of Mistral has a very narrow field of view to reject decoys and interference, the seeker can tilt in the range of +/-38°. On the launcher, the missile runs up the gyro in 2 seconds, and the total reaction time is 5 seconds. The missile applies a cooled all-aspect two-color IR-seeker and is equipped with laser proximity and impact fuzes (Figure 6-37).

The Mistral Coordination Post (MCP) is designed to be used with a portable Mistral system as well as the vehicle-mounted one as an area-based AD system for defense of military units and important facilities. In Ukraine, it is positioned around the infrastructure objects such as transformer stations which are often targeted by the Russian Shaheed 136/Geran suicide drones.

The MCP provides target designation and fire control for eleven Mistral firing units. The MCP is mounted on a truck chassis or any other off-road chassis.

There is a Mistral-based six-missile version called Sadral, with a stabilized fully automated rapid-reload launcher. A TV and forward-looking infrared fire-control director are integrated into the launcher. Its function is in the way that the image produced by both directors appears on the operator console screen allowing the missiles to lock onto the target.

France have delivered some numbers of MANPADS and announced more.

Many foreign-supplied AD systems place a strain on the training of the Ukrainian operators and maintenance troops. The AD system is a symbiosis of equipment, tactics, and manpower. The Western "allies" can deliver what is available (not the brand-new models because these are intended for domestic use and there are limited stocks) but training the crews in both combat roles and maintenance is a time-consuming process and it takes many months for individuals to become fully proficient. Maintenance is an acute problem because Russia is targeting those centers and existing Ukrainian ones are turned into piles of rubble. The other option is the use of foreign volunteers but AD systems' crews have been killed and wounded in such numbers that it is far riskier for foreigners to be there in comparison with Saudi Arabia, for example. As the war progresses, it may be over before at least a portion of the Ukrainian crews are fully proficient in the use of the supplied hardware and can inflict some damage on the Russian war machine.

The Javelin's tandem high-explosive anti-tank (HEAT) 8.4kg warhead can defeat modern tanks up to 2.5km distance by a top attack, hitting them from above, where their armor is thinnest and is also useful against fortifications in a direct-attack flight (Figures 7-2, 7-3).

This warhead utilizes an explosive-shaped charge to create a stream of deformed metal formed from conical-shaped metallic liners. The result is a narrow high-velocity particle stream that can penetrate armor.[3]

The Javelin counters the advent of explosive reactive armor (ERA) widely used on the Russian tanks. ERA boxes or tiles lying over a vehicle's main armor explode when struck by a warhead. This explosion does not harm the vehicle's main armor but causes steel panels to fly across the path of a HEAT round's narrow particle stream, disrupting its focus and leaving it unable to cut through the main armor. The Javelin uses two shaped charge warheads in tandem. The weak, smaller-diameter HEAT precursor charge detonates the ERA, clearing the way for the much larger diameter HEAT warhead, which then penetrates the target's primary armor (Figure 7-3).

A two-layered molybdenum liner is used for the precursor and a copper liner for the main warhead.

To protect the main charge from the explosive blast, shock, and debris caused by the impact of the missile's nose and the detonation of the precursor charge, a blast shield is used between the two charges. This was the first composite-material blast shield and the first that had a hole through the middle to provide a less diffuse jet.

The missile tracks its target without assistance from the operator by coupling an onboard imaging IR system (separate from the command-and-launch unit (CLU) imaging system) with an onboard tracking system.

The operator uses the CLU's IR system to find and identify the target, then switches to the missile's independent IR system to set a track box around the target and establish a lock. The gunner places brackets around the image for locking. The seeker stays focused on the target's image, continuing to track it as the target moves or the missile's flight path alters, or attack angles change. The seeker consists of three main components: focal plane array image sensor, cooling and calibration, and stabilization.

The tracker is key to guidance/control for a hit. The tracker compares the signals from detector elements in the seeker where readout integrated circuits create a video frame that is sent to the tracker system for processing. The tracker determines the need to correct to keep the missile on target by comparing the individual frames. The tracker must be able to determine which portion of the image represents the target.

The target is initially defined by the gunner, who places a configurable frame around it. The tracker then uses pattern recognition algorithms to of view to reject decoys and interference, the seeker can tilt in the range of +/-38°. On the launcher, the missile runs up the gyro in 2 seconds, and the total reaction time is 5 seconds. The missile applies a cooled all-aspect two-color IR-seeker and is equipped with laser proximity and impact fuzes (Figure 6-37).

The Mistral Coordination Post (MCP) is designed to be used with a portable Mistral system as well as the vehicle-mounted one as an area-based AD system for defense of military units and important facilities. In Ukraine, it is positioned around the infrastructure objects such as transformer stations which are often targeted by the Russian Shaheed 136/Geran suicide drones.

The MCP provides target designation and fire control for eleven Mistral firing units. The MCP is mounted on a truck chassis or any other off-road chassis.

There is a Mistral-based six-missile version called Sadral, with a stabilized fully automated rapid-reload launcher. A TV and forward-looking infrared fire-control director are integrated into the launcher. Its function is in the way that the image produced by both directors appears on the operator console screen allowing the missiles to lock onto the target.

France have delivered some numbers of MANPADS and announced more.

Many foreign-supplied AD systems place a strain on the training of the Ukrainian operators and maintenance troops. The AD system is a symbiosis of equipment, tactics, and manpower. The Western "allies" can deliver what is available (not the brand-new models because these are intended for domestic use and there are limited stocks) but training the crews in both combat roles and maintenance is a time-consuming process and it takes many months for individuals to become fully proficient. Maintenance is an acute problem because Russia is targeting those centers and existing Ukrainian ones are turned into piles of rubble. The other option is the use of foreign volunteers but AD systems' crews have been killed and wounded in such numbers that it is far riskier for foreigners to be there in comparison with Saudi Arabia, for example. As the war progresses, it may be over before at least a portion of the Ukrainian crews are fully proficient in the use of the supplied hardware and can inflict some damage on the Russian war machine.

Chapter 7

Anti-Armor Systems

Javelin

When it was the first time announced that Ukraine would receive thousands of US-made Javelin anti-tank missiles,[1] the missile acquired an almost a mythical status as a "Russian tank killer" and was even nicknamed "St Javelin" by the Ukrainian and Western media (Figure 7-1). NATO warehouses are depleted while transports are poured into Ukraine. But what really is Javelin? Is it another or the very first "wonder weapon" that is going to turn the tide of the war, or is it just another marketing boost for an ordinary system?

The FGM-148 Javelin, or AAWS-M,[2] is a US-made portable anti-tank missile system. It is a fire-and-forget design that uses automatic infrared guidance that allows the user to seek cover immediately after launch.

Figure 7-1: "St Javelin" badge (left); Javelin launch (right). (*Source*: Euronews and Ukrainian MoD)

ANTI-ARMOR SYSTEMS

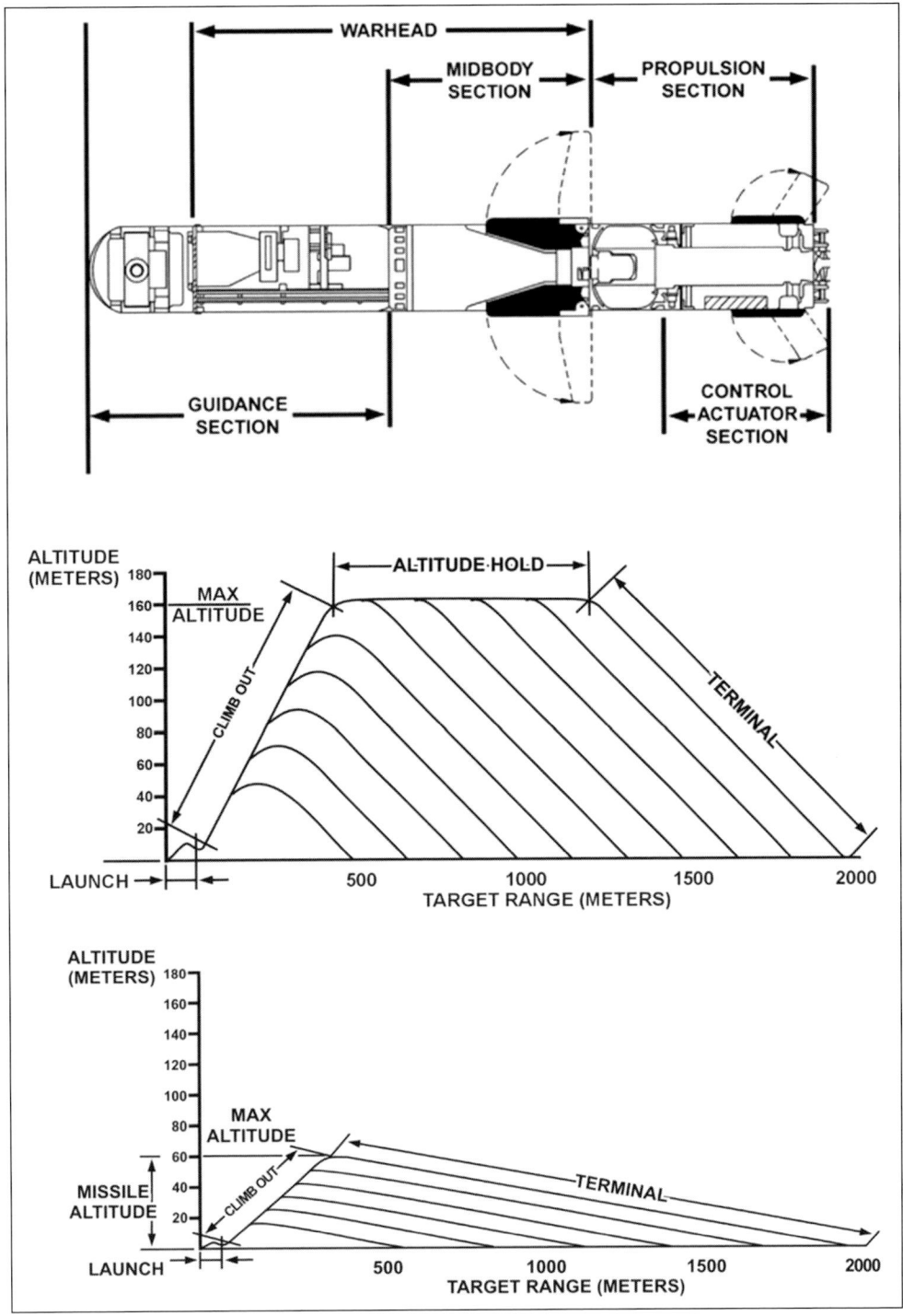

Figure 7-2: Javelin cutaway (top); attack trajectories altitudes profiles (middle and bottom). (*Source*: US Javelin manual)

The Javelin's tandem high-explosive anti-tank (HEAT) 8.4kg warhead can defeat modern tanks up to 2.5km distance by a top attack, hitting them from above, where their armor is thinnest and is also useful against fortifications in a direct-attack flight (Figures 7-2, 7-3).

This warhead utilizes an explosive-shaped charge to create a stream of deformed metal formed from conical-shaped metallic liners. The result is a narrow high-velocity particle stream that can penetrate armor.[3]

The Javelin counters the advent of explosive reactive armor (ERA) widely used on the Russian tanks. ERA boxes or tiles lying over a vehicle's main armor explode when struck by a warhead. This explosion does not harm the vehicle's main armor but causes steel panels to fly across the path of a HEAT round's narrow particle stream, disrupting its focus and leaving it unable to cut through the main armor. The Javelin uses two shaped charge warheads in tandem. The weak, smaller-diameter HEAT precursor charge detonates the ERA, clearing the way for the much larger diameter HEAT warhead, which then penetrates the target's primary armor (Figure 7-3).

A two-layered molybdenum liner is used for the precursor and a copper liner for the main warhead.

To protect the main charge from the explosive blast, shock, and debris caused by the impact of the missile's nose and the detonation of the precursor charge, a blast shield is used between the two charges. This was the first composite-material blast shield and the first that had a hole through the middle to provide a less diffuse jet.

The missile tracks its target without assistance from the operator by coupling an onboard imaging IR system (separate from the command-and-launch unit (CLU) imaging system) with an onboard tracking system.

The operator uses the CLU's IR system to find and identify the target, then switches to the missile's independent IR system to set a track box around the target and establish a lock. The gunner places brackets around the image for locking. The seeker stays focused on the target's image, continuing to track it as the target moves or the missile's flight path alters, or attack angles change. The seeker consists of three main components: focal plane array image sensor, cooling and calibration, and stabilization.

The tracker is key to guidance/control for a hit. The tracker compares the signals from detector elements in the seeker where readout integrated circuits create a video frame that is sent to the tracker system for processing. The tracker determines the need to correct to keep the missile on target by comparing the individual frames. The tracker must be able to determine which portion of the image represents the target.

The target is initially defined by the gunner, who places a configurable frame around it. The tracker then uses pattern recognition algorithms to

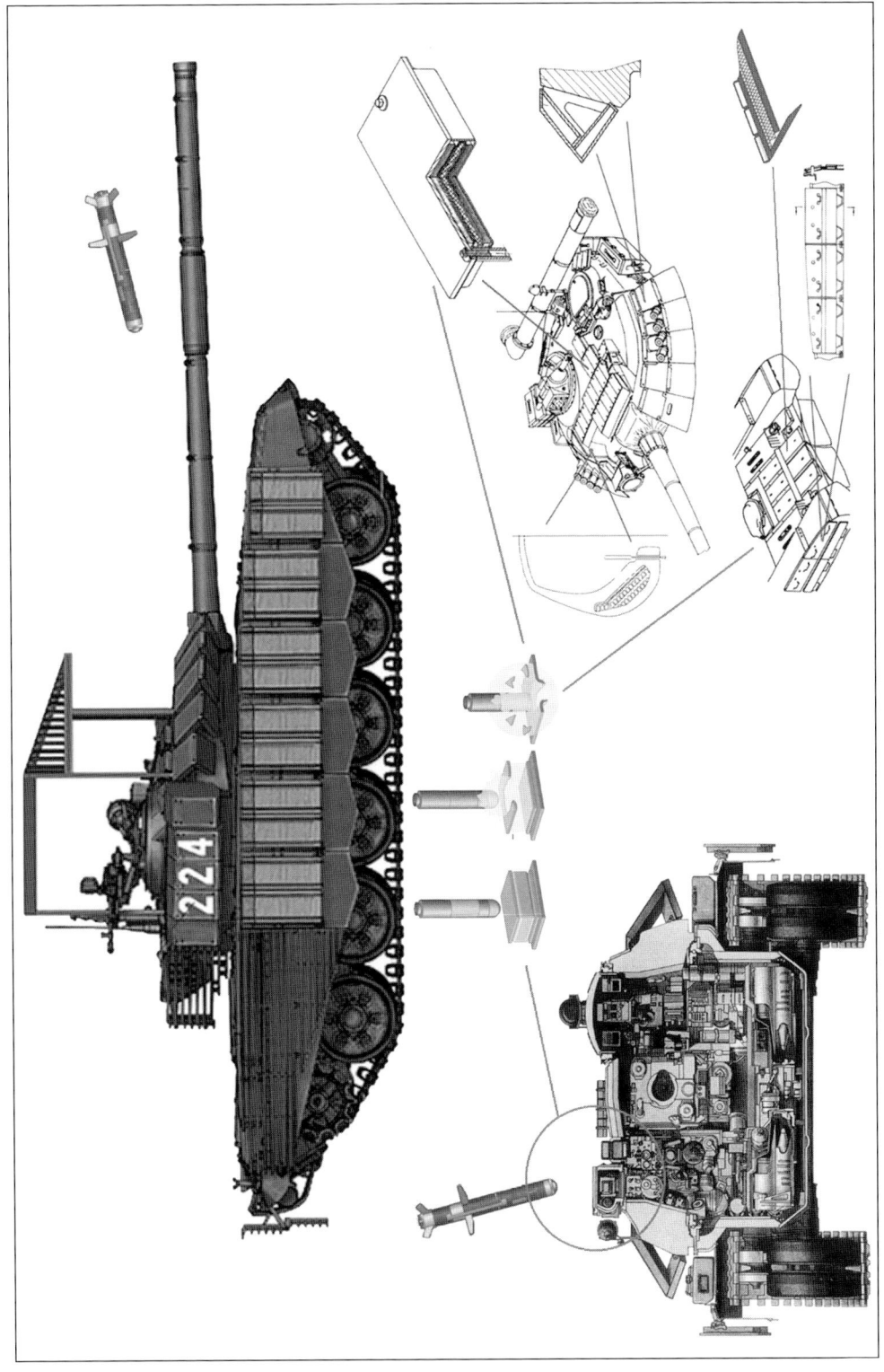

Figure 7-3: Javelin attack profiles. Low profile can attack beneath the rooftop cage. Top profile can attack through the rooftop cage at the thinnest turret top armor.

compare that region of the frame based on image, geometric, and movement data to the new image frames being sent from the seeker.

The missile is equipped with four movable tail fins and two fixed wings at mid-body. To guide the missile, the tracker locates the target in the current frame and compares this position with the aim point. If this position is off-centre, the tracker computes a correction and passes it to the guidance system, which makes the appropriate adjustments to the four movable tail fins. To guide the missile, the system has sensors that check that the fins are positioned as requested. If not, the deviation is sent back to the controller for further adjustment.

There are three stages in the flight managed by the tracker:

1. An initial phase after launch,
2. A mid-flight phase that lasts for most of the flight, and
3. A terminal phase in which the tracker selects the most effective point of impact.

With guidance algorithms, the autopilot uses data from the seeker and tracker to determine when to transition the missile from one phase of flight to another. Depending on whether the missile is in top-attack or direct-attack mode, the profile of the flight can change significantly. The top-attack mode requires the missile to climb sharply after launch and cruise at a high altitude then dive on the top of the target (curveball). In direct-attack mode (fastball) the missile cruises at a lower altitude directly at the target. The exact flight path which takes into account the range to the target is calculated by the guidance unit.

Javelin may also harm the operator because the launch motor uses a standard NATO propellant with the presence of lead and lead oxide in the exhaust which means that the operators need to hold their breath after firing for their safety.

Out of 5,500+ delivered missiles, almost a quarter have been captured and the Russians have even issued an operator manual in Russian so that the missiles can be used against the previous owners.[4]

NLAW

NLAW[5] is a missile system that has been optimized from the outset to combat tanks and other armored vehicles. The aim was to develop a weapon that gives individual soldiers the capability to combat a modern tank in all conflict situations and in all environments (Figure 7-4).

The development of NLAW began in 1999 and it has been in production since 2008. The weapon is used by the Swedish and British armies and thereby constitutes an anti-tank complement to the existing light and crew-operated medium-range systems.

ANTI-ARMOR SYSTEMS

Figure 7-4: NLAW transport container (left); launcher and missile (right). (UK MoD)

NLAW is a top-attack, PLOS-guided,[6] fire-and-forget missile, which is preloaded into a disposable launch tube. NLAW is handled and fired by one person and can be fired from confined spaces. The effective range is 20–600m, which more than covers the requirements for an individual soldier's combat range. The maximum firing range is 1,000m, beyond which the missile is designed to auto-destruct. The missile requires no target lock-on or IR signature before firing.

NLAW is a one-man weapon similar to other anti-tank RPGs but with the capability to take out a tank in a single shot in any attitude, even if the tank is equipped with reactive armor, is hidden in a protected or firing position, located in a built-up area or in woodland, or is concealed, for example, behind a wall of concrete. In doing this with the specific mode of attack it targets the less-protected areas.

In the Ukrainian service it still didn't achieve saint-like status, but Javelin found its role. At the beginning of the war, numerous Russian columns were ambushed and a significant number of vehicles were destroyed or damaged especially on the roads and in urban areas, but as the war has progressed the role of NLAW has reduced. There are numerous reports of the missile failing to activate or damage tanks. In any case, for the time being, it will be in use on both sides (the Russians have captured significant quantities and turned them against the previous owners (Figure 7-5)).

Both Javelin and NLAW are effective weapons if used properly. NLAW has a shorter range, and fewer penetration capabilities but is far less expensive, thus it can be supplied in much higher numbers than Javelins, and it can be used in space-constrained areas. Both systems may support each other in the anti-tank combat units.

Figure 7-5: Unusual application – NLAW container used as a water tank. (*Source*: Author's archive)

Stugna

The Skif (Stugna-P) is a Ukrainian anti-tank guided missile system developed by the Luch Design Bureau. The first missile guidance device was developed and manufactured by the Belarusian design bureau Peleng, based in Minsk, while the Stugna-P uses a domestic Ukrainian one (Figure 7-6).

The Skif is designed to destroy modern armored targets with combined carried or monolithic armor, including explosive reactive armor (ERA). Skifs can attack both stationary and moving targets. They can attack from both long-range (up to 5km in the daytime) and close-range (100m). They can attack point targets such as weapon emplacements, lightly armored objects, and helicopters. The Skif has two targeting modes: manually steered, and automated fire-and-forget that uses no manual tracking of a target.

The PDU-215 control panel is a briefcase-like laptop computer with a control panel, holding a small joystick and a flat-panel display, which is connected to the firing unit by a cable, allowing it to be used at distances up to 50m away. Two firing modes are available: manual and fire-and-forget. Fire-and-forget provides automatic control of the missile flight using a targeting laser beam.

The system uses two calibers of missiles: 130mm and 152mm. The RK-2S warhead is a tandem charge HEAT high-explosive anti-tank. It was declared that it can penetrate 800mm RHA. It can also use HE-FRAG RK-2OF and RK-2M-OF warheads to attack light armored vehicles and infantry positions. It is equipped with a thermal imager. During operations in woodland and

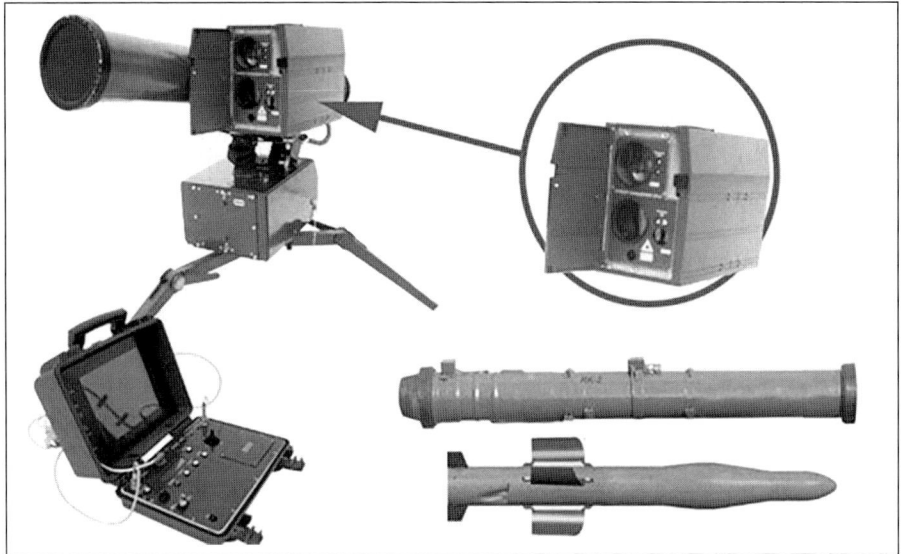

Figure 7-6: Stugna ATGM. (*Source*: Ukrainian MoD and Luch)

urban areas it is a crew transported, but once the fight moves to open ground, the system is mounted on light platforms for mobility.

Compared with NLAW and Javelin, it has a greater range and heavier warhead, but requires more crew members. Stugna is "budget-friendly" because it costs a third of the price of the Javelin.

The missile system became "famous" on 5 April 2022, when the crew documented the downing of a Ka-52 helicopter (Figure 7-7).

Ukrainian sources claimed that on 25 April, in the battle near Izyum, four tanks were destroyed or damaged in 4 minutes by one Stugna-P crew. Another source claimed a hit on a Russian tank 300m beyond the maximum range.

In general, these systems in combination with other older systems represent a solid anti-tank capability for the Ukrainian Army.

Figure 7-7: Stills from Stugna attacks: Doening Ka-52 (top); BTR-80 attack (bottom). (*Source*: Ukrainian MoD)

ANTI-ARMOR SYSTEMS

Brimstone

Brimstone is a ground-attack missile developed for the RAF. The basic design is intended for fire-and-forget use against armor. The challenge was in the differentiation of the moving targets and for that a millimetric-wave active radar homing seeker was developed. The missile is equipped with a tandem shaped charge warhead. Three Brimstone missiles are carried on a single weapon station, allowing a single aircraft to carry many missiles (Figure 7-8).

The warhead weighs 6.3kg of which 100g is for the first stage to break the reactive armor and the rest is in the second larger charge designed to penetrate the base armor. The RAF used it in combat (Afghanistan and Libya) with 90 percent efficiency according to the UK MoD.

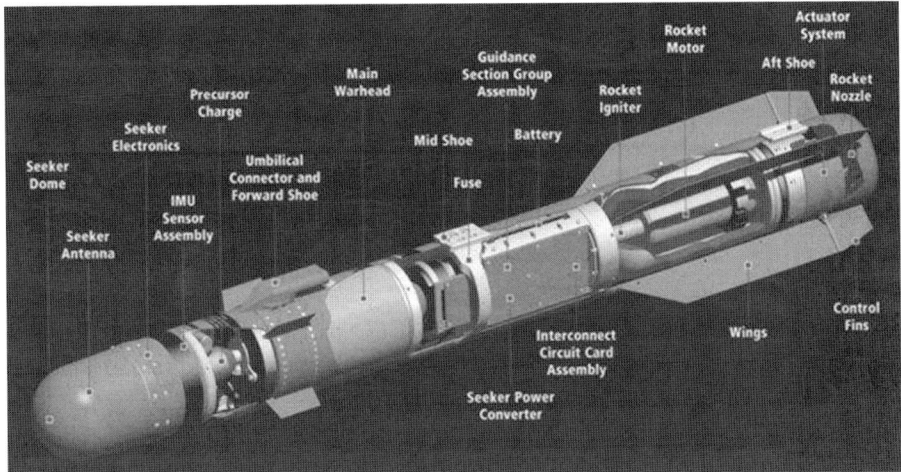

Figure 7-8: Brimstone cutaway (top); vehicle platform launch (bottom). (Ukrainian MoD)

Brimstone is programmable to adapt to particular mission requirements. This capability includes the ability to find targets within a certain area (such as those near friendly forces). In addition to the semi-autonomous ability to decide its targets, the Brimstone can determine where on a target to best impact causing the most damage. If used from the air launched platform, the missile's targeting system requires an algorithm to ensure targets are hit in staggered order.

Brimstone can be fired in several attack profiles: direct or indirect against single targets, a column of targets, or against an array of targets. The latter utilizes a salvo-attack capability for multiple kills per engagement.

Besides the air launched platforms, there are also ship-launched and ground-launched ones.

In April 2022, the UK MoD supplied ground-launched Brimstones to the Ukrainian military. On 17 May 2022, it was claimed that ground-launched Brimstone missiles had destroyed two Russian tanks, operating behind their lines, however, this claim was not supported by any evidence. The Ukrainian military is using Brimstones, but the quantities are very limited. A few missiles failed to acquire the targets and crashed almost intact preserving all vital system components. The Russians immediately collected them and they were thoroughly inspected and evaluated by their experts (Figure 7-9).

Figure 7-9: Captured intact Brimstone missile. (*Source*: anna-news.info)

9K121 Vikhr

Without a doubt, the 9K121 Vikhr[7] system with 9M127 missile (Figure 7-10) is the most important anti-tank system for the airborne platform in the Russian inventory. The missile can be launched from Mi-28NM, Ka-52 helicopters, and Su-25T/TM aircraft.

The missile is intended to engage any type of armored or unarmored target at a range of up to 8km when launched from a helicopter and up to 10km when fired from a fixed wing aircraft.

The Vikhr-1 missile is part of the Vikhr-M system, which also includes an automatic sight and a depressible launcher.

The automatic sight uses TV and IR channels for target sighting, a laser beam channel for missile control (laser beam-riding guidance), a laser rangefinder, an automatic target tracking unit, a digital computer, and a system for stabilization and aiming the sighting and beam channels. The

Figure 7-10: 9M127 missile. (*Source*: topwar.ru)

automatic sight provides day and night target detection, identification and tracking, and missile guidance, and generates exact information for gun and missile firing. The missile is equipped with a HEAT fragmentation warhead with a contact and a proximity fuze, an air dynamic control actuator, control electronics, a motor, and a laser detector. It is kept in a sealed launching transporting container.

The multi-purpose warhead (two-stage HEAT and an additional fragmentation sleeve) allows the missile to engage armored, airborne, and ground targets alike. This is an advantage compared with the previous 9M120 Ataka-V complex. The use of the proximity fuze allows a near miss of up to 5m and makes it possible to engage an air target at speeds of 500m/s making it a universal helicopter launched weapon.

The guidance laser beam control system provides for its precise guidance owing to data transmission to the missile in the course of its launch, which is excluded in homing systems. The laser guidance principle is identical to that used by 9M117 Bastion or 9M119 Svir anti-armor missiles. The Vikhr missile-control system has low jamming susceptibility because its receiver faces the carrier, thereby protecting it from most jamming signals.

The high pinpoint target hit probability (reported 0.95 against stationary targets) is provided by the automatic target tracking system and highly accurate missile-control system that makes allowance for changes in the parameters of the carrier and the target while firing.

The missiles can be fired singly or in pairs (at the same target to increase lethality). The high flight speed allows it to engage targets rapidly. The system can launch Vikhr missiles against two to four targets in 30 seconds and starting at a range of 10km, which increases its lethality to three to four times that of earlier systems. In Ukraine, Vikhr is a killer of Ukrainian equipment. The extended range allows the platform to attack from a distance neutralizing the SHORAD or point AD assets.

9K135 Kornet

The 9K135 Kornet is a modern Russian anti-tank-guided weapon system widely used in the war in Ukraine.

The 9M133 missile is equipped with a tandem HEAT warhead, has a diameter of 152mm, and is considered the largest and most powerful ATGM ever built. This warhead is of such a size and concept that it can defeat any modern and in-development tank with advanced Chobham armor or tanks equipped with the latest ERA (Figure 7-11).

The Russian Army has been using it since 1998. It was designed to replace the ubiquitous 9K113 Konkurs which is still in use in some second-tier Russian units as well as the former Warsaw Pact countries.

ANTI-ARMOR SYSTEMS

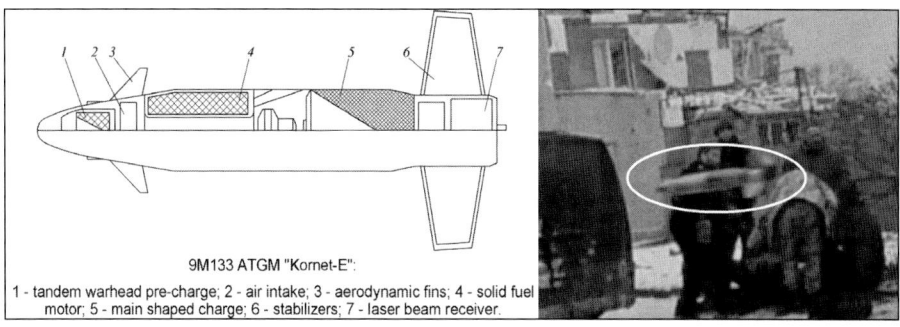

9M133 ATGM "Kornet-E":
1 - tandem warhead pre-charge; 2 - air intake; 3 - aerodynamic fins; 4 - solid fuel motor; 5 - main shaped charge; 6 - stabilizers; 7 - laser beam receiver.

Figure 7-11: 9M133 Kornet E ATGM cutaway. The insert shows Kornet just before the hit on the Ukrainian minivan. Only one soldier survived the hit. The missile was launched 4km away.

The Kornet is deployed by a two-man team, but a single person can assemble and fire it. The two-man setup involves one carrying the launch tube loaded with a missile while the other carries the fire-control system and day/night sight on its adjustable tripod. The Kornet was designed to conceal its operator who could aim it while either crouched down or lying prone behind cover. This is why the launch tube is mounted above the fire-control system.

Besides its powerful warhead, the Kornet's great advantage in comparison with the previous Soviet models as well as the modern NATO ATGM is its extreme range. The FGM-148 Javelin, for example, can only fire up to 2.5km away, while the original Kornet-E had a maximum range of 5.5km. The Ukrainian Stugna's range is slightly shorter, but it is fielded in a very limited number.

The Kornet has an impressive combat record having destroyed numerous US-made Abrams tanks and Israeli-made Merkavas as well as hundreds of Ukrainian tanks and armored vehicles even before the outbreak of the war in 2022.

The system comes in several modifications:

- Kornet-EM is an upgraded version with a laser beam riding guidance system and a range of 8–10km. There are two different missiles. A standard anti-tank missile with a tandem HEAT warhead has a range of 8km. It penetrates 1,100–1,300mm behind ERA-protected armor or 3–3.5m of concrete (which is important in engaging fortifications). The second missile has a thermobaric warhead and a range of 8km. The third missile has a blast-fragmentation warhead and a range of 10km,
- Kornet-M is an improved version available in man-portable and vehicle-mounted configurations. It uses an improved tripod launcher and sights. It uses the same missiles as the Kornet-EM,

- Kornet-D is a mobile version based on the GAZ Tigr armored vehicle. The Tigr has two separate launchers with four missiles in each. This missile is also used on the new unmanned turrets of the Armata heavy IFV, Kurganets-25 IFV, and Boomerang APC. Kornet-D1 is an improved anti-tank missile carrier, fitted with an improved Kornet-M system. Kornet-T is based on the BMP-3.

One of the latest modifications is the 9M133F-1 missile with a thermobaric warhead. Hits on Ukrainian positions by these missiles are particularly devastating, exploiting all the advantages of thermobaric warheads with the precision of a sniper.

Izdeliye-305

This is the latest and relatively unknown helicopter launched multi-purpose missile used by the Russian forces. It was designated as the lightweight missile project Izdeliye-305 "LMUR,"[8] a project that was halted a few times but has now resurfaced in combat use in Ukraine (Figure 7-12).

The LMUR has a canard configuration. Wings are folded for transport and unfolded when the missile is mounted on a helicopter. Rear-looking datalink antennas are mounted on the rear wings. Compared with other helicopter launched missiles such as the 9M120-1 Ataka and 9M127-1 Vikhr, the Izdeliye-305 is heavier (105kg compared with 48.5kg and 59kg respectively). Its warhead is also heavier (at 25kg compared with 7.4kg and 8.6kg respectively). The Izdeliye-305 uses both a shaped charge and a high-explosive warhead.

The maximum range is 14.5km. It is equipped with optical/thermal imaging seeker. It can be used in two different modes:

1. The target is marked by the operator before launch, and the carrier helicopter can turn away directly after the missile launch,
2. The missile is launched without it being locked on a target. It first flies in its direction, using inertial guidance with satellite navigation providing corrections. The image from the seeker is transmitted back to the helicopter via a datalink pod called the AS-BPLA.[9] The operator can select the target and change it while the missile is flying toward its area.

The Russians are using these missiles on Mi-8, Mi-28, and Ka-52 helicopters. Besides tactical aviation, FSB also uses these missiles.

In Ukraine, numerous videos have been published showing the missile's extraordinary precision, hitting buildings, warehouses, armored and soft-skin vehicles as well as pontoon bridges. Its exceptional range and precision are serious problems for the Ukrainian forces. It is expected that many more of these missiles will be seen in the future.

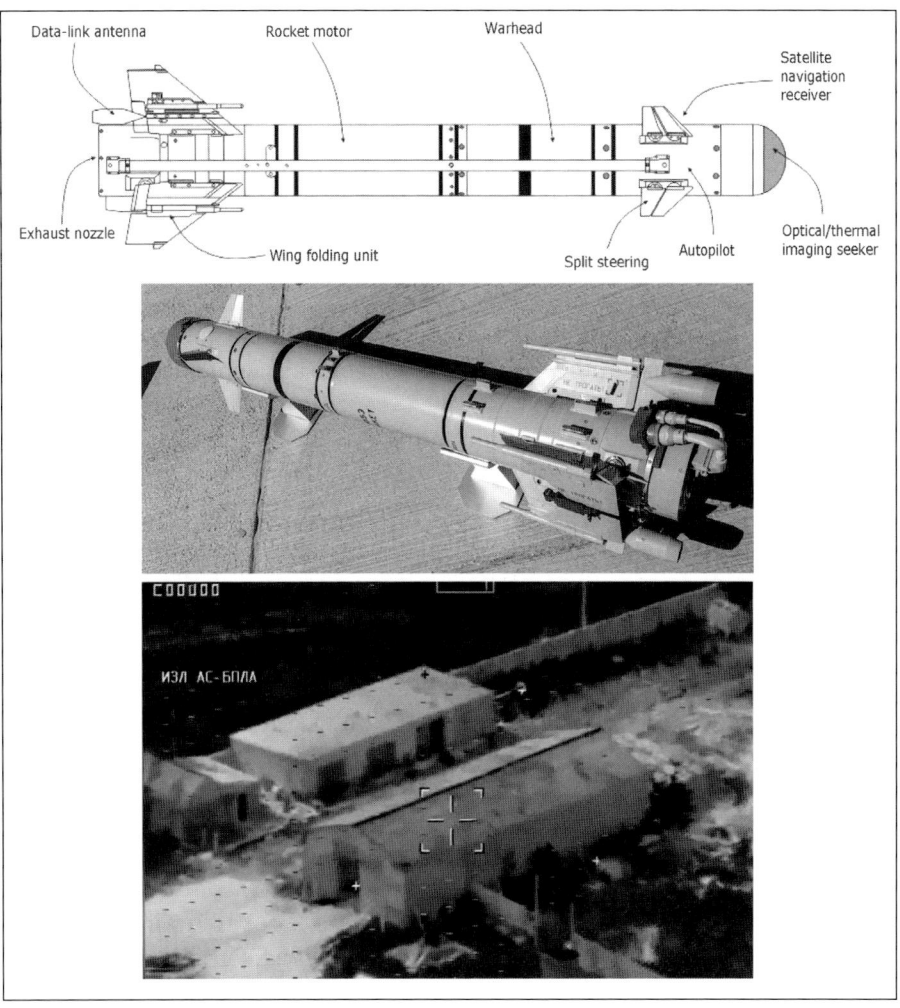

Figure 7-12: Izdeliye-305 (9A-7755). (*Source*: Russian MoD)

Chapter 8

Air-to-Air Missiles

Air-to-air combat in Ukraine is rare as time goes on. It is evident that the Russian Air Force (RuAF) dominates the sky and in all engagements has downed Ukrainian airplanes and helicopters. This is opposite to how this is presented by the Western media, which glorifies fictitious Ukrainian aces such as the "Ghost of Kiev" and even publishes videos (which are from video games). The reality is very different. Older Ukrainian interceptors with same-age missiles can't compete with the RuAF's modern interceptors and much better air-to-air missiles.

Ukraine inherited large quantities of ex-Soviet missiles but after thirty years of no modernization, the state of the arsenal is highly questionable. Since the outbreak of hostilities, many have been destroyed in warehouses, but some small quantities are available for the remaining interceptors.

Russia is employing beyond-the-visual-range combat utilizing superior interceptors and weaponry and controlling the zone of operations. As Ukraine is a large country, the RuAF can't control the whole territory but commands the front line, successfully destroying all Ukrainians who can master flying. Inferior Ukrainian MiG-29s, Su-24s, Su-25s, and Su-27s are no match for the Russian Su-30SMs, Su-35Ss, and MiG-31s (Figure 8-1).

Both sides use short- and medium-range missiles. Russia has the upper hand using long-range missiles.

The short-range missile in use is the R-73 (Figure 8-2), which is a heat-seeking missile with a sensitive, cryogenic cooled seeker with a substantial "off-boresight" capability: the seeker can detect targets up to 40° off the missile's centerline. It can be targeted by a helmet-mounted sight allowing pilots to designate targets by looking at them. The minimum engagement range is about 300m, with a maximum aerodynamic range of nearly 30km at altitude. A Ukrainian MiG-29 used this missile to hit a Russian drone Shahed-136, but when the drone exploded, debris damaged the plane and the pilot was forced to eject. This is the first time in history that a drone downed an airplane.

Figure 8-1: Su-30SM with 2 R-27R, 2 R-27T, and 2 R-73 (top); Su-35S launching R-37M (bottom). (*Source*: Russian MoD)

The R-27 medium-range missile (Figure 8-3) is manufactured in different configurations that include infrared-homing (R-27T, R-27ET), semi-active-radar-homing (R-27R, R-27ER), and active-radar-homing (R-27EA) versions. The R-27 family of missiles are produced by both Russian and Ukrainian manufacturers. The R-27 missile is carried by the MiG-29 and Su-27 fighters.

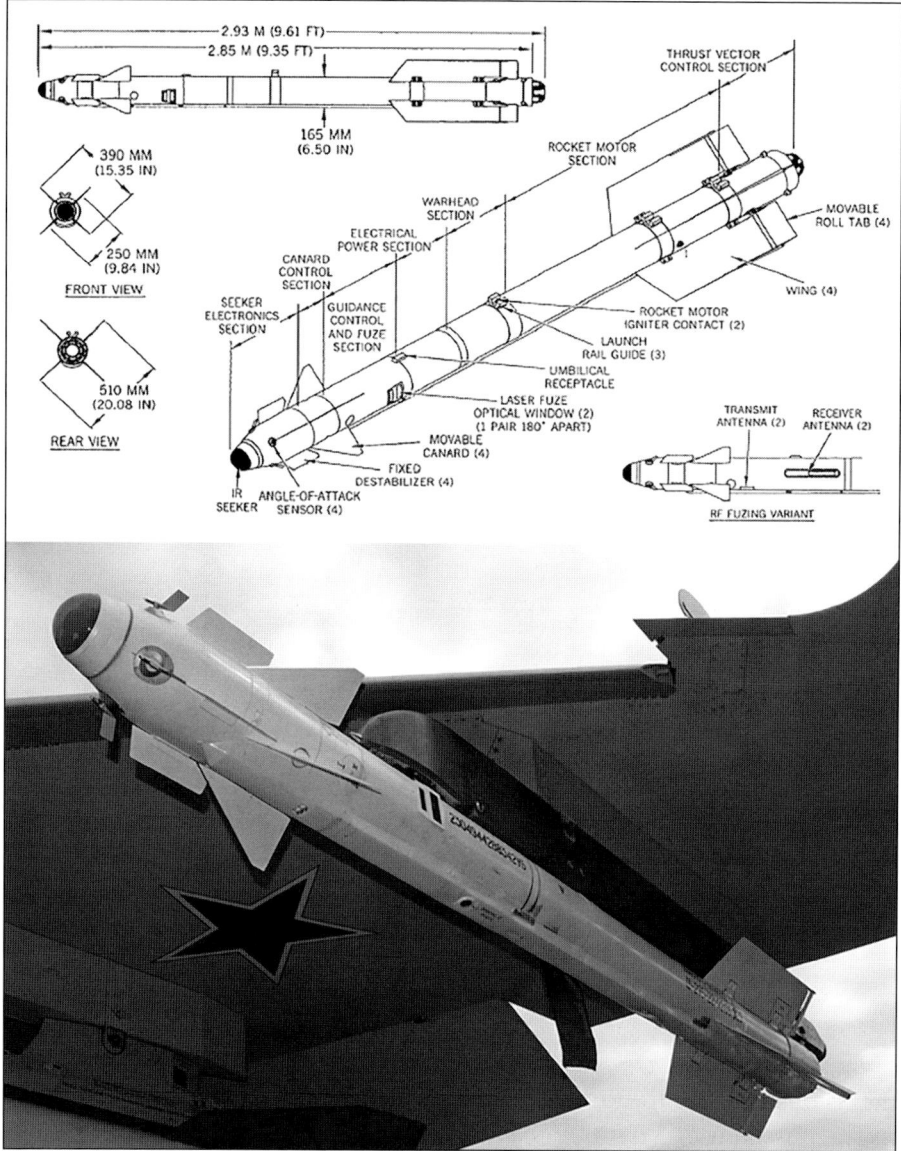

Figure 8-2: R-73. (*Source*: Russian MoD and Author's archive)

The R-77 (Figure 8-3) is an active radar-homing, medium-range, beyond-visual-range missile. Work began on it in the 1980s, but was not completed before the Soviet Union fell. Production was further disrupted in 2014 when Ukraine stopped deliveries of some components. The RuAF developed R-77-1 without Ukrainian-made components and since 2015 it has been in full production.

The aerodynamics combine vestigial cruciform wings with grid fins used as tail control surfaces. The flow separation which occurs at high angles

AIR-TO-AIR MISSILES

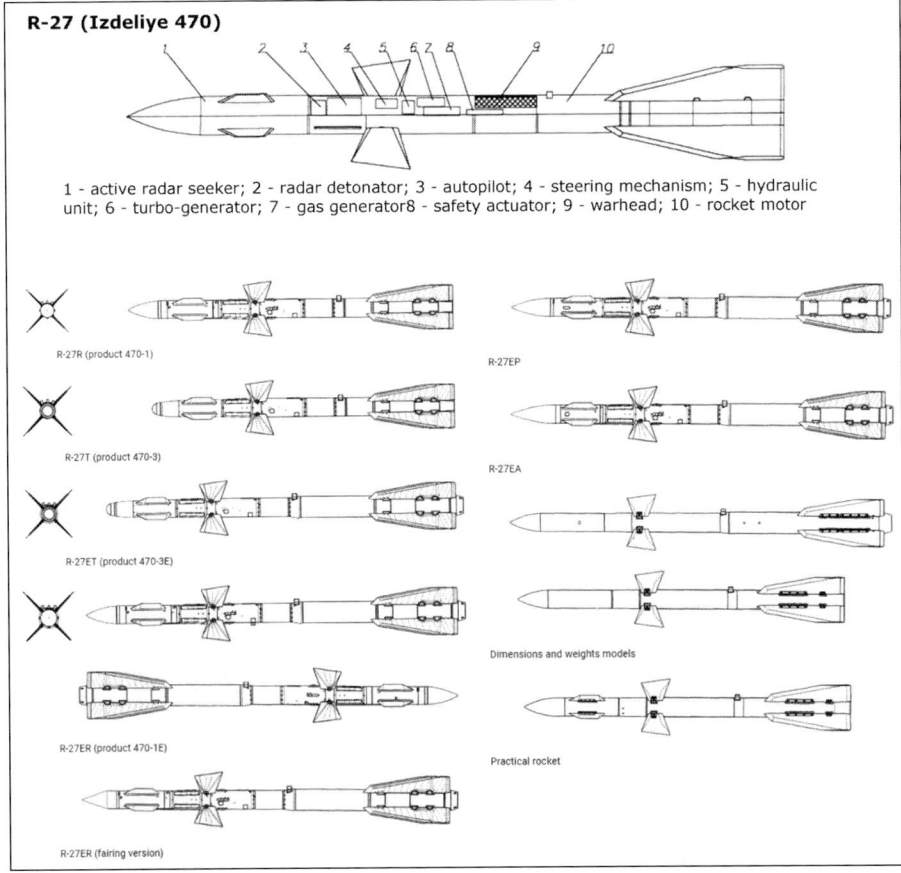

Figure 8-3: R-27 family.

of attack enhances its turning ability, giving the missile a maximum turn rate of up to 150° per second. However, the grid fins also increase drag and radar cross-section. Updated variants of the R-77, such as the Izdeliye-180 that is destined for the Sukhoi Su-57, will use conventional fins instead.

The missile uses a multi-function Doppler-monopulse active radar seeker. The radar features two modes of operation. Over short distances, the missile will launch in an active "fire-and-forget" mode. Over longer distances, the missile is controlled by an inertial guidance autopilot with occasional encoded datalink updates from the launch aircraft's radar on changes in spatial position or G of the target. As the missile comes within 20km of its target, the missile switches to its active radar mode. The host radar system maintains computed target information in case the target breaks the missile's lock-on.

The main user is the Su-35S, usually carrying a couple of R-77 missiles, between IR seeking R-27T under the inner pylons and R-73 under the outer ones.

The R-33 (Figure 8-4) is a long-range missile primarily used by the MiG-31 interceptor.

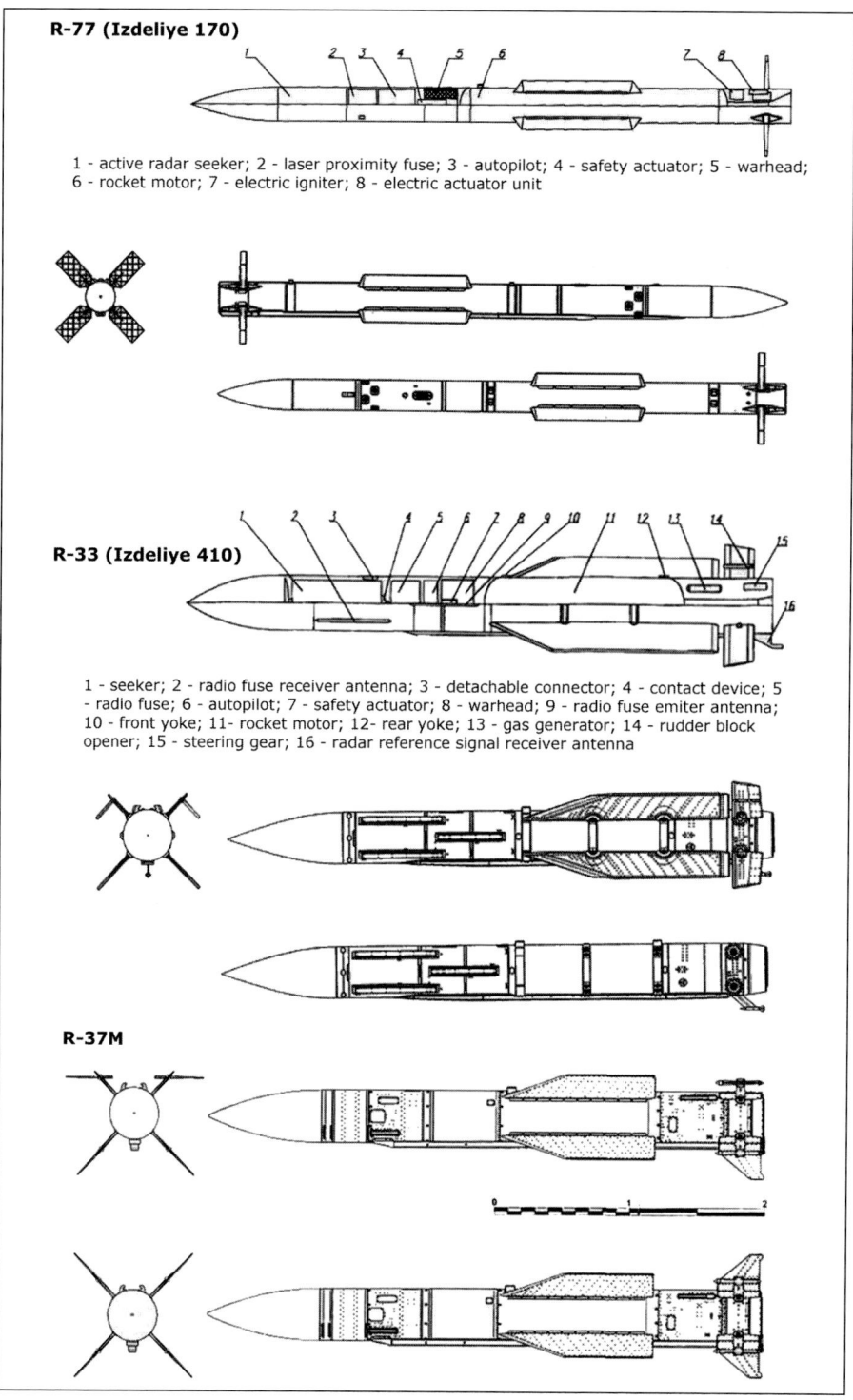

Figure 8-4: R-77, R-33, and R-37.

It uses a combination of semi-active radar homing for initial acquisition and mid-course updates, and inertial navigation to reach the target at an extreme range. The MiG-31 Zaslon phased array radar allows four missiles to be guided simultaneously at separate targets.

The R-37 (developed from R-33) is a long-range hypersonic missile (Figure 8-4). The missile and its variants have also had the names K-37, Izdeliye-610, and RVV-BD.[1]

It is designed to shoot down NATO AWACS, EW aircraft, and refueling tankers. The R-37M version has a jettisonable rocket booster that increases the range to 300–400km.

The Russian and Indian media claim that on 19 October 2022, the Su-57 stealth fighter shot down a Ukrainian Su-27 using the R-37M missile.

Su-35S fighters carry two R-73s in the central wing pylon, two R-77s slung underneath the engine nacelles, and two R-37s on the hardpoints between the engines, with an option to carry a few more missiles, such as a Kh-31 anti-radar missile.

The R-37 is a deadly threat to Ukrainian aircraft. As recently as August 2022 Russian Su-35S or MiG-31s combat patrols shot down 4xMiG-29s, 6xSu-25s, a Su-24, and an Su-27. A combination of hypersonic velocity, extreme range, and an advanced seeker that can detect and engage low-altitude targets effectively closed the sky for the Ukrainian Air Force.

Appendix

Abbreviations

AD	Air Defense
ATACMS	Army Tactical Missile System
ATGM	Anti-Tank Guided Missile
CEP	Circular Area of Probability
CP	Command Post
CV	Combat Vehicle
DoD	Department of Defense
DSMAC	Digital Scene Matching Area Correlator
ELINT	Electronic Intelligence
EO	Electro-Optical
ERA	Explosive Reactive Armor
EW	Electronic Warfare
GLONNAS	Global Navigation Satellite System
HE	High Explosive
HE-FRAG	High Explosive Fragmentation
HEAT	High Explosive Anti-Tank
HIMARS	High Mobility Artillery Rocket System
HUD	Head-up Display
IADS	Integrated Air Defense System
MANPADS	Man Portable Air Defense System
MLRS	Multiple Launch Rocket System
MoD	Ministry of Defense
MRL	Multiple Rocket Launcher
OED	Opto Electronic Device
PGM	Precise Guided Munition
PrSM	Precision Strike Munition

ABBREVIATIONS

RCS	Radar Cross Section
RuAF	Russian Air Force
SA	Surface-to-Air
SAM	Surface-to-Air Missile
SEAD	Suppression of Air Defense
SHORAD	Short Range Air Defense
TEL	Transporter Erector and Launcher
TELAR	Transporter Erector Launcher and Radar
TLC	Transport Launch Container
UAES	Universal Automation Equipment System
UAV	Unmanned Aerial Vehicle
UBCP	Universal Battery Command Post
UHF	Ultra-High Frequency
VHF	Very High frequency

Most Common Russian Abbreviations

ASU	Avtomatizirovanya Sistema Upravleniya	Automated Control System
BM	Boveya Mashina	Combat Vehicle
GDL	Gazo Dynamicjeskaya laboratoria	Gas Dynamics Lab
GIRD	Grupa Istrazhivaniya Reaktivnog Dvizheniya	Group for Study of Reactive (jet) Propulsion
GKAT	Gosudarstveni Komitet Aciacionoy Tehniki	State Aviation Technics Committee
GRAU	Glavnoe Raketno Artilerisko Upravlenie	Main Rocket and Artillery Directorate
ISBU	Informatsionnaya Sistema Boevogo Upravleniya	Combat Control Information System
KBP	Konstruktorskoe Biro Proborostroeniya	Instrument Design Bureau
NII	Nauchno-Isleditelyskii Institut	Scientific Research Institute
NPO	Naucho-Proizvodstveno Obyedinenie	Scientific and Manufacturing Enterprise
NVO	Niskovisotni Obnaruzhitely	Low-level Surveillance Radar

OKB	Opitnoe Konstruktorskoe Biro	Research Design Bureau
OTRK	Operaticny Takticheskii Raketni Kompleks	Operation Tactical Missile Complex
PBU	Punkt Boevogo Upravleniya	Combat Command Post
PKB	Proektno-Konstruktorkoe Biro	Project-Design Bureau
PO	Proizvodstvenoe Obyedineniye	Manufacturing Enterprise
PU	Puskovaya Ustanovka	Launcher
PVO	Protivovazdushnaya oborona	Air Defense
PZRK	Perenosni Zenitni Raketni Kompleks	MANPADS
REB	Radio-Elektronaya borba	Electronic Warfare
RLO	Radiolokator Obnaruzheniya	Surveillance/tracking radar
RLS	Radiolokatsionaya Stanitsa	Radar Station
RPN	Radilokator Podsveta i Navedeniya	Surveillance, tracking and guidance radar
RSZO	Reaktivnii Sistem Zalpovoga Ognya	Multiple Launch Rocket System
SNR	Stanitsa Navedeniya Raket	Missile Guidance Station
SPU	Samohodnaya Puskovaya Ustanovka	Self-propelled Launcher
TOS	Tyazhelovi Ognemetni Sistem	Heavy Flamethrower
TPK	Transportno-Puskovoi Kontainer	Transport-Launch Container
TsKB (CKB)	Tsentralnii Konstrukorskoe Biro	Central Design Bureau
TsNII (CNII)	Tsentralnii Naucho-Isledovatelskii Institut	Central Scientific Research Institute
VKS	Vozdusho-Kosmicheskoi Sili	Aerospace forces
VMF	Voeno Morskoi Flot	Navy

ABBREVIATIONS

V-PVO	Voiskova Protivovazdusha Oborona	Army Air Defense
VVKO	Vozdushno Kosmicheskaya Oborona	Aerospace defense
VVS	Voeno Vazdushiy Sil	Air Force
ZAK	Zenitniy Artilleriskiy Kompleks	Air Defense Artillery Complex
ZRK	Zenitno-Raketni Kompleks	Air Defense Missile Complex
ZRS	Zeninto-Raketnaya Sistema	Air Defense Missile System

NATO Codenames for Soviet/Russian-Made Air-Defense Missile Systems

9K33 Osa-AKM	SA-8 "Gecko"
9K31 Strela-1	SA-9 "Gaskin"
S-300P/PS/PT	SA-10 "Grumble"
9K37 Buk	SA-11 "Gadfly"
S-300V	SA-12 "Gladiator" and "Giant"
9K35 Strela-10	SA-13 "Gopher"
9K36 Strela-3	SA-14 "Gremlin"
9K330/9K331/9K332 Tor	SA-15 "Gauntlet"
9K310 Igla-1	SA-16 "Gimlet"
9K37 Buk-M1-2	SA-17 "Grizzly"
9K38 Igla	SA-18 "Grouse"
2K22 Tunguska	SA-19 "Grison"
S-300PM/PMU Favorit	SA-20 "Gargoyle"
S-400 Triumf	SA-21 "Growler"
Pantsir-S1	SA-22 "Greyhound"
S-300VM "Antey-2500"	SA-23 "Gladiator/Giant"
9K338 Igla-S	SA-24 "Grinch"
9K333 Verba	SA-25
9K317 BUK M3 Viking	None Assigned (Viking used)
9K79 Tochka-U	SS-21 "Scarab"
9K720 Iskander	SS-26 "Stone"

NATO Codenames for S-300 and S-400 Missiles

5V55K/KD	Grumble mod 0
5V55R/RD	Grumble mod 1
48N6/E	Gargoyle mod 0
48N6D/E2	Gargoyle mod 1
48N6DM/E3	Growler
9M96/E/D/E2	None Assigned
40N6	None Assigned

Notes

Special Military Operation

1. Excerpts from Wikipedia.

Chapter 1: Introduction to Warheads

1. I. Balagansky, *Damaging Effects of Weapons and Ammunition*, 2022.
2. Geneva International Centre for Humanitarian Demining, "Explosive Weapon Effects" (2017), Global CWD Repository, 149, https://commons.lib.jmu.edu/cisr-globalcwd/149.
3. Ibid.
4. Ibid.
5. Ibid.
6. Ibid.
7. Ibid.
8. *Cratering by Explosion, Compendium*.
9. Geneva International Centre for Humanitarian Demining, "Explosive Weapon Effects."
10. Ibid.
11. Ibid.
12. Ibid.
13. Ibid.

Chapter 2: Operational-Tactical Missile Systems

1. Very simplified, a rocket is an unguided system with a path (trajectory) that can't be adjusted, while the missile is basically a rocket that has some kind of guidance system that allows trajectory corrections.
2. In Russian – Operativno-Takticheskii Raketni Kompleks (OTRK), Оперативно-тактические ракетные комплексы.

3. Sam Cranny-Evans and Dr Sidharth Kaushal, "The Iskander-M and Iskander-K: A Technical Profile," *Commentary*, RUSI, 8 August 2022.
4. Ibid.
5. Ibid.
6. Informatsionnaya Sistema Boyevogo Upravleniya.
7. Ibid
8. Ibid.
9. Ibid.
10. Ibid.

Chapter 3: MLRS

1. Wikipedia.
2. C. Mihailescu et al., "The Analysis of Dispersion for Trajectories of Fire-extinguishing Rocket," *Electromecanica*, Ploesti, Romania.
3. Ibid.
4. BM-21 stands for Боевая машина-21 (Boyevaya Mashina – 21; Combat Vehicle – 21).
5. Grad is the Russian name for hail.
6. A.V. Karpenko, *Sovremennyye Reaktivnyye Sistemy Zalpovogo Ognya*, 2010.
7. Geneva International Centre for Humanitarian Demining, "Explosive Weapon Effects."
8. Ibid.
9. Ibid.
10. Ураган – Hurricane.
11. Тулгоснииточмаш, Тульский государственный научно-исследовательский институт точного машиностроения – Tula state scientific and research precision machine institute.
12. Смерч – Tornado.
13. S.V. Gurov, *Reaktivnyye Sistemy Zalpovogo Ognya, Obzor* (2021).
14. Ibid.
15. Ibid.
16. The author was personally involved in this operation.
17. General reference from https://en.wikipedia.org/wiki/M270_Multiple_Launch_Rocket_System.
18. FM 6-60 MCRP 3-1.6.24, Tactics, Techniques and Procedures for MLRS Operations.
19. A quote by Joseph Stalin.

Chapter 4: Thermobaric Weapons

1. Balagansky, *Damaging Effects of Weapons and Ammunition*.

NOTES

2. Thomas M. Klapötke, *Chemistry of High-Energy Materials* (2017).
3. RPO-A Shmel (Bumblebee) stands for Russian "реактивный пехотный огнемёт-А Шмель (РПО-А Шмель)," Rocket-propelled Infantry Flamethrower-A.
4. Karez is the Pashto term for the manmade underground water system.
5. Rural settlement of semi-nomadic Turkic peoples of Central Asia and Azerbaijan. Used also for an Afghan village.
6. TOS stands for Russian "Тжёлая Огнемётная Система" (ТОС) meaning "Heavy Flamethrower System;" Gurev, *Reaktivnyye Sistemy Zalpovogo Ognya*.
7. https://www.wired.com/story/russia-ukraine-blast-trauma/.

Chapter 5: Guided Missiles

1. Russian крылатая ракета – krilyati raket.
2. Kh is from the pronunciation of the Russian letter "X."
3. Kalibr or Russian Калибр means caliber.

Chapter 6: Surface-to-Air Missiles

1. Norwegian Advanced Surface-to-Air Missile System, also known as the National Advanced Surface-to-Air Missile System developed by Kongsberg Defence & Aerospace (KDA) and Raytheon.
2. Advanced Medium Range Air-to-Air Missile.
3. Norwegian abbreviation for Tactical Data Communication.
4. InfraRed Imaging System Tail/Thrust Vector-Controlled.
5. HAWK – Homing All the Way Killer.
6. D. Borojevic, M. Mihajlovic, Z. Vukosavljevic, *Three Fingers of Death: 2K12 KUB (SA-6 Gainful) Missile System* (2022).
7. Short Range Air-Defence.

Chapter 7: Anti-Armor Systems

1. Only the most modern anti-tank guided missiles on both sides are discussed. There are many anti-armor systems in use starting with the older guided missile systems up to the man-portable weapons such as the whole set of RPGs that are detailed in the other book about the artillery in the conflict by the same author.
2. Advanced Anti-Tank Weapon System-Medium.
3. Penetration is classified but it is believed that it is about 760mm rolled homogeneous steel armor.
4. The author inspected the Javelin system and interweaved some users. Even though the system is very advanced and effective, it appears that

there are many undocumented issues and most users complained that often the missile can't be launched and when launched the problem is a short range that requires an operator to be close to the target which may work in urban areas but in the open field and often under the enemy fire it is very difficult to achieve a hit. Russian operators are not overly impressed by the Javelin's performance and think that it is inferior to the domestically made long-range anti-armor systems. One of the great disadvantages is that the Javelin missile is extremely expensive (approximately $240,000) so the extensive launching practiced by Ukrainians and misses may not be economically justified.
5. Next Generation Light Antitank Weapon.
6. Predicted Line-Of-Sight. The missile's guidance electronics unit automatically receives target speed data from the gunner's aiming movement and calculates and predicts the target route as well as the flight path to the target. After launch, the missile flies autonomously to the target.
7. Whirlwind.
8. Russian for light multipurpose guided missile (Легкая многоцелевая управляемая ракета).
9. Russian for communication equipment with an unmanned aerial vehicle (Аппаратура связи с беспилотным летательным аппаратом).

Chapter 8: Air-to-Air Missiles

1. Ракета Воздух-Воздух Большой Дальности (Raketa Vozduh-Vozduh Bolshoy Dalnosti, "Long-range air-to-air missile."

Bibliography

Air Defense Artillery Reference Handbook, FM 3-01.11 (FM 44-100-2), 2007

Asanin, V., *Raketi Otechestvenogo Flota*, 2010; В. Асанин, *Ракеты отечественного флота*

Australian Strategic Policy Institute, *Man-Portable Air Defence Systems (MANPADS)*, 2008

Balaganskiy, I.A., *Deystviye Sredstv Zashchity i Obshchestvennogo Pitaniya*, 2011; Игорь Андреевич Балаганский, *Действие средств поражения и боеприпасов, Учебники НГТУ*, 2011

Balagansky, I., *Damaging Effects of Weapons and Ammunition*, 2022

Baranovskii, M.N., *Reaktivnaya Sistema Zalpovogo Ognya 9K57 Uragan. Osnovi Ustroistva i Podgotovki k Boevomu Primeneniyu*; М.Н. Барановский, *Реактивная система залпового огня 9К57 Ураган. Основы устройства и подготовки к боевому применению*

Bernard, R. and Crayton, C., *Projectile Penetration in Soil and Rock Analysis for Non-Normal Impact*, 1979

Bogomolov, A.I., *Osnovi Ustroistva i Raschet Reaktivnih Sistem, Texbook*, 2003; А.И. Богомолов, *Основания устройства и расчет реактивных систем: Учебник. – Пенза: ПАИИ*, 2003

Borojevic, D., Mihajlovic, M., and Vukosavljevic, Z., *Three Fingers of Death: 2K12 KUB (SA-6 Gainful) Missile System*, 2022

Chistyakov, M.N., *Artilleria*, 1953

Coghe, F., "Efficiency of Different CAGE Armour Systems," article, Appl. Sci., https://doi.org/10.3390/app12105064, 2022

Cooper, P., *Explosives Engineering*, 1996

Cranny-Evans, Sam S. and Kaushal, Dr Sidharth, "The Iskander-M and Iskander-K: A Technical Profile," *Commentary*, RUSI, 8 August 2022

Dullum, Ove, *The Rocket Artillery Reference Book*, 2010

Elcin, S.N., *Raketa 9M38M1, Ustroistvo i funkcioniranie*

Geneva International Centre for Humanitarian Demining, "Explosive Weapon Effects," 2017, Global CWD Repository, 149, https://commons.lib.jmu.edu/cisr-globalcwd/149

GICHD (group of authors), *Explosive Weapon Effects, Final Report,* 2017

Gordon, John et al., *Comparing U.S. Army Systems with Foreign Counterparts,* 2015

Grau, L.W. and Jalali, A.A., "Underground Combat: Stereophonic Blasting, Tunnel Rats and the Soviet-Afghan War," *Engineer,* November 1998

Grau, L.W. and Smith, T., "A 'Crushing' Victory: Fuel-Air Explosives and Grozny," *Marine Corps Gazette,* August 2000

Gurov, S.V., *Reaktivnyye Sistemy Zalpovogo Ognya. Obzor,* 2021
https://www.wired.com/story/russia-ukraine-blast-trauma/ (how explosion actually kill)

Jaramaz, S., *Physics of Explosion,* 2003

Javelin – Close Combat Missile System, Medium, TC 3-22.37 (FM 3-22.37), 2013

Karlos, V. and Solomos, G., *Calculation of Blast Loads for Application to Structural Components,* 2013

Karpenko, A.V., *Sovremennyye Reaktivnyye Sistemy Zalpovogo Ognya,* 2010

Kinney, G.F. and Graham, K.J., *Explosives Shocks in Air,* 1985

Klapötke, Thomas M., *Chemistry of High-Energy Materials,* 2017

Laad, O. and Knight, D., "Effect of Off-Axis Pulsed Energy Deposition on the Kinzhal Missile," article, AIAA, 2021

Lloyd, M., *Conventional Warhead Systems, Physics and Engineering Design (Progress in Astronautics and Aeronautics)* (Vol. 179), 1998

Low Altitude Air Defense (LAAD) Gunner's Handbook MRCP 3-25.10A, 2011

Makarovskiy, V. and Perov, K., *Sovetskiye Aviatsionnyye Rakety Vozdukh-Zemlya,* 2005; В. Макаровский, К. Перов, *Советские авиационные ракеты воздух-земля,* 2005

Manuylenko, V.G. and Udin, Ye.G., *Teoreticheskiye Osnovy Krylatykh Upravlyayemykh Raket,* 2020; В.Г. Мануйленко, Е.Г. Удин, *Теоретические основы крылатых управляемых ракет,* Санкт-Петербург, 2020

Markovskiy, V., *Krylatyye Rakety SSSR i Rossii (Voyna i my. Aviakollektsiya),* 2016; Виктор Марковский, *Крылатые ракеты СССР и России (Война и мы. Авиаколлекция) – Яуза,* 2016

MBDA, Brimstone 2 Advanced Multi [Role] Precision Strike Weapon, catalogue, 2021

Mihailescu, C. et al., "The Analysis of Dispersion for Trajectories of Fire-extinguishing Rocket," *Electromecanica,* Ploesti, Romania

Mihajlović, M. and Aničić, D.S., *Shooting Down the Stealth Fighter,* 2002

Mihajlović, M., *Defending Putin's Empire: Russia's Air Defence System,* 2023

Mihajlović, M., *Jetliner Down: Tor-M1 missile system which downed Ukrainian PS752 flight,* 2019

Mohamed, A.K. et al., *Study of Performance of Some Selected TBXs,* 15th International Conference on ASAT Technology, 2013

NATO EOD Center of Excellence, Former Warsaw Pact *Ammunition Handbook,* Vol. 2, 2015

Valetskiy, O., *Oruzhiye Sovremennykh Voyn: Boyepripasy, Sistema Upravleniya Zadachami i Merami Protivodeystviya Ikh Primeneniyu*, 2015; Олег Валецкий, *Оружие современных войн: Боеприпасы, системы управляемого вооружения и меры противодействия их применению*. Пушкино, 2015

Orlov, A.P., *Osnovi Ustroistva i Funkcionirovaniya Reaktivnih Sistem Zalpovogo Ognya*, 2002; А.П. Орлов, *Основы устройства и функционирования реактивных систем залпового огня*, Тула, 2002

Orlov, A.P., *Osnovi ustroistva i finkcionirovania snaryadov RSZO*

Pavlyuk, Yu.S., *Ballisticheskoye Proyektirovaniye Raket*, 1996; Ю.С. Павлюк, *Баллистическое проектирование ракет*, Челябинск, 1996

Redmon, Danny Ray, *Tactical Missile Conceptual Design*, 1980

Rooke, A., Carnes, B. and Davis, L., *Cratering by Explosion, Compendium*, 1974

Selivanov, V.V., *Boyepripasy*, 1–2 toma, 2016; В.В. Селиванов, *Боеприпасы*, Том 1–2, 2016

Selivanov, V.V., *Boepripasi, Compendium*, 2012

Shcherbakov, B.F., *Nazemnyye Operativno-Takticheskiye Raketnyye Kompleksy*, 2008; Б.Ф. Щербаков, *Наземные оперативно-тактические ракетные комплексы*, Санкт-Петербург, 2008

Shcherbakov, B.F. and Rumyantsev, B.V., *Protivotankovyye Raketnyye Kompleksy: Uchebnoye Posobiye*, 2010; Б.Ф. Щербаков, Б.В. Румянцев, *Противотанковые ракетные комплексы: учебное пособие*, Санкт-Петербург, 2010

Shirokorad, A.B., *Ognennyy Mech Rossiyskogo Flota-Yauza*, 2004; А.Б. Широкорад, *Огненный меч Российского флота-Яуза*, Эксмо, 2004

Shunkov, V., *Boyevaya Moshch' Rossii. Sovremennaya Voyennaya Tekhnika*, 2017; Шунков, Виктор, *Боевая мощь России. Современная военная техника*, Эксмо, Москва, 2017

Shunkov, V., *Polnaya Entsiklopediya Sovremennogo Vooruzheniya Rossi*, 2017; *Полная энциклопедия современного вооружения России*

Simic, D. et al., "Thermobaric Effects of Cast Composite Explosives of Different Charge Masses and Dimensions," *Central European Journal of Energetic Materials*, 2016, 13(1), pp. 161–82

Sukharevsky, O.I., *Electromagnetic Wave Scattering by Aerial and Ground Radar Objects*, 2014

Vasilyev, S.V., Dyudaev, K.N., Petrunin, A.V., and Seleznev, A.G., *Osnovi Teorii Postoeniya Korabelnih Kompleksov Krilatih Raket, Chast 1, Ustroitsvo Raket I Puskovih Ustanovok*, 2019

Vuorio, Kristian Oskar, *Use of Thermobaric Weapons*, 2015

Whelan, A.J., "The Development of a Warhead into an Integrated Weapon System to Provide and Advanced Battlefield Capability," thesis, 2011

Wildegger-Gaissmaier, A., "Aspects of Thermobaric Weaponry," *ADF Health*, Vol. 4, 2013

Index

2K22 246
3M-14 43, 175, 176, 178, 182
3M-54 175, 176, 182
40N6 218
48N6DM/E3 220
48N6E 220
48N6E2 220
5V55K/KD 210, 212
5V55R/RD 210, 212
9A310 225, 230
9A317 226
9A82 214
9A83 214
9K121 267
9K270 35, 37, 40
9K310 (Igla-1) 248
9K317 (Buk-M3 Viking) 224, 225
9K33 Osa 241, 242
9K330 243
9K331 243
9K333 (Verba) 250
9K338 (Igla-S) 247
9K35 (Strela-10) 246
9K38 Igla 247, 249
9K714 Oka 35
9K79 25, 35
9M133 268, 269
9M723 35, 38, 40, 42, 45, 46
9M728 38, 42, 43
9M331 243, 245
9M38/9M38M 16, 224, 225, 227–9

9M79M 25
9M82 214, 215, 217
9M83 214, 215, 217
9M96/E/D/E2 218, 220

aeroballistic (missile) 193, 194, 217, 224
ABM (anti-ballistic missile) 214
AGM-88 201, 203, 205
AIM-120 234, 235, 237
AMRAAM 234–6
Aspide 241
ASTER 239
ATGM 19, 22, 268, 269
AWACS 199, 221, 277

Bastion (Russian cruise missile) 186
Bastion (Ukrainian MLRS) 65, 66, 83
beam riding 253, 267, 269
beyond-the-visual-range 272
blast effect 11, 14, 203
BM-13 (Katyusha) 49, 53, 59, 62
BM-21 57, 58, 59, 62, 63, 65, 71
BM-27 76, 83
BM-30 88, 90, 105, 106, 109
Brimstone 265, 266
Buk 224
Buk-M1 45, 209, 224
Buk-M1-2 224
Buk-M3 224, 225, 226, 230

INDEX

cluster munition 3, 40, 42, 79, 80, 113
cluster warheads (for BM-30 Smerch) 95
Command Post 24, 37, 46, 88, 105, 110, 235
Continuous Wave (CW) 214, 227
cratering 6, 10
CV (Combat Vehicle) 64

DSMAC 42

Electronic Countermeasures (ECM) 175, 186, 214, 241
ELINT (Electronic Intelligence) 127, 184, 193
EW (Electronic Warfare) 163
explosion effect 2, 5

FGM-148 256, 269
fragmentation 1, 4, 6, 13, 14, 23, 25, 61

GLONNAS 42, 43, 57, 96, 107, 180
GPS-guided 116, 117
Grad (BM-21) 58, 59, 61–3, 68, 71, 73
GRAU (Main Rocket and Artillery Directorate) 61, 76, 185

HARM 201, 203–5
Harpoon 190, 191, 193
HAWK 198, 239–41
HE (High Explosive) 1, 2, 5, 11, 13, 25, 27, 40, 59, 79, 96, 136, 182, 216, 258, 270
HEAT (High-Explosive Anti-Tank) 17, 66, 130, 258, 263, 268
HE-FRAG (High-Explosive Fragmentation) 25, 63, 71, 75, 76, 94, 184, 189, 227, 263
HIMARS 112, 117, 124, 126, 127
hypersonic 193–5, 239, 277

Igla 247–50
improvised launchers 127–8

IRIS-T 209, 237
Iskander-M 37, 40, 156, 195
Izdeliye-180 272
Izdeliye-305 270
Izdeliye-610 289

Javelin 256–60

Kalibr 175–8, 182
Ka-52 130, 264, 267, 270
Kh-22 156–62
Kh-29 184
Kh-31 198, 199
Kh-32 161, 162
Kh-38 184
Kh-47M 193
Kh-55 162–70
Kh-58 198
Kh-59 172–5
Kh-101 167
Kinzhal 193–7
Kornet 268–70

LMUR 270
long-range missile 57, 162, 272, 275

M142 112, 113, 117, 120
M270 112–17
MANPAD 247–55
medium range (missile) 272, 274
Mi-28 267, 270
MiG-29 203–5
MiG-31 195, 272, 275, 277
MIM-104 221, 223, 238
Mistral 254, 255
MLRS 49–127

NASAMS 234–6
NII (Scientific Research Institute) 59, 88, 224
NLAW 260-262
NPO (Scientific and Manufacturing Enterprise) 162, 175, 179, 185

OKB (Research Design Bureau) 156
OSA-AKM 241, 242
OTRK-21 35
OTRK-23 Luna 35

P-800 (Oniks/Yakhont) 185, 186, 188
PAC-3 223, 224
Pantsir-S1 231–3
Patriot 197, 221-224, 238
PrSM (Precision Strike Munition) 116, 117

R-27 247, 273, 275
R-33 275, 277
R-37 277
R-73 272, 275, 277
R-77 274, 275, 277
R-360 Neptune 188–90
Radar Cross Section (RCS) 167, 234, 247, 275
RDX 132, 138
RM-70 67

S-8 129, 130
S-300P/PS/PT 209–13
S-300PM 210
S-300V 214–17
S-400 209, 217, 220, 221
SAMP-T 238, 239
SCALP 106–208
SEAD (Suppression of Air Defence) 198, 206
shaped charges 1, 17–22
Shmel (RPO-A) 138–40
short-range ballistic missile 35, 194
SHORAD 241–7
shrapnel 1, 95
Smerch (BM-30) 55, 88–112
StarStreak 252–4
Stinger 250–2

Storm Shadow 206–8
Stugna 263, 264
Su-24 184, 199, 200, 206–8, 217, 272, 277
Su-25 184, 231, 250, 267, 272, 277
Su-27 160, 203, 206, 221, 272, 273, 277
Su-30 184, 272
Su-35 176, 206, 272, 275, 277
Su-57 185, 275, 277
Surface-to-Air Missile (SAM) 209–47

TEL 37, 38, 116, 226
TELAR 214, 224, 226
Thermobaric 23, 132–54, 270
TLC (Transport-Launch Container) 215
Tochka-U 25–35
Tor 243-246
Tornado-G 63–5
Tornado-S 107
TOS 139-150
Tosochka (TOS-2) 141, 150, 152
Tu-95 160, 163, 167, 169
Tunguska 246
TZM 29, 90, 94, 140, 142

UAV 76–88
UCAV (Unmanned Combat Aerial Vehicle) 205
UHF (Ultra-High Frequency) 234
Uragan (BM-27) 76–87

V-500R 210
Vikhr 267, 268
Viking 225

Yakhont 185, 186, 188

ZRN-01 130